PARLEY'S
HISTORY
OF THE
WORLD

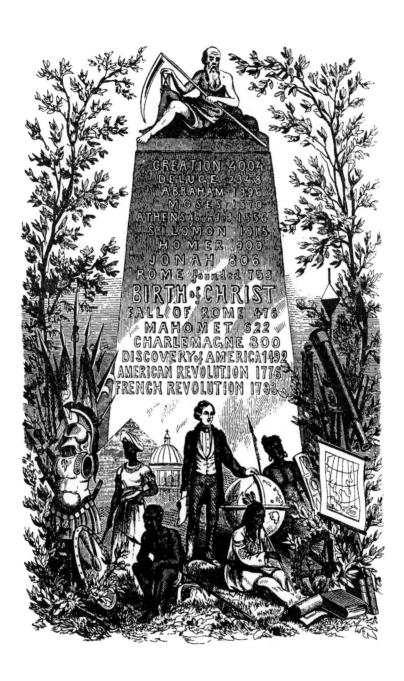

CREATION 4004
DELUGE 2348
ABRAHAM 1996
MOSES 1570
ATHENS founded 1556
SOLOMON 1015
HOMER 900
JONAH 806
ROME founded 753
BIRTH of CHRIST
FALL OF ROME 476
MAHOMET 622
CHARLEMAGNE 800
DISCOVERY of AMERICA 1492
AMERICAN REVOLUTION 1776
FRENCH REVOLUTION 1793

PARLEY'S
COMMON SCHOOL HISTORY OF THE WORLD.

A PICTORIAL

HISTORY OF THE WORLD

ANCIENT AND MODERN

FOR THE USE OF SCHOOLS

BY SAMUEL G. GOODRICH

AUTHOR OF PICTORIAL HISTORIES OF THE UNITED STATES, ENGLAND, GREECE,
ROME, FRANCE, ETC.

Illustrated by Engravings

Originally published 1881

PRINTED BY HEARTHSTONE PUBLISHING
P.O. Box 815, Oklahoma City, OK 73101

Printed in the United States of America
ISBN 1-57558-099-3

The design of this work is to furnish a CLEAR OUTLINE OF UNIVERSAL HISTORY suited to common schools. It is intended for beginners, and is therefore written in a simple style, and to render it convenient both for the pupil and teacher, it is divided into brief paragraphs and short chapters. Ample questions for examination are appended to the work.

It will be seen that a pupil may commit the whole volume to memory during a winter's schooling; and if, in this brief space, a clear outline of Universal History may be established in the memory, it is obvious that the subject is worthy the attention of every person interested in education.

In this edition, the whole work has been carefully revised, and is illustrated throughout by new engravings.

DEPARTMENT OF PUBLIC INSTRUCTION,
Baltimore, Md., July 22d, 1865.
At a meeting of the State Board of Education, held this day, "GOODRICH'S PICTORIAL HISTORY OF THE UNITED STATES" was adopted as a Text-Book to be used in the Public Schools throughout the State.　　　　W. HORACE SOPER, Clerk

OFFICE OF THE CONTROLLERS OF PUBLIC SCHOOLS, FIRST DISTRICT OF PENNSYLVANIA
Philaelphia, April 2d, 1868.
At a meeting of the Controllers of the Public Schools, First District of Pennsylvania, held at the Controllers' Chamber, Tuesday, March 10th, 1868, the following resolution was adopted:
Resolved, That "GOODRICH'S PICTORIAL HISTORY OF UNITED STATES," "GOODRICH'S HISTORY OF THE WORLD," "GOODRICH'S PICTORIAL CHILD'S HISTORY," and "MITCHELL'S PHYSICAL GEOGRAPHY," be introduced to be used in the schools of this District.
From the Minutes,　　　　　　　　H. W. HALLIWELL, Secretary

CONTENTS

ASIA

CHAPTER   PAGE

Foreword by N. W. Hutchings 15

I. Introduction 17

II. The Creation. Garden of Eden. Geography of Asia.
The Earth Peopled. The Deluge 19

III. How Noah and his Family came out of the Ark. The
People settle in the Land of Shinar. The Tower
of Babel 22

IV. More about the Tower of Babel 23

V. About the great Assyrian Empire, and the Reign of
Queen Semiramis 25

VI. Queen Semiramis sets forth to conquer the world, but
is defeated by the King of the Indies 28

VII. About Ninias. Reign of Sardanapalus, and
overthrow of the First Assyrian Empire 29

VIII. Extent of Assyria and Babylonia. Notices of
other Countries in ancient times 31

IX. Cyrus conquers Babylon. His death 32

X. Reign of Cambyses 33

XI. About Darius. Expedition of Xerxes into Greece 34

XII. Affairs of Persia till the Saracen Conquest 37

XIII. Modern History of Persia 38

XIV. About the Hebrew, or Jews. Origin of the Hebrews.
The Removal of Jacob and his Children to Egypt 40

XV. The Bondage in Egypt. Flight of the Hebrews, and
Destruction of Pharaoh and his Host 42

XVI. About the Wanderings of the Israelites in the
Wilderness 45

XVII. Overthrow of the Midianites. Samson, Judge of Israel 47

XVIII. Samson's Exploits and Death 48

XIX. Beginning of the Reign of Saul 50

XX. Combat of David and Goliath 52

7

CHAPTER   PAGE

   XXI. The Reign of David. Wisdom of Solomon 53
  XXII. The Building of the Temple. Visit of the Queen
        of Sheba 55
 XXIII. The Decline of the Jewish Nation 57
 XXIV. The Hebrew Prophets... 58
  XXV. Crucifixion of the Saviour. Destruction of Jerusalem 60
 XXVI. Early History of China 63
XXVII. Anecdotes of the Chinese Emperors........................... 65
XXVIII. Cities of China. Manners of the Chinese..................... 67
 XXIX. Origin of the Arabs. Rise of Mohammed 69
  XXX. Sequel of the History of the Saracens 71
 XXXI. About Syria, Phoenicia, and Asia Minor 72
XXXII. About Asia Minor, or Natolia 74
XXXIII. A Brief View of Several Nations 76
XXXIV. Review of the History of Asia 78
 XXXV. Chronology of Asia 81

                            AFRICA
 XXXVI. About the Geography of Africa. The Inhabitants........... 85
XXXVII. Early Sovereigns of Egypt 86
XXXVIII. Egyptian Architecture and Sculpture 90
 XXXIX. The Ptolemies and Queen Cleopatra......................... 92
    XL. Sequel of the Egyptian History................................ 94
   XLI. Sketches of Ethiopian History 95
  XLII. Origin of the Barbary States and their Piracies
        on the Christians 96
 XLIII. Curious Facts and Fables about Africa....................... 98
 XLIV. History of the Slave Trade 100
  XLV. Chronology of Africa 101

                            EUROPE
 XLVI. Introductory Remarks on its Geography and
        other Matters 103
XLVII. About Greece. Where it is situated. Appearance
        of the Country. Climate 106
XLVIII. Extent of Greece. First Settlement of the Country 109
 XLIX. The Grecian Lawgivers 110
     L. War with Persia 112
    LI. Affairs of Athens 113

CHAPTER		PAGE
LII.	Beginning of the Theban War	115
LIII.	Sequel of the Theban War	116
LIV.	Grecian Religion or Mythology	117
LV.	The Grecian Philosophers	119
LVI.	The Grecian Philosophers continued	121
LVII.	Something more about the Greek Philosophers. The Greek Poets	123
LVIII.	About the Mode of Life among the Ancient Greeks	124
LIX.	Philip of Macedon conquers Greece	127
LX.	Conquests of Alexander the Great	129
LXI.	Sequel of Alexander's Career	131
LXII.	Greece Invaded by the Gauls	132
LXIII.	End of Grecian Independence	134
LXIV.	Modern History of Greece	135
LXV.	About Italy as it now is	136
LXVI.	Founding of Rome by Romulus. Its early State	140
LXVII.	Battle of the Horatii and Curiatii	142
LXVIII.	From the Reign of Ancus Marius, till the Expulsion of the Kings	143
LXIX.	The Story of Coriolanus	145
LXX.	Rome Invaded by the Gauls. The first Punic War	146
LXXI.	Second and third Punic Wars	149
LXXII.	Scipio's Triumph	150
LXXIII.	Sylla and Marius	152
LXXIV.	Cneius Pompey and Julius Caesar	153
LXXV.	Caesar usurps the Supreme Power	154
LXXVI.	Assassination of Julius Caesar	155
LXXVII.	Consequences of Caesar's Death	157
LXXVIII.	About the great Power and Extent of the Roman Empire in the Time of Augustus	159
LXXIX.	The Means by which Rome acquired its Power	161
LXXX.	Rome under the Emperors	163
LXXXI.	Fall of the Western Empire of the Romans	164
LXXXII.	Progress of the Decline of Rome	166
LXXXIII.	Manners and Customs of the Ancient Romans	167
LXXXIV.	About Religion. Deities. Temples. Marriages	169
LXXXV.	About Funeral Rites and Ceremonies	171

CHAPTER   PAGE

LXXXVI. Roman Farms. Mode of Plowing. Farmhouses.
Grain. Cattle. Superstitions of the Farmers.
Gardens. Vines 173

LXXXVII. Country Houses. Description of Pliny's Villa.
Aqueducts 174

LXXXVIII. Military Affairs of the Romans. Division of the Army.
The Imperial Eagle. Music. Arms. Dress.
Military Rewards. Crowns. The Triumph 176

LXXXIX. About Naval Affairs. The War Galley. Commerce.
Shows of Wild Beasts. Exhibitions of Gladiators 178

XC. Sports. Chariot Racing. The Circus. Carriages.
Private Entertainments. Supper Rooms. Convivial
Parties. Luxuries 180

XCI. About Theaters. Clocks and Watches. The Fine Arts.
Books and Writing. Costume. Conclusion 182

XCII. Rome under the Popes 184

XCIII. About several other Italian States 185

XCIV. About the Ottoman Empire. Turkey in Europe.
Turkey in Asia. About the Climate, People, and
Other Things 187

XCV. About the Saracens. How the Turks overturned the
Saracen Empire, and how the Ottoman Turks founded
the Ottoman Empire. About Bajazet, Timour, and
other remarkable Characters 188

XCVI. Sequel to the Turkish History 190

XCVII. Early History of Spain. The Moorish Conquest 192

XCVIII. Wars between the Moors and the Spaniards 195

XCIX. The Invincible Armada. Curious Death of a Spanish
King. Recent Affairs of Spain. 197

C. A short Story about Portugal 198

CI. Description of France. Its Climate. Cities. Manufactures. Manners and Customs of the People 200

CII. About the Gauls and other Tribes of Barbarians. How
the Southern Parts of Europe were first settled, and
how the Northern Parts were settled afterward 202

CIII. Story of the Barbarians continued 203

CIV. The Gauls. Origin of the modern French Nation
Little King Pepin 205

CHAPTER		PAGE
CV.	About Clovis and Little King Pepin	206
CVI.	The Reign of Charlemagne	207
CVII.	About the Crusades or Holy Wars	209
CVIII.	About the Feudal System	211
CIX.	About Chivalry, or Knight-Errantry	213
CX.	More about Chivalry	215
CXI.	King Philip and Pope Boniface. Wars of the French and English	217
CXII.	The Reign of several French Kings	219
CXIII.	The Reigns of Louis the Grand and his Successor	220
CXIV.	The French Revolution	222
CXV.	The Rise of Napoleon Bonaparte	224
CXVI.	The Fall of Bonaparte	226
CXVII.	Recent Affairs of France	227
CXVIII.	About Germany	229
CXIX.	About the ancient Tribes of Germany, Charlemagne, etc.	230
CXX.	Affairs of Switzerland	232
CXXI.	Sequel of German History	233
CXXII.	About Austria, Hungary, etc.	235
CXXIII.	About Hungary, Bohemia, the Tyrol, etc.	236
CXXIV.	About Prussia	238
CXXV.	History of Prussia	239
CXXVI.	Description of Russia	240
CXXVII.	Description of Russia continued	242
CXXVIII.	The Reign of Peter the Great	243
CXXIX.	The Successors of Peter the Great	245
CXXX.	About Sweden	247
CXXXI.	Charles the Twelfth and his Successors	249
CXXXII.	About Lapland, Norway, and Denmark	250
CXXXIII.	Brief Notice of several Kingdoms and States	253
CXXXIV.	Kingdom of Great Britain and Ireland	254
CXXXV.	About London and other Cities of England, Wales Scotland, and Ireland	255
CXXXVI.	Origin of the British Nation. The Druids	258
CXXXVII.	Saxon and Danish Kings of England	260
CXXXVIII.	Norman Kings of England	262
CXXXIX.	English Wars and Rebellions	263

CHAPTER   PAGE

CXL. The Lancastrian Kings of England 265
CXLI. Wars of the Roses 266
CXLII. Reigns of the Tudor Princes 268
CXLIII. The Reign of Elizabeth 269
CXLIV. Accession of the House of Stuart 271
CXLV. Wars of the King and Parliament 272
CXLVI. The Protectorate and the Restoration 274
CXLVII. The Revolution of 1688 and other matters 276
CXLVIII. The Hanoverian Kings of Great Britain 277
CXLIX. The Story of Wales 279
CL. The History of Scotland 281
CLI. About Ireland 283
CLII. Various Matters and Things..284
CLIII. Review. The Dark Ages. Important Inventions, etc....286
CLIV. Chronology of Europe 289

AMERICA

CLV. About America 295
CLVI. The first Inhabitants of America......................................297
CLVII. Discovery of America by Columbus 298
CLVIII. A few words about Iceland and Greenland. Settle-
ments of the French in America 300
CLIX. The French Colonies Conquered by English 302
CLX. Description of the United States 304
CLXI. Settlement and Colonial History of New England 306
CLXII. Affairs of New England continued 308
CLXIII. Early History of Virginia 309
CLXIV. Braddock's Defeat, and other Matters 311
CLXV. Causes which led to the Revolution 312
CLXVI. Account of the Battle of Lexington 313
CLXVII. The Battle of Bunker Hill 315
CLXVIII. Progress of the War. Capture of Burgoyne 316
CLXIX. The Story of Benedict Arnold and Major André 317
CLXX. War in the South. Surrender of Cornwallis 319
CLXXI. Affairs of the United States since the Revolution...........320
CLXXII. The Great Rebellion 322
CLXXIII. The Great Rebellion continued 324
CLXXIV. The Great Rebellion continued.......................................327

CHAPTER		PAGE
CLXXV.	The Great Rebellion concluded	329
CLXXVI.	General Remarks on the History of the United States	331
CLXXVII.	About South America. El Dorado, and the Fountain of Youth	332
CLXXVIII.	History of the Mexican Territories. Texas. Guatimala	334
CLXXIX.	Spanish Peruvian Territories	336
CLXXX.	Account of Brazil	337
CLXXXI.	The West Indies	339
CLXXXII.	West Indies continued	340
CLXXXIII.	West Indies continued	342
CLXXXIV.	Chronology of America	343

OCEANIA

CLXXXV.	About Oceania. The Malaysian Islands	346
CLXXXVI.	The Australasian Division of Oceania	347
CLXXXVII.	Polynesia. The Sandwich Islands	349
CLXXXVIII.	Polynesia continued. The Society Islands	350
CLXXXIX.	Story of the Bounty concluded	352
CLXL.	Chronology of Oceania	353
CLXLI.	General Views	354
	Index	358

FOREWORD

HISTORY! What is history?

Webster's New World Dictionary tries to answer this question: "1) An account of what has happened; narrative; 2) What has happened in the life of a people, country, institution, etc.; 3) All recorded events of the past; 4) The branch of knowledge that deals systematically with the recording, analyzing and explaining of past events; 5) Known or recorded past."

Parley's History of the World was published or compiled by S. G. Goodrich in 1854. It was used as a textbook for beginning history students in the Common Schools. The historical premises exemplified in this book were evidently readily accepted without question at the time it was used as a history textbook. However, not only would this book not be accepted in any public school system today, it would probably be permitted in only a very few Christian schools. And, not even the first sentence in this book would be permitted in any public school textbook in the United States. The reason is that Goodrich begins his history of the world with the statement: "In this book I am going to tell my readers the history of this world on which we live: how God created it, and placed human beings upon it. . . ."

In 1854 the history of the world began when God created it. In 1854 the history of the human race began when God created Adam and Eve. This occurred, as stated in this 1854 history book, 4004 B.C. This textbook references the Bible as a credible record of both the world and humankind's past. And, what better place to start to present the history of the human race than with the first human.

Contemporary science cannot accept the proposition that God created the world. In fact, contemporary science cannot accept the reality of God, because God cannot be analyzed in a test tube. Evolutionists, who rule over the publications of present day textbooks, cannot have man appearing on the earth 4004 B.C. To get rid of the Creator they must have man appearing first in the form of a single cell amoeba in a slime pit and developing and evolving over billions and billions of years. Therefore, revisionists must get rid of all these "mythological" references to a God who made the world and things therein. This was the first major revision in our history, geography, and science textbooks.

Next, since 1854, the moral and ethical standards of the American people have changed drastically. In 1854 there were very few divorces; very few abortions, if any; very few illegitimate children; and even if there were exceptions, they were judged to be sinful and immoral by public standard. Also, in 1854, only seventy years after the end of the Revolutionary War of Independence, the citizenry understood that this nation was a republic and the Constitution was the unchanging law of the land. Slowly but surely after the turn of the twentieth century the social and political change agents began to exert influence upon the nation's textbooks and public schools. Instead of our founding fathers being brave and stalwart Christians whose faith and fortitude founded a great nation, the revisionists remade them into philandering, self-serving, hypocritical deists.

Anyone watching the multitude of TV quiz shows would surely note that the questions usually missed by the contestants under forty are questions about history or geography. The world governance planners know that it is easier to build a new structure on level, plain ground rather than on an old building. Therefore, it is better not to teach any history or geography at all. On the other hand, when history is taught in our nation, as well as other nations, there is the utmost corruption. For example, the history books in Israel will tell you of a proud and highly civilized race of people who were cruelly and unjustly killed and driven off their land two thousand years ago. After being persecuted for two thousand years, these people have returned to fulfill their mission and destiny. The history book Palestinian children use will claim there never was a true Jewish nation, that they never lived in Jerusalem, nor was there a Jewish temple on the Temple Mount. Therefore, the Jews have no right to Palestinian land.

As the readers progress through this history book, I am sure they will soon understand that the textbooks of 1854 have little in common with the textbooks today. The question that the contemporary revisions cannot answer is that if the textbooks of 1854, and before, were so bad, how did we become such a great nation.

Sure, we might question the historicity of some of the traditional accounts in this book just as we would question some of the politically and anti-Christian revisions in modern textbooks. But on a whole, I have found this textbook to be far superior, and infinitely more interesting and reliable, more honest and accurate in presentation, than any in our public schools today.

—N. W. Hutchings

PETER PARLEY'S
HISTORY OF THE WORLD

PETER PARLEY TELLING ABOUT HISTORY AND GEOGRAPHY

CHAPTER I—INTRODUCTION

1. IN THIS BOOK I am going to tell my readers the history of this world on which we live: how God created it, and placed human beings upon it, and how these multiplied and increased, and covered the earth with many nations, and kingdoms, and tribes.

2. Here is a map (*page 18*), or picture, which shows the form of the earth. It represents one half, or one side, only. Here we see the Continent of America, on which we live. To the east of it, we see the Atlantic Ocean: to the west of it, we see the Pacific Ocean. In these oceans are many islands.

Questions—CHAP. I—1. What does Parley propose to tell about it this book?   What is the meaning of history?   *Answer—History is an account of important events that have taken place.*   What events will this book tell about?

MAP OF THE WESTERN HEMISPHERE

3. Before I proceed with the history, I wish to tell my readers something about the geography of the world on which we live. This is a vast sphere or globe, twenty-four thousand miles in circumference. It takes a whole year for a man to go round it.

4. The surface of the world is divided into land and water; the land consists of continents and islands, and the water of seas and oceans, lakes and rivers.

5. The map on page 19 represents the Eastern Continent, which is divided into Europe, Africa, and Asia.

6. To the west of Europe and Africa is the Atlantic Ocean. To the east of Asia is the Pacific Ocean.

Questions—2. What is the form of the earth? What does the above map of the Western Continent represent? What continent do we see on this map? Where do we see the Atlantic Ocean? Where do we see the Pacific Ocean? 3. What is geography? *Ans.—A description of the earth.* How many miles is it around the earth? 4. How is the surface of the earth divided? What does the land consist of? What does the water consist of? 5. What does the map of the Eastern Continent (*page 19*) represent? How is the Eastern Continent divided?

MAP OF THE EASTERN HEMISPHERE

7. To the south of Asia is the Indian Ocean. The Southern Ocean lies toward the southern part of the globe: the Northern Ocean lies toward the northern part of the globe.

CHAPTER II—ASIA

The Creation—Garden of Eden—Geography of Asia—
The Earth Peopled—The Deluge

1. The story of the Creation is very beautifully told in the opening chapter of the Bible. In this account we are told that, ages ago, God created the heavens and the earth, and all things in them.

2. Having created the sea, and the land, and the plants, and the animals, He at last completed His great work by the creation of two human

---

Questions—6. Where do we see the Atlantic Ocean on the map?   Where do we see the Pacific Ocean?   7. Where is the Indian Ocean?   The Southern Ocean?   The Northern Ocean?

Chap. II—1. Where is the story of the Creation told?   *Here let the teacher require the pupil to read the first chapter of Genesis.*   What are we told in this account?

SCENES IN ASIA

beings, called Adam and Eve. These were superior to all other created beings: so God placed them in a beautiful garden called Eden, and gave them
dominion over the earth and all the animals therein.

3. This garden was in a lovely valley, near the river Euphrates, in Asia,
and in this region the earliest events of human history took place. Here the
first nations were founded; here were Nineveh, and Babylon, and Jerusalem, which we read of in the Bible.

4. I wish, therefore, that my readers would remember that Asia is one
of the Grand Divisions of the earth, situated to the east of the United States,
nearly six thousand miles. In order to go to it, we must cross the Atlantic
Ocean, as well as the Mediterranean Sea.

5. If any of my readers ever visit Asia, they will find almost every variety of climate there, as in our own country, here in America. They will also

---

Questions—2. What beings did God create, after he had created the earth and other
things? Were Adam and Eve superior to other created beings? Where did God place
Adam and Eve? What did he give them dominion of? 3. Where was the Garden of Eden?
Note—*The Garden of Eden is supposed to have been between the rivers Euphrates and
Tigris, a little north of the Persian Gulf.* Where did the earlier events of history take
place? Where were the first nations founded? What great cities were there in this valley?
4. What is Asia? Where is Asia situated? What ocean and what sea do we cross in going
to Asia?

MAP OF ASIA

find many different nations and tribes there, having among them very different complexions, and manners, and customs.

6. Well, Adam and Eve were for a time the only human beings on this vast globe; yet they did not feel alone, for God was with them. At length they had children, Cain, Abel, Seth, and others. Some of these had children, and their descendants, after many years, became very numerous.

7. These dwelt in the neighborhood of the river Euphrates, and here they built towns, cities, and villages. But they became very wicked. They forgot to worship God, and were unjust and cruel.

Questions—5. What kind of a country is Asia as to climate? What of the nations and tribes of Asia? 6. What of Adam and Eve? What of the children of Adam and Eve? What of their descendants? 7. Where did the descendants of Adam and Eve live? What did they do?

8. The Creator therefore determined to cut off the whole human family, with the exception of Noah and his children, both as a punishment to the disobedient, and as a warning to all future nations that evil must follow sin.

9. Noah was told of the coming destruction, and therefore built an ark, or great ship, into which he gathered his family: he also took into the ark a single pair of the various kinds of land animals. It then began to rain, until all the countries of the earth were covered with a deluge of water.

10. The Bible tells us, in the seventh chapter of Genesis, that all flesh that moved upon the earth, both of fowl and of cattle, and of beast, and of every creeping thing that creepeth upon the earth, and every man, perished. Noah only remained alive, and those that were with him in the ark.

11. Thus the nations were cut off, and the world once more had but a single human family upon it.

12. These events happened a long time ago. Adam and Eve were created about six thousand years ago, and sixteen hundred and fifty-six years afterward, the deluge took place.

CHAPTER III—ASIA—Continued
How Noah and his Family came out of the Ark— The People settle in the Land of Shinar—The Tower of Babel

1. THE PEOPLE who lived before the flood are called *Antediluvians*. We know nothing about them except what is told in the Bible. It is probable that they extended over but a small part of Asia, and that no human beings dwelt either in Africa, Europe, or America, before the flood.

2. After a while the waters subsided, and Noah's ark rested upon the top of a tall mountain, situated in Armenia, called Ararat.

3. The people and animals now came out of the ark, and from them the world was again stocked with inhabitants. The animals spread themselves abroad, and after many centuries they were extended into all countries.

Questions—8. What did God do?   Why did God cause the people to perish by means of a deluge?   9. What can you tell of Noah?   What of the rain?   10. What was the effect of the deluge?   11. What of the nations of the earth?   What of Noah and his family?   12. How long since the creation of Adam and Eve?   How long after the creation of Adam and Eve did the deluge take place?

Chap. III—1. What are the people called who lived before the flood?   Where do we get our knowledge of the antediluvians?   What countries is it probable the antediluvians inhabited?   2. Where did the ark rest?   3. What of the people and animals in the ark?

4. Noah had three sons, Shem, Ham, and Japheth. These, with their families, proceeded to the country of Shinar, a beautiful and fruitful land, which lay to the south, near what is now called the Persian Gulf.

5. Here they settled themselves on the borders of the river Euphrates, probably the same country that had been inhabited by the antediluvians. It is in this region that the first nations were formed, as I have before told you.

6. The people increased very rapidly, and, at the end of a hundred years from the deluge, they were quite numerous. Most of Noah's family were at this time alive. They had told their descendants how the world had been overflowed with water, which destroyed all the land animals and all the people, except those that were in the ark.

7. All who remembered the deluge, or had heard of it, were afraid that the wickedness of mankind would again be punished in a similar way. They therefore resolved to build a tower, that they might mount upon it, and save themselves from destruction.

8. Accordingly, they laid the foundation of the edifice called the Tower of Babel, on the eastern bank of the river Euphrates. Perhaps they expected to raise the tower so high that the top would touch the blue sky, and enable them to climb into heaven.

9. Their building materials were bricks that had been baked in the sun. Instead of mortar, they cemented the bricks together with a sort of slime or pitch, which was abundant in that country.

CHAPTER IV—ASIA—CONTINUED
More about the Tower of Babel

1. THE WORKMEN labored very diligently, and piled one layer of bricks upon another, till the earth was a considerable distance beneath them. But the blue sky, and the sun, and the stars, seemed as far off as when they first began.

2. One day, while these foolish people were at their labor, a very wonderful thing took place. They were talking together as usual, but, all of a

---

Questions—4. What of Noah's sons and their families? What of Shinar? 5. Where were the first nations formed? 6. What of the increase of the people? What did Noah's family tell the people? 7. Why did the people resolve to build a great tower? 8. Where did they lay the foundation of the Tower of Babel? What did the people expect? 9. What were the materials of which Babel was built?

CHAP. IV—1. What of the workmen upon the tower?

THE PEOPLE GOING TO VARIOUS COUNTRIES

sudden, they found it impossible to understand what each other said.

3. If any of the workmen called for bricks, their companions at the bottom of the tower might mistake their meaning, and bring them pitch. If they asked for one sort of tool, another sort was given them. Their words appeared to be mere sounds without any sense, like the babble of a little child, before it has been taught to speak.

4. These strange events caused such confusion that they could not go on building the tower. They therefore gave up the idea of climbing to heaven, and resolved to wander to different parts of the earth.

5. It is likely that they formed themselves into several parties, each consisting of those who could talk intelligibly together. They set forth on

OBSERVATION—The preceding story about the Tower of Babel is famous in history, and we often allude to it in our common speech. The strange confusion of language among the people is called *"Confusion of tongues,"* and *Babel* is often used to mean *confusion of jargon.* This story also explains how mankind became first divided in different nations and tribes, and how they began to speak different languages.

Questions—2. What strange thing happened while the people were building the Tower of Babel? 3. Describe the confusion among the workmen. 4. What was the effect of this confusion of tongues?

their journey in various directions.

6. As each company departed, they probably threw a sad glance behind them at the Tower of Babel. The sun was perhaps shining on its lofty summit, as it seemed to rise into the very midst of the sky; and we may believe that it was long remembered by these exiles from their country.

7. The descendants of Shem are supposed to have distributed themselves over the country near to the Euphrates, and founded the nations there. The descendants of Ham took a westerly direction, and proceeded to Africa. They settled in Egypt, and laid the foundation of a great nation there. The descendants of Japheth proceeded to Greece, Rome, and other countries, and thus laid the foundation of several European nations.

CHAPTER V—ASIA—Continued
About the great Assyrian Empire, and the Reign of Queen Semiramis

1. WHEN THE REST of mankind were scattered into different parts of the earth, there were a number of people who remained near the Tower of Babel. They continued to inhabit the land of Shinar, which was a warm country, and very fertile. In the course of time they extended over a much larger tract of country, and built towns and cities there.

2. This region received the name of Assyria. Here was the first of the great empires of the earth. Its boundaries varied at different times, but its place on the map at page 27 may be seen near the two rivers Tigris and Euphrates, to the north of the Persian Gulf.

3. Ashur, the grandson of Noah, was the first ruler of Assyria. In the year 2221 B.C., that is, Before Christ, he built the city of Nineveh, and surrounded it with walls a hundred feet high. It was likewise defended by fifteen hundred towers, each two hundred feet in height. The city was so large, that a person would have traveled sixty miles merely in walking round it.

4. But the city of Babylon, two hundred and fifty miles south of Nineveh, and which was founded about the same time as that city, was supe-

---

Questions—5. How did the multitude arrange themselves for their departure? 6. What did the people do, as they departed from the valley of Shinar? 7. What of the descendants of Shem? Of Ham? Of Japheth?

CHAP. V—1. Did all the people leave the land of Shinar after the confusion of languages? Did the people of the land of Shinar increase? What did they do? 2. What name did the country around Shinar recieve? What was the first empire or great nation of the earth? 3. Who was the first ruler of Assyria? What city did he build? Describe the city of Nineveh.

QUEEN SEMIRAMIS GOING TO WAR

rior to it, both in size and beauty. It was situated on the river Euphrates. The walls were so thick that six chariots drawn by horses could be driven abreast upon the top, without danger of falling off on either side. In this country, we do not surround our cities with walls; but in ancient times, walls were necessary to protect the people from their enemies.

5. In the city of Babylon, there were magnificent gardens, belonging to the royal palace. They were constructed in such a manner that they appeared to be hanging in the air without resting on the earth. They contained large trees, and all kinds of fruits and flowers.

6. There was also a splendid temple dedicated to Belus, or Baal, who was the chief idol of the Babylonians. This temple was six hundred and sixty feet high, and it contained a golden image of Belus, forty feet in height.

7. The city of Babylon, which I have been describing, was first built by Nimrod, that mighty hunter, of whom the Bible tells us. But the person who made the beautiful gardens and palaces, and who set up the golden

---

Questions—4. Where was the city of Babylon? Describe this wonderful city. Why did the ancients surround their cities with walls? 5. What of the hanging gardens? 6. The temple of Belus?

QUESTIONS ON THE MAP AT PAGE 27—*This map shows the portions of the earth known to the ancients—that is, the nations which existed two or three thousand years ago. The names of countries are mostly different now from what they were then. The countries occupied by ancient Assyria and Babylon now belong to Turkey.* Which way was Assyria from the Mediterranean Sea? Which way from Persia? From Arabia? From Syria? From Armenia? etc.

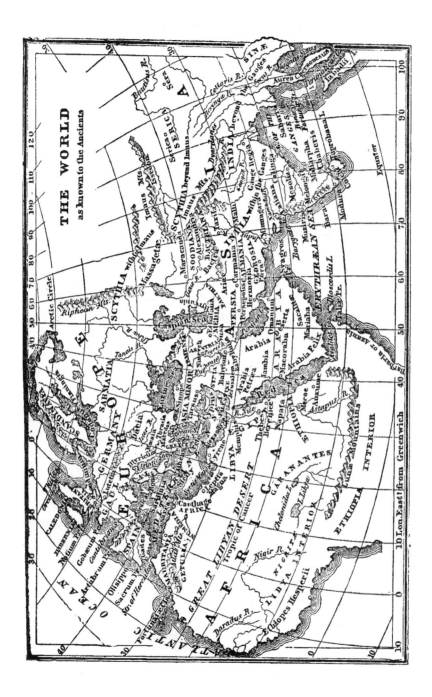

image of Belus, was a woman, named Semiramis.

8. She had been the wife of Ninus, king of Assyria; but when King Ninus died, Queen Semiramis became sole ruler of the empire, which had conquered Babylon and the country round about. She was an ambitious woman, and could not content herself to live quietly in Babylon, although she had taken so much pains to make it a beautiful city.

9. She was tormented with a desire to conquer all the nations of the earth. So she collected an immense army, and marched against the rich and powerful King of the Indies, who lived in what we now call Hindostan, a country lying to the southeast of Assyria.

CHAPTER VI—ASIA—Continued
Queen Semiramis sets forth to conquer the world,
but is defeated by the King of the Indies

1. When the King of the Indies, who, as I have said, was very rich and powerful, heard that Queen Semiramis was coming to invade his dominions, he mustered a vast number of men to defend them. Besides his soldiers, he had a great many elephants.

2. Each of these enormous beasts was worth a whole regiment of soldiers. They were taught to rush into the battle, and toss the enemy about with their trunks and tusks, and trample them down with their huge feet.

3. Now Queen Semiramis had no elephants, and therefore she was afraid that the King of the Indies would overcome her. She endeavored to prevent this misfortune by a very curious contrivance. In the first place, she ordered three thousand brown oxen to be killed.

4. The hides of the dead oxen were stripped off, and sewed together in the shape of elephants. These were placed upon camels, and when the camels were drawn up in battle array, they looked pretty much like a troop of great brown elephants. Doubtless, the King of the Indies wondered where

---

Editor's Note—Although believed true at the time of original publication, the story of Semiramis related here has no basis in biblical fact.

Questions—7. Who built Babylon? Who made the hanging gardens, the image of Belus, etc? 8. What of Semiramis? Was she contented with Babylon? 9. What foolish and wicked desire had she? What did she do? Where did the King of the Indies live? In which direction was India from Assyria?
Chap. VI—1. What did the King of the Indies do when he heard that Semiramis was going to make war upon his kingdom? What sort of an army had he? 2. What of the elephants? 3–4. By what contrivance did Semiramis endeavor to match the elephants of the King of India?

Queen Semiramis had caught them, as there were no elephants in Assyria.

5. When the battle was beginning, the King of the Indies, with his real elephants, marched forward on one side, and Queen Semiramis, with her camels and ox-hides, came boldly against him on the other.

6. But when the Assyrian army had marched close to the host of the Indians, the latter perceived that there was no such thing as an elephant among them. They therefore laid aside all fear, and rushed furiously upon Queen Semiramis and her soldiers.

7. The real elephants put the camels to flight; and then, in a great rage, they ran about, tossing the Assyrians into the air, and trampling them down by the hundreds. Thus the Assyrian army was routed, and the King of the Indies gained a complete victory.

8. Queen Semiramis was sorely wounded; but she got into a chariot, and drove away at full speed from the battlefield. She finally escaped to her own kingdom, but in a very sad condition.

9. She then took up her residence in the palace at Babylon. But she did not long enjoy herself in the beautiful gardens which she had suspended in the air. It is said that her own son, whose name was Ninias, put his mother to death, that he might get possession of the throne, and reign over the people.

10. Such was the melancholy end of the mighty Queen Semiramis. How foolish and wicked it was for her to spend her life in trying to conquer other nations, instead of making her own people happy. But she had not learned that golden rule, "Do to others as you would have done to you."

CHAPTER VII—ASIA—Continued
About Ninias—Reign of Sardanapalus, and overthrow of the First Assyrian Empire

1. AFTER NINIAS had wickedly murdered his mother, he became king of Assyria. His reign began about the year 2000 B.C., or about three hundred and fifty years after the deluge.

2. Ninias was not only a very wicked man, but a very slothful one. He did not set out to conquer kingdoms like his mother, but shut himself up in his palace, and thought of nothing but how to enjoy himself.

Questions—5–6. Describe the battle.   7. What was the result of the battle?   8. What of Semiramis?   9. What was the fate of Queen Semiramis?

CHAP. VII—1. What of Ninias?   When did his reign begin?   2. What was the character of Ninias?   What did he do?

3. He knew that his people hated him, and therefore he kept many guards in his palace; but he was afraid to trust even his guards. Whether he was murdered at last, or whether he died quietly in his bed, is more than I can tell, for history does not inform us.

4. After the reign of Ninias, there was an interval of eight hundred years, during which it is impossible to say what happened in the kingdom of Assyria. It is probable that most of the kings were like Ninias; that they wasted their time in idle pleasures, and never did any thing worthy of remembrance.

5. Some years afterward, there was a king upon the throne of Assyria, whose name was Sardanapalus. He is said to have been a beautiful young man; but he was slothful and took no care of his kingdom, and made no attempt to promote the welfare of his people.

6. At last he ceased to go outside of his palace, and lived all the time among the women. In order to make himself more fit for their company, he painted his face, and sometimes put on a woman's dress. In this ridiculous guise, the great King Sardanapalus used to sit down with the women, and help them to spin.

7. But while Sardanapalus was feasting, and dancing, and painting his face, and dressing himself like a woman, and helping the women to spin, a terrible destruction was impending over his head.

8. Arbaces, governor of the Medes, and Belesis, the governor of Babylon, made war against this unworthy monarch, and besieged him in the city of Nineveh. Sardanapalus saw that he could not escape, and that if he lived any longer he should probably become a slave.

9. So, rather than be a slave, he resolved to die. He therefore collected his treasures, and heaped them into one great pile in a splendid hall of his palace, and then set fire to the pile. The palace was speedily in a blaze, and Sardanapalus, with his favorite officers, and a multitude of beautiful women, were burnt to death.

10. Thus ended the First Assyrian Empire, the first that makes a figure in history, about the year 900 B.C.—that is, Before Christ. After a time, a new empire arose, of which Nineveh was the capital. This is called the Second Assyrian Empire, and I will give a brief account of it.

Questions—3. What else can you tell of Ninias?   4. What of Assyria for eight hundred years after Ninias?   5. What of Sardanapalus?   6. How did he live?   8. What of Arbaces?   9. What did Sardanapalus do?   10. What was the end of the First Assyrian Empire?   Do you think it was right for Sardanapalus to live only for his own pleasure, and not try to make his people happy?   Does not his story show that even a king cannot be idle without bringing destruction upon his people, and misery upon himself?

SENNACHERIB IN FRONT OF HIS PALACE

CHAPTER VIII—ASIA—CONTINUED
Extent of Assyria and Babylonia—
Notices of other Countries in ancient times

1. By THIS TIME, it will be understood, that the nations and kingdoms of Asia had become very numerous. Not only was the country of Assyria very populous, but Babylonia, of which Babylon was the capital, was also a great empire. This was several times conquered by the Assyrians, and the history of the two countries is frequently blended together, as if they were one empire.

2. To the east of Assyria was Media; to the southeast was Persia; to the west were Palestine and Syria; to the north was Armenia—all populous and powerful countries. About this time, too, Egypt, in Africa, was at the height of its prosperity, and Rome and Greece, in Europe, were rising into power.

3. But Assyria, after a long time, revived from its overthrow, and become once more a powerful empire. Several of its kings made war on the Israelites, and are mentioned in the Old Testament. Among them were Pul, Tiglath-pilesar, Shalmaneser, Sennacherib, and several others.

Questions—CHAP. VIII—1. What of Asia at the time of the overthrow of Sardanapalus? 2. What of Assyria? Of Babylon? What of Media? Palestine? Syria? Persia? Armenia? Egypt? Rome? Greece? (*see map, p. 27*).

4. At last, in the year 606 B.C., the King of the Medes and the King of Babylon united their forces, and made war on Assyria. They captured Nineveh and overturned the empire, which from this time became extinct.

5. The conquerors completely destroyed Nineveh, and in a few centuries it was almost forgotten. Its site became a mere heap of ruins, and these were at last so covered with soil, that the place where Nineveh was built became a matter of doubt.

6. But a few years since, an Englishman by the name of Layard caused excavations to be made on the east bank of the Tigris, near the present town of Mosul, and here he found the ruins of a superb palace, supposed to be that of Sennacherib.

7. This spot is now known to be the site of the ancient Nineveh. Many curious things have been found there, which show how the ancient Assyrians worshipped, and how they made war, and how they dressed themselves, and many other interesting things.

CHAPTER IX—ASIA—CONTINUED
Cyrus conquers Babylon—His death

1. SOON AFTER the overthrow of the Second Assyrian Empire and the final destruction of Nineveh, Persia began to rise into importance. The first inhabitants of that country were descended from Elam, the eldest son of Shem. They were therefore called Elamites. Very little is known of their history till about eighteen centuries after the deluge. Cyrus, a great conqueror, then ascended the throne of Persia.

2. Cyrus continued to extend his empire in all directions. Media, Parthia, Mesopotamia, Armenia, Syria, Canaan, and parts of Arabia, were subdued, and made subject to his kingdom. One of his chief exploits was the taking of the city of Babylon, the capital of Babylonia. The walls of this great city were so thick and high, that it would have been impossible for an enemy either to break them down, or to climb over them. It was, therefore, a very difficult matter to capture this strong place.

3. Now, the channel of the river Euphrates ran directly through the

---

Questions—3. What of Assyria?   Mention some of the Assyrian kings named in the Bible.   4. What took place in the year 606 B.C.?   5. What of the great city of Nineveh?   6. What of Mr. Layard?   7. What information do we gather from the discoveries of Mr. Layard?

CHAP. IX—1. What of Persia, soon after the overthrow of the Second Assyrian Empire? What of the early history of Persia?   2. What of the conquests of Cyrus?   What was one of his chief exploits?   What of the walls of Babylon?

center of Babylon. Cyrus therefore caused deep ditches to be dug around the city, so that he could draw off all the water of the river, and leave the channel dry. When the ditches were completed, he waited for a proper time to draw off the river.

4. On a certain night, Belshazzar, king of Babylon, made a great festival. His guards, and nearly all the inhabitants, were eating and drinking, thoughtless of the enemy on the outside of their walls. The Persians seized this opportunity to throw open the dams of the ditches.

5. The whole water of the Euphrates immediately flowed into them. Cyrus put himself at the head of the Persian army, and where the mighty river had so lately rushed along, there in its channel were now the trampling footsteps of an innumerable host. Thus the Persian troops entered the city.

6. The guards of the royal palace were surprised and slain. The astonished Belshazzar heard the clash of arms, and the shrieks of dying men, as he sat with his nobles in the banquet-hall. But it was too late to escape. They were all slaughtered, and their blood was mingled with the wine of the festival. Thus Babylon was taken, and for a long time was one of the capitals of Persia. All the surrounding nations also became subject to Persia.

7. Cyrus afterward marched against the Scythians, a brave nation who dwelt to the northeast of the Caspian Sea. But Tomyris, their queen, collected an army, and fought a bloody battle with the Persians. Cyrus was defeated, and taken prisoner. The son of the Scythian queen had been killed in the battle, and she resolved to avenge his death. She ordered her attendants to kill Cyrus, which was done in a horrible manner.

CHAPTER X—ASIA—Continued
Reign of Cambyses

1. CAMBYSES, the son of Cyrus, seems to have been a worse man than his father. He was addicted to drinking wine, and Prexaspes, a favorite courtier, hinted to him that he injured his health and faculties by this practice. When Prexaspes had done speaking, Cambyses called for wine, and drank off several large goblets. "Now we shall see," said he, "whether the

---

Questions—3. What of the river Euphrates? What did Cyrus do to this river? 4. What of King Belshazzar? 5–6. When Cyrus opened the dams of the ditches, what happened? 7. Where did the Scythians live? Their character? What else can you tell of Cyrus? CHAP. X—1. What of Cambyses? What story can you tell of him?

wine has dimmed my sight or rendered my hand unsteady!"

2. He then called for a bow and arrow, and ordered the son of Prexaspes to stand at the further end of the hall. The boy did so; and while his father looked on, the cruel Cambyses took aim at the poor child, and shot an arrow directly through his heart!

3. I am very sorry, my dear young reader, to tell you such horrible stories as these. I would not tell them but that they are true, and they may teach us good and useful lessons. They may show us how wicked and miserable even kings may be.

4. They may also make us rejoice that we live in an age when such things do not happen. You must recollect that I am telling you of what took place many ages since. The people were then thought to be merely the playthings of their kings, and only made to serve them. Since that time, Christ has come and told us that it is the will of God that each man should do to another as he would be done by.

5. It is true that in many countries, particularly in Asia, the divine laws of Christ are not much known; but in most places, the kings are better than they were in the time of Cambyses. In our happy country we have no kings, and therefore the stories I am telling you about the cruelties of the ancient monarchs of Asia appear very shocking.

6. But I must go on with my story. Cambyses made war against the Egyptians. At the siege of one of their cities, he contrived a very cunning method to take the place. The Egyptians believed that cats and dogs were sacred, and they worshipped them as divine. This foolish superstition induced Cambyses to collect a great many cats and dogs, and place them in front of his army.

7. The Egyptians were afraid to discharge their arrows, lest they should kill some of these sacred animals. The Persians, therefore, marched onward, with the dogs barking and the cats mewing before them, and the city was taken without the slightest resistance.

8. The chief deity of the Egyptians was a bull, to whom they had given the name of Apis. Cambyses killed this holy bull, and bestowed the flesh on some of his soldiers for dinner. Soon afterward, to the great joy of the Egyptians, he killed himself accidentally with his own sword.

Questions—3. What lessons may we learn from these painful tales of ancient kings? 4. What was thought of the people in these ancient times? What has Christ since told us? 5. Where are the laws of Christ not known? What of kings now? 6–7. How did Cambyses capture an Egyptian city? 8. What of the Egyptian god Apis? How was Cambyses slain?

DARIUS ORDERING THE THREE YOUNG MEN TO BE KILLED

CHAPTER XI—ASIA—Continued
About Darius—Expedition of Xerxes into Greece

1. ANOTHER KING of the Persians was named Darius. He was likewise a cruel tyrant. When he was going on an expedition against the Scythians, he compelled an old man's three sons to join his army. These were all the children the old man had. He came into the king's presence, and earnestly entreated that one of his sons might be left at home.

2. "I am very poor and infirm," said the old man. "I am unable to work. If you take away all my three children, I shall starve to death." "Indeed," answered King Darius, in a very compassionate tone, "then they shall all three remain with you !" Immediately he ordered the three young men to be slain, and gave their dead bodies to their poor old father.

3. While Darius was preparing to make war on Greece, he fell sick and died. His successor was his son Xerxes. This monarch invaded Greece with nearly two millions of men on land, and more than half a million on board his fleet.

4. You may well believe that a king who could collect so large an army, had great wealth and power. At this time the Persian Empire was of vast extent, but still Xerxes wished to conquer other nations. His chief capital was Persepolis, one of the most splendid cities that ever existed.

Questions—CHAP. XI—1-2. What of Darius?   Tell a story of his cruelty.   3. Who was the successor of Darius?   How large was the army of Xerxes when he invaded Greece? *Where is Greece?—Ans. In Europe.   How far from Persia?—Ans. About fifteen hundred miles.   In which direction from Persia?—Ans. Northwest.*

5. Here Xerxes had magnificent palaces; he had gold and silver in abundance; he had precious stones more than he could count; he was indeed surrounded with pomp and magnificence; but all these could not bring contentment. He was still desirous of conquering other nations, and for this purpose he collected the greatest army of which history gives us any account.

6. When Xerxes arrived in Greece, it so happened that a great mountain, called Mount Athos, stood directly in the way that he wished his ships to sail. He therefore wrote a letter to the mountain, commanding it to get out of the way; but Mount Athos would not stir one step.

7. In order to bring his land forces from Asia into Greece, Xerxes built a bridge of boats across a part of the sea called the Hellespont. But the waves broke the bridge to pieces, and Xerxes commanded the sea to be whipped for its disrespectful conduct.

8. The greater part of the cities of Greece submitted to Xerxes; but Sparta and Athens made a stubborn resistance. Though they could muster but few soldiers, these were far more valiant than the Persians.

9. At Thermopylae, Xerxes wished to lead his army through a narrow passage between a mountain and the sea. Leonidas, king of Sparta, opposed him with six thousand men. Seventy thousand Persians were slain in the attempt to break through the pass.

10. At last, Leonidas found that the Persians could not be kept back any longer. He therefore sent away all but three hundred men, and with these he remained at the pass of Thermopylae. The immense host of the Persians came onward like a flood; and only one soldier of the three hundred Spartans escaped to tell that the rest were slain.

11. But Xerxes did not long continue to triumph in Greece. His fleet was defeated at Salamis, and his army at Plataea. In escaping, he was forced to cross the Hellespont in a little fishing vessel; for the sea, in spite of its being whipped, had again broken his bridge for boats.

12. Not long after his return to Persia, the proud Xerxes was murdered in his bed. This event happened in the year 465 B.C. His son and successor, Artaxerxes, made peace with the Greeks.

13. The story of Xerxes may teach us the folly of ambition. Had he

---

Questions—4. What of the Persian Empire in the time of Xerxes? What of Persepolis? In which direction was it from Babylon? Jerusalem? 5. What of the wealth and magnificence of Xerxes? What was the greatest army ever known? 6. What of Mount Athos? 7. What of the Hellespont? 8. What of Greece? 9. What of Thermopylae? 10. What of Leonidas? 11. What of Salamis? Plataea? How did Xerxes return?

been content with staying at home and governing his people so as to make them happy, he might have been happy himself. But, having too much, he still strove to acquire more, and thus brought misery upon himself and millions of his fellow-men.

CHAPTER XII—ASIA—CONTINUED
Affairs of Persia till the Saracen Conquest

1. BETWEEN ONE and two centuries after the death of Xerxes—that is, about 330 years before Christ—Persia was invaded by Alexander the Great, king of Macedon. Darius the Third was then king of Persia. Being defeated by Alexander, two of his own subjects bound him with golden chains, and put him in a covered cart.

2. They intended to murder Darius, and get possession of the kingdom. But Alexander came suddenly upon the conspirators, and forced them to take flight. As they rode away, they discharged their darts at Darius, and slew him.

3. After this time, Persia became subject to the Parthians, whose country had formerly been a province of the Persian Empire. It continued under the government of the Parthian kings nearly five hundred years. About the year 230 after the Christian era, a Persian, named Artaxerxes, excited a rebellion, and made himself king.

4. His descendants occupied the throne for many generations. One of the most distinguished was Chosroes, or Khosrou the Great, who lived about five hundred and fifty years after Christ. He made war against the Romans, and ravaged their provinces in Asia.

5. One of his successors was likewise named Khosrou. This hateful monster caused his own father to be beaten to death. But Heaven punished him by the wickedness of his eldest son, whose name was Siroes. He dethroned his father, and murdered all his brothers in his presence.

6. Siroes then ordered his father to be thrown into a dungeon. Here,

Questions—12. What of the death of Xerxes? When did this event happen? Who succeeded Xerxes? 13. What may the story of Xerxes teach us? How might he have been happy? How did he bring misery upon himself and others?

CHAP. XII—1. When was Persia invaded by Alexander the Great? Who was then king of Persia? What happened to Darius? 2. How was he killed? 3. To whom did Persia become subject after the death of Darius? How long did it continue under the government of Parthia? Which way is Parthia from Persia? When did Artaxerxes make himself king? 4. What of his descendants? Khosrou the Great? When did he live? What did he do?

instead of killing the old king at once, he tormented him for a long time by pricking him with the points of arrows! Khosrou died at last, in great agony.

7. These things may seem too shocking to tell; but it is perhaps necessary that my young readers should know how very cruel men may become when given up to the influence of passion. Let us be thankful that the religion of Christ has taught us to look upon such crimes as were often practiced by the Persian kings, with horror and disgust.

8. Isdegerdes, who ascended the throne in the year 632 of the Christian era, was the last of this dynasty of Persian kings. During his reign, the Saracens, a warlike people of Arabia, who had adopted the faith of Mohammed, invaded Persia, and conquered it. Isdegerdes was killed in battle.

9. Persia then became a part of the Saracen Empire. It was ruled by the caliphs, who resided at Bagdad, a splendid city which they built on the river Tigris.

10. This celebrated place was founded A.D. 673, and once contained two millions of inhabitants. It was then filled with costly buildings, but these are now mostly in ruins. The modern city is poorly built, and comparatively insignificant.

CHAPTER XIII—ASIA—Continued
Modern History of Persia

1. IN THE YEAR 1258 of the Christian era, the empire of the Saracens was subverted by the Tartars. Persia was governed by them for a considerable time. It was afterward ruled by monarchs called Sophis, or Shahs. The first of these was named Ishmael, a man of Saracen descent. He took possession of the throne by violence, and reigned twenty-three years.

2. The greatest of these monarchs was named Shah Abbas. He ascended the throne in 1586. Abbas fought against the Turks, and gained many splendid victories. He also deprived the Portuguese of their possessions in the East.

Questions—5. What of one of the successors of Khosrou the Great? What wickedness did Siroes commit? 7. How may men become very cruel? For what should we be thankful? 8. When did Isdegerdes ascend the throne? What of him? Who were the Saracens? What did the Saracens do during Isdegerdes' reign? How was Isdegerdes killed? 9. Of what empire did Persia become a part? How was it ruled? Where did the caliphs live? 10 What of Bagdad?

CHAP. XIII—1. What of the empire of the Saracens in the year 1258? How was Persia governed? What of Ishmael?

A GROUP OF MODERN PERSIANS

3. The best of this family of kings was Shah Husseyn; and he was also the last, and most unfortunate. He began to reign in the year 1694. Husseyn and his subjects met with many disasters; and he was at length compelled to surrender his throne to a rival.

4. But before he took off the crown from his head, Husseyn went on foot through the principal streets of Ispahan, which was then the capital. The people thronged around him with tears and lamentations. The excellent and kind-hearted monarch endeavored to comfort them.

5. He told them that the new king, whose name was Mahmoud, would not love them better than he himself had done, but that he would know better how to govern them, and how to conquer their enemies. So the good Husseyn took off his crown, which had been only a trouble to him, and bade his people farewell.

6. In 1730, Kouli Khan took possession of the throne of Persia. He called himself Nadir Shah. He was a famous conqueror and tyrant, and was assassinated in his tent after a reign of about seventeen years.

7. Since his death, there has been much bloodshed in Persia. Ambitious men have often aspired to the throne, and involved the country in civil war.

8. The king generally resides in the city of Teheran. But he has a beautiful palace at Ispahan, called the Palace of Forty Pillars. Each of the forty

Questions—2. Who was Shah Abbas? When did he ascend the throne? What did he do? 3. What of Shah Husseyn? 4–5. Describe the manner in which he surrendered his crown. 6. When did Kouli Khan come to the throne? What other name had he? What of him? 7. What of Persia since the death of Kouli Khan?

pillars is supported by four lions, of white marble. The whole edifice looks as if it were built of pearl, and silver, and gold, and precious stones.

9. I have now done with the story of Persia. Like that of most other eastern countries, it abounds in tales of cruelty, battle, and bloodshed. In ancient times, the people worshiped the sun, and bowed down to idols. But, for more than a thousand years, they have been believers in a false prophet, called Mohammed.

10. They have never become acquainted with the religion of Jesus Christ, which teaches us to be gentle and forgiving one to another; and thus cruelty has ever been common among them.

11. The climate of Persia is mild, and the country abounds in beautiful and fragrant trees, shrubs, and flowers. The people are less warlike than in former times. The rich live in splendid palaces, and the poor in mud huts. The kingdom is small, compared with the vast empire of Xerxes. Persepolis, the ancient capital, is now a heap of ruins. Teheran and Ispahan, the two principal cities, are of comparatively modern date.

12. From what I have told you, you will not like the Persian character; yet it is not altogether bad. The people are very fond of reading, and telling instructive stories; many of these were written ages since, and are exceedingly beautiful. The people also have a taste for poetry, and they appear to be fond of the beauties of nature, and to have a love of virtue.

CHAPTER XIV—ASIA—Continued
About the Hebrews, or Jews—Origin of the Hebrews—
The Removal of Jacob and his Children to Egypt

1. The founder of the Hebrew nation was Abraham, the son of Terah. He was born about two hundred years after the deluge. The country of his birth was Chaldea, which formed the southern part of the Assyrian Empire.

2. The rest of the inhabitants of Chaldea were idolators, and worshiped the sun, moon, and stars; but Abraham worshiped the true God whom we

---

Questions—8. Where does the King of Persia generally reside? Describe the palace of the emperor. 9. What of the story of Persia? What was the worship of the ancient Persians? What is now the religion of the people? 10. What has always been common among them? 11. What of the climate of Persia? The soil? People? How does the extent of the country compare with what it was in the time of Xerxes? What of Persepolis? Teheran? Ispahan? 12. What of the Persian character?

Chap. XIV—1. What of Abraham? When was he born? How long ago?—*Ans. Nearly four thousand years.* What was the native country of Abraham?

40

ABRAHAM

worship. In the early part of his life he was a herdsman on the Chaldean plains. When his father was dead, God commanded him to leave his native country, and travel westward to the land of Canaan.

3. This region was afterward called Palestine. It lies north of Arabia, and is on the eastern border of the Mediterranean Sea. It is nearly six thousand miles southeasterly from New York. It was a rich and fertile country, and God promised Abraham that his descendants should dwell there.

4. Many years of Abraham's life were spent in wandering to and fro. His wife Sarah went with him, and they were followed by a large number of male and female servants, and by numerous flocks and herds. They dwelt in tents, and had no settled home.

5. Abraham and Sarah had one son, named Isaac. His father loved him fondly; but when God commanded him to sacrifice the child, he prepared to obey. But an angel came down from heaven and told him not to slay his son.

Questions—2. What of the worship of the Chaldeans? Of Abraham? What of the early life of Abraham? What did God command Abraham to do? Which way was Canaan from Chaldea? How far was Chaldea from Canaan?—*Ans. About five hundred miles.* 3. Where is the land of Canaan? What is it now called? Which way is it from where you live? How would you go to the land of Canaan or Palestine?—*Ans. Across the Atlantic Ocean and the Mediterranean Sea.* 4. What of the life of Abraham? Who went with him from Chaldea to Canaan?

6. The life of Abraham was full of interesting events, but I have not room to relate them all here. He lived to be a hundred and seventy-five years old, and then died at Hebron, in Canaan. His burial place was in a cave at Machpelah, where Sarah had been buried many years before.

7. The Jews and the Arabians are descended from this ancient patriarch. They have always called him Father Abraham. It is said that, to this day, they show the place where Abraham and Sarah lie buried, and that they consider it a holy spot. Many travelers at the present day go to see it.

8. Isaac, the son of Abraham, left two children, Esau and Jacob. The younger, Jacob, persuaded his brother to sell his birthright for a mess of pottage. He likewise obtained a blessing, which his father intended to bestow on Esau.

9. Jacob had twelve sons, whose names were Reuben, Simeon, Levi, Dan, Judah, Naphthali, Gad, Asher, Issachar, Zebulon, Joseph, and Benjamin. The posterity of each of these twelve afterward became a separate tribe among the Hebrews.

10. My young reader must look into the Bible for the beautiful story of Joseph and his brethren. I can merely tell him that Joseph was sold into captivity, and carried into the land of Egypt, and that there he was the means of preserving his aged father and all his brothers from death by famine. He died 1635 B.C.

11. Jacob and his twelve children removed to Egypt, and took up their residence there. It was in that country that the Hebrews first began to be a nation; so that their history may be said to commence from this period. Jacob died 1689 B.C.

CHAPTER XV—ASIA—CONTINUED
The Bondage in Egypt—Flight of the Hebrews, and Destruction of Pharaoh and his Host

1. EGYPT, you know, is in Africa. It has many cities, and a famous river called the Nile runs through the country. But this land is less populous now than in the time of Joseph. It was then full of people, and they were the

---

Questions—5. What of Isaac? 6. What else of Abraham? 7. What of the Jews? 8. What of Isaac? What did Esau do? What is meant by birthright?—*Ans. The eldest son, in ancient times, enjoyed many privileges over his younger brothers. These Esau sold to Jacob for a single meal of victuals. Thus, Jacob became the head of the Jewish people.* 9. Who were the twelve sons of Jacob? What of the descendants of these twlve sons of Jacob? 10. Can you tell the story of Joseph, as related in Genesis, chap. 37, etc.? 11. Where did Jacob go with his family? Which way was Egypt from Canaan? How far?—*Ans. About two hundred miles.*

most learned and civilized of all the nations of the earth. There are many ruins to be seen in Egypt, which show that the palaces and cities of ancient times were very splendid.

2. But I must tell you of the Hebrews. Pharaoh, the good king of Egypt, died, and Joseph likewise. Another king then ascended the throne, who hated the Hebrews, and did all in his power to oppress them.

3. The Egyptians treated them like slaves. All the hardest labor was performed by the Hebrews. It is thought by some writers that the immense piles of stone, called the Pyramids, were built by them. These vast edifices are still standing on the banks of the Nile.

4. The cruel King of Egypt was named Pharaoh, like his predecessor. One of the most wicked injuries that he inflicted on the Hebrews was the following:

5. He commanded that every male child should be thrown into the river Nile the instant he was born. The reason for this horrible cruelty was, that the Hebrews might not become more numerous than the Egyptians, and conquer the whole country.

6. One of the Hebrew women, however, could not make up her mind to throw her son into the Nile. If she had positively disobeyed the king's order, she would have been put to death. She therefore very privately made a little ark, or boat, of bulrushes, placed the child in it, and laid it among the flags that grew by the river's side.

7. In a little while the king's daughter came down to the river to bathe. Perceiving the ark of bulrushes, she went with her maids to fetch it. When the looked into it, they found a little Hebrew boy there!

8. The heart of the princess was moved with compassion, and she resolved to save his life. She hired his own mother to nurse him. She gave him the name of Moses, and, when he grew old enough to be put in school, she caused him to be instructed in all the learning of the Egyptians. At that period they were the most learned people on earth.

9. But, though he himself was so well treated, Moses did not forget the sufferings of the other Hebrews. He remembered that they were his breth-

---

Questions—CHAP. XV—1. What of Egypt?   Which way does it lie from you?   How far is it from New York to Egypt?—*Ans. Nearly six thousand miles.*   Which way does the Nile flow?   In which of the four quarters of the globe is Egypt?   In which part of Africa is Egypt?   What of Egypt in the time of Joseph?   2. How were the Hebrews treated after the death of Joseph?   3. What of the pyramids?   How high is the tallest of the Egyptian pyramids?—*Ans. About five hundred feet.*   4–5. What cruelty did Pharaoh inflict upon the Hebrews?   6. What did one of the Hebrew women do?   7. What of Pharaoh's daughter?   8. What of Moses?

MOSES FOUND IN THE BULRUSHES

ren, and he resolved to rescue them from their oppressors.

10. He and his brother Aaron received power from God to perform many wonderful things, in order to induce Pharaoh to let the Hebrews depart out of Egypt. Ten great plagues were inflicted on the Egyptians; and these were so terrible, that at last Pharaoh gave the Hebrews leave to go.

11. But scarcely were they gone, when the king was sorry that he had not still kept them in Egypt, that he might oppress them, and compel them to labor for him as before. He therefore mustered his warriors, and rode swiftly after the fugitives.

12. When he came in sight of them, they were crossing the Red Sea, which lies between Egypt and Arabia. The Lord had caused the waters to roll back, and form a wall on each side. Thus there was a path of glistening sand for the Hebrews through the very depths of the sea.

13. Pharaoh and his army rode onward, and by the time that the fugi-

---

Questions — 9. What did he resolve to do?   10. What of Moses and Aaron?   To what did Pharaoh consent?   11. Did he change his mind?   What did he do?   12. Which way was the Red Sea from Egypt?   What miracle did God perform?   How did the Hebrews cross the Red Sea?

tives had reached the opposite shore, the Egyptians were in the midst of the wonderful passage.

14. As the Hebrews fled, they looked behind them. There was the proud array of the Egyptian king, with his chariots and horsemen, and all his innumerable army, and Pharaoh himself riding haughtily in the midst.

15. The affrighted Hebrews looked behind them again, and, lo! the two walls of water had rolled together. They were dashing against the chariots, and sweeping the soldiers off their feet. The waves were crested with foam, and came roaring against the proud and wicked king. In a little time the sea rolled calmly over Pharaoh and his host, and thus they all perished, leaving the Jews to proceed on their journey.

16. This was a terrible event, but Pharaoh had been very cruel; he therefore deserved his fate. This story may teach us that not only wicked rulers, but those who follow them, have reason to fear the judgments of Heaven.

CHAPTER XVI—ASIA—Continued
About the Wanderings of the Israelites in the Wilderness

1. IT WAS NOW two hundred and fifteen years since Jacob had come to settle in Egypt. His descendants had multiplied so rapidly that, at the time of their departure, the Hebrew nation are supposed to have amounted to at least two millions of people. Moses, their leader, was eighty years old, but his step was steady; and, though of meek and humble manners, he was a man of great wisdom and firmness of character.

2. The Hebrews intended to go directly from Egypt to the land of Canaan. This latter country is now called Palestine. Before reaching it, the children of Israel were to pass through a part of Arabia.

3. In order that they might not go astray, a vast pillar of mist, or cloud, moved before them all day long; and at night the pillar of cloud was changed to a pillar of fire, which threw a radiance over the regions through which they journeyed.

4. The country was desolate and barren, and often destitute of water,

---

Questions—15. What became of Pharaoh and his army?

CHAP. XVI—1. How long was it from the time Jacob settled in Egypt to the departure of the Israelites? What was the number of the Israelites at this time? How old was Moses? What was his character? 2. In which direction is Canaan from Egypt? What country lies between Canaan and Egypt? In what country did the Hebrews wander? 3. How were the Hebrews guided?

but the Lord fed the people with manna and with quails; and when they were thirsty, Moses smote upon a rock, and the water gushed out abundantly. This was a great relief, for the climate there was exceedingly hot. Besides all this, the Hebrews received divine assistance against the Amalekites, and were enabled to conquer them in battle.

5. But, in spite of these various mercies, the Israelites were an ungrateful and rebellious people. They often turned from the worship of the true God, and became idolators.

6. At the very time when the Lord was revealing himself to Moses on the summit of Mount Sinai, the people compelled Aaron to make a golden calf. They worshipped this poor image instead of Jehovah, who had brought them out of Egypt.

7. On account of their numerous sins, the Lord often inflicted severe punishments upon them. Many were slain by pestilence, and some were swallowed up in the earth. The remainder were compelled to wander forty years in the deserts of Arabia, though the whole distance in a direct line from Egypt to Canaan was but about three hundred miles.

8. Before they came to the land of Canaan, most of those who had fled out of Egypt were dead. Their children inherited the promised land, but they themselves were buried in the sands of the desert. Even Moses was permitted merely to gaze at the land of Canaan from the top of Mount Pisgah. Here he died, at the age of one hundred and twenty years.

9. After the death of Moses, Joshua, the son of Nun, became the leader of the Israelites. Under his guidance they entered the promised land, and subdued the people who inhabited it. The territory of Canaan was then divided among the twelve tribes of Israel.

Questions—4. What sort of country did they travel through? How were they fed? When they could find no spring or river, how were they supplied with water? Why was this supply of water necessary? What other divine assistance was rendered to the Hebrews? 5. Were the Hebrews grateful for all the mercies bestowed upon them? 6. What did they do when Moses was on Mount Sinai? Were not the Hebrews very foolish and wicked to worship the image of a calf rather than to worship God? When children disobey their parents, and seek their own pleasure rather than do their duty, are they not like the Hebrews in this instance? 7. What evil resulted from the disobedience of the Hebrews? Do you not know that evil always follows disobedience? How long did the Hebrews wander? What is the distance, in a straight line, from Egypt to Canaan? 8. Did most of the Hebrews who left Egypt reach Canaan? What of Moses? Where is Mount Pisgah? 9. Who became leader after the death of Moses? How was the land of Canaan divided?

CHAPTER XVII—ASIA—Continued
Overthrow of the Midianites—Samson, Judge of Israel

1. AFTER THEIR SETTLEMENT in Canaan, the Israelites lived under the authority of Judges. These were their rulers in time of peace, and their generals in war. Some of them were very remarkable personages, and did many things worthy of remembrance.

2. The name of one of the judges was Gideon. While he ruled Israel, an army of Midianites invaded the country, and oppressed the people for seven years. But the Lord instructed Gideon how to rescue the Israelites from their power.

3. Gideon chose three hundred men, and caused each of them to take an earthen pitcher, and put a lamp within it. With this small band he entered the camp of the Midianites by night. There was an immense army of them, sleeping in their tents, without apprehending any danger from the conquered Israelites.

4. But their destruction was at hand. Gideon gave a signal, and all his three hundred men broke their pitchers, at the same time blowing a loud blast upon trumpets which they had brought. This terrible clamor startled the Midianites from their sleep.

5. Amid the clangor of the trumpets, they heard the Israelites shouting, "The sword of the Lord and of Gideon." A great panic seized upon the Midianites. They doubtless imagined that all the Hebrew army had broken into their camp.

6. Each man mistook his neighbor for an enemy; so that more of the Midianites were slain by their own swords than by the swords of the men of Israel. Thus God wrought a great deliverance for his people.

7. The most famous of all the judges of Israel was named Samson. He was the strongest man in the world; and it was a wonderful circumstance that his great strength depended upon the hair of his head.

8. While he continued to wear his hair long, and curling down his neck, he had more strength than a hundred men put together. But if his hair were to be cut off, he would be no stronger than any single man.

9. In the days of Samson, the Philistines had conquered the Israelites. Samson disliked them on account of the injuries which they inflicted upon

Questions—CHAP. XVII—1. How were the Hebrews governed after their settlement in Canaan? What of the judges? 2. What of Gideon? 3–6. Tell how Gideon contrived to overcome the Midianites. 7. What of Samson? In what did his strength lie?

his countrymen. He made use of his great strength to do them all the harm in his power.

CHAPTER XVIII—ASIA—Continued
Samson's Exploits and Death

1. On one occasion Samson slew a thousand of the Philistines, although he had no better weapon than the jawbone of an ass. At another time, when they had shut him up in the city of Gaza, he took the gates of the city upon his shoulders, and carried them to the top of a distant hill.

2. But though Samson hated the Philistines, and was always doing them mischief, there was a woman among them whom he loved. Her name was Delilah. She pretended to love Samson in return; but her only object was to ruin him.

3. This woman used many persuasions to induce Samson to tell her what it was that made him so much stronger than other men. At first Samson deceived her. He said that if he were bound with seven green withes, his strength would depart; or that if he were tied with new ropes, he should be as weak as an ordinary man.

4. So Delilah bound him first with seven green withes, and afterward with new ropes. But Samson snapped the withes like burnt tow, and the ropes like thread. At length, however, Delilah prevailed upon him to tell her the real source of his great strength.

5. When she had found out the secret, she cut off the hair of his head while he was sleeping, and then delivered him to her countrymen, the Philistines. These put out his eyes, and bound him with fetters of brass, and he was forced to labor like a brute beast in the prison.

6. Samson was able to work very hard; for pretty soon his hair began to grow, and so his wonderful vigor returned. Thus he became the strongest man in the world again.

7. One day the Philistines were offering a great sacrifice to their idol, whose name was Dagon. They feasted, and their hearts were merry. When their mirth was at its height, they sent for poor blind Samson, that he might amuse them by showing specimens of his wonderful strength.

Questions—9. What of the Philistines? Why did Samson dislike them?

Chap. XVIII—1. With what weapon did Samson kill a thousand Philistines? What of the gates of Gaza? 2. What of Delilah? 3. How did Samson deceive her? 5. How did Delilah deprive Samson of his strength? What did the Philistines do to Samson? 6. What happened when Samson's hair grew again? 7–11. Tell how Samson destroyed the Philistine temple.

This map represents Palestine, or the land of Canaan, as it was about the time of our Saviour. The teacher will put such questions upon it here, as he may deem necessary.

SAMSON BREAKING THE WITHES

8. Samson was accordingly brought from prison and led into Dagon's temple. His brazen fetters clanked at every step. He was a woeful object with his blinded eyes. But his hair had grown again, and was curling upon his brawny shoulders.

9. When Samson had done many wonderful feats of strength, he asked leave to rest himself against the two main pillars of the temple. The floor and galleries above were all crowded with Philistines. They gazed upon this man of mighty strength, and they triumphed and rejoiced, because they imagined he could do them no more harm.

10. But while they gazed, the strong man threw his arms round the two pillars of the temple. The edifice trembled as with an earthquake. Then Samson bowed himself with all his might, and down came the temple with a crash like thunder, overwhelming the whole multitude of the Philistines in its ruins.

11. Samson was likewise crushed, but in his death it appears that he triumphed over his enemies, and lay buried beneath the dead bodies of lords and mighty men.

CHAPTER XIX—ASIA—Continued
Beginning of the Reign of Saul

1. Many other judges ruled over Israel, in the space of about four hun-

Questions—Chap. XIX—1. For how long a time were the Hebrews governed by judges?

dred years from the time that Moses led the Hebrews out of Egypt. But at length they became dissatisfied with this mode of government, and demanded that a king should be placed over them.

2. Samuel was then the judge of Israel. He was an old man, and a wise one; and besides the wisdom that he had collected in the course of a long life, he possessed wisdom from on high.

3. When the people demanded a king, Samuel endeavored to convince them that they were much better off without one. He described the tyrannical acts which kings have been in the habit of committing, whenever they have had the power to do so.

4. But the Israelites would not hearken to this wise and good old man. They still wished for a king. They imagined that none but a king would govern them well in time of peace, or fight successfully against their enemies in war.

5. Samuel, therefore, consulted the Lord, and was directed to find out a king for the Israelites. The person who was fixed upon was a young man named Saul, the son of Kish. He possessed great beauty, and was a head taller than any other man among the Israelites. Samuel anointed his head with oil, and gave him to the Israelites as their king.

6. For a considerable time King Saul behaved like a wise and righteous monarch. But at length he began to disobey the Lord, and seldom took the advice of Samuel, although that good old priest would have been willing to direct him in every action of his life.

7. In the course of Saul's reign, the Israelites were often at war with the neighboring nations. At one time, when the Philistines had invaded the country, there was a great giant in their host, whose name was Goliath, of Gath.

8. He was at least ten or twelve feet high, and was clothed from head to foot in brazen armor. He carried an enormous spear, the iron head of which weighed as many as thirty pounds.

9. Every day did this frightful giant stride forth from the camp of the Philistines, and defy the Israelites to produce a champion who would stand against him in single combat. But, instead of doing this, the whole host of Israel stood aloof from him, as a flock of sheep from a lion.

Questions—2. What of Samuel?   3. What did he do when the people demanded a king?   4. What did the Israelites think?   5. What of Saul?   6. What did Saul do?   7–9. What of Goliath?

CHAPTER XX—ASIA—CONTINUED
Combat of David and Goliath

1. AT LAST a young shepherd, by the name of David, happened to come to the camp of the Israelites, and heard the terrible voice of Goliath, as he thundered forth his challenge.

2. Young as he was, David had already slain a lion and a bear; and, with the help of the Lord, he thought himself able to slay this gigantic Philistine. He therefore obtained leave of King Saul to accept the challenge.

3. But, instead of wearing the king's armor, which Saul would willingly have lent him, David went to the battle in his shepherd's garb. He did not even buckle on a sword.

4. When the two combatants came into the field, there was the youthful David on the side of the Israelites, with a staff in one hand and a sling in the other, carrying five smooth stones in a shepherd's scrip or pouch.

5. On the side of the Philistines, strode forth the mighty Goliath. He glistened in his brazen armor, and brandished his great iron-headed spear till it quivered like a reed. When the giant spoke, his voice growled almost like thunder rolling overhead.

6. He looked scornfully at David, and hardly thought it worth his while to lift up his spear against him. "Come hither," quoth the giant, "and I will feed the fowls with your flesh!"

7. But little David was not at all abashed. He made a bold answer, and told Goliath that he would cut off his head, and give his enormous carcass to the beasts of the field. This threat so enraged the giant that he put himself in motion to slay David.

8. The young man ran forward to meet Goliath, and, as he ran, he took a smooth stone from his scrip, and placed it in his sling. When at a proper distance, he whirled the sling, and let drive the stone. It went whizzing through the air, and hit Goliath right in the center of the forehead.

9. The stone penetrated to the brain; and down the giant fell at full length upon the field, with his brazen armor clanging around him. David then cut off Goliath's head with his own sword. The Philistines were affrighted at their champion's overthrow, and fled.

10. The men of Israel pursued them, and made a prodigious slaughter. David returned from the battle carrying the grim and grisly head of Goli-

---

Questions — CHAP. XX — 1. Who was David? What did he do? 2. What had David done? What did he think? 3–10. Tell the story of David and Goliath.

COMBAT BETWEEN DAVID AND GOLIATH

ath by the hair. The Hebrew women came forth to meet him, danced around him, and sung triumphant anthems in his praise.

CHAPTER XXI—ASIA—Continued
The Reign of David—Wisdom of Solomon

1. David had won so much renown by his victory over Goliath, that Saul became envious of him, and often endeavored to kill him. But Jonathan, the son of Saul, loved David better than a brother.

2. During the lifetime of Saul, David was forced to live in exile. But, after a reign of about twenty-four years, King Saul was slain on the mountains of Gilboa, in a disastrous battle with the Philistines. Jonathan was likewise killed.

3. When David heard of these sad events, he expressed his sorrow by weeping and rending his garments. Yet he gained a kingdom by the death

---

Questions—Chap. XXI—1. Why was Saul envious of David? What did Saul do? What of Jonathan? 2. How was David obliged to live? What of Saul? Jonathan?

of Saul and Jonathan; for the men of Judah first elected him to reign over them, and afterward the whole people of Israel chose him for their king.

4. A great part of David's life was spent in war. He gained many victories, and enjoyed high renown as a gallant leader. He conquered many of the surrounding nations, and raised his kingdom to a higher pitch of power than it ever enjoyed before or afterward. But he also won a peaceful kind of fame, which will last while the world endures.

5. He won it by his heavenly poesy; for King David was the sweet Psalmist of Israel; and in all the ages since he lived, his psalms have been sung to the praise of the Lord. It is now about three thousand years since David died; yet to this hour every pious heart loves to commune with God in the beautiful words of this inspired man.

6. In the latter part of his life, David was much grieved by the rebellious conduct of his son Absalom. But it grieved him more when Absalom was slain by Joab, who found him hanging by his long hair on the branches of an oak, and pierced his body with three darts.

7. When David had reigned forty years, and was grown a very old man, he died in his palace at Jerusalem. The kingdom was inherited by his son Solomon. This prince was very young when he ascended the throne, but he was wiser in his youth than in his riper years.

8. Not long after he became king, two women came into his presence bringing a little child. Each of the women claimed the child as her own, and they quarreled violently, as if they would have torn the poor babe asunder. It seemed impossible to find out whose the child really was.

9. "Bring hither a sword," said King Solomon; and immediately one of the attendants brought a sharp sword. "Now," continued Solomon, "that I may not wrong either of these women, the thing in dispute shall be equally divided between them. Cut the child in twain, and let each take half."

10. But when the real mother saw the keen sword glittering over her poor babe, she gave a scream of agony. "Do not slay the child!" she cried. "Give it to this wicked woman. Only let it live, and she may be its mother!"

11. But the other woman showed now pity for the child. "I ask no more than my just rights," she said. "Cut the child in two! I will be content with

---

Questions—3. What effect had these events upon David?   Who became king of Israel after the death of Saul?   4. How was a great part of David's life spent?   To what condition did he bring the Hebrew nation?   What better fame did he acquire than that of a conqueror?   5. Who was the author of the Psalms?   What can you say of the Psalms? How long since David lived?   6. What of Absalom?   7. How long did David reign?   Who succeeded him?   What of Solomon?   8–11. Tell the story of the child.

half." Now, Solomon had watched the conduct of the two women, and he knew the true mother by her tenderness for the poor babe. "Give the child alive to her who would not have it slain," he said. "She is its mother."

CHAPTER XXII—ASIA—Continued
The Building of the Temple—Visit of the Queen of Sheba

1. KING DAVID, as I before told you, had increased the power and wealth of the Hebrew nation, so that it was now a great kingdom. Silver and gold were very abundant in the country, and King David had made preparations for the building of a splendid temple, to be dedicated to the worship of the true God.

2. The chief event of Solomon's life was the building of this temple. This was done by the special command of the Lord. It was now four hundred and eighty years since the Israelites had come out of Egypt; and in all that time there had been no edifice erected to the worship of God.

3. Solomon made an agreement with Hiram, king of Tyre, that he would give him a yearly supply of wheat and oil, in exchange for cedar and fir. Tyre was a great commercial city on the coast of the Mediterranean Sea, to the northward of Jerusalem. It belonged to Phoenicia, a country which has the credit of having first engaged in commerce.

4. With the timber which he procured from Tyre, and with a large quantity of hewn stone, Solomon began to build the temple. The front of this building was one hundred and twenty feet long, thirty-five feet broad, and forty-five feet high, with a porch or entrance of much greater height. It extended around a large square, and, with the various buildings attached to it, covered twenty acres of ground.

5. But no pen can describe the richness and admirable splendor of this sacred edifice. The interior was constructed of the most costly kinds of wood; and the walls were carved with figures of cherubim and other beautiful devices. The walls and floors were partly overlaid with gold.

Questions—CHAP. XXII—1. What had David done? What of silver and gold among the Hebrews? 2. What was the chief event of Solomon's reign? By whose command was the temple built? 3. What agreement did Solomon make with Hiram, king of Tyre? What of Phoenicia? In what part of Canaan was Jerusalem? How far from the Mediterranean Sea?—*Ans. About thirty-five miles.* Where was Tyre? In which direction is Jerusalem from Babylon? From Egypt? 4. With what did Solomon begin to build the temple? Where was the temple of Solomon built?—*Ans. On a hill in Jerusalem called Mount Moriah.* Describe the extent of the temple. 5. Describe the interior of the temple.

6. The temple was furnished with altars, and tables, and candlesticks, and innumerable other articles, all of the purest gold. The whole edifice must have shone almost as if it had been built entirely of that precious metal.

7. Seven years were employed in building this temple. It was just about three thousand years from the creation that it was finished, and one thousand years before the birth of Christ. When it was finished, Solomon assembled all the chiefs, and elders, and great men of Israel, in order to dedicate it. The priests brought the ark, containing the two tables of stone which God had given to Moses more than four centuries before.

8. The ark was now placed in the holiest part of the temple. It rested beneath the broad wings of two cherubim that were overlaid with gold. No sooner was the ark in its place than a cloud issued forth and filled the temple. This was a token that the Lord was there.

9. After the building of the temple, Solomon became so renowned for his wisdom and magnificence, that the Queen of Sheba came from her own dominions to visit him. Her country is supposed to have been in Africa, to the southward of Egypt.

10. She traveled with a great multitude of attendants; and she had likewise a train of camels, laden with gold and precious stones, and abundance of spices. The sweet perfume of the spices scented the deserts through which she passed.

11. When she came to Jerusalem, she beheld Solomon seated on a great throne of ivory overlaid with pure gold. His feet rested on a golden footstool. There were lions of gold about the throne. The king had a majestic look, and the Queen of Sheba was astonished at his grandeur; but when they had talked together, she admired his wisdom even more than his magnificence. She acknowledged that the half of his greatness had not been told her.

12. If the Queen of Sheba could have seen Solomon a few years afterward, she would have beheld a lamentable change. He turned from the true God, and became an idolator. This wise and righteous king, who had built the sacred temple, now grew so wicked that he built high places for the worship of heathen deities.

Questions—6. With what was the temple furnished? 7. How long were they in building the temple? How long after the creation was the temple finished? How long before Christ? How long ago? Describe the dedication of the temple. 9. What of the Queen of Sheba? Where is it supposed she came from? 10. Describe her visit to Solomon. 12. What change took place in Solomon?

13. For this reason God determined to take away the chief part of the kingdom from his descendants. Accordingly, when Solomon was dead, ten of the tribes of Israel revolted against his son Rehoboam.

CHAPTER XXIII—ASIA—CONTINUED
The Decline of the Jewish Nation

1. IN CONSEQUENCE of the revolt of the ten tribes, Rehoboam reigned only over the two tribes of Judah and Benjamin, these being called the Kingdom of Judah. Besides the loss of so large a part of his kingdom, he suffered other misfortunes. Shishak, king of Egypt, made war against him, and took Jerusalem. He carried away the treasures of the temple and of the palace.

2. The other ten tribes of Israel, which had revolted from Rehoboam, were thenceforward governed by kings of their own, the country being called the Kingdom of Israel. Most of these kings were wicked men, and idolators. Their palace and seat of government was in the city of Samaria.

3. When the kingdom of Israel had been separated from that of Judah about two hundred and fifty years, it was conquered by Shalmaneser, king of Assyria. He made slaves of the Israelites, and carried them to his own country, and most of them never returned to the land of Canaan.

4. The people of the two tribes of Judah and Benjamin continued to reside in Canaan. They were now called Jews. The royal palace and seat of government was at Jerusalem. Some of the Jewish kings were pious men, but most of them offended God by their sinfulness and idolatry.

5. The whole nation of the Jews were perverse, and underwent many severe inflictions from the wrath of God. In the year 601 B.C., Nebuchadnezzar, king of Babylon, took Jerusalem. He destroyed the temple, and carried the principal people captive to Babylon.

6. Afterward, when Zedekiah was king, Jerusalem was again besieged and taken by Nebuzaradan, a general under Nebuchadnezzar. He broke

---

Questions—13. What evil followed the idolatry of Solomon?

CHAP. XXIII—1. Who was Rehoboam? Into what two kingdoms was the Hebrew nation divided during his reign? What name was given to the two tribes? What of Shishak? 2. What name was given to the ten tribes which revolted? How was the kingdom of Israel governed? In which part of Canaan were the ten tribes? In which part was the kingdom of Judah? What of the kings of Israel? Where did these kings dwell? Where was Samaria? How far from Jerusalem?—*Ans. Forty miles.* 3. What of Shalmaneser? 4. What were the people of Judah now called? Where was the seat of government? What of the kings of Judah? 5. What of the Jewish nation? What of Nebuchadnezzar?

down the walls of the city, and left nothing standing that could be destroyed. The Jews remained captive in Babylon seventy years.

7. When Babylon was taken by Cyrus, king of Persia, the Jews were permitted to return to their own country. They rebuilt the temple, and resumed their ancient manner of worship. Till the time of Alexander the Great, about 330 B.C., the nation was dependent on the kings of Persia.

8. It is said that Alexander the Great intended to take Jerusalem. But as he advanced with his army, the High Priest came forth to meet him, in his robes of office, at the head of a long train of Levites and people. Alexander was so struck with their appearance that he agreed to spare the city.

9. In the course of the two next centuries the Egyptians invaded the Jewish kingdom, and afterward the Syrians reduced the inhabitants to bondage. They suffered great calamities from the tyranny of these conquerors.

10. But in the year 166 before the Christian era, Judas Maccabaeus, a valiant Jewish leader, drove the Syrians out of the country. When the King of Syria heard of it, he took an oath that he would destroy the whole Jewish nation. But, as he was hastening to Jerusalem, he was killed by a fall from his chariot.

11. The descendants of Judas Maccabaeus afterward assumed royal authority, and became kings of the Jews. In less than a century, however, the country was subdued by Pompey, a celebrated Roman general. He conferred the government on Antipater, a native of Edom.

12. In the year 37 before the Christian era, the Roman senate decreed that Herod, the son of Antipater, should be king of the Jews. It was this Herod who commanded that all the young children of Bethlehem should be slain, in order that the infant Jesus might not survive. The period of that blessed infant's birth was now at hand.

CHAPTER XXIV—ASIA—Continued
The Hebrew Prophets

1. I must now glance backward, and say a few words respecting a class of men who had appeared at various times among the Hebrews. These men

---

Questions—6. What of Nebuzaradan? How long did the Jews remain captive in Babylon? 7. What of Cyrus? What did the Jews do on their return from captivity? How long was the nation dependent upon Persia? 8. What of Alexander the Great? 9. What happened after the time of Alexander? 10. What of Judas Maccabaeus? What of the King of Syria? In which direction from Syria was Canaan? 11. What of the descendants of Judas Maccabaeus? What of Pompey? Whom did he appoint to govern Judah? 12. When did the Roman senate appoint Herod king of the Jews? What of Herod?

were called prophets. They held intercourse with God, and he gave them the knowledge of things that were to happen in future years.

2. One of the most remarkable of the prophets was named Elijah. Many wonderful things are told of him. While he was dwelling in a solitary place, the ravens brought him food. He restored the son of a poor widow from death to life.

3. He denounced God's vengeance against the wicked king Ahab, and foretold that the dogs should eat the painted Jezebel, his queen. And all this was so. He caused fire to come down from heaven and consume two captains, with their soldiers. He divided the river Jordan by smiting it with his mantle, and passed over on dry ground.

4. At last, when his mission on earth was ended, there came a chariot of fire, and horses of fire, and carried Elijah by a whirlwind up to heaven.

5. Elijah's mantle fell from the fiery chariot. It was caught up by a person named Elisha, and he likewise became a very celebrated prophet. He cursed some little children because they laughed at his bald head, and soon afterward two she-bears tore forty and two of them in pieces.

6. When Elisha was dead, and had lain many months in his sepulchre, another dead man happened to be let down into the same darksome place. But when the corpse touched the hallowed bones of the prophet Elisha, it immediately revived, and became a living man again.

7. Jonah was another prophet. A whale swallowed him, and kept him for three days in the depths of the ocean, and then vomited him safely on dry land. Isaiah was also a prophet. He foretold many terrible calamities that were to befall Israel and Judah, and the surrounding nations. Jeremiah bewailed in plaintive accents the sins and misfortunes of God's people.

8. The prophet Daniel foretold the downfall of Belshazzar, king of Babylon. He was afterward cast into a den of lions in Babylon, at the command of King Darius. The next morning the king looked down into the den, and there was Daniel, alive and well!

9. King Darius then ordered Daniel to be drawn out of the den, and his false accusers to be thrown into it. The moment that these wicked persons touched the bottom, the lions sprang forward and tore them limb from limb.

10. Many other prophets appeared at various times, and most of them

---

Questions—Chap. XXIV—1. What of the prophets? 2. What is told of Elijah? 5. What of Elisha? 7. What of Jonah? Isaiah? Jeremiah? 8. What of Daniel? 10. What can you say of the prophets? Of what did the prophets all speak?

THE PROPHET ELIJAH

performed such wonderful works that there could be no doubt of their possessing power from on high. Now, it was remarked that all these prophets, or nearly all, spoke of a King, or Ruler, or other illustrious Personage, who was to appear among the Jews.

11. Although they foretold the most dreadful calamities to the people, still there was this one thing to comfort them. A descendant of King David was to renew the glory of the Jewish race, and establish his sway over the whole world.

12. This great event was expected to happen in about fifteen hundred years after Moses led the Israelites out of Egypt. And it did then happen. When the appointed period had elapsed, there appeared a Star in a certain quarter of the heavens.

13. Three Wise Men from the East beheld the star, and were guided by it to a stable in the little village of Bethlehem. It was about five miles from Jerusalem. There, in a manger, lay the infant Jesus!

CHAPTER XXV—ASIA—CONTINUED
Crucifixion of the Saviour—Destruction of Jerusalem

1. THE greatest event, not only in the history of the Jews, but in the history of the world, had now taken place. This was the coming of the Saviour. But my readers must not expect me to relate the whole story of this

---

Questions—11. What cheering prospect did the prophets hold out to the Jews? 12. About how long after Moses did Christ appear? What of a star in the east? 13. What of Bethlehem? Whom did the Wise Men find in a stable?

divine Personage in the little book which I am now writing.

2. The Jews rejected him. They had been looking for an earthly potentate; and when they beheld the meek and lowly Jesus, they despised and hated him. From the time that he proclaimed himself the Messiah, they sought to take his life.

3. They brought him before the judgment seat of Pontius Pilate, who was then the Roman governor of Judea. Pilate sentenced him to death, and the Saviour of the world was crucified between two thieves. He however rose from the dead, after being buried three days, and ascended into heaven!

4. Such is the brief history of Jesus Christ. After his death, his apostles proceeded to preach his Gospel throughout the land of Canaan and other countries. Of all the apostles, Paul was the most active and successful.

5. He visited various parts of Palestine, Syria, Asia Minor, and Greece. At length he was sent as a prisoner to Rome, to be tried by the emperor. He went with other prisoners in a small vessel nearly the whole length of the Mediterranean Sea.

6. In the course of the voyage, the vessel was wrecked upon the island of Malta, during a terrible gale. After this, the vessel proceeded on its voyage, and Paul reached Rome, sixty-one years A.D. Here he remained in prison a long time; but many persons came to visit him, and he preached to them all the doctrines of Christianity. Paul was at length released, but it is believed that he was beheaded by order of the emperor Nero.

7. The apostles had now sown the seeds of the Gospel in many countries, and the fruits began to appear. Nearly all the civilized world were worshipers of the Roman gods; but this heathen faith gradually gave way before the Gospel, and, in process of time, Christianity was diffused over nearly the whole of Europe.

8. Long before the crucifixion of Christ, the Jews had become completely subject to the Roman power. But, about forty years after his death, they rebelled against their masters.

Questions—CHAP. XXV—1. What is the greatest event that has occurred on the globe? How long since Christ was born? How long after the creation did Christ appear?—*Ans. Four thousand and four years.* How long after the flood?—*Ans. Two thousand three hundred and forty-eight years.* 2. How did the Jews receive Christ? 3. What of Pilate? The crucifixion? 4. What did Christ's apostles do after his death? What of Paul? 5. What countries did Paul visit? Where was he at length sent? 6. Where was Paul's vessel wrecked? When did he arrive at Rome? To whom did he preach Christianity? What is supposed to have been his fate? 7. What had the apostles done? What of the worship of heathen deities? What of Christianity?

CRUCIFIXION OF THE SAVIOUR

9. Titus, the Roman general, immediately marched to besiege Jerusalem. A most dreadful war ensued. The inhabitants were shut up in the city, and soon were greatly in want of food. Hunger impelled one of the Jewish women to devour her own child. When Titus heard of it, he was so shocked that he vowed the destruction of the whole Jewish race, and more than a hundred thousand persons perished during this frightful siege!

10. At length the city was taken in the nighttime, and set on fire. The flames caught the temple. The hills on which Jerusalem is situated were all blazing like so many volcanoes. The blood of the slaughtered inhabitants hissed upon the burning brands.

11. Ninety-seven thousand Jews were taken prisoners. Some were sold as slaves. The conquerors exposed others to be torn in pieces by wild beasts. A few people remained in Jerusalem, and partly rebuilt the city. But it was again destroyed by a Roman emperor named Adrian. He leveled the walls and houses with the earth, and sowed the ground with salt.

12. The Jews were scattered all over the world. This catastrophe had

Questions—11. What of Adrian?

long been prophesied. There are now between four and five millions of them in different parts of the earth. They still keep their religion, and many of their old customs. Jerusalem has been partially restored, but it is now very different from what it was in the time of our Saviour, being quite an inferior city.

CHAPTER XXVI—ASIA—Continued
Early History of China

1. THE TERRITORY of the Chinese Empire is nearly the same at the present day that it has been for several centuries. It is bounded on the north by Asiatic Russia, on the east by the Pacific Ocean, and on the south by the Chinese Sea and Farther India. On the west there are mountains and sandy deserts, which divide it from Tibet and Tartary.

2. This empire is very ancient, and has continued longer than any other that has ever existed. It is also the most populous empire in the world, containing about three hundred and fifty millions of people! Its history goes back four thousand years from the present time. The name of its founder was Fohi, whom some writers suppose to have been the same as Noah.

3. There have been twenty-two dynasties, or separate families of em-

A GROUP OF CHINESE

Questions—12. What became of the Jews? What event had been foretold by the prophets? What of Jerusalem?

CHAP. XXVI—1. What of the Chinese empire? Boundaries? What divides it from Tibet and Tartary? Which way is China from Persia? Hindostan? Siberia? The Birman empire? 2. What of the antiquity and duration of the Chinese empire? How far back does its history extend? Who was its founder? What do some writers suppose?

perors, who have successively ruled over China. If their history were to be particularly related, it would fill at least twenty-two great books. Yet few of the emperors did anything worthy of remembrance.

4. Before the time of Fohi, the Chinese believe that men lived pretty much like brutes; that they had no settled homes, but wandered up and down in the forests, seeking for food; and when they caught any animals or birds, that they drank the blood, and devoured even the hair and feathers.

5. We find nothing very remarkable about the Chinese emperors till the reign of Chaus, who lived about a thousand years before the Christian era. He was extremely fond of hunting, and used to gallop into the midst of the rice fields in pursuit of game. In this manner he did so much mischief, that his subjects resolved to destroy him.

6. There was a large river, which the emperor was often in the habit of crossing. On the shore of this river the people placed a boat, as if for the accommodation of Chaus. The next time that the emperor returned from hunting, he and his attendants got on board the boat, and set sail for the opposite shore.

7. But the boat had been contrived on purpose for his destruction. In the middle of the river it fell to pieces, and all on board were drowned. Thus, to the great joy of his subjects, the emperor Chaus went down among the fishes, and never again came a-hunting in the rice fields.

8. The emperor Ching, who reigned about two thousand years ago, built a great wall in order to protect his dominions against the Tartars. It was forty-five feet high, and eighteen feet thick, and it extended over mountains and valleys, a distance of fifteen hundred miles. This wall still remains, though in a ruinous state.

9. When Ching had completed the wall, he thought himself so very great an emperor, that none of his predecessors were worth remembering. He therefore ordered all the historical writings and public records to be burnt. He also caused four hundred learned men, who were addicted to writing histories, to be buried alive.

10. If the emperor Ching could have caught poor old Peter Parley, he certainly would have buried him likewise, with his four hundred learned brethren; and so the world would have lost this Universal History!

Questions—3. What of the dynasties or families that have ruled over China?   4. What do the Chinese suppose was the state of China before the time of Fohi?   5. When did Chaus live?   What of him?   6–7. Relate the manner in which the people destroyed him?`   8. When did the emperor Ching live?   Describe the great wall.   Does it still remain? 9. What orders did he give respecting historical books, records, and learned men?

CHAPTER XXVII—ASIA—Continued
Anecdotes of the Chinese Emperors

1. THE MOST FAMOUS man China has ever produced, was Confucius, who was born about five hundred years before Christ. He was a learned man, and had many disciples or scholars, who attended his lectures and traveled about with him. He composed several books, which are held in great reverence, even to this day, by the learned Chinese.

2. The emperor Vati lived about the time of the Christian era. This emperor was desirous of reigning till the world should come to an end, and perhaps longer. He therefore spent his time in endeavoring to brew a liquor that would make him immortal. But, unfortunately, before the liquor was fit to drink, the emperor died.

3. Another emperor, instead of attending to the affairs of the nation, applied himself wholly to study. His prime minister took advantage of his negligence, and raised a rebellion against him. When the emperor heard the shouts of the rebels, he shut his book, and put on his armor. But, on ascending the ramparts of the city, he saw that it was too late to resist. He then returned to his library, which contained one hundred and forty thousand volumes.

4. The emperor knew that these books had been the means of his losing the vast empire of China, by withdrawing his attention from the government. He therefore set fire to them with his own hands, and the whole library was consumed. The rebels afterward put him to death.

5. The emperor Si-given began to reign in the year 617 after the Christian era. He dwelt in a magnificent palace. After the emperor's death, his son came to the palace, and was astonished at its splendor and beauty. "Such a residence is good for nothing but to corrupt a monarch, and render him proud!" exclaimed he. Accordingly he commanded this great and costly edifice to be burnt to the ground.

6. Chwang-tsong, who had been a brave soldier, was made emperor about eight hundred years ago. He was a person of very frugal habits. It was one of his singularities, but he never slept on a bed, but always on the bare ground, with a bell fastened to his neck. If he turned over in his sleep,

---

Questions—CHAP. XXVII—1. What of Confucius?   2. What of the emperor Vati? How did he spend his time?   3–4. Tell the story of a very learned emperor.   5. When did Si-given begin to reign?   Where did he dwell?   What did his son do?   6. What of Chwang-tsong?   What curious fact is related of him?

CONFUCIUS

the ringing of the bell would awaken him; and he then considered it time to get up.

7. In the year 1209, Genghis Khan, the famous Mogul conqueror, invaded China with an immense army of Tartars. He and his descendants conquered the whole empire, and the latter governed it for many years.

8. The emperor Ching-tsa ascended the throne three or four centuries ago. A mine was discovered during his reign, and precious stones of great value were dug out of it. Some of them were brought to the emperor, but he looked scornfully at them.

9. "Do you call these precious stones?" cried he. "What are they good for? They can neither clothe the people, nor satisfy their hunger." So saying, he ordered the mine to be closed up, and the miners to be employed in some more useful kind of labor.

10. About a hundred years ago, in the reign of Yong-tching, there was the most terrible earthquake that had ever been known. It shook down nearly all the houses in the city of Pekin, and buried one hundred thousand people. A still greater number perished in the surrounding country.

11. In 1840, a war between Great Britain and China broke out, which continued for two years. The British government sent an expedition against the Chinese, which took Canton, and several other places. The war continued till 1842, when peace was made. Soon after, a treaty of commerce was

---

Questions—7. When did Genghis Khan invade China? What of him and his descendants? 8–9. What of the emperor Ching-tsa? Relate the story of the mine. 10. What happened in the reign of Yong-tching? 11. What happened in 1840? What of the British government.

made between China and the United States.

12. Mr. Cushing went to China and negotiated this treaty on the part of our country. It is said that he was one day invited by a mandarin to dinner. Mr. Cushing was curious to know what a particular dish was, and not speaking Chinese, inquired: "Quack?—quack, quack?"

13. The mandarin understood him, and, shaking his head solemnly, replied: "Bow, wow!" I am not sure that this story is true, but as the Chinese eat young dogs, it may be true.

14. In 1852 a great insurrection began in China, headed by a native Chinese, Tae-ping-wang. This man had acquired some notion of the Bible, and in his proclamations he set forth some doctrines similar to those of Christianity.

15. This rebellion was not suppressed until July 1864, when Nankin, which had been made the rebel capital, was taken, and Tae-ping-wang committed suicide. During the progress of this rebellion, China was for a short time engaged in wars with England and France: she is now (1881) at peace with all the world.

CHAPTER XXVIII—ASIA—Continued
Cities of China—Manners of the Chinese

1. I MUST NOW give you a short account of the cities and people of China as they are at this day. Nankin was formerly the capital of China. Pekin, which contains two millions of inhabitants, is now the capital. The emperor's palace stands in a part of Pekin called the Tartar city.

2. The walls of Pekin are built of brick, and are nearly one hundred feet high, so that they hide the whole city. They are so thick, that sentinels on horseback ride round the city on the top of the wall. There are nine gates, which have marble arches, and are prodigiously high.

3. The people of China have an olive complexion, with black hair, and small black eyes. The chief part of their dress is a long loose robe, which is fastened round the body with a silken girdle. In this girdle they carry a knife, and two sticks for eating instead of a knife and fork.

4. There are some horrible customs among them. For instance, if par-

---

Questions—12–13. What of Mr. Cushing and his treaty between the United States and China? 14. What of Tae-ping-wang? 15. What of other wars?

Chap. XXVIII—1. What was formerly the capital of China? What is now? How many inhabitants does Pekin contain? Where is the emperor's palace? 2. What of the walls of Pekin? The gates? 3. What of the people of China? Their dress?

ents have a greater number of children than they can conveniently support, they are permitted to throw them into a river!

5. The people are not nice about what they eat. Dog meat is publicly sold in the streets for food. Indeed there is a certain kind of dog fatted for this purpose. Rats and mice are frequently eaten. There is a sort of bird's nest which is made into a jelly, and is considered a great delicacy.

6. The Chinese ladies are chiefly remarkable for their little feet. A grown woman in China is able to wear smaller shoes than a young child in America. But their feet are kept merely for show, and are almost good for nothing to walk with.

7. Religion among the Chinese is in a very sad condition. The people are given up to idolatry. Almost all religions are tolerated, although but little reverence is paid to any. There are more temples than can be easily numbered. Most of the educated Chinese have no other religion than the moral teachings of Confucius.

8. When a Chinese wishes to be married, he buys a wife of her parents, but he is not permitted to see her till she is sent home. The young lady is brought to her husband's door in a palankeen. He puts aside the curtains of the palankeen, and peeps in at his new wife. If he does not like her looks, he sends her back again.

9. In China there are some very singular punishments. Sometimes a wooden frame, weighing two hundred pounds, is put round a man's neck. He is compelled to carry it about with him wherever he goes; and, so long as he wears it, he can neither feed himself, nor lie down.

10. One of the most curious customs of China was that of excluding foreigners from the country. A few American and European merchants were permitted to reside at Canton, but they were obliged to leave their wives at Macao. No other strangers were permitted in the kingdom. The Chinese think their manners and customs are the best in the world, and they do not wish foreigners to come and introduce new notions. By the treaty of peace with Great Britain in 1842, five ports were, however, opened to strangers.

11. China has a great many large cities, and these are filled with almost countless numbers of inhabitants. They have many ingenious arts

---

Questions—4. What of the customs of the Chinese? 5. What of food? 6. What of the ladies? 7. What of religion in China? Temples? 8. What is done when a man wishes to be married? 9. What of punishments in China? 10. What custom is there respecting foreigners? Where do the wives of merchants reside? Why do not the Chinese wish foreigners to come among them? What of the treaty of China with Great Britain in 1842?

and manufacturers; they till the earth with great skill, and their gardens are managed with special care.

12. Tea is brought to us from China, with a great variety of other articles. You will not be surprised that we get so many things from China, when you remember that the country contains, as I have said, three hundred and fifty millions of people, that is, six times as many as there are in all America.

CHAPTER XXIX—ASIA—Continued
Origin of the Arabs—Rise of Mohammed

1. THE ARABS are descended from Ishmael, a son of Abraham. It was foretold of him, that "his hand should be against every man, and every man's hand against him." In all ages this prophecy has been fulfilled among his posterity; for they appear to have been enemies to the rest of mankind, and mankind enemies of them.

2. Arabia consists of several separate states or nations. The whole country is bounded on the north by Palestine, Mesopotamia, etc.; on the east by the Persian Gulf and the Gulf of Ormuz, on the south by the Indian Ocean, and west by the Red Sea.

3. The Arabs have always been wandering tribes, and have dwelt in tents, amid the trackless deserts which cover a large portion of their country. Their early history is very imperfectly known. The first event that is worth recording, was the birth of Mohammed. This took place at Mecca, a city on the borders of the Red Sea, in the year 570 of the Christian era.

4. Till the age of twenty-five Mohammed was a camel-driver in the desert. He afterward spent much of his time in solitude. His dwelling was a lonesome cave, where he pretended to be employed in prayer and meditation. When he was forty years old, he set up for a prophet.

5. He publicly proclaimed that God had sent him to convert the world to a new religion. The people of Mecca would not at first believe Mohammed. He was born among them, and they knew that he had been a camel-

---

Questions—11. What of the cities of China? Manufacturers? Do the people understand agriculture? 12. Where do we get our tea? What is the population of China?

CHAP. XXIX—1. From whom are the Arabs descended? What was prophesied of Ishmael? Has the prophecy been fulfilled? 2. Of what does Arabia consist? How is it bounded? 3. How have the Arabs always lived? What of their early history? When and where was Mohammed born? 4. Of what profession was Mohammed? How did he live before he was forty years old? 5. What did he then do? What of the people of Mecca? What did Mohammed pretend?

GROUP OF ARABS

driver, and was no holier than themselves. Besides, he pretended that he had ridden up to heaven on an ass, in company with the angel Gabriel; and many of his stories were as ridiculous as this.

6. So the men of Mecca threatened to slay Mohammed, and he was therefore forced to flee to Medina, another city of Arabia. There, in the course of two or three years, he made a great number of converts. He told his disciples that they must compel others to adopt his religion by force, if they refused to do so by fair means.

7. This conduct brought on a war between the disciples of Mohammed and all the other Arabians. Mohammed won many victories, and soon made himself master of the whole country, and of Syria besides.

8. Mohammed was now not only a pretended prophet, but a real king. He was a very terrible man, even to his own followers; for, whenever he was angry, a vein between his eyebrows used to swell, and turn black. This gave him a grim and frightful aspect.

9. His power continued to increase; but he died suddenly, at the age of sixty-three. He was buried at Medina. It is said that his coffin may be seen there in a mosque to this day, and that it is suspended in the air by a loadstone. Many pilgrims go every year to visit the place.

Questions—6. Why did Mohammed flee to Medina? What means did he take to make converts in Medina? 7. What was the effect of this conduct? What victories did Mohammed win? 8. Describe Mohammed. 9. When did he die? Where was he buried? What is said of his coffin?

10. The religion of Mohammed was diffused over a great part of Asia and Africa, and is still believed by many millions of people. Its precepts are contained in a book called the Koran. Mohammed affirmed that the angel Gabriel brought him the doctrines contained in this book from heaven.

CHAPTER XXX—ASIA—Continued
Sequel of the History of the Saracens

1. Those of the Arabians who followed Mohammed were named Saracens. After their leader's death, they conquered the whole of what is now called Turkey in Asia, and many other countries. The capital of their empire was the city of Baghdad, on the river Tigris, which I have already mentioned.

2. One of the successors of Mohammed was Ali, his son-in-law. He was opposed by Ayesha, Mohammed's widow. This woman was suspected of having murdered her husband.

3. She raised an army and led them to battle against Ali. During the conflict, Ayesha sat in a sort of cage or litter, on the back of a camel. The camels' reins were held by one of her soldiers; and it is said that seventy soldiers were killed, one after another, while holding the rein. Finally, Ali was victorious, and confirmed his sway over all the disciples of Mohammed, and over the countries which they had won.

4. The Saracen Empire was thus established. The kings were called caliphs. They reigned at Baghdad for the space of six hundred and twenty years. One of the most distinguished of them was Mahmud Gazni. He was a great conqueror, and added a part of India to his dominions.

5. A poor man once complained to Mahmud Gazni that a soldier had turned him and his family out of doors, and had kept possession of his house all night. When the caliph, Mahmud Gazni, heard this, he suspected that the soldier was his own son. "If he ill-treats you again, let me know," said he.

6. Accordingly, a few nights afterward, the poor man told the caliph

---

Questions—10. Where is the religion of Mohammed followed? What is the Koran? What did Mohammed affirm? Where is Mecca? Medina?

Chap. XXX—1. Who were the Saracens? What of them? What was the capital of their empire? 2. Who was Ali? Who opposed him? Who was Ayesha? 3. Describe the conflict between Ali and Ayesha. Who was victorious? 4. Who were the caliphs? Where did they reign? What of Mahmud Gazni? 5–7. Relate the story of the poor man and Mahmud Gazni.

that the same soldier had turned him out of his house again. The caliph took his cimeter and went to the house; but before entering, he caused all the lights to be extinguished, so that his heart might not be softened by the sight of the offender.

7. When all was darkness, he entered the house, and struck the soldier dead with his cimeter. "Now, bring a light," cried the caliph. His attendants did so. Mahmud Gazni held a torch over the bloody corpse of the soldier, and found that his suspicious were correct. He had killed his own son!

8. The last of the caliphs was named Mostasem. He was so proud and vainglorious that he considered his subjects unworthy to behold his face. He therefore never appeared in public without wearing a veil of golden tissue. Whenever he rode through the streets, thousands would flock to get a glimpse of his golden veil.

9. But at length, Hulaki, chief of the Tartars, took the city of Baghdad. He stripped off the golden veil of the caliph Mostasem, and put him alive into a leathern bag. The bag, with the poor caliph in it, was dragged by horses through the same streets where he had formerly ridden in triumph.

10. Thus perished the caliph Mostasem, being bruised to death on the pavements. With him ended the empire of the Saracens, in the year 1258 of the Christian era.

11. But the termination of this empire did not put an end to the religion of Mohammed. This continued to flourish, and finally extended over nearly all the countries of Asia and Africa, as I have stated.

CHAPTER XXXI—ASIA—CONTINUED
About Syria, Phoenicia, and Asia Minor

1. I will now give you a short account of Syria, which lay to the north of Palestine. It was bounded north by Asia Minor, on the east by the river Euphrates and Arabia, on the south by Palestine and a part of Arabia, and west by the Mediterranean Sea.

2. Syria is frequently mentioned in the Bible. The people were engaged in almost constant wars with the Jews, from the time of David, nearly to the time of Christ, when it became a Roman province.

Questions—8. Who was Mostasem? What can you say of him? 9. How did he die? 10. When did the empire of the Saracens end? 11. What of the religion of Mohammed?

Chap. XXXI—1. Where was Syria situated? How was it bounded? 2. What of the people of Syria?

72

GROUP OF SYRIANS

3. At this period its capital was Antioch, which was one of the most splendid cities in the world. This was the native place of Luke, and here both Peter and Paul lived for some time. Here, too, the followers of Christ were first called Christians.

4. Damascus, another city of Syria, one hundred and thirty-six miles northward of Jerusalem, appears to have been known ever since the time of Abraham. It is frequently mentioned in the Bible; and here St. Paul was miraculously converted to the Christian faith.

5. This city was famous in later times for making the best swords, sabers, and other cutlery; but the art which the people once possessed is now lost. The inhabitants of this city were also celebrated for manufacturing beautiful silks, to which the name of *damask* was given, from the place where they were made.

6. Another place in Syria mentioned in the Bible, was Tadmor, sometimes called "Tadmor in the Desert"; this was built by Solomon for the convenience of his traders; it was ten miles in extent, but it is now in ruins. The splendid remains of this place, consisting of columns and other things, beautifully sculptured in stone, show that it must have been a rich and

Questions—3. Capital of Syria? What great events took place at Antioch? 4. What of Damascus? What took place there? 5. What was Damascus celebrated for in ancient times?

powerful city. In modern times it is called Palmyra.

7. At a distance of thirty-seven miles northwest of Damascus are the remains of Balbec, a very splendid city in the time of the apostles, and then called Heliopolis. It is now in ruins, and contains scarcely more than a thousand inhabitants.

8. I must not forget to mention Phoenice, or Phoenicia, which lay along the border of the Mediterranean Sea; it contained the cities of Tyre, Sidon, Ptolemais, and other celebrated places. In very early times, the Phoenicians were famous for taking the lead in commerce, navigation, and other arts. They were then an independent nation, but in after times their country became a province of Syria.

9. Syria is at the present day governed by the Turks, and, like every other country under the sway, is stamped with an aspect of desolation and decay. The term Syria is now applied, not only to what anciently bore that name, but to Palestine also.

CHAPTER XXXII—ASIA—Continued
About Asia Minor, or Natolia

1. ASIA MINOR, or Natolia, as it is now called, lies at the northeastern corner of the Mediterranean Sea; it is a kind of peninsula, bounded on the north by the Euxine or Black Sea; on the west by the Aegean Sea; and on the east by Syria, Mesopotamia, and Armenia.

2. It is about six hundred miles in length, from east to west, and four hundred in breadth. It is at present under the government of Turkey, and its inhabitants are mostly believers in Mohammed. The chief city now is Smyrna, to which many vessels go from this country, and bring back figs, dates, and other things.

3. Asia Minor appears to have been settled in very early times. Several kingdoms have arisen and flourished here at different periods, but it has never been the seat of any great empire. The kingdom of Lydia, in Asia Minor, existed as early as eight hundred years before Christ. Ardysus, who reigned seven hundred and ninety-seven years B.C., appears to have been one of its earliest kings.

Questions — 6. What of Tadmor? 7. What of the ruins of Balbec? 8. What of Phoenicia? What did it contain? 8. What of the Phoenicians? 9. What of Syria? To what is this name now applied?

CHAP. XXXII—1. Give the situation and boundaries of Asia Minor. 2. Its extent. Government. Inhabitants. What of Smyrna? 3. What of Asia Minor? What of Lydia? Ardysus?

4. The last king of Lydia was Croesus, who was a friend of men of learning. Aesop, the author of many of our pleasing fables, lived at his court, and was a great favorite with him. Croesus was also so famous for his great riches, that to this day we say, "As rich as Croesus." But, in spite of his wealth, he was conquered by Cyrus, king of Persia, 548 B.C.

AESOP

5. From this period, Lydia, with a great part of Asia Minor, continued subject to the Persian Empire till the time of Alexander, about 330 B.C., when it was conquered by that famous leader.

6. Three hundred years before Christ, Pontus, which had once been a part of Lydia, became an independent country. It continued to flourish for many years, and Mithridates VII successfully maintained a war with the Romans for a long time.

7. By his skill and courage he baffled the best generals of the empire. But at length, in the year 64 B.C., he was conquered, and his kingdom, with the rest of Asia Minor, was subjected to Roman dominion.

8. Notwithstanding the wars in Asia Minor, the country became filled with people, and superb cities rose up in various parts of it. Ephesus, situated in Lydia, was a splendid place, and it had a temple dedicated to the

---

Questions—4. What can you tell of Croesus? 5. What of Lydia? By whom was it conquered? 6. What of Pontus? Mithridates VII? 7. By whom was Mithridates conquered?

heathen goddess Diana, so magnificent, that it was called one of the Seven Wonders of the world.

9. This temple was one hundred and twenty years in building; but a man named Erostratus, wishing to make himself remembered forever, set it on fire, and it was burnt to the ground.

10. There were also many other fine cities in Asia Minor, several of which are mentioned in the New Testament. Among these was Tarsus, the birthplace of Paul; also, Pergamos, Thyatira, Sardis, Philadelphia, and Laodicea, which are spoken of in the book of Revelation.

11. These places are all sunk into poverty and insignificance, and some of them are mere heaps of ruins. Sardis, once the proud capital of Croesus, has experienced more misfortunes that almost any other place on the globe; it has been burned to the ground by hostile armies, it has been overturned by earthquakes, and devastated by war. A few fragments of walls and columns are the only remains of its former grandeur.

12. Through the labors of Paul, Barnabus, Silas, Timothy, Luke, and perhaps others, Christianity was early planted in nearly all the divisions of Asia Minor. The country is very beautiful by nature, but the present inhabitants are blind worshipers of Mohammed, and are barbarous in their manners and customs.

CHAPTER XXXIII—ASIA—Continued
A Brief View of Several Nations

1. I have now related the history of the most celebrated countries of Asia. But there are several other territories, and some of them very extensive, of which I can say only a few words in this little book.

2. In the ancient times, the Scythians inhabited the northern parts of Asia. They were a warlike yet savage people, and very expert with the bow and arrow. Many of the Asiatic and European kings endeavored to subdue them, but were generally defeated.

3. At different times, vast numbers of the Scythians used to overrun the more civilized countries that lay south of them. A tribe of Scythians founded the powerful empire of Parthia, which afterward extended its sway

---

Questions—8. What of Ephesus? 9. Temple of Diana? How was it destroyed? 10. What other cities were there in Asia Minor? 11. What can you say of these cities now? 12. Who planted Christianity in Asia Minor? What of the country and inhabitants?

Chap. XXXIII—2. What of the Scythians? Where did they live?

76

over Persia and other countries. This empire began in the year 250 B.C., and continued five hundred years.

4. In more modern times, the regions inhabited by the Scythians have been called Tartary, and the people Tartars. The modern inhabitants are not much more civilized than the ancient ones. More than one celebrated conqueror has arisen among the Tartars.

5. India, which we call the East Indies, was very little known to the people who lived westward of it in ancient times. Semiramis invaded it, and likewise Alexander the Great, and several other conquerors. The people of the present day, called Hindus, are an interesting people, but are addicted to idolatry.

6. India or Hindostan is a great country, containing a hundred and forty millions of people. Within the last hundred years, the English have gained great power in this part of the world. They made war against the native princes, and having reduced them to subjection, now rule over them and their people.

7. The Turks, or Ottomans, are a people who had their origin in Asia. But, as they have been settled in Europe during several centuries, it will be more proper and convenient to speak of them in the history of that quarter of the globe.

8. Japan is an extensive empire containing twenty-six millions of inhabitants. These live to the east of China, upon several islands, of which Niphon is the largest. The people live crowded together in large cities, and resemble the Chinese in their religion, manners, and customs.

9. It is uncertain whether the ancient nations knew any thing of this empire, and its early history is almost unknown. It is probable it has remained with little change for thousands of years. Its existence was first ascertained by the Europeans about the year 1400; but as strangers are not permitted to travel in the country, very little is found out concerning it. A treaty of peace and commerce was made between the country and the United States, in 1854.

10. There are several other kingdoms of Asia, of which the history is little known, or quite uninteresting. Among these are Siam, Cochin China,

---

Questions—3. What of Parthia? 4. What is the name given to the countries formerly inhabited of the Scythians, Parthians, etc.? Do the Tartars remain nearly the same as the ancient inhabitants? 6. What of India or Hindostan? *Which way is it from China? From Persia? From Palestine? (see map, p. 27)* What of the English in Hindostan? 7. What of the Turks or Ottomans? 8. What of Japan? *Direction of the Japanese isles from Hindostan? Persia? Palestine? (see map p. 27)*

ANCIENT SCYTHIANS

and the Birman Empire, called Farther India, with Afghanistan, Beloo–chistan, and other others.

11. Besides these, there are the northern portions of Asia, which go under the general name of Siberia; these are occupied by various tribes of Tartars, who appear to have wandered over these regions for ages, leaving no story behind them, together with a few Russians, who have settled in the country. The Emperor of Russia rules over these vast dominions.

CHAPTER XXXIV—ASIA—Continued
Review of the History of Asia

1. Let us now go back and review the history of Asia. In this quarter of the globe, the most wonderful events in the history of mankind have happened. Here Adam and Eve were created; and on the banks of the Euphrates all the people dwelt who lived before the flood.

2. It was in Asia that the ark of Noah rested; and here again the people began to build cities, and establish nations. Here the first great empire arose. Here the Jewish nation had its origin; and nearly all the events related in the Old Testament took place here.

3. It was in Asia that the religion which teaches us that there is one

---

Questions—10. What other nations of Asia are there, of which the history is little known? 11. What of the northern portions of Asia?

only living and true God, had its origin; and here Jesus Christ appeared, to establish this religion, and seal the truth of revelation with his blood.

4. It was in Asia that Mohammed commenced and established his religion, which is now believed by one-quarter of the human race. Several other religions had their origin in Asia.

5. In Asia, some of the greatest empires have existed, of which history gives us any account. The Assyrian Empire, as I have before said, is the first on record. This was followed by the Persian Empire, which seemed to swallow up all the surrounding nations. China, the most populous empire on the globe, has endured longer than any other.

6. The Saracens, who extended their dominion over many countries, had their origin in Asia. The Turks, who have reigned over Palestine, Mesopotamia, Syria, Asia Minor, a part of Europe, and a part of Africa, for nearly five hundred years, had their origin in Asia.

7. There is one portion of Asia which is, perhaps, more full of historical interest than any other on the face of the globe. It is that which lies between the Mediterranean on the west, Armenia on the north, Persia on the east, and Arabia on the south. Here is the spot on which the first inhabitants dwelt; here was the place where the first nations were formed; here the miracles recorded in the Bible took place; here the prophets dwelt; here Jesus Christ lived, preached, and died.

8. But, although Asia was peopled before any other part of the world, and though the inhabitants have been favored by miracles, and the presence of a Divine Teacher, they are far behind the nations of Europe and America in the knowledge of religion, and the various arts which make life comfortable and happy.

9. In all parts of Asia, there are many people who are full of superstition, and there are very few who worship God in sincerity and truth. Jesus Christ is hardly known among the many millions of people in Asia; and though some of the rich men, kings, and princes live in gorgeous palaces, and are decked with gold and jewels, yet the mass of the people live as they have done for ages, ignorant, poor, and degraded.

10. The most remarkable feature in the history of Asia is, that, while

---

Questions—CHAP. XXXIV—1–4. What remarkable events have occurred in Asia? 5. What is the first empire recorded in history? What of the Persian Empire? What of China? 6. What of the Saracens? What of the Turks? 7. What portion of Asia is the most interesting on the globe? Why is this portion of country thus interesting? 8. How has Asia been particularly favored? In what respects are the inhabitants of Asia behind those of Europe and America? 9. What is the state of the people in Asia?

BRAHMA   VISHNU

the country has seen many revolutions and changes, the condition of the people remains nearly the same. In our country and in Europe, there is a constant improvement. Every year brings some new art, invention, or institution for the benefit of society.

11. But in Asia it is not so. Whoever is king, the people are but slaves. Education makes slow progress, liberty is unknown, truth is little valued, virtue is not prized, and that thing which we call comfort, and which makes our homes so dear to us, is not to be found in that vast country, so favored by Providence, and so richly endowed by nature.

12. It would seem that the real difficulty in Asia is, that, while they are destitute of the knowledge of the Gospel, they have many false religions. Mohammedanism prevails over a great part of this portion of the globe; and it is remarkable that no country has ever been happy or well governed where this religion prevailed.

13. Hindus believe in Brahmanism, which teaches them that there is one principle deity, called Brahma, and several other inferior deities, called Vishnu, Siva, etc. They make strange images of these, and worship them. The priests are called Brahmins, and instruct the people in many vain ceremonies and cruel superstitions.

Questions — 10. What is remarkable in the history of Asia? What is said of this country and of Europe? 11. How does Asia differ from Europe and America? 12. What is the condition of Asia? What of Mohammadanism? What is a remarkable fact? 13. In what religion to the Hindus believe? What does Brahminism teach? What of the Brahmins?

14. Besides these religions, there is the worship of Buddha, represented by the Grand Lama, who lives in a great temple at Lassa, in Tibet. The Chinese believe in Buddha, and other nations believe in other deities.

15. Thus nearly the whole of Asia is involved in darkness as to the character of God, and the destiny of man; and thus we see, that the conduct of mankind is such as might be expected, where such ignorance and such error prevail.

CHAPTER XXXV—ASIA—Continued
Chronology of Asia

1. CHRONOLOGY is a record of the dates when historical events happened. By studying chronology, you therefore learn the time at which the creation took place, when Abraham went from Chaldea to Canaan, when Christ was born, and other things.

2. Now, in order to have a clearer view of the progress of history, it is very important to place before us a table of chronology; and if we wish to remember history for a long time, it is well to fix this table in the memory.

3. I will now give you a brief view of the chronology of Asia. By this you will notice some curious things. You will see that Solomon and Chaus of China lived at the same time; that Solomon began the temple exactly three thousand years after the creation, etc.

	B.C.
Creation of the world	4004
Deluge	2348
Confusion of tongues	2247
Ashur founds the empire of Assyria	2221
Ninias, king of Assyria, began to reign	2000
Abraham born	1996
Abraham sets out from Chaldea to go to Canaan	1921
Jacob removes with his family to Egypt	1705
Death of Jacob	1689
Death of Joseph	1635
Moses born	1570
Departure of the Israelites from Egypt	1491
Death of Moses	1447

Questions—14. Where is the temple of the Grand Lama?   In what deity do the Chinese believe?   15. In what error is nearly the whole of Asia involved?   What do we see as respects the conduct of mankind?

CHAP. XXXV—1. What is chronology?   Its uses?

B.C.

Death of Joshua	1426
Saul proclaimed king of Israel	1100
King David born	1085
Solomon began to reign	1015
Temple of Solomon built	1004
Chaus, emperor of China, began to reign	1000
Death of Sardanapalus; first Assyrian empire overthrown	888
Jonah the prophet sent to preach to the Ninevites	806
Ardysus, first king of Lydia, in Asia Minor	797
Shalmaneser conquered the kingdom of Israel, and carried the chief inhabitants into captivity	720
Isdegerdes made king of Persia	630
Second Assyrian empire overthrown	606
Lydia conquered by Cyrus, king of Persia	548
Babylonian empire overthrown	538
Jews return from Babylon	536
Persian empire established by Cyrus the Great	536
Death of Cyrus	529
Cambyses succeeds his father Cyrus	529
Darius begins to reign	522
Xerxes defeats Leonidas at Thermopylae	480
Death of Xerxes	465
Alexander invades Persia	330
Kingdom of Syria founded by Seleucus	312
Pontus becomes independent under Mithridates II	300
Empire of Parthia founded	250
Artaxerxes made king of Persia	230
Judas Maccabaeus drives the Syrians out of the Jewish Kingdom	166
Chang, emperor of China	67
Pontus, with other parts of Asia Minor, conquered by the Romans	64
Syria and Canaan conquered by the Romans	61

Questions—2. What benefit can we gain by placing before us a chronological table? What is the advantage of fixing a chronological table in the memory? 3. What curious things do we learn from a chronological view of Asia.

The teacher may now proceed to ask such questions as he deems proper, in regard to the several events noticed in the table: it may be well to turn to the pages where the details are given respecting the events, and interrogate the pupil upon them. Questions like the following may be useful: How long from the birth of Abraham to that of Moses? From that of Moses to that of David? From the beginning to the end of the Saracen empire? etc.

B.C.

Herod, king of the Jews 37

Vati, emperor of China 33

Jesus Christ was born 4004 years after the Creation: this period is called the Christian era. It is the custom in all Christian countries to date from the birth of Christ — B.C. means before Christ; A.C. means after Christ; A.D. stands for Anno Domini, that is, in the year of our Lord. Thus, we say A.D. 1858, by which we mean in the year of our Lord, or from the birth of Christ, 1858 years.

A.D.

Jesus Christ born 0

Christ crucified 33

Paul arrives at Rome 61

Destruction of Jerusalem by Titus 70

Birth of Mohammed 570

Si-given, emperor of China, began to reign 617

Mohammed obliged to fly from his enemies 622
  (This is called the Hegira [he-ji-ra], and is the era from
  which the Turks date, as we do from the birth of Christ.)

Death of Mohammed 632

Saracen Empire established 638

Baghdad, the seat of the caliphs, founded 672

Chosroes, or Khosrou the Great, king of Persia, began to reign 660

Chwang-tsong, emperor of China, began to reign 1037

Genghis Khan invaded China 1209

Saracen empire overturned by the Turks 1258

Japan discovered by Europeans 1400

Shah Abbas ascended the throne of Persia 1586

Shah Husseyn ascended the throne of Persia 1694

Kouli Khan made king of Persia 1730

Yong-tching came to the throne of China 1737

War between China and Great Britain 1840

Canton taken 1841

Peace between Great Britain and China 1842

Treaty between China and the United States 1844

Rebellion in China of Tae-ping-wang 1852

Treaty between United States and Japan 1854

War between China and Great Britain 1858

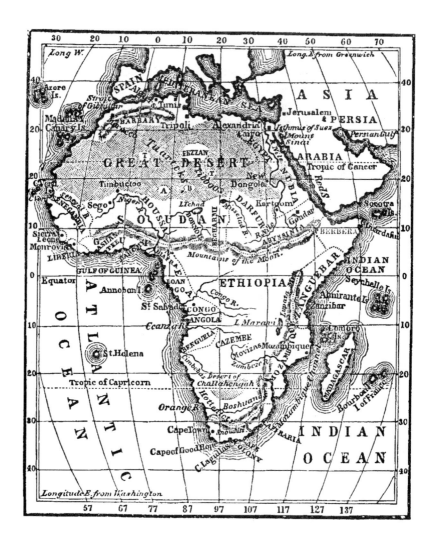

MAP OF AFRICA

AFRICANS

CHAPTER XXXVI—AFRICA
About the Geography of Africa—The Inhabitants

1. AFRICA IS ONE of the Six Grand Divisions of the globe. It is an immense extent of country, and includes nearly one-fourth of all the land on earth. It is separated from America by the Atlantic Ocean; the part nearest to our country is about three thousand miles from New York or Boston.

2. It is separated from Europe by the Mediterranean Sea, and from Asia by the Red Sea. It is, however, attached to Asia by a narrow neck of land, called the Isthmus of Suez.

3. Africa is less known than any other grand division of the globe. Many portions of the interior have never been visited by Europeans. The greater part of the inhabitants are negroes, of which there are many tribes.

4. The climate being warm, they need little shelter or clothing. Their houses are therefore poor mud huts, or slight tenements, made of leaves or branches of trees. Their dress is often but a single piece of cloth tied around

Questions—CHAP. XXXVI—1. What of Africa? How is it separated from America? How far is the nearest point from New York or Boston? 2. How is it separated from Europe? Asia? What neck of land joins it to Asia? 3. Is Africa well known? What of the inhabitants?

the waist. They are, however, a cheerful race.

5. Besides the negroes, there are several other races of Africans. The inhabitants from Egypt to Abyssinia appear to consist of the original Egyptian people, mixed with Turks, Arabs, and others. The people of the Barbary States are the descendants of the ancient Carthaginians, mingled with the Saracens who conquered the country, together with Turks and Arabs.

6. The immense Desert of Sahara—which is almost as extensive as the whole United States—with part of the adjacent regions, appears to be occupied by wandering tribes of Arabs, who move from place to place with their houses and camels, like the people of Arabia, for pasturage or plunder.

7. The central parts of Africa abound in wild animals, such as lions, panthers, leopards, elephants, rhinoceroses, zebras, and quaggas. The woods are filled with chattering monkeys, the thickets are infested with monstrous serpents, ostriches roam over the deserts, various kinds of antelopes and deer, in vast herds, graze upon the plains, hippopotami are seen in the lakes and rivers, and crocodiles abound in the stagnant waters. Wild birds of every hue meet the eye of the traveler in nearly all parts of the country.

CHAPTER XXXVII—AFRICA—CONTINUED
Early Sovereigns of Egypt

1. THE NATIVES of Africa are supposed to be descended from Noah's son, Ham, who went thither and settled in Egypt after the building of the tower of Babel, this country being near the land of Shinar. The kingdom of Egypt is very ancient, and according to general tradition, was founded by Menes, one of the children of Ham, about 2188 B.C. In the Bible he is called Misraim.

2. Egypt is bounded north by the Mediterranean Sea, east by the Red Sea, south by Nubia, and west by the desert. The Nile runs through the midst of Egypt, from the south to the north. This river overflows its banks once a year, and thus fertilizes the country, for it very seldom rains in Egypt.

3. Menes, or Misraim, the first king of Egypt, turned aside the Nile from its original channel, and built the city of Memphis where the river

---

Questions—4. What of the climate? Houses? Dress? What of the negroes? 5. What of other races? Describe them. 7. What of animals in Central Africa? CHAP. XXXVII—1. From whom are the natives of Africa descended? By whom and when was Egypt founded? What of Menes? 2. How is Egypt bounded? What of the Nile? Does it often rain in Egypt?

EGYPTIANS

had formerly flowed. He was so great a monarch that the people worshiped him as a god, after his death.

4. The history of Egypt is very obscure during a considerable time after the reign of Menes. From the year 2084 to the year 1825 before the Christian era, it was governed by rulers who originally led the lives of shepherds, and were therefore called Shepherd Kings. They are also known in history under the name of *Hyksos.*

5. These kings to whom are attributed the building of some of the great cities and great monuments of Egypt, were afterward driven from the country. An Ethiopian woman, named Nitocris, became queen of this country, in the year 1678 before the Christian era. Her brother had been murdered by the Egyptians, and she resolved to avenge him.

6. For this purpose Queen Nitocris built a palace under ground, and invited the murderers of her brother to a banquet. The subterranean hall, where the banquet was prepared, was brilliantly illuminated with torches. The guests were the principal men in the kingdom.

7. The scene was magnificent, as they sat feasting along the table. But

---

Questions—3. Where and by whom was Memphis built? What was thought of Menes? 4. What of the history of Egypt? 5. What of the Shepherd Kings? What of Nitocris? 6–7. How did she revenge her brother's death?

MAP OF EGYPT

suddenly a rushing and roaring sound was heard overhead, and a deluge of water burst into the hall. Queen Nitocris had caused a river to flow through a secret passage, and it extinguished the torches, and drowned all the company at the banquet.

8. The most renowned monarch that ever reigned over Egypt was Sesostris, who is also called Ramses. The date of his reign is not precisely known, but there are carvings in stone, lately found in Egypt, which are more than three thousand years old, and supposed to present portraits of him. They are, doubtless, the oldest portraits in existence. This king formed the design of conquering the world, and set out from Egypt with more than

ANCIENT EGYPTIAN CHARIOT

half a million of foot soldiers, twenty-four thousand horsemen, and twenty-seven thousand armed chariots.

9. His ambitious projects were partially successful. He made great conquests, and wherever he went, he caused marble pillars to be erected, and inscriptions to be engraved on them, so that future ages might not forget his renown.

10. The following was an inscription on most of the pillars: SESOSTRIS, KING OF KINGS, HAS CONQUERED THIS TERRITORY BY HIS ARMS. But the marble pillars have long ago crumbled into dust, or been buried under the earth; and the history of Sesostris is so obscure, that some writers have even doubted whether he ever made any conquests at all.

11. But other writers assure us that he returned to Egypt after his wars, bringing with him a multitude of captives, and long trains of camels, laden with treasure, and that he then built magnificent temples, and constructed canals and causeways.

12. When Sesostris went to worship in the temple, he rode in a chariot which was drawn by captive kings. They were harnessed like horses, four abreast; and their royal robes trailed in the dust as they tugged the heavy

Questions—8. What can you say of Sesostris? What of his army? 9. His ambition? 10. What inscription was engraved on the marble pillars raised by Sesostris? Are the pillars still standing? What do some writers doubt? 11. What do others say?

chariot along. But at length the proud Sesostris grew old and blind. He could no longer look around him and see captive kings drawing his chariot, or kneeling at his footstool. He then became utterly miserable, and committed suicide.

CHAPTER XXXVIII—AFRICA—CONTINUED
Egyptian Architecture and Sculpture

1. THE ANCIENT HISTORY of Egypt is so obscure, and yet so full of wonderful tales, that we might doubt it altogether, and believe it but the marvelous invention of fanciful storytellers, were it not for the vast ruins and stupendous monuments still to be found in different parts of the country. These show that between three and four thousand years ago, this country was filled with millions of people, and that there were cities here of the most wondrous magnificence.

2. Thebes appears to have been more magnificent than any other city, either in ancient or modern times. It was called the city of a hundred gates; and such was the immense population, that through each of these gates, in time of war, marched two hundred armed chariots, and two thousand horsemen.

3. Thebes was ruined in the time of Cambyses, king of Persia, who lived about twenty-four hundred years ago. Yet the remains of the city are still visible, scattered over a space of many miles on each side of the Nile. Some of the pillars of the temples are eleven feet in diameter.

4. One of the Egyptian kings caused his subjects to dig a great lake, forty-five miles in circumference. Another king constructed a labyrinth of marble, containing three thousand chambers, fifteen hundred of which were under ground.

5. In the upper chambers of this labyrinth were kept the sacred crocodiles, and all the other animals which the Egyptians worshiped. In the subterranean chambers lay the dead kings of Egypt.

6. The catacombs are likewise very wonderful. They are galleries hewn out of the rock, and extend a great way beneath the ground. The dead

---

Questions—12. How was the chariot of Sesostris drawn? What was the fate of this despotic king?

CHAP. XXXVIII—1. What of the ancient history of Egypt? What of ruins and monuments? What do they prove? 2. What of Thebes? What about the population of Thebes? 3. Who destroyed Thebes? Remains? Pillars? 4. Describe the works of some of the kings. What of the labyrinth? 5. What were kept in the labyrinth?

bodies of persons who died thousands of years ago are found in the catacombs, and they are nearly as well preserved now as when they were first buried. They are called *mummies;* and many of them, supposed to be three thousand years old, have been brought to Europe and America.

7. Everybody has heard of the pyramids of Egypt. These immense edifices, of which there are about eighty, are still standing on the banks of the Nile. The largest is five hundred feet high, and covers eleven acres of ground.

8. The pyramids are so old that it is impossible to tell with certainty when they were erected, or by whom. It is generally supposed that the ancient kings of Egypt intended them as their sepulchres, thinking that thus they should be famous forever. But though the pyramids have not decayed, the names of those kings are forgotten.

9. On a plain near Thebes are two enormous stone statues, somewhat like a man and woman. These are fifty feet high. No one can look upon them but with wonder.

10. The Sphinx is one of the most curious among the Egyptian antiquities. It was originally the gigantic head of a woman, on the body of a lion; but the lower part is now buried in the sand. The part which remains above ground is the head and neck. These are twenty-seven feet high, and are made of solid rock. At a distance, they look as if a great flat-nosed woman were rising out of the sand.

11. The ruins of the temple of Luxor, forming a part of ancient Thebes, are so grand as to strike the beholder with awe. The remains of one of the temples are, doubtless, the most remarkable existing relics of antiquity.

12. At the time when they constructed these marvelous works, the ancient Egyptians possessed more learning and science than any other people. Their superior knowledge caused them to be looked upon as magicians by the people of other countries.

13. The Egyptians had, indeed, many absurd superstitions. Their chief goddess was Isis, and another deity was Osiris. Of these they made strange images, and worshiped them. Isis was greatly reverenced, and the people dedicated many splendid temples to her worship.

Questions — 6. Describe the catacombs. What are mummies? 7–8. What of the pyramids? What was the probable cause of their erection? 9. What of statues near Thebes? 10. Describe the Sphinx. 11. What of the ruins of Luxor? 12. What of the Egyptians at the time we are speaking of? How were they looked upon by the people of other countries? 13. What of the superstitions of the Egyptians? Isis and Osiris?

CHAPTER XXXIX — AFRICA — CONTINUED
The Ptolemies and Queen Cleopatra

1. IN THE HISTORY of the Hebrews or Jews I have told of their bondage in Egypt, and of their miraculous escape. A long while afterward, an Egyptian king, named Shishak, took Jerusalem, and robbed Solomon's temple of its treasures.

2. A very famous king of Egypt was named Amenophis. He is supposed to be the same with Memnon, in honor of whom a temple with a gigantic statue was erected, of which some remains are still to be seen at Thebes. This statue was said to utter a joyful sound at sunrise, and a mournful sound when the sun set. Some modern travelers imagine that they have heard it.

3. In the year 525 before the Christian era, Egypt was conquered by Cambyses, king of Persia. He compelled Psammenitus, who was then king of Egypt, to drink bulls' blood. It operated as a poison, and caused his death.

4. Three hundred and thirty-two years before the Christian era, Egypt was conquered by Alexander the Great, king of Macedon. Here he built a famous city, called Alexandria, which was for many centuries one of the most splendid places in the world. But the ancient city is in ruins, and modern Alexandria is far inferior to it.

5. Alexander appointed Ptolemy, one of his generals, to be ruler of the country. From Ptolemy were descended a race of kings, all of whom were likewise called Ptolemy. They reigned over Egypt two hundred and ninety-four years. The last of these kings was Ptolemy Dionysius, whose own wife made war against him. A battle was fought, in which Ptolemy Dionysius was defeated. He attempted to escape, but was drowned in the Nile. His wife, whose name was Cleopatra, then became sole ruler of Egypt.

6. She was one of the most beautiful women that ever lived, and her talents and accomplishments were equal to her personal beauty. But she was very wicked. Among other horrid crimes, Cleopatra poisoned her brother, who was only eleven years old. Yet, though all the world knew what an abandoned woman she was, the greatest heroes could not or would

---

Questions—CHAP. XXXIX—1. Who was Shishak? What did he do? 2. Who was Amenophis? What of the statue of Memnon? 3. When and by whom was Egypt conquered? Fate of Psammenitus? 4. When did Alexander conquer Egypt? What of Alexandria? 5. What of Ptolemy and his descendants? How long did they reign in Egypt? Who was Ptolemy Dionysius? His wife? 6. What of Cleopatra? What cruelty did she commit? What made Cleopatra irresistible?

CLEOPATRA

not resist the enticements of her beauty.

7. When Mark Antony, a Roman general, had defeated Brutus and Cassius, at Philippi, in Greece, he summoned Cleopatra to come to Cilicia, on the northeastern coast of the Mediterranean. He intended to punish her for having assisted Brutus.

8. As soon as Cleopatra received the summons, she hastened to obey. She went on board a splendid vessel, which was richly adorned with gold. The sails were made of the costliest silk. Instead of rough, sunburnt sailors, the crew consisted of lovely girls, who rowed with silver oars; and their strokes kept time to melodious music.

9. Queen Cleopatra reclined on the deck, beneath a silken awning. In this manner she went sailing along the river Cydnus. Her vessel was so magnificent, and she herself so lovely, that the whole spectacle appeared like a vision.

10. Mark Antony was first warned of her approach by the smell of delicious perfumes, which the wind wafted from the silken sails of the vessel. He next heard the distant strains of music, and saw the gleaming silver oars.

Questions — 7. Who was Mark Antony? Why did he wish to punish Cleopatra? 8–10. Give an account of the arrival of Cleopatra at Cilicia.

11. But when he beheld the beauty of the Egyptian queen, he thought of nothing else. Till Mark Antony met Cleopatra, he had been an ambitious man and a valiant warrior. But from that day forward he was nothing but her slave.

12. Owing to Cleopatra's misconduct and his own, Antony was defeated by Octavius, another Roman general, at Actium, in Greece. He then killed himself, by falling on his sword. Cleopatra knew that if Octavius took her alive, he would carry her to Rome, and expose her to the derision of the populace.

13. She resolved not to endure this ignominy. Now in Egypt there is a venomous reptile, called an asp, the bite of which is mortal, but not very painful. Cleopatra applied one of these reptiles to her bosom. In a little while her body grew benumbed, and her heart ceased to beat; and thus died the beautiful and wicked Queen of Egypt. This event occurred thirty years before Christ.

CHAPTER XL—AFRICA—CONTINUED
Sequel of the Egyptian History

1. AFTER THE DEATH of Cleopatra, Egypt became a province of the Roman empire. It continued to belong to that power, and to the portion of it called the Eastern Empire, till the year 640 after the Christian era. It was then conquered by the Saracens. It remained under their government upward of six centuries.

2. The Saracen sovereigns were dethroned by the Mamelukes, whom they had trained up to be their guards. The Mamelukes ruled Egypt till the year 1517, when they were conquered by the Turks. They kept possession of Egypt till the year 1798. It was then invaded by Napoleon Bonaparte, with an army of forty thousand Frenchmen.

3. The Turks, ever since their conquest of Egypt, had kept a body of Mamelukes in their service; these made a desperate resistance. A battle was fought near the pyramids, in which many of them were slain, and others were drowned in the Nile. Not long after this victory, Bonaparte went

Questions—11. What was the character of Antony till he met Cleopatra? 12. Where was Antony defeated? Who was Octavius? Fate of Antony? Why did Cleopatra determine to kill herself? 13. What caused her death? How long was this before Christ?

CHAP. XL—1. What was the state of Egypt from Cleopatra's death to its subjugation by the Mamelukes? 2. How long did the Mamelukes govern Egypt? When and how long did the Turks govern Egypt? What happened in 1798?

back to France, and left General Kleber in command of the French army.

4. General Kleber was a brave man, but a severe one, and his severity cost him his life. He had ordered an old Mussulman, named the Sheik Sada, to be bastinadoed on the soles of his feet. Shortly afterward, when the general was in a mosque, a fierce Arab rushed upon him, and killed him with a dagger.

5. In 1801, the English sent Sir Ralph Abercrombie with an army to drive the French out of Egypt. General Menou was then the French commander. Sir Ralph Abercrombie beat him at the battle of Aboukir, but was himself mortally wounded.

6. In the course of the same year the French army sailed from Egypt back to France. The inhabitants lamented their departure, for the French generals had ruled them with more justice and moderation than their old masters, the Turks. Egypt is now governed by a successor of Mehemet Ali, who bears the title of pashaw, but the country is tributary to the Turkish Empire.

7. The present capital of Egypt is Grand Cairo. It is much inferior to what it was in former times, but still it contains about three hundred thousand inhabitants. Alexandria, built by Alexander the Great, as I have before said, is now much reduced, but the ruins around it show that it was once a splendid city.

8. There is no part of the world that seems more gloomy to a traveler than Egypt. The present aspect of the towns and cities is that of poverty in the midst of the most splendid ruins.

CHAPTER XLI—AFRICA—Continued
Sketches of Ethiopian History

1. ALL THE INTERIOR parts of Africa were anciently called Ethiopia. But, properly speaking, Ethiopia comprised only the countries now called Nubia, and some adjacent territories. This region lies south of Egypt, and extends along the shore of the Red Sea. The first inhabitants of Ethiopia are supposed to have emigrated from Arabia Felix—that is, Arabia the Happy. Their

---

Questions—3. What battle was fought? What of Bonaparte after the victory? 4. What of General Kleber? 5. What took place in 1801? 6. What happened in the same year? Why were the Egyptians sorry to have the French leave them? How is Egypt governed now? How is the country considered? 7. What is the capital of Egypt? What of Grand Cairo? Population? What of Alexandria? 8. How does Egypt appear to a traveler?

early history is almost unknown.

2. Ethiopia, or at least a portion of it, was formerly called Sheba, and from thence it is supposed that the Queen of Sheba went to visit Solomon. About forty years ago, it is said that one of her descendants was king of Abyssinia.

3. It used to be the custom to confine the Ethiopian princes on a high mountain, which was named Geshen. It was very lofty and steep, and looked like an enormous castle of stone. No person could ascend this mountain, or come down from it, unless he were raised or lowered by means of ropes.

4. The princes lived on the summit of the mountain, in miserable huts. The greater part of them never came down till their dying day. But whenever the king died, one of the princes was summoned to the throne. Perhaps, however, he found himself no happier in the royal palace, than in his hut on the summit of Mount Geshen.

5. The Ethiopians were believers in the Jewish religion till the middle of the fourth century after the Christian era. Candace, the queen of the country, was then converted to Christianity, and her subjects followed her example.

6. Abyssinia is a part of what was anciently called Ethiopia, and Christianity appears to have been introduced here many centuries ago. The inhabitants still profess to be Christians, but their mode of worship is mixed up with many Jewish practices. They also, like the Roman Catholics, make the Virgin Mary and the saints their intercessors before God.

7. The people of this portion of Africa are not generally negroes. They are of an olive complexion, and have long hair and agreeable features.

CHAPTER XLII—AFRICA—CONTINUED
Origin of the Barbary States and their Piracies on the Christians

1. THE BARBARY STATES are Morocco, Algiers, Tunis, and Tripoli. They are bounded on the north by the Mediterranean Sea, east and south by the desert, and west by the Atlantic Ocean. These countries were inhabited in

---

Questions—CHAP. XLI—1. What was anciently called Ethiopia?   In which direction is it from Egypt?   Where was Ethiopia, properly speaking, situated?   Who were the first inhabitants of Ethiopia?   2. What was Ethiopia formerly called?   What of the Queen of Sheba?   3. What was once the custom?   4. How did the princes live?   What happened when the king died?   5. Till what time did the Ethiopians believe in the Jewish religion? What of Candace?   6. What of the worship of the people of Ethiopia at the present time? 7. What of their personal appearance?

the time of the Romans. Morocco was called Mauritania; and Algiers, Numidia. These regions were first settled by colonies from Phoenicia, Greece, and other countries.

2. In this region stood the celebrated city of Carthage in ancient times. Its site was about ten miles northeast of the present city of Tunis. It was founded by some Phoenicians, eight hundred and sixty-nine years before the Christian era. The Phoenicians, as I have told you, were the first people who engaged in commerce, and founded colonies for the purpose of carrying on trade.

3. In the history of Rome I shall tell you how Carthage was destroyed. The Romans erected a new city where it had formerly stood. This was conquered and destroyed by the Saracens, who then built the city of Tunis. In the year 1574, Tunis was seized by the Turks.

4. The city of Algiers was built by the Saracens, in the year 944. The government, called the Regency of Algiers, was founded in 1518, by two Turks, named Horue and Hagradin. They were brothers, and both bore the name of Barbarossa, or Red-Beard.

5. The country now called Morocco was conquered by the Saracens about the same time with the other Barbary states. So also was Tripoli. All these states, except Morocco, afterward fell into the hands of the Turks.

6. During a long period, the Barbary states were in the habit of fitting out vessels to cruise against the ships of other nations. Their prisoners were sold as slaves, and never returned to their own country, unless a high ransom was paid for them.

7. The Americans were the first who made any considerable resistance to these outrages. In the year 1803, Commodore Preble sailed to the Mediterranean Sea with a small American fleet. He intended to attack Tripoli; but one of his frigates, the Philadelphia, got aground in the harbor.

8. The Turks took possession of the Philadelphia. But one night, Lieutenant Decatur entered the harbor of Tripoli, and rowed toward the captured vessel, with only twenty men. He leaped on board, followed by his crew, and killed all the Turks, or drove them overboard: the Philadelphia was then set on fire.

Questions—CHAP. XLII—1. What are the Barbary states? How are they bounded? 2. Where did ancient Carthage stand? Who founded it? 3. Who erected a new city? What did the Saracens do? When was Tunis seized by the Turks? 4. When and by whom was Algiers built? What was done in 1518? Who were called Barbarossa? 5. What of Morocco and Tripoli? Which of the Barbary states fell afterward into the hands of the Turks? 6. What were these states in the habit of doing? 7. What was done in 1808? What of Commodore Preble? 8. What of the Philadelphia? What did Decatur do?

9. After this exploit, Commodore Preble obtained some gun-boats from the King of Naples, and with these and the American vessels, he made an attack on the fortifications of Tripoli. The Bashaw of Tripoli was forced to give up his prisoners.

10. In the year 1815, Commodore Decatur—the same who had burnt the Philadelphia—was sent with a fleet against Algiers. He captured their largest vessels, and compelled the Algerines, and the Tripolitans also, to agree never more to make slaves of Americans.

11. In 1816, Algiers was battered by an English fleet under the command of Lord Exmouth. This was the severest chastisement that the Algerines had ever received at that period. But in 1830, the French sent a large naval and military force against Algiers, commanded by Marshal Beaumont.

12. The war continued for seventeen years, an Arab leader, by the name of Abd-el-Kader was defeated and taken prisoner; so the country was conquered, and Algiers, under the name of *Algeria,* is now a province of France.

CHAPTER XLIII—AFRICA—Continued
Curious Facts and Fables about Africa

1. Most of the other regions of Africa can hardly be said to have any history. The inhabitants possess no written records, and cannot tell what events have happened to their forefathers.

2. The ancient had very curious notions about Africa, for they had visited only the northern parts, and contented themselves with telling incredible stories about the remainder. They supposed that toward the eastern shore of the continent, there were people without noses, and others who had three or four eyes apiece.

3. In other parts of Africa there were said to be men without heads, but who had eyes in their breasts. Old writers speak also of a nation whose king had a head like a dog. There was likewise said to be a race of giants, twice as tall as common men and women.

4. But the prettiest of all these fables is the story of the Pygmies. These

---

Questions—9. What attack was made upon Tripoli?   What of the bashaw?   10. What was done in the year 1815?   What agreement did the Tripolitans and Algerines make?   11. When was Algiers battered by the English fleet?   What took place in 1880?   12. What of Abd-el-Kader?   What of Algiers now?

Chap. XLIII—1. What of the inhabitants of most parts of Africa?   2–3. What were the ideas of the ancients concerning Africa?

little people were said to be about a foot high, and were believed to dwell near the source of the river Nile. Their houses were built something like birds' nests, and their building materials were clay, feathers, and eggshells.

5. These pygmies used to wage terrible wars with the cranes. An immense army of them would set out on an expedition, some mounted on rams and goats, and others on foot.

6. When an army of the Pygmies encountered an army of the cranes, great valor was displayed on both sides. The cranes would rush forward to the charge flapping their wings, and sometimes one of them would snatch up a Pygmy in his beak, and carry him away captive.

7. But the Pygmies brandished their little swords and spears, and generally succeeded in putting the enemy to flight. Whenever they had a chance, they would break the eggs of the cranes, and kill the unfledged young ones without mercy.

8. Until within a few years, the moderns have not known much more about the interior of Africa than the ancients did. They have now acquired considerable knowledge respecting it; but the subject belongs rather to geography than history. Nearly the whole of the central part of Africa, through which the river Niger flows, is called Nigritia. It is inhabited by several different nations.

9. The principle city of Nigritia is called Timbuktu. No white people have ever visited it, except one American, one Englishman, and one Frenchman. The name of the latter was M. Caillié. He was there in 1827, and describes the city as built in the shape of a triangle, and situated eight miles from the Niger.

10. The houses are only one story high, and are built of round bricks baked in the sun. The poor people and slaves dwell in huts of straw, shaped something like beehives. All around the city, there is an immense plain of yellowish-white sand.

11. There are English and French settlements on the western coast of Africa. There was formerly a Dutch settlement at the southern extremity of the continent, but the English have had possession of it since the year 1806. This is called Cape Town, and is situated at the Cape of Good Hope.

Questions—4. What is the prettiest of all these fabulous stories? 5–7. Give some account of the Pygmies. 8. What knowledge have the moderns of the interior of Africa? Where is Nigritia? What of the inhabitants? 9. What of Timbuktu? Who have visited it? What does M. Caillié say of it? 10. Describe it. 11. What of settlements? What of Cape Town? How long have the English had possession of it?

CHAPTER XLIV—AFRICA—Continued
History of the Slave Trade

1. The most painful part of the history of Africa is that which belongs to the slave trade. From the earliest ages, when human society was yet in a rude state, it was the custom to make slaves of those who were taken in war. This practice was continued in after times, and thus, for thousands of years, slavery was established in nearly all the nations of the earth. In ancient Greece and Rome the slaves constituted a large part of the inhabitants.

2. But in those countries where the Christian religion prevailed, slavery came into general disuse. In 1482, however, the Portuguese began the traffic of the African slave trade, and the English followed in 1563. Thus slavery was established in the American colonies.

3. For at least two hundred years, this traffic was carried on to a great extent. The custom was for vessels to go to the western coast of Africa, and purchase of the African princes such prisoners as they had for sale. Sometimes, however, the captains of the vessels would rob the people of their children, or they would go on shore with a body of armed men, and carry away the inhabitants of a whole village.

4. The poor negroes thus taken from their homes and separated forever from all they held dear, were crowded into the vessels bound for America or the West Indies. On the passage they were often half-starved, and sometimes suffered from disease, or unkind treatment. Such was frequently their distress, that they would jump into the sea, or beat out their own brains in despair.

5. In modern times, the principal civilized nations have made laws to suppress the slave trade, and it is now treated as piracy by them. America was the first nation to set the example which led to this state of things. Some bad men still carry on the slave trade, but they do it secretly, well knowing that they would be not only held in detestation, but be severely punished, if they were detected in their evil doings.

Questions—CHAP. XLIV—1. What is painful in the history of Africa? What was the custom in the earliest ages? How was slavery established? 2. What effect had the Christian religion upon slavery? When did the Portuguese engage in the slave trade? The English? 3. How long was the traffic carried on? What was the custom? What was done by captains of vessels? 4. Describe the state of the negroes. 5. What of the slave trade now?

CHAPTER XLV — AFRIC A — Continued
Chronology of Africa

1. The following table exhibits the dates of the most remarkable events in the history of Africa.

	B.C.
Egypt settled by Misraim	2188
Nitocris reigned queen of Egypt	1678
Departure of the Israelites from Egypt	1491
Cambyses conquers Egypt	525
Cambyses destroys Thebes	520
Alexander conquers Egypt	332
Death of Cleopatra	30

	A.D.
Egypt conquered by the Saracens	670
Algiers built	944
Mamelukes came into power	1250
The Portuguese begin to traffic in slaves	1482
Egypt conquered by the Turks	1517
A government founded at Algiers, called the Regency of Algiers	1518
The English begin to traffic in slaves	1563
Tunis seized by the Turks	1574
Napoleon invades Egypt	1798
Sir Ralph Abercrombie drives the French out of Egypt	1801
Tripoli attacked by Commodore Preble	1803
The English take Cape Town from the Dutch	1806
Commodore Decatur attacks Algiers	1815
Lord Exmouth attacks Algiers	1816
Caillié, a Frenchman, goes to Timbuktu	1827
City of Algiers taken by Marshal Beaumont	1830

MAP OF EUROPE

Questions on the Map—Tell the direction of the following places from London: France; Austria; Asia Minor; Moscow; Finland; Turkey; Italy; Norway; Warsaw; Caspian Sea; Asia; Paris; Ireland.

SCENES IN EUROPE

CHAPTER XLVI—EUROPE
Introductory Remarks on its Geography and other Matters

1. EUROPE IS CONSIDERED the third Grand Division of the globe. It is the smallest in extent, being about one-quarter as large as Asia, one-third as large as Africa, and but little larger than the whole United States. It is part of the Eastern Continent, and is only separated from Asia by the Ural Mountains. It is separated from Africa by the Mediterranean Sea. At the Straits of Gibraltar, the distance from Europe to Africa is but twenty-one miles.

2. But although Europe is the smallest Grand Division of the globe, it has nearly three hundred millions of inhabitants, and is much superior to Asia, Africa, and most parts of America, in civilization. It abounds in fine cities, fine roads, good houses, useful manufacturers, and most other things that are necessary to the comfort and happiness of mankind.

3. In all parts of Europe except Turkey, the Christian religion prevails. If you were to travel in Asia or Africa, you would meet with no churches, or

Questions—CHAP. XLVI—1. Which is the third Grand Division of the globe? The smallest? How large is Europe compared with Asia? Africa? The United States? How is it separated from Asia? From Africa? How far is the nearest point of Europe from Africa?

only now and then one, where the true God is worshiped. But you would see a great many mosques dedicated to the false religion of Mohammed, and a great many temples where the people bow down to idols of wood, stone, or metal.

4. But in Europe, the traveler everywhere meets with churches, and these show that the people are Christians. In Europe, also, there are many colleges, academies, and schools, which prove that the people set a high value upon education. It is a fact which I wish you to remember, that in all parts of the world where you find churches, you find that the people are more or less advanced in civilization and the arts, which render mankind happy.

5. This may show to us that the Christian religion tends to make people wiser and happier; and this is rendered still more clear by the fact that in all those countries where the Christian religion is unknown, the greater part of the people are ignorant, degraded, and miserable.

6. As Europe is the smallest of the Grand Divisions of the earth, so it was behind Asia and Africa in being settled and civilized. Long after the Assyrian Empire had risen to great power and splendor, long after Babylon and Nineveh had flourished on the banks of the Euphrates and Tigris, long after Egypt had become a mighty kingdom, long after Thebes, Memphis, and other magnificent cities had risen upon the borders of the Nile, Europe continued to be inhabited only by wandering tribes of savages.

7. Greece was the first portion of Europe that was settled. About the time that Moses led the Israelites out of Egypt, the Greeks began to build houses, found cities, and emerge from the savage into a more civilized state. By degrees they advanced in knowledge and refinement, and at length became the most polished people in the world.

8. Afterward Rome, situated in Italy, became a mighty city, and the Roman people extended their empire over the greater part of Europe, and the most civilized portions of Asia and Africa. Carthage, Egypt, Greece,

---

Questions—3. What of religion in Europe? What of Asia and Africa? What of churches? Mosques? Temples? 4. What does the traveler meet in Europe? What do churches show? What do colleges, schools, etc., show? What do you find where there are churches? 5. What effect has the Christian religion? What of countries where the Christian religion is unknown? 6. What of Europe? What was the condition of Europe until after the empires of Asia and Egypt had long flourished? 7. What part of Europe was first inhabited? About what time did the Greeks begin to emerge from the savage into a civilized state? Progress of the Greeks? 8. What of Rome? What countries became subject to Rome?

Asia Minor, Palestine, Syria, and other Asiatic countries, bowed to the Roman yoke.

9. Rome was the most splendid empire of all ancient times. But as it crushed other kingdoms beneath its feet, so, in turn, imperial Rome was itself trampled down by the northern nations of Europe. Great ignorance followed this event, and the different nations and tribes of Europe seemed like broken and crushed limbs and members of the great empire, almost without life.

10. But these separate fragments of the human family grew up in due time to be separate nations, and these advanced in knowledge until they reached the condition in which we now find them.

11. Europe may be divided into two parts, the northern and southern. In the former, the climate is about as cold as it is in our middle and eastern states. In the latter, it is about as warm as in the southern states. The principal kingdoms in the northern section of Europe are Russia, Norway, Sweden, Prussia, several German states, Denmark, Holland, Belgium, Switzerland, France, and Great Britain.

12. Among the southern kingdoms of Europe are Portugal, Spain, Italy, Greece, and Turkey. In these latter countries the soil is generally fertile, and here grapes, olives, oranges, lemons, melons, and other delicious fruits, are abundant.

13. Here, too, all the wants of man for food are easily supplied, and so warm and gentle is the climate, that the people do not find it necessary to build tight houses, and put on thick clothing, and provide stores against the winter.

14. In the northern parts of Europe, the people find it necessary to cultivate the soil with care, and lay up in summer a store of provisions against the long, cold winter. They build themselves good houses, they furnish them with many convenient articles, and thus, by their industry and care, they live more happily than those who inhabit the gentler climes of the south.

15. The wild animals of Europe resemble those of this country, though

Questions—9. What was Rome? What happened to the empire? What followed the destruction of the Roman empire? 10. What of the several nations of Europe? 11. How may Europe be divided? Climate in northern Europe? Southern Europe? Principle nations in northern Europe? *Direction of each of these from England?* 12. The southern climate of Europe? *Direction of each of these from England?* 13. Climate in southern Europe? Effect of the climate upon the people? 14. What of the northern parts of Europe? Condition of the people?

105

they are in some respects different. The trees, plants, shrubs, and flowers are similar to those we find here, though not exactly the same.

16. If you were to go to Europe, you would everywhere feel that you were in a strange land, but still many things would remind you of your own home in America. But if you were to go to Asia or Africa, the houses, the fields, the dress of the people, and all their manners and customs, would impress you with the idea that you were in a strange land, far from your native country.

CHAPTER XLVII—EUROPE—CONTINUED
About Greece—Where it is situated—Appearance of the Country—Climate

1. GREECE IS A SMALL strip of land extending into the Mediterranean Sea. It lies almost exactly east of New York, at the distance of about five thousand miles. It is nearly at an equal distance from Asia Minor on the east, and Italy on the west.

2. Greece is bounded on the north by Macedonia, which is now a part of Turkey; on every other side it is bounded by the sea. To the south and east of it are a great number of islands, some of which are extremely beautiful.

3. Several of these have towns and cities upon them, and one, called Antiparos, is remarkable for a grotto beneath the earth, which appears like a beautiful palace. When lighted up with lamps, it seems a vast hall, with a thousand pillars and ornaments of silver.

4. Some of the islands of Greece have been thrown up from the sea, and others which formerly existed have disappeared. These strange things have been caused by volcanic fires under the sea. Nothing can be more wonderful than the scenes which have sometimes been exhibited by these convulsions of nature.

5. In the southern part of Greece, and among the islands, the climate is as mild as in Virginia, and here the country abounds in all sorts of delicious fruits. In the northern part, the climate is somewhat colder.

Questions—15. Wild animals of Europe? Vegetation? 16. What if you were to go to Europe? Asia? Africa?

CHAP. XLVII—1. What is Greece? Direction and distance from New York? In what direction from Asia Minor? From Italy? 2. How is Greece bounded on the north? East? South? West? What of the islands? 3. What of Antiparos? 4. What of volcanic islands? 5. Climate in the southern part of Greece? Northern?

6. If you were to travel through Greece, you would discover that it is naturally very beautiful. Along the shores, you would meet with many little bays and harbors, and you would easily believe that the people living there would be tempted by the placid water to become seamen. You would accordingly find a large portion of the inhabitants to be seafaring people.

MODERN GREEKS

7. In the interior of the country you would meet with lofty mountains, whose tops in winter are covered with snow. You would meet with smiling valleys, bright, rapid streams, and steep hillsides covered with olive groves, vineyards, and fig trees.

8. You would often meet with the ruins of temples and other edifices, built by the ancient Greeks two or three thousand years ago.

9. These would show you, that the former inhabitants of this country were among the most remarkable people that ever lived. It is of these I am now going to tell you.

Questions—6. What of the shores of Greece?   To what pursuit are many of the present Greeks devoted?   7. What of the interior of Greece?   8. What of the present inhabitants of Greece?   What of ruins of temples, etc.?   9. What would these ruins prove?

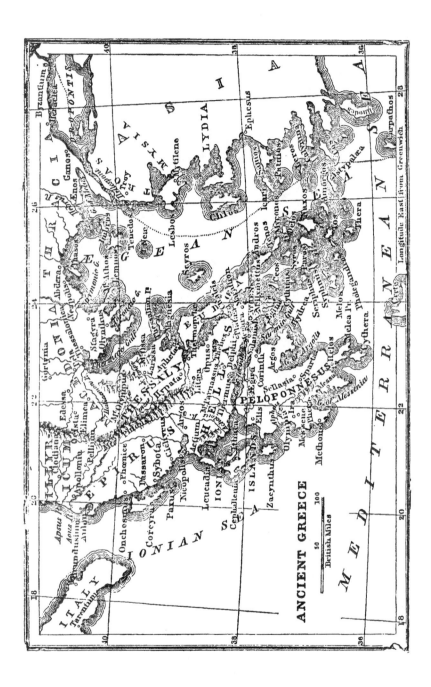

ANCIENT GREECE

CHAPTER XLVIII—EUROPE—Continued
Extent of Greece—First Settlement of the Country

1. Though Greece is one of the most famous countries on the face of the globe, it is not very extensive; its boundaries varied at different times, but it never exceeded four hundred miles in length, and about one hundred and fifty in width. That portion to which the name of Greece is properly applied, was not much larger than the state of New York.

2. I must now carry you back to the first settlement of this country, which took place four thousand years ago. When the human race was scattered from the tower of Babel, it is supposed that some of the family of Japheth, Noah's youngest son, traveled from Asia into Europe. As Greece lay nearer to the land of Shinar than the other parts of Europe, it was probably settled first.

3. The Greeks themselves believed that their ancestors had sprung up out of the earth. The first inhabitants were mere savages. They dwelt in wretched huts, and fed on acorns. Their garments were the skins of wild beasts.

4. There are so many fables about the early history of Greece, that I shall pass very briefly over the first three or four centuries. Cecrops, an Egyptian, seems to have been the first who introduced civilization among the Greeks. He came, with a number of his countrymen, and founded the city of Athens. This event took place about fifteen hundred and fifty-six years before the Christian era.

5. Thirty or forty years afterward, Cadmus came from Phoenicia and built the city of Thebes. He was one of the greatest benefactors of the Greeks, for he taught them the cultivation of the vine, the manufacture of metals, and the use of the alphabet.

6. Other parts of Greece were also settled by colonies from foreign nations. The country then consisted of a number of small kingdoms, which

---

Questions—Chap. XLVIII—1. What of the extent of Greece? Its greatest length? Width? 2. How long since Greece was first settled? Who are supposed to have been the first inhabitants of Greece? *In which direction was Greece from the land of Shinar? From Egypt? (See Map, p. 27).* 3. What did the Greeks believe of their ancestors? What of the first inhabitants of Greece? 4. Who introduced civilization among the Greeks? What city was founded by Cecrops? When did this take place? *In what part of Greece was Athens? Does Athens still exist?—Ans. Yes.* 5. What of Cadmus? *In which direction was Thebes from Athens? N.B. You must remember that there was a famous city in Egypt named Thebes.*

had little or no connection with one another. These were frequently at war among themselves.

7. Twelve of these little kingdoms, or states, soon united themselves into a confederacy. Their deputies held a meeting twice a year, in order to consult respecting the welfare of the country. They were called the council of the Amphictyons. By means of this council, the different states were kept at peace with each other, and were united against foreign enemies.

8. One of the famous events of Grecian history was the Argonautic expedition. It is said that a prince named Jason, with a company of his friends, sailed to Colchis, which lay eastward of the Black Sea. Their object was to find a wonderful ram with a fleece of gold; but the whole story is supposed by some to be a fable.

9. The Trojan war was still more famous than the expedition in search of the golden fleece. Troy was a large city on the Asiatic side of the Hellespont, which is now called the Dardanelles [*dar-da-nelz ´*]. Paris, the son of the Trojan king, had stolen away the wife of Menelaus, a Greek prince.

10. All the Grecian kings combined together to punish this offense. They sailed to Troy in twelve hundred vessels, and took the city after a siege of ten years. This event is supposed to have occurred eleven hundred and ninety-three years before the Christian era.

11. But most historians are of opinion that the Trojan war was a much less important affair than Homer—from whom we get the story—has represented it to be. Poets do not always tell the truth; and Homer was the father and chief of poets. He was a blind old man, and used to wander about the country, reciting his verses.

CHAPTER XLIX—EUROPE—Continued
The Grecian Lawgivers

1. ONE OF THE PRINCIPAL states of Greece was called Sparta or Lacedaemon [*las-e-de ´-mon*]. It was founded by Lelex, 1516 B.C. It had a code of laws from Lycurgus, who lived nearly nine centuries before Christ. He was strict and severe, but wise and upright.

Questions—6. How were other parts of Greece settled? What of Greece at that time? 7. What did twelve of the Grecian states do? What of the Amphictyonic Council? What effect had this council? 8. What of the Argonautic expedition? 9. What of the Trojan war? 11. What of Homer?

CHAP. XLIX—1. What of Sparta? Laws? When did Lycurgus live? What was his character?

2. Lycurgus ordered that all the Spartans should eat together at public tables. The reason of this law was, that the rich citizens might not feast luxuriously at home, but that rich and poor should fare alike. As for the children, they were not allowed anything to eat, unless they could steal it. This wicked custom was adopted with the idea that it would train up the young Spartans to be cunning in war.

3. In order that the people might not be avaricious, Lycurgus forbade any gold or silver to be coined into money. All the money was made of iron. It could not very easily be carried in the pocket, for a Spartan dollar weighed as much as fifty pounds.

4. The children were all brought up at public expense. They were allowed to stand near the dinner tables and listen to the wise conversation of their parents. The Spartans were very anxious that their children should abhor drunkenness.

5. They showed them the disgusting effects of this pernicious vice, by causing their slaves to drink intoxicating liquors. When the children had witnessed the ridiculous conduct of the drunken slaves, they were careful never to reduce themselves to so degraded a condition.

6. When Lycurgus had completed his code of laws, he left Sparta. Previous to his departure, he made the people swear that they would violate none of the laws till he should return. But he was resolved never to return.

7. He committed suicide by starving himself to death; and his remains were thrown into the sea by his command, so that the Spartans might not bring back his dead body. Thus, as Lycurgus never could return, the Spartans were bound by their oath to keep his laws forever.

8. They did keep them during five hundred years; and, all that time, the Spartans were a brave, patriotic, and powerful people. Many of their customs, however, belonged rather to a savage than a civilized nation.

9. Athens had two celebrated lawgivers, Draco and Solon. The laws of Draco were so extremely severe that they were said to be written with blood, instead of ink. He punished even the smallest offenses with death. His code was soon abolished.

10. Solon's laws were much milder. Almost all of them were wise and

---

Questions—2. Why did Lycurgus wish the Spartans to eat in public? What of the children? Why were they encouraged to steal? 3. What laws were made respecting money? What of a Spartan dollar? 4. How were children brought up? 5. How were they taught to abhor drunkenness? 6. What did Lycurgus make the Spartans swear before he went away? 7. What was the fate of the Spartan lawgiver? 8. How long did the Spartans keep his laws? 9. What of Draco and Solon? The laws of Draco?

good laws, and would have been advantageous to the people. But the Athenians had so much fickleness and levity, that they were continually proposing alterations in them.

11. Athens was at this time a republic—which is, you know, a government carried on by persons chosen by the people; but soon after Solon had made his laws, the supreme power was usurped by Pisistratus, an ambitious citizen. He and his sons ruled Athena fifty years.

CHAPTER L—EUROPE—Continued
War with Persia

1. About five centuries before the Christian era, Darius, king of Persia, made war against Greece. His generals invaded the country with a fleet of six hundred vessels, and half a million of men. There were scarcely any troops to oppose them, except ten thousand Athenians.

2. Darius felt so certain of conquering Greece, that he had sent great quantities of marble with his army. He intended that it should be carved into pillars and triumphal arches, and other trophies of victory. He had also commanded his generals to send all the Athenians to Persia in chains.

3. The Athenian general was named Miltiades. He led his little army against the immense host of the Persians, and encountered them at Marathon. This was a small town on the seashore, about fifteen miles northeast of Athens.

4. While their countrymen were fighting, the aged people, and the women and children, remained at Athens in the utmost anxiety. If Miltiades were to lose the battle, they knew that the Persians would chase his routed army into the city, and burn it to ashes.

5. Suddenly, a soldier, covered with blood, ran into the marketplace of the city. He was sorely wounded; but he had come all the way from the army to bring the news. He was ghastly pale, and the people feared that the Persians had won the day, and that the soldier was a fugitive.

6. They gathered round him, eagerly asking about Miltiades and the

---

Questions—10. What of Solon's laws? 11. What was the government of Athens? Who usurped the supreme power? What of the government of Athens for fifty years?

Chap. L—1. When did Darius make war against Greece? What of the Persian force? The Athenian? 2. What of marble? What did Darius command? 3. Who was the Athenian general? Where was Marathon? 4. What of those who remained at Athens? 5. What messenger was sent from Marathon? *Which way is Marathon from Athens? From Sparta? — (See Map, p. 108).*

army. The soldier leaned heavily upon his spear. He seemed too much ex-hausted to give utterance to the news he had brought.

7. But exerting all his strength, he cried out, "Rejoice, my country-men! The victory is ours!" and, with that exulting shout, he fell down dead.

8. The Athenians showed themselves ungrateful to the brave Miltiades. All that he demanded as a reward for rescuing his native land from slavery, was a crown of olive leaves, which was esteemed a mark of honor among the Greeks. But they refused to give him one; and he was afterward con-demned, on some frivolous pretense, to pay a fine of fifty talents, which was a very large sum. As Miltiades had not so much money in the world, he perished in prison.

9. After the battle of Marathon, the Persians were driven out of Greece, and Darius died while he was preparing to invade the country again. His son Xerxes renewed the war. In the history of Persia, I have already told of the invasion of Greece by Xerxes with two millions of men, and of the mis-fortunes which befell him there.

CHAPTER LI—EUROPE—Continued
Affairs of Athens

1. AFTER THE PERSIAN war, Cimon, Aristides, and Pericles were the three principal men of Athens. Pericles at length became the chief person in the republic. Athens was never more flourishing than while he was at the head of the government.

2. He adorned the city with magnificent edifices, and rendered it fa-mous for learning, poetry, and beautiful works of art, such as temples, stat-ues, and paintings. But the Athenians were fickle, and generally ungrate-ful to their public benefactors; and they sometimes ill treated Pericles.

3. In the latter part of his administration, a terrible plague broke out in Athens. Many of the citizens fell down and died, while passing through the streets. Dead bodies lay in heaps, one upon another.

4. The illustrious Pericles was one of the victims of this pestilence. When he lay at the point of death, his friends praised him for the glorious

Questions—7. What news did the messenger bring? 8. How did the Athenians treat Miltiades? His fate? 9. What of the Persians after the battle of Marathon? What of Darius? Xerxes? What may you read in the history of Persia?

Chap. LI—1. Who were the three principal men of Athens? What of Pericles? 2. What did he do for Athens? What was the general character of the Athenians? 3. What of the plague?

deeds which he had achieved. "It is my greatest glory," replied Pericles, "that none of my acts have caused a citizen of Athens to put on mourning."

5. Three years before the death of Pericles, a war had commenced between Athens and Sparta. These were now the two principal states of Greece, and they had become jealous of each other's greatness. A fierce war followed, in which all the states of that part of Greece called Peloponnesus were engaged. This bloody strife lasted twenty-eight years.

6. In the course of this war, Alcibiades made a conspicuous figure among the Athenians. He was the handsomest and most agreeable man in Athens. At one period he was greatly beloved by the people, and possessed almost unlimited power. But he was ambitious and destitute of principle.

7. He was the cause of much trouble, not only in his native city, but all over Greece. At last, when he had lost the good will of everybody, he retired to a small village in Phrygia, in Asia Minor, and dwelt there with a woman named Timandra.

8. His enemies sent a party of assassins to murder him. These set fire to the house in which he lived. Alcibiades was a brave man, and he rushed out, sword in hand, to fight the assassins. But they stood at a distance, and pierced him through with javelins. They then went away, leaving Timandra to bury him.

9. The Peloponnesian war brought great misfortunes upon the Athenians. The Spartans conquered them, and burnt the city; and while this work of destruction was going forward, the victors caused gay tunes of music to be played.

10. The Athenians were now placed under the government of thirty Spartan captains. These were called the Thirty Tyrants of Athens; but they held their power only three yars. Thrasybulus, a patriotic Athenian, then incited his countrymen to regain their freedom.

11. The thirty tyrants were expelled; and Thrasybulus was rewarded with a wreath made of two twigs of an olive tree, which, as I have before said, was esteemed a great mark of honor. Athens again became prosperous, and its former government was restored in the year 403 before the Christian era.

Questions—4. What did Pericles say on his death bed? 5. What was begun three years before the death of Pericles? What of Athens and Sparta? How long did the Peloponnesian war last? *What part of Greece was called Peloponnesus?—(see Map of Greece, p. 108). What states were included in the Peloponnesus?—Ans. Arcadia, Laconia, Messenia, Elis, Argolis, Achaia, Sicyon, and Corinth.* 6. What of Alcibiades? 7. What happened to him? 8. How did he die? 9. What of the Peloponnesian war? Sparta? 10. What of the thirty tyrants? Thrasybulus? 11. How was he rewarded for expelling the thirty tyrants? What took place in 403 B.C.?

CHAPTER LII—EUROPE—Continued
Beginning of the Theban War

1. Not long after this period, Thebes became the most distinguished city of Greece. It was the capital of the kingdom of Boeotia [be-o´-she-a]. A war between Thebes and Sparta had originated in the following manner: Phoebidas [feb´-i-das], a Spartan general, had wrongfully taken possession of Cadmea, a fortress belonging to Thebes. The Thebans demanded that it should be given up; but the Spartans garrisoned it strongly, and resolved to hold it as their own.

2. A brave and patriotic young man of Thebes, named Pelopidas, contrived a scheme to get back the fortress. He and eleven companions put on their breastplates, and girded their swords around them, but clothed themselves in women's garments over their armor. In this garb they went to the gate of Cadmea, and were admitted.

3. The magistrates and Spartan officers were assembled at a splendid festival. Archias, the Spartan commander, sat at the head of the table. He and his friends were wholly occupied with the enjoyment of the banquet. They took scarcely any notice when the twelve figures in female attire entered the hall.

4. At the moment when the mirth and festivity of the Spartans was at its height, the strangers tore off their female garb. Instead of twelve women, there stood twelve young warriors. The light of the festal torches flashed back from their bright breastplates. Their naked swords were in their hands.

5. Pelopidas and his eleven companions immediately attacked the Spartan banqueters. Their surprise hindered the Spartans from making an effectual resistance. Archias and many others were struck dead, almost before they could rise from the table.

6. Thus the Thebans gained possession of the fortress. But Sparta immediately began a war against Thebes. Many of the other states of Greece lent their assistance to the Spartans. It appeared probable that the Thebans would be conquered and utterly ruined.

7. But they had a brave and skillful general, named Epaminondas. With only six thousand Thebans, he encountered twenty-five thousand Spartans, commanded by Cleombrotus, their king. The battle was fought at

Questions—Chap. LII—1. What of Thebes? *In what part of Greece was Boeotia?* How did the war between Thebes and Sparta originate? 2. What of Pelopidas? Describe the scheme of Pelopidas and his companions. 5. Did this bold undertaking succeed? 6. What state made war upon Thebes? Other states?

Leuctra. The Thebans gained a complete victory, and killed Cleombrotus and fourteen hundred of his men.

CHAPTER LIII—EUROPE—CONTINUED
Sequel of the Theban War

1. EPAMINONDAS, the Theban general, was one of the best men that lived in ancient times. His private virtues were equal to his patriotism and valor. It is said of him that a falsehood was never known to come from his lips— one of the highest praises that can be bestowed on any man.

2. It might be supposed that the Thebans would have felt the utmost gratitude toward Epaminondas, whose valor had saved his country; and it is true that the most virtuous part of the people honored him according to his merits; but I am sorry to tell you that a great and good man is very apt to have enemies.

3. His virtues and his greatness are a reproach to the vicious and the mean, and therefore they hate him, and seek to destroy him. So it happened with Epaminondas, and so it has happened in all ages.

4. Epaminondas had many enemies among the Thebans. They at first attempted to have him sentenced to death because he had kept the command of the army longer than the law permitted. But as his only motive had been to preserve Thebes from ruin, his judges concluded to let him live.

5. Nevertheless, in order to disgrace him as much as possible, he was appointed to clean the streets of Thebes. Epaminondas was not mortified; for he knew that the Thebans might disgrace themselves by such ingratitude, but could not disgrace him. He therefore set about discharging the duties of his new office, and the great and victorious general was accordingly seen clearing away the filth from the streets.

6. But the war was not yet at an end; and the Thebans soon found that they could not do without Epaminondas. They made him throw away his broom, and take the sword again. He was placed at the head of the army with greater power than he had possessed before.

Questions—7. What of Epaminondas? His army? The Spartan force? Who was the Spartan leader? Were the Thebans victorious?

CHAP. LIII—1. Character of Epaminondas? 2. Were the Thebans grateful to him? 3. Why do the wicked hate a great and good man? 4. What did the Thebans attempt? 5. How did they attempt to disgrace Epaminondas? Was he mortified? What did he do? 6. What did the Thebans find? What did they do?

116

7. So long as Epaminondas was their general, the Thebans were the most powerful people of Greece. The last victory that he gained was at Mantinea. But it cost the Thebans dear; for while Epaminondas was fighting in the thickest of the battle, a Spartan soldier thrust a javelin into his breast.

8. The Thebans and Spartans fought around the wounded Epaminondas, the latter wishing to put an end to his life, and the former to bear him from the field. The Spartans were driven back, and some of his soldiers carried Epaminondas in their arms to his tent.

9. The javelin remained sticking in the wound, for the surgeons declared that he would die the moment that it should be drawn out. Epaminondas lay in great pain; but he thought little of his own agony, and was anxious only for the success of his countrymen.

10. At last a messenger came from the battlefield, and told him that the Spartans were flying, and that Thebes had won a glorious victory. "Then all is well!" said Epaminondas. As he spoke, he drew the javelin out of his wound, and instantly expired.

11. This event took place in the year 363 before the Christian era. After the death of Epaminondas, the Thebans were no longer formidable to the rest of the Greeks.

CHAPTER LIV—EUROPE—Continued
Grecian Religion or Mythology

1. MY HISTORY has now reached the period when the glory of Greece was at its height; and I shall soon have to speak of its decline. Before doing so, I think it proper to give a slight account of the religion of the Greeks, and some other interest particulars.

2. The Greeks believed that there were three classes of deities—the Celestial, the Marine, and the Infernal. The first, as they fancied, dwelt in the sky, the second in the sea, and the third in the dreary regions under the earth. Besides these, there were inferior kinds of deities, who haunted the woods, or lived in fountains and streams.

Questions—7. What of Thebes while Epaminondas was general? What was his last victory? How was he wounded? 8. By whom was he carried from the field? 9. What of the javelin? 10. Describe the death of Epaminondas. 11. When did this happen? What of the Thebans after the death of Epaminondas?

CHAP. LIV—1. At what period was the glory of Greece at its height? 2. In what deities did the Greeks believe? What were the three classes? Where did each of them dwell? What of inferior deities?

JUPITER AND HIS GODS AND GODDESSES ON MOUNT OLYMPUS

3. The deities whose home was in the sky, were Jupiter, Apollo, Mars, Mercury, Bacchus, Vulcan, Juno, Minerva, Venus, Diana, Ceres, and Vesta. The greatest of all the gods was Jupiter. When it thundered and lightened, the Greeks supposed that Jupiter was angry, and was flinging his thunderbolts about.

4. The Olympic games were instituted by the Greeks, in honor of Jupiter. These games were celebrated every four years. They consisted of races on foot and on horseback, and in chariots, and of leaping, wrestling, and boxing. It was considered a very great honor for a person to gain a prize at the Olympic games.

5. Apollo was the son of Jupiter. He was supposed to be the driver of the sun, which had four horses harnessed to it, and went round the world every day. It was pretty much like a modern stagecoach, except that it carried no passengers.

6. Besides being the coachmen of the sun, Apollo was likewise the god of music and poetry, and of medicine, and all the fine arts. He also presided over the famous oracle at Delphos, whither people used to come from all parts of the world to find out the events of futurity.

Questions—3. Who were the celestial deities?　What of Jupiter?　4. What of the Olympic games?　5. What of Apollo?　His chariot?　6. What more can you tell of Apollo?

7. Mars was the god of war, and Mercury the god of thieves, and Bacchus was the god of drunkards, and Vulcan the god of blacksmiths. Vulcan seems to have been one of the best and most useful of the heathen deities, for he was an excellent blacksmith, and worked hard at his anvil.

8. Venus was the goddess of beauty. Her statues were made in the form of a beautiful woman. She had a son named Cupid, who was a mischievous little deity, and used to shoot at people with a bow and arrow.

9. Neptune was the chief of the marine deities. It was supposed that he had a huge scallop shell for a chariot, and that his horses had the tails of fishes. Whenever he rode over the waves, a tribe of sea monsters surrounded his chariot.

10. Pluto was the deity who presided in the infernal regions. He used to sit on a throne of brimstone, looking very stern and awful. In one hand he held a scepter, and in the other two keys. Besides these gods, the Greeks believed in heroes, who were half gods and half men. Of these, Hercules was very famous for his wonderful feats of strength.

11. Unless I were to write a large book on this one subject, it would be impossible for me to tell you all about the fanciful gods of ancient Greece, and the strange and foolish things they are said to have done. The only use of such a book would be, to show how necessary it was that the true God should reveal himself to men, since they could contrive no better religion than these absurd though sometimes amusing fables.

12. Ridiculous as their deities were, the Greeks honored them with magnificent temples. Many of the churches and other public buildings in Europe and America are built on the plan of the old Grecian temples. The Grecian sculptors also carved marble statues of their deities, some of which were grand and beautiful.

CHAPTER LV—EUROPE—Continued
The Grecian Philosophers

1. THE GRECIAN PHILOSOPHERS were men who pretended to be wiser than mankind in general. There were a great many of them, who lived in various ages. I shall speak of some of the most remarkable, in this and the following chapters.

Questions—7. What of Mars? Mercury? Bacchus? Vulcan? 8. What of Venus? Cupid? 9. What of Neptune? Where did he dwell? How is he represented? 10. Who was Pluto? Where did he dwell? What of him? 12. How did the Greeks honor their false gods? What of temples? What can you say of the Grecian statues?
CHAP. LV—1. Who were the Greek philosophers?

2. The philosopher Thales was born between six and seven hundred years before the Christian era. In his time there were seven philosophers, who were called the Seven Wise Men of Greece; and Thales was considered the wisest of them all.

3. One night, while the great philosopher was taking a walk, he looked upward to contemplate the stars. Being much interested in this occupation, he strayed out of his path, and tumbled into a ditch. An old woman who lived in his family ran and helped him out, all covered with mud. "For the future, Thales," said she, "I advise you not to have your head among the stars, while your feet are on the earth!" Some people think that the old woman was the wiser philosopher of the two.

4. Another philosopher was named Pittacus. He was the first temperance man on record; for, though there were many sorts of delicious wines in his country, he never drank any thing but water.

5. The philospher Bias lived in the year 617 B.C. Some fishermen once found a golden vase in the belly of a large fish. On the vase were engraved these words—"To the wisest." It was therefore sent to Bias, who was thought to be at least as wise as anybody.

6. But Bias did not care for gold or riches. When his native city was taken by the enemy, all the other inhabitants endeavored to hide their most valuable property. Bias alone gave himself no trouble. "Riches are but play-things," said he. "My only real treasures are my own thoughts."

7. Epimenides was a very wonderful philosopher. My readers must not put too much faith in the story which I am going to tell them. It is as follows: One day, when Epimenides was young, his father sent him in search of a sheep that was lost. After finding the sheep, Epimenides entered a cave by the wayside, and sat down, for he was tired, and the sun was very hot. In this cave he fell asleep, and slept a good deal longer than he intended.

8. It was no less than fifty-seven years before he awoke. When he closed his eyes he was a young man, but he was old and gray when he opened them again. He left the cave and went back to the town where he had formerly lived.

9. But his father was long ago dead; his brother, who had been a child when he went away, was an old man now; and the town was full of houses

---

and people that he had never seen before. These were certainly very wonderful changes, considering that they had all happened while Epimenides was taking a nap.

CHAPTER LVI—EUROPE—Continued
The Grecian Philosophers continued

1. THE PHILOSOPHER Pythagoras believed that when people died, their souls migrated into the bodies of animals or birds. He affirmed that his own soul had once lived in the body of a peacock.

2. Heraclitus of Ephesus was called the dark philosopher, because all his sayings were like riddles. He thought that nothing was wisdom which could be understood by common people.

3. This wise man considered the world as such a wretched place, that he never could look at anybody without shedding tears. And at last he retired to a cave among the mountains, where he lived on herbs and roots, and was as miserable as his heart could wish.

4. Democritus, who lived not long after Heraclitus, was quite a different sort of philosopher. Instead of shedding tears, he laughed so continually that his townsmen thought him mad. And, to say the truth, I think so too.

5. The philosopher Anaxagoras believed that the sky was made of stones,

DISCOVERY OF THE SHOE OF EMPEDOCLES

Questions—CHAP. LVI—1. What did Pythagoras believe? 2. What of Heraclitus? 4. What of Democritus? How did he differ from Heraclitus?

and that the sun was a great mass of red-hot iron. This may seem very strange; but in those ancient times the people did not know the shape of the earth.

6. The philsopher Empedocles went and lived near Mount Aetna, in Sicily. He was a man of very grave and majestic appearance, and everybody knew him, because he used to wear a crown of laurel about his head. People generally acknowledged him to be a very wise man; but not content with this, he wanted to be thought a god.

7. One day, after he had prepared a great festival, Empedocles disappeared, and was never seen again. The people took it for granted that he had ascended to heaven. But shortly afterward, there was an eruption of Mount Aetna, and an old shoe was thrown out of the crater. On examination, it was found out that this shoe had belonged to Empedocles. It was now easy to guess at the fate of the foolish old man. He had thrown himself into the crater of the blazing volcano, in order that people might think that he was a god and had gone to heaven.

8. Socrates was one of the wisest and best philosophers of Greece. Indeed he was so wise and good, that the profligate Athenians could not suffer him to live. They therefore compelled him to drink poison.

9. Diogenes [*di-oj´-e-neze*] was the queerest philosopher of all. He was

ALEXANDER AND DIOGENES

Questions—5. What did Anaxogoras believe? 6. Where did Empedocles live? What did he wish to be thought? 7. What means did he take to make the people think him a god? 8. What of Socrates? His death?

called Diogenes the Dog—either because he lived like a dog, or because he had a currish habit of snarling at everybody.

10. His doctrine was, that the fewer enjoyments a man had, the happier he was likely to be. This philosopher went about barefoot, dressed in very shabby clothes, and carrying a bag, a jug, and a staff. He afterward got a great tub, which he used to lug about with him all day long, and sleep in at night.

11. One day, Alexander the Great came to see Diogenes, and found him mending his tub. It happened that Alexander stood in such a manner as to shade Diogenes from the sun, and he felt cold. "Diogenes," said Alexander, "you must have a very hard time of it, living in a tub. Can I do anything to better your condition?" "Nothing, except to get out of my sunshine," replied Diogenes, who disdained to accept any other favor from the greatest monarch in the world.

CHAPTER LVII—EUROPE—Continued
Something more about the Greek Philosophers—The Greek Poets

1. I could tell you much more about the Grecian philosophers, but I have not room. I must not forget, however, to mention Plato, who was born 429 years B.C., and was for eight years the pupil of Socrates.

2. This great man, like many other Grecian philosophers, was a sort of schoolmaster, and many young men came to be taught by him. He delivered his lectures in a grove near Athens, called Academus, from which circumstance the word *academy* has since been applied to the higher class of schools.

3. So great was his reputation, that the first young men from various parts of the world came to be his pupils. He had very sublime ideas of religion, virtue, and truth; and he delivered these with so much sweetness and eloquence, that his listeners were enchanted. The Greeks spoke of him as Plato the Divine.

4. There were other celebrated philosophers in Greece, but I must leave them now, and tell you of the poets. Homer, the best poet of ancient times, one of the best that ever lived, I have already mentioned. When this great man was born, how he lived, or where he died, are matters of uncertainty.

Questions—9. What of Diogenes?   10. His doctrines?   How did he live?   11. Tell an anecdote of Diogenes.
Chap. LVII—1. When was Plato born?   Whose pupil was he?   2. What else of Plato?   3. What of his ideas, and his mode of expressing them?   4. What of Homer?

5. The general opinion is, that he lived about the year 900 B.C., and was a wandering minstrel, who went about from place to place reciting and singing his verses. The Iliad and Odyssey, his two poems, were composed in separate parts, and, but for the care of Lycurgus, who had them collected, would doubtless have been lost. They celebrate the actions of heroes and imaginary gods, and are full of the liveliest interest.

6. There were many other poets in ancient Greece, some of whom acquired great celebrity. Among these was Anacreon, who wrote about love; Pindar, who composed sublime odes; and Theocritus, who sang about shepherds and shepherdesses, living very pleasantly in the country. There were also some poets who wrote pieces for the stage.

7. You already know that the Greeks were in many respects very ignorant, and entertained many absurd notions. They did not know that the earth is a great globe or ball, that it turns round every day, and that the sun, moon, and stars are also great worlds moving about in the sky.

8. You would not therefore expect in their poetry to find any useful information about geography or astronomy. Yet they lived in a beautiful country, and their mountains, streams, and valleys were often the subject of their songs.

9. Their religion, too, though full of absurdity, furnished materials for the poets. They described the gods and goddesses as dwelling upon the mountains, or skipping along the valleys, or gliding amid the waters. Thus every object of nature derived a new interest from the vivid fancy of these poets.

10. To this day the verses of the Greek poets are remembered, and the places mentioned by them are often visited by travelers, who look upon them with emotion, on account of the beautiful fictions they inspired more than two thousand years ago.

CHAPTER LVIII—EUROPE—Continued
About the Mode of Life among the Ancient Greeks

1. BUT WE MUST now leave poets and philosophers, and take a view of the private life of the ancient Greeks. The men wore an inner garment

---

Questions—5. When is it Homer lived? How did he live? What of his poems? 6. What of Anacreon? Pindar? Theocritus? Other poets? 7. What did the Greeks not know? 8. What of the poetry of the ancient Greeks? 9. What use did the Grecian poets make of their mythology? What effect had the poems of the ancient Greeks? Are the poems of the ancient Greeks still remembered? 10. Are the places mentioned in these poems rendered more interesting to travelers of the present time who visit them?

called a tunic, over which they threw a mantle; their shoes or sandals were bound under their feet with thongs or ropes. In ancient times the Greeks went with their heads uncovered; but afterward they used hats, which were tied under the chin.

2. The women always covered their heads with a veil, which came down upon the shoulders. They wore in their hair golden grasshoppers, and earrings were suspended from their ears. The rest of their dress consisted of a white tunic fastened with a broad sash, and descending in folds down to their heels.

3. The Greeks usually made four meals a day: the morning meal, which was taken at the rising of the sun; the next at midday; the afternoon repast, and the supper, which was the principal meal, as it was taken after the business of the day.

4. In the early ages, the food of the Greeks was the fruits of the earth, and their drink water; the flesh of animals was introduced at a later period. This brought on the luxuries of the table, and some of the cities of Greece became renowned for producing excellent cooks. The Spartans, as we have before mentioned, ate at public tables. Their chief food consisted of black broth.

5. The poor sometimes fed on grasshoppers, and the extremities of leaves. In general, the Greeks were very fond of flesh. Their usual drink was water, either hot or cold, but most commonly the latter, which was sometimes cooled with ice. Wines were very generally used, and even perfumed wines were introduced at the tables of the rich.

6. Before the Greeks went to an entertainment, they washed and anointed themselves; when they arrived, the entertainer took them by the hand, or kissed their lips, hands, knees, or feet, as they deserved more or less respect. It must be observed concerning the guests, that men and women were never invited together.

7. They sat at meat either quite upright, or leaning a little backward; but in more degenerate ages, they adopted the Asiatic custom of reclining on beds or couches. As soon as the provisions were set on the table, and

---

Questions—Chap. LVIII—1. What did the men wear among the ancient Greeks? Their shoes? Headdress? 2. Headdress of the women? What ornaments did they wear? The rest of their dress? 3. The meals of the Greeks? 4. What was the food of the Greeks in early ages? What of flesh? Luxuries of the table? What of the Spartans? 5. What of the poor? Were the Greeks fond of meat for food? What of their drink? Wine? 6. What of entertainments? Men and women?

before the guests began to eat, a part was offered as a sort of firstfruits to the gods.

8. They had a custom, similar to ours, of drinking healths, not only to those present, but to their absent friends; and at every name they poured a little wine on the ground, which was called a libation.

9. The entertainment being ended, a hymn was sung to the gods. After this, the company was amused with music, dancing, and mimicry, or whatever could tend to excite mirth or cheerfulness.

10. The houses of the rich were built of stone, and many of them were highly ornamented. A large part of the people, however, lived in huts made of rough stone laid in clay.

11. In war, the Greeks fought with various weapons. Some of the soldiers had bows and arrows; some had javelins or spears, which they hurled with great force and precision of aim, and some had slings, with which they threw stones. They usually carried shields for warding off the weapons of their enemies.

12. You must recollect that, in these ancient times, gunpowder was not known and muskets and cannon were, therefore, not in use. In battle, the warriors often engaged in close conflict, foot to foot, and breast to breast. The strife was, therefore, very exciting, and the men usually fought with furious courage.

13. As mankind were very much given to making war upon one another, it was the custom in all countries to surround the cities with high walls for defense. This practice, indeed, continued for many ages, and if you ever go to Europe, you will see that the principal cities of France, Germany, and many other countries, are still secured in this way.

14. In modern times, when an army attacks a city, it batters down the walls with cannon-shot, or by undermining them, placing gunpowder beneath, and then setting it on fire. But in the olden times of Greece, the warriors used battering rams, consisting of heavy beams with ponderous stones at one end. These were driven by main strength against the walls, and thus, after many efforts, they were demolished.

Questions—7. How did they sit at table? How do the people of Asia sit at table? Did the Greeks adopt this Asiatic custom? What was done before beginning to eat? 8. What of drinking healths? 9. What followed the eating? 10. What of the inhabitants of the rich? Of the poor? 11. What weapons were used by the Greeks in war? 12. What of gunpowder? How did the warriors engage one another in conflict? 13. What was the custom regarding cities? What are to be seen in Europe? 14. How do the moderns attack a walled city? How did the ancients destroy the walls of a city?

CHAPTER LIX—EUROPE—Continued
Philip of Macedon conquers Greece

1. I SHALL NOW resume the history of Greece, at the point where I left off. The reader will recollect that I had just finished speaking of the Theban war.

2. Not long after the close of that war, the states of Greece became involved in another, which was generally called the Sacred War. The people of Phocis had been sentenced, by the Amphictyonic council, to pay a heavy fine for plowing a field which belonged to the temple of Apollo, at Delphos.

PHILIP OF MACEDON

3. Rather than pay the fine, the Phocians resolved to go to war. The people of Athens, Sparta, and Achaia assisted the Phocians. The Thebans, Locrians, and the Thessalians took the part of the Amphictyonic council, and Philip, king of Macedon, was induced to fight on the same side.

4. The kingdom of Macedon is numbered by some historians among

---

Questions—CHAP. LIX—2. What of the Sacred War? Cause of it? 3. What states fought on the side of the Phocians? What on the side of the Amphyctionic Council? On which side did Philip, king of Macedon, fight?

the states of Greece; but others consider it a separate country. Although it was founded about five hundred years before this period, it had never been very powerful till Philip mounted the throne.

5. Philip was ambitious and warlike. No sooner had he marched his army into Greece, than he determined to make himself ruler of the whole country. The Greeks were not now so valiant as they had been; and there were no such men as Leonidas, Miltiades, or Epaminondas, to lead them to victory.

6. The man that gave Philip more trouble than any other, was Demosthenes, an Athenian. He was one of the most eloquent orators that ever lived; and he uttered such terrible orations against Philip, that the Athenians were incited to resist him in battle. It is from these orations against the Macedonian king that severe speeches have since been called *philippics*.

7. But the Athenians were beaten at Chaeronea, in the year 338 before the Christian era. Thenceforward, Philip controlled the affairs of Greece, till his death. Perhaps, after all, he was a better ruler than the Greeks could have found among themselves.

8. But he had many vices, and among the rest, that of drinking to excess. One day, just after he had risen from a banquet, he decided a certain law case unjustly. The losing person cried out, "I appeal from Philip drunk, to Philip sober!" And, sure enough, when Philip got sober, he decided the other way.

9. A poor woman, who had some business with Philip, tried in vain to obtain an audience. He put her off from one day to another, saying he had no leisure to attend to her. "If you have no leisure to do justice, you have no right to be king!" said the woman. Philip was struck with the truth of what the woman said, and he became more attentive to the duties of a king.

10. He lived only about two years after he had conquered the Greeks. There was a young nobleman named Pausanias, a captain of the guard, who had been injured by one of Philip's relations. As Philip would not punish the offender, Pausanias resolved that he himself should die.

Questions—4. What of Macedon?   Where was it situated?   When was it founded?
Which way did Philip's army march from Macedon to Greece?   5. What of Philip?   On what did he determine?   What of the Greeks at this time?   6. What of Demosthenes? What effect had his oratory on the Athenians?   What is the origin of the word *philippic?* 7. Where were the Athenians beaten?   When did the battle take place?   *Where is Chaeronea?   Direction from Thebes?   Athens?   Sparta?*   How long did Philip rule Greece?   8–9. What of Philip?   Relate some anecdotes of him.   10. What of Pausanias?

11. On the day of the marriage of Philip's daughter, the king was entering the public theater, where the nuptial festivities were to be celebrated. At this moment Pausanias rushed forth, with his sword drawn, and stabbed him to the heart.

12. The Athenians greatly rejoiced at the news of Philip's death. They publicly voted that a golden crown should be given to Pausanias, as a reward for having murdered him. All the other states of Greece likewise revolted against the power of Macedon.

CHAPTER LX—EUROPE—Continued
Conquests of Alexander the Great

1. But the successor of Philip, the new king of Macedon, though only twenty years old, was well worthy to sit on his father's throne. He was Alexander, afterward surnamed the Great. Young as he was, he had already given proofs of the valor which so soon made him conqueror of the world. He was a famous horseman, and had a horse named Bucephalus, which went with him in wars, and was almost as celebrated as his rider.

ALEXANDER AND BUCEPHALUS

Questions—11. Describe the death of Philip.   12. What did the Athenians do?   Other states?

Chap. LX—1. Who was the new king of Macedon?   Of what had he given proofs?   What of Bucephalus?

2. Alexander subdued the Grecian states in the course of one campaign. He was then declared generalissimo of the Greeks, and undertook a war against Persia. The army which he led against that country consisted of thirty-five thousand men.

3. He crossed the Hellespont, and marched through Asia Minor toward Persia. Before reaching its borders, he was met by the Persian king, Darius, who had collected an immense army. Alexander defeated him, and killed a hundred and ten thousand of his soldiers.

4. Darius soon assembled a mightier army than before. He had now half a million of men. He advanced to battle in the midst of his troops, seated on a lofty chariot, which resembled a moving throne. Around him were his life-guards all in splendid armor.

5. But when the Persians saw how boldly the Macedonian horsemen advanced, they took to flight. Poor King Darius was left almost alone on his lofty chariot. He had but just time to get on horseback, and gallop away from the battle. Shortly afterward, he was slain by two of his own subjects, as I have told you in the history of Persia.

6. After the victory, Alexander marched to Persepolis, which was then the capital of Persia. It was a rich and magnificent city. In the royal palace there was a gigantic statue of Xerxes, but the Macedonian soldiers overthrew it, and tumbled it upon the ground.

7. While he remained at Persepolis, Alexander gave himself up to drunkenness and licentious pleasures. One night, at a splendid banquet, an Athenian lady persuaded the conqueror to set fire to the city. It was accordingly burnt to the ground.

8. When Persia was completely subdued, Alexander invaded India, now Hindostan. One of the kings of that country was named Porus. He is said to have been seven feet and a half in height. This gigantic king led a great army against Alexander.

9. Porus was well provided with elephants, which had been trained to rush upon the enemy, and trample them down. Alexander had no elephants, but his usual good fortune did not desert him. The army of Porus was routed,

---

Questions—2. After what exploit was Alexander declared generalissimo of the Greek? What of the army which he led against Persia? *Which way is Persia from Macedon?* 3. What sea and country did the army cross to reach Persia? Who opposed Alexander? How many of Darius' army were killed? 4. Describe the march of Darius and his half-million of troops. 5. What became of Darius? 6. Where did Alexander go after his victory? Where was Persepolis? *Direction from Athens?* What of the statue of Xerxes? 7. What happened at Persepolis? 8. What country did Alexander next invade? *Direction of India from Greece? Persia?* What of Porus?

and he himself was taken prisoner, and loaded with chains.

10. In this degraded condition, the Indian king was brought into the victor's tent. Alexander gazed with wonder at the enormous stature of Porus. Although so great a conqueror, he was himself only of middle size. "How shall I treat you?" asked Alexander of his prisoner. "Like a king!" said Porus. This answer led Alexander to reflect how he himself should like to be treated, had he been in a similar situation; and he was induced to behave generously to Porus.

CHAPTER LXI—EUROPE—Continued
Sequel of Alexander's Career

1. In the early part of his career, Alexander had shown many excellent and noble traits of character. But he met with such great and continual success in all his undertakings, that his disposition was ruined by it. He began to consider himself the equal of the gods.

2. Yet so far was Alexander from being a god, that some of his actions were unworthy of a man. One of his worst deeds was the murder of Clitus, an old officer who had fought under King Philip. He had once saved Alexander's life in battle; and on this account he was allowed to speak very freely to him.

3. One night, after drinking too much wine, Alexander began to speak of his own exploits; and he spoke more highly of them than old Clitus thought they deserved. Accordingly he told Alexander that his father Philip had done much greater things than ever he had done.

4. The monarch was so enraged, that he snatched a spear from one of his attendants, and gave Clitus a mortal wound. But when he saw the old man's bloody corpse extended on the floor, he was seized with horror. He had murdered the preserver of his own life!

5. Alexander's remorse, however, did not last long. He still insisted on being a god, the son of Jupiter Ammon; and he was mortally offended with a philosopher named Callisthenes, because he refused to worship him. For no other crime, Callisthenes was put into an iron cage, and tormented till he killed himself in despair.

Questions—9. What animals had Porus in his army? Who conquered? What became of Porus? 10. Describe the meeting between Alexander and Porus.

Chap. LXI—1. What of Alexander? What ruined his disposition? How did he consider himself? 2. What of the actions of Alexander? Who was Clitus? 3–4. Give an account of the murder of Clitus. 5. What did Alexander insist upon being called? What of Callisthenes?

6. After Alexander's return from India to Persia, he met with a great misfortune. It was the loss of his dearest friend, Hephestion, who died of a disease which he had contracted by excessive drinking. For three days afterward, Alexander lay prostrate on the ground, and would take no food.

7. He erected a funeral pile of spices and other precious materials, so that it was as costly as a palace would have been. The lifeless body of Hephestion was placed on the summit. Alexander then set fire to the pile, and stood mournfully looking on while the corpse of his friend was reduced to ashes.

8. It would have been well if he had taken warning by the fate of Hephestion. But Alexander the Great was destined to owe his destruction to the wine cup. While drinking at a banquet in Babylon, he was suddenly taken sick, and death soon conquered the conqueror.

9. As to the merits of Alexander, I pretty much agree with a certain pirate, whom the Macedonian soldiers once took prisoner. Alexander demanded of this man by what right he committed his robberies. "I am a robber by the same right that you are a conqueror," was the reply. "The only difference between us is, that I have but a few men, and can do but little mischief; while you have a large army, and can do a great deal!"

10. It must be confessed that this is the chief difference between most conquerors and robbers. Yet, when Alexander died, his body was deposited in a splendid coffin, at Alexandria, in Egypt, and the Egyptians paid him divine honors, as if he had been the greatest possible benefactor to the world.

CHAPTER LXII—EUROPE—Continued
Greece invaded by the Gauls

1. WHEN ALEXANDER lay on his deathbed, his attendants asked to whom he would bequeath the empire, which now extended from Greece to India, including a great many nations. His answer was, "To the most worthy."

2. But there appears to have been no very worthy man among those whom he left behind him; and even if there had been, the unworthy ones would not have consented to yield him the whole power. Alexander's empire was, therefore, divided among thirty-three of his chief officers.

Questions—6. What of Hephestion? What was the cause of his death? 7. What did Alexander do with the body of Hephestion? 8. What caused Alexander's death? Where did he die? *Where is Babylon? Directions from Macedon? India?* 9. Tell the story of the pirate. 10. What was done when Alexander died?
CHAP. LXII—1. What was asked of Alexander on his deathbed? His reply? 2. How was the empire divided?

3. But the most powerful of these officers were determined to have more than their share; and in the year 312 b.c. four of them had got possession of the whole. Alexander had then been dead eleven years. All his children and relatives had been destroyed by his ambitious officers.

4. The Greeks, when they heard of Alexander's death, had attempted to regain their liberty. But their struggles were unsuccessful; and the country was reduced to subjection by Cassander, who had been general of Alexander's cavalry. Cassander died in a few years. Thenceforward, the history of Greece tells of nothing but crimes and revolutions, and misfortunes.

5. In the year 278 before the Christian era, the Gauls invaded Greece. They were a barbarous people, who inhabited the country now called France. Their general's name was Brennus; and their numbers are said to have been a hundred and sixty-five thousand men.

6. Brennus met with hardly any opposition. He marched to Delphos, intending to steal the treasures that were contained in the famous temple of Apollo. "A deity, like Apollo, does not want these treasures," said Brennus. "I am only a man, and have great need of them."

7. Accordingly, he led his barbarians toward the temple. The stately marble front of the edifice was seen at a short distance before them. It was considered the holiest spot in Greece. Here was the mysterious oracle, from which such wonderful prophecies had issued.

8. A wild shout burst from the army of the Gauls, and they were on the point of rushing forward to the temple. But suddenly a violent storm arose. The thunder roared, and the wind blew furiously. At the same moment a terrible earthquake shook the ground beneath the affrighted Gauls.

9. A band of Greeks had assembled, to fight in defense of the temple. When they saw the disorder of the barbarians, they attacked them, sword in hand. It had grown so dark that the Gauls could not distinguish friends from foes. They killed one another, and the whole army was destroyed.

10. Such is the story which the old historians tell about this battle; it is doubtless much exaggerated, for some of the particulars appear hardly credible. But, at any rate, this was the last great victory that the ancient Greeks ever achieved over their enemies.

Questions—3. What took place in the year 312 b.c.? What of Alexander's children and relatives? 4. Who put Greece under subjection? Who was Cassander? What of the history of Greece after his death? 5. When did the Gauls invade Greece? Who was their general? What of their army? 6. *Where was Delphos? Direction from Athens? Sparta? Thebes?* What famous temple was at Delphos? 7. Describe the march toward the temple. 8. What affrighted the Gauls? 9. What of the Greeks? How were the Gauls destroyed? 10. What may be said of this victory over the Gauls?

CHAPTER LXIII—EUROPE—Continued
End of Grecian Independence

1. The Greeks had now almost entirely lost their love of liberty, as well as the other virtues which had formerly distinguished them. In proof of this, I will relate the story of Agis, the young king of Sparta.

2. King Agis was anxious for the welfare of Sparta, and he greatly desired to restore the ancient laws which Lycurgus had enacted. But the Spartans were now vicious and cowardly. They hated the very name of Lycurgus, and resolved not to be governed by his severe laws.

3. They therefore seized the virtuous young king, and dragged him to prison. He was condemned to death. The executioner shed tears at the moment when he was going to kill him. "Do not weep for me," said Agis; "I am happier than my murderers."

4. A little while after Agis was killed, his mother and grandmother came to the prison to see him, for they had not heard of his death. They were led to his dungeon; and the murderers of Agis immediately strangled them both, and threw their dead bodies upon his.

5. Some time after this horrible event, the Spartans had a king called Nabis. He was such a cruel monster, that Heaven seemed to have made him a king only for the punishment of the people's wickedness. Nabis had an image in his palace. It resembled his own wife, and was very beautiful; it was likewise clothed with magnificent garments, such as were proper for the queen to wear. But the breast and arms of the image were stuck full of sharp iron spikes.

6. These, however, were hidden by the rich clothes. When king Nabis wished to extort money from any person, he invited him to his palace, and led him up to the image. No sooner was the stranger within reach, than the image put out its arms and squeezed him close to its breast.

7. This was done by means of machinery. The poor man might struggle as hard as he pleased; but he could not possibly get away from the cruel embrace of the statue. There he remained, with the iron spikes sticking into his flesh, until his agony compelled him to give Nabis as much money as he asked for.

8. When such enormities were committed by the kings of Greece, it

---

Questions—Chap. LXIII—1. What of the Greeks? Who was Agis? What did he desire? What of the Spartans? 3. What did they do to Agis? Describe his death. 4. What of the mother and grandmother of Agis? 5. What of Nabis? 6. What did Nabis do when he wanted to extort money out of any one?

was time that the country should be governed by other masters. My readers will not be sorry to hear that this soon happened. One hundred and forty-six years before the Christian era, Greece submitted to the authority of Rome.

9. Thus I have given you a very brief account of ancient Greece. Its history is full of interest, and full of instruction. I hope you will hereafter read the whole story in some larger work than mine.

CHAPTER LXIV—EUROPE—Continued
Modern History of Greece

1. From this time forward, the history of Greece is connected with that of other nations. The Greeks had no longer any power, even in their own native country. But they were still respected, on account of the poets, and historians, and sculptors, who appeared among them.

2. But, in course of time, the genius of the Greeks seemed to have deserted them, as well as their ancient valor. They were then wholly despised. I have not space to relate any of the events that occurred to them while they were governed by the Romans.

3. Between three and four hundred years after the Christian era, the Roman dominions were divided into the eastern and western empires. The capital of the eastern empire was Constantinople. The territory of ancient Greece was included under this government, and it was sometimes called the Greek Empire.

4. About a thousand years elapsed, and nothing happened of such importance that it need be told in this brief history. But, about the year 1450, the Turks invaded the eastern empire of the Romans. Greece then fell beneath their power. During almost four centuries the Greeks were treated by the Turks like slaves.

5. At last, in the year 1821, they rebelled against the tyranny of the Turks. A war immediately broke out. It continued a long time, and was carried on with the most shocking cruelty on both sides.

6. Many people from other countries went to assist the Greeks. The ancient renown of Greece made friends of all who were acquainted with

Questions—8. When was Greece conquered by the Romans?
Chap. LXIV—1. What of the Greeks? Why were they respected? 2. What happened in course of time? 3. When were the Roman dominions divided? 4. What happened about 1450? Into whose power did the Greeks then fall? How were they treated? 5. What took place in 1821?

135

her history. Lord Byron, the illustrious English poet, lost his life in Greece, for the sake of this famous land.

7. The Turks, now greatly excited, resolved not to give up the country. The Greeks, on the other hand, determined either to drive away their oppressors, or to die. But they would not have succeeded if England, France, and Russia had not taken their part.

8. The fleets of these three nations formed a junction off the coast of Greece. They were all under the command of the English admiral, Sir Edward Codrington. In October 1827, they attacked a Turkish fleet of more than two hundred vessels, in the bay of Navarino [nav-a-ree´-no].

9. The Turks were entirely beaten, and their vessels were sunk or burned. In consequence of their losses in this battle, they were unable to continue the war. Greece was therefore evacuated by the Turks.

10. But as the Greeks were not considered entirely fit to govern themselves, a king was selected for them by England, France, and Russia. The new king was a young German prince of eighteen, named Otho. He was placed on the throne in the year 1829, and reigned till 1863, when he was succeeded by George I, son of the king of Denmark. At the same time the Ionian Islands were incorporated with the kingdom.

CHAPTER LXV—EUROPE—CONTINUED
About Italy as it now is

1. ITALY IS A STRIP of land or peninsula on the south of Europe, extending into the Mediterranean Sea. It is fancied to have the shape of a boot, the island of Sicily at the toe. It has a beautiful climate, the seasons being very mild.

2. If you were to go to this country, you would be charmed with the beauty of the sky, and the balmy softness of the air. You would find grapes so abundant that you could buy a delicious bunch, as large as you could eat, for a few cents; and if you wished for wine, you could get a bottle for ten cents.

Questions—6. Who assisted the Greeks? Why did Greece find so many friends? What of Byron? 7. What of the Turks? The Greeks? Who took part with Greece? 8. Who commanded the combined fleet of England, France, and Russia? When did they attack the Turks? 9. What of the Turks? Were they obliged to leave Greece? 10. Who chose a king for the Greeks? What is his name? When did he come to the throne? By whom and when was he succeeded?

CHAP. LXV—1. What is Italy? Its shape? Where is Sicily? Climate of Italy? 2. What of the air and sky in Italy? What of grapes? Wine?

SCENES IN ITALY

3. You would find, in short, that Italy abounds in pleasant fruits, and in every species of production required for the comfort of man. You would find the people—men, women, and children—living a great part of the time in the open air, often singing, and sometimes dancing in groups beneath the trees.

4. But, in the midst of these signs of cheerfulness, you would observe a great deal of poverty, and you would soon discover that many of the people are indolent, ignorant, and superstitious.

5. In the cities, many of which are large, and filled with thousands of people, you may notice costly churches and splendid palaces, many of them built of marble. The union of nearly all of Italy under one government, that has lately taken place, has given the people great satisfaction, and raised their hopes as to the future.

6. At Florence, Rome, Naples, and other large cities, you would find collections of pictures and statues, which surpass in beauty everything of

---

Questions—3. Fruits? Other productions? The people? 4. What would you discover after observing the people of Italy carefully? 5. What of the cities?

QUESTIONS ON THE MAP—Boundaries of Italy? Tell the direction of the following places from Rome—Naples; Sicily; Sardinia; Island of Sardinia; Island of Corsica; Turin; Lombardy; Venice; Tuscany; Florence; Leghorn; Switzerland; Austria; France.

the kind in the world. These pictures are the works of famous artists, who have lived in Italy within the last five hundred years.

7. The statues are the productions of sculptors who have lived, at various periods, within the last two thousand years. Some of them, indeed, are supposed to have been executed by Grecian artists who lived in the time of Pericles.

8. But in all Italy there is nothing that will excite so much interest as the ruins of ancient Rome, many of which are still to be seen in the modern city. These, like the ancient remains of Egypt and Greece, would delight you with their beauty, and astonish you by their grandeur and magnificence.

9. The most remarkable edifice of modern times to be found in Italy is the church of St. Peter's, at Rome, the height of which is nearly five hundred feet. Near this is the Vatican, a famous palace inhabited by the pope, who governs Rome and a small territory round it, and is the head of the Catholic Church.

10. If you were to go to Naples, you would see at the distance of a few miles a famous mountain called Vesuvius, from which smoke, flame, and torrents of melted lava have periodically issued for ages. Sometimes whole towns and cities in the neighborhood have been buried beneath the burning masses.

11. If you were to go to the island of Sicily, you would find another volcanic mountain called Etna, which also pours out, from time to time, immense volumes of smoke, fire, and lava. Yet on the very sides of these mountains the people dwell in thickly-settled villages, and here you will find rich vineyards, beautiful gardens, and groves of figs, oranges, and olives.

12. Having visited Italy, you will return to America with many wonderful tales to tell of this famous peninsula that lies in the shape of a boot in the Mediterranean Sea; but you will still be contented and happy to settle down in your native country, where beggars are seldom seen, where poverty and wretchedness are rare, and where everything speaks of prosperity.

13. You may remember with admiration the desolate ruins of Rome, the marble palaces of Venice and Naples, but you would not wish to live

---

Questions—6–7. What of pictures and statues? 8. What of the ruins of Rome? 9. What of St. Peter's? The Vatican? The pope? 10. What of Vesuvius? 11. What of Etna? Where is the island of Sicily? 12. With what feelings would you return to America after visiting Italy?

where even these splendid edifices oppress the heart with gloom. You would much rather live among the more cheerful and thriving villages and towns of our own country. The truth is, that Italy has been badly governed for ages, and the people have become indolent and weak. Let us hope that they will yet become more worthy of the beautiful country they inhabit.

CHAPTER LXVI—EUROPE—Continued
Founding of Rome by Romulus—Its early State

1. I SHALL NOW proceed to tell you the history of Rome, one of the most celebrated empires of antiquity. Like the history of all ancient countries, it abounds in tales of battle, bloodshed, injustice, and crime. Over such horrid scenes I should be glad to draw a vail; but these things have really happened, and it is the duty of the faithful storyteller to hide nothing which is necessary to give a true picture of what he undertakes to exhibit.

2. The famous city of Rome stands on the River Tiber, in Italy. Its distance from the sea is about sixteen miles. It is supposed to have been founded by Romulus, in the year 752 B.C. Romulus was the captain of about three thousand banditti, or outlaws. These men built some huts on a hill called the Palatine, and inclosed them with a wall. This was the origin of the most famous city the world ever saw.

3. It is said that this wall was so low, that Remus, the brother of Romulus, leaped over it. "Do you call this the wall of a city?" cried he, contempuously. Romulus was so enraged, that he struck his brother dead; and this was the first blood that crimsoned the walls of Rome.

4. When Romulus and his fellow-robbers were comfortably settled in their new houses, they found themselves in want of wives. At this time Italy was inhabited by many rude tribes. Among these were the Sabines, who lived in the neighborhood of Rome. These would not allow their young women to marry the Romans; but Romulus contrived a scheme to get wives by force.

5. He invited the whole Sabine people to witness some games and sports. Accordingly, the Sabines came; and, as they suspected no mischief, they brought with them almost all of the marriageable young women of their country.

Questions—Chap. LXVI—1–2. What of the empire of Rome?   What of its history?   On what river is Rome?   How far is it from the sea?   When and by whom was Rome founded? Who was Romulus?   What did the outlaws do?   What is the origin of Rome?   3. What happened between Romulus and Remus?   4. Of what did Romulus and his men feel the want?   What of the Sabines?

6. At first, the Sabines were highly delighted with the feats of strength and agility which were performed by the Romans to entertain them. But, in a little while, Romulus gave a signal; and all his men drew their swords, and rushed among the peaceable spectators.

7. The Sabines were of course taken by surprise, and could make no effectual resistance. Each of the Romans caught up the handsomest young woman he could find, and carried her away. There was no longer any scarcity of wives in Rome.

8. This outrageous act of violence caused a war between the Romans and Sabines. The latter mustered a large army, and would probably have exterminated Romulus and his banditti; but when they were about to engage in battle, the young wives of the Romans rushed into the field.

9. They besought the two hostile parties to make peace. They said that whichever side might gain the victory it would bring nothing but sorrow to them; for, if the Sabines should conquer, their husbands must lose their lives; or if the Romans should win the day, their kindred would perish.

10. Both parties were much moved by these entreaties. The Sabines saw that the young women had become attached to their husbands; and therefore it would be a pity to separate them, even if it could be done without bloodshed. In short, the matter ended peaceably, and an alliance, which you know is a friendly treaty, was formed.

11. The first government of Rome consisted of a king and senate. Romulus was chosen king, and reigned thirty-seven years. There are different accounts of the way in which his reign terminated.

12. Some historians pretend that, while Romulus sat in the senate-house giving wise instructions in regard to matters of state, the hall was suddenly darkened by an eclipse of the sun. When the sun shone out again, the chair of Romulus was perceived to be empty; and it was said he had been taken up into heaven.

13. Others say that Romulus attempted to make himself a tyrant, and that therefore the senators pulled him down from his chair of state, and tore him in pieces. This story appears more probable than the former. At all events, king Romulus suddenly disappeared and was never seen again in the city which he had founded.

Questions—5–7. Give an account of the carrying off of the Sabine women.   8. What did this act cause?   How was the war prevented?   9. What did the young wives of the Romans say?   10. What effect had their entreaties?   11. What of the first government of Rome?   Who was chosen king, and how long did he reign?   12. What do some historians pretend?   13. What do others say?

HORATII AND CURIATII

CHAPTER LXVII—EUROPE—CONTINUED
Battle of the Horatii and Curiatii

1. THE SECOND KING of Rome was Numa Pompilius. He was a wise and good king, and a great lover of peace. He spent forty-three years in making excellent laws, and instructing the people in agriculture and other useful arts.

2. The peaceful Numa was succeeded by Tullus Hostilius. He was a warlike monarch. During his reign the Romans engaged in hostilities with the Albans, who inhabited a neighboring city.

3. It was agreed that the war should be decided by a battle between three champions on each side. In the army of the Albans there were three brothers, each named Curiatius; and in the Roman army there were three brothers by the name of Horatius.

4. These Horatii and Curiatii were fixed upon as the champions. They fought in an open plain; and on each side stood the ranks of armed warriors, with their swords sheathed, anxiously watching the combat.

5. At first it seemed as if the Curiatii were going to win the victory. It is true they were all three wounded; but two of the Horatii lay dead upon the

---

Questions—CHAP. LXVII—1. Who was the second king of Rome? What of him? 2. What of Tullus Hostilius? 3. How was the war between the Romans and the Albans to be decided? Who were the Horatii and Curiatii?

field. The other Horatius was still unhurt. He appeared determined not to perish like his two brothers; for he was seen to turn and flee. At the flight of their champion, the Romans groaned with shame and despair; for if he should lose the battle, they were all to be made slaves.

6. The three Curitaii pursued the fugitive. But their wounds had rendered them feeble. They staggered along, one behind the other, so that they were separated by considerable distances. This was what Horatius desired. Though he could not have beaten all three together, he was more than a match for them singly.

7. He now turned fiercely upon the foremost, and slew him. Then he encountered the second, and smote him dead in a moment. The third met with the same fate. The Alban army now turned pale, and dropped their weapons on the field; for their champions were defeated, and they had lost their freedom.

8. The exulting Romans greeted Horatius with shouts of triumph. He returned toward Rome amid a throng of his countrymen, all of whom hailed him as their benefactor. But as he entered the city, he met a young woman wringing her hands in an agony of grief. This was his sister. She was in love with one of the Curiatii, and when she saw Horatius, she shrieked aloud, and reproached him bitterly for having slain her lover.

9. The victor still held the bloody sword with which he had killed the three Alban champions. His heart was still fierce with the frenzy of the combat. He could not bear that his sister should bewail one of the dead enemies, instead of her two dead brothers; nor that she should darken his triumph with her reproaches. Accordingly, in the frenzy of the moment, he stabbed her to the heart.

10. Horatius was condemned to die for this dreadful crime; but he was afterward pardoned, because his valor had won for Rome such a great deliverance. But the disgrace of his guilt was far more than the honor of his victory.

CHAPTER LXVIII—EUROPE—Continued
From the Reign of Ancus Martius, till the Expulsion of the Kings

1. AFTER THE DEATH of Tullus Hostilius, the Romans elected Ancus

---

Questions—4–5. Describe the struggle between these combatants. Who fled from the battle? 6. What did the three Curiatii do? What of Horatius? 7. What was the fate of the Curiatii? 8. How was Horatius greeted? What of his sister? 9. Why did Horatius kill her? 10. What of Horatius? Why was he pardoned?

Martius to be king. He was succeeded by Tarquin the Elder, whose father had been a rich merchant. The next king was Servius Tullius. When Servius had reigned forty-four years, he was murdered by Tarquin, his son-in-law, who was ambitious of being king.

2. Tullia, the wife of Tarquin and daughter of Servius, rejoiced at her father's death, for she wished to be queen. She rode out in her chariot in order to congratulate her wicked husband. In one of the streets through which the chariot was to pass, lay the dead body of the poor old king. The coachman saw it, and was desirous of turning back. "Drive on!" cried the wicked Tullia.

3. The coachman did so; and as the street was too narrow to permit him to turn out, the chariot passed directly over the murdered king. But Tullia rode on without remorse, although the wheels were stained with her father's blood.

4. Her husband now ascended the throne, and was called Tarquin the Proud. The Romans abhorred him, for he was a hateful tyrant. Several almost incredible stories are told respecting his reign.

5. One day, it is said, that a woman of singular aspect entered the king's presence, bringing nine large books in her arms. No one knew whence she came, nor what was contained in her books. She requested the king to buy them. But the price was so high, that Tarquin refused; especially as he did not know what the books were about.

6. The unknown woman went away and burnt three of her books. She then came back, and again offered the remaining ones to Tarquin. But she demanded as much money for the six as she had before asked for the whole nine; and Tarquin of course refused to buy them.

7. The woman went away a second time. But shortly afterward she was again seen entering the palace. She had now only three volumes left; and these she offered to the king at the same price which she had before asked for the whole nine.

8. There was something so strange and mysterious in all this, that Tarquin concluded to give the woman her price. She put the three volumes into his hands, and immediately disappeared.

9. The books were found to be the oracles of a sibyl, or prophetess. They were therefore looked upon with superstitious reverence, and were preserved in Rome during many ages; and in all difficult and perplexing

Questions—CHAP. LXVIII—1. Who was king after Tullus Hostilius? Who next? Who killed Servius Tullus? 2–3. What of Tullia? Describe her wicked act. 4. What was Tarquin called? What of him? 5–9. What strange story can you tell of him?

cases, the rulers looked into these old volumes, and read, as they supposed, the secrets of their country's fate.

10. The above story is probably a fable. So also is that of the discovery of a man's head, while the workmen were digging the foundation of the temple of Jupiter. Yet the Romans firmly believed that a human head was found there under the earth, and that it looked as fresh as if just cut off.

11. When Tarquin the Proud had reigned more than twenty years, he and his family were driven out of Rome by the people. This event was brought about by the wickedness of his son Sextus, whose conduct had caused a noble Roman lady to commit suicide. Her name was Lucretia.

12. The expulsion of the Tarquins took place in the year 509 before the Christian era. The Romans never had another king. Beside the senate, the government now consisted of two magistrates called consuls, who were chosen every year. Brutus and Collatinus were the first.

13. Brutus gave a terrible example of his justice and patriotism. His two sons had engaged in a conspiracy to make Tarquin king again. Brutus, who was a judge when they were brought to trial, condemned them both to death, and had them executed in his presence.

CHAPTER LXIX—EUROPE—Continued
The Story of Coriolanus

1. ACTS OF HEROISM were commong among the Romans, in those days. A young man, named Mutius Scaevola, gained great credit for his fortitude. He had been taken prisoner by the troops of the king of Etruria, or Tuscany, who was at war with Rome. Porsenna threatened to torture him, unless he would betray the plans of the Roman general.

2. A fire was burning close beside the prisoner. He immediately put his hand into the midst of the flames, and held it there till it was burnt off. By this act, he showed Porsenna that no torture could induce him to turn traitor.

3. Almost from the first foundation of Rome, the inhabitants had been divided into two classes; one called patricians, and the other plebeians. The senate and most of the rich men were included among the patricians. The consuls were also chosen from this class.

Questions—10. What of a man's head? 11. How long did Tarquin reign? What of him and his family? What of Sextus? 12. What took place 509 years B.C.? How long from the founding of Rome to the death of her last king? What of the government of Rome after the Tarquins? Who were the first consuls? 13. What act did Brutus perform? CHAP. LXIX—1–2. Relate the anecdote of Mutius Scaevola.

4. Thus the patricians had nearly all the power in their hands. This caused frequent quarrels between them and the common people, or plebeians. But at length it was ordained that five magistrates, called tribunes, should be annually chosen by the plebeians.

5. These tribunes took away a great deal of power from the patricians, and were therefore hated by them. Coriolanus, a valiant, but proud patrician, endeavored to have the office of the tribunes abolished. But they were more powerful than he, and succeeded in procuring his banishment.

6. Coriolanus left the city, and went to the territories of the Volsci, who were bitter enemies of the Romans. There he gathered a large army, and advanced to besiege Rome. His countrymen were greatly alarmed when they heard that the banished Coriolanus was returning so soon, and in so terrible a manner.

7. They therefore sent an embassy to meet him, consisting of the oldest senators. But these venerable men could make no impression on Coriolanus. Next came an embassy of priests; but they met with no better success.

8. Coriolanus still marched onward, and pitched his tent within a short distance of the Roman walls. He was gazing toward the city, and planning an attack for the next day, when a third embassy appeared. It was a mournful procession of Roman ladies.

9. At their head walked Veturia, who was the mother of Coriolanus; and Vergilia, his wife, was also there, leading his children by the hand. When they drew near, his mother knelt down at his feet, and besought him not to be the ruin of his native country.

10. Coriolanus strove to resist her entreaties, as he had resisted those of the senators and priests. But though his heart had been proud and stubborn against them, it was not so against his mother.

11. "Mother," cried he, "I yield! You have saved Rome, but you have destroyed your son!" And so it proved; for the Volsci were enraged at his retreat from Rome, and they murdered him at Antium.

CHAPTER LXX—EUROPE—Continued
Rome invaded by the Gauls—The first Punic War

1. In process of time, the Roman government underwent various

Questions—3. What two classes were there in Rome? What of the class of the patricians? Who were the plebeians? 4. What caused quarrels between the patricians and plebeians? From which class were the tribunes chosen? 5. What of the tribunes? 6–10. Tell the story of Coriolanus. 11. What was his fate?

146

THE GAULS AT ROME

changes. The will of the plebeians had far greater influence than the will of the patricians. It may be added, that the prosperity of Rome increased at home and abroad.

2. But in the year 385 B.C., a great calamity befell the city. It was taken by an army of Gauls, inhabitants of the country now called France. When Brennus, their general, had entered Rome, he marched with his soldiers to the senate-house.

3. There he beheld an assemblage of gray-bearded senators, seated in a noble hall, in chairs of ivory. Each held an ivory staff in his hand. These brave old men, though they could make no resistance, considered it beneath their dignity to run away from the invaders.

4. The Gauls were awe-struck by their venerable aspect. But finally, one of the soldiers, being ruder than his companions, took hold of the long gray beard of an aged senator, and pulled it. The old gentleman, whose name was Papyrius, was so offended at this insult, that he uplifted his ivory staff, and hit the soldier a blow on the head.

5. But that blow cost Rome dear. The Gauls immediately massacred Papyrius and the other senators, and set fire to the city; and almost the whole of it was reduced to ashes. You must bear in mind that, at this time, Rome had become an immense city. It contained some fine edifices; the most splendid of these was called the Capitol; this was not taken by the

Questions—CHAP. LXX—1. What can be said of the prosperity of Rome? 2. What befell the city 385 B.C.? What of Brennus? 3–4. What happened in the senate-house?

Gauls.

6. All the bravest of the Romans assembled there, and resolved to defend it to the last. Yet the enemy had nearly got possession of it in the night. But as they were creeping toward the gate, they awoke a large flock of geese; and their cackling alarmed the sentinels.

7. In consequence of this fortunate event, a goose was thenceforth considered a very praiseworthy and honorable fowl by the Romans. I am not sure but what they thought it a sin to have roast goose for dinner.

8. The Gauls were driven out of Rome, and were soon vanquished by Camillus, a brave and patriotic Roman. It is said that not a single man of them got back to their own country, to tell the fate of his companions.

9. The Romans were almost continually at war. Their valor and discipline generally rendered them successful; but sometimes they met with misfortunes. In a war with the Samnites, a Roman army was captured, and forced to pass under the yoke, which was a sign of subjection. This was the highest possible ignominy.

10. But at length all the other states and kingdoms of Italy were reduced under the Roman power. Afterward, the most formidable enemy of Rome was Carthage. This was a powerful city on the African coast, near where Tunis now stands. It was situated nearly south of Rome, across the Mediterranean Sea, at the distance of about four hundred miles.

11. The wars between Rome and Carthage were called Punic wars. The first began in the year 264 B.C., and lasted twenty-three years. Many battles were fought on land, and some by sea.

12. The Carthaginians were a cruel people. Whenever their generals lost a battle, they were crucified. Regulus, a Roman general, was taken by them, and underwent horrible torments. They cut off his eyelids, and then exposed his naked eyes to the burning sun. He was afterward put into a barrel, the inner sides of which were set with iron spikes.

13. A peace was at last concluded between Rome and Carthage. The doors of the temple of Janus, at Rome, had not been shut for five hundred years; for they always stood open while the Romans were at war. But now they were closed and barred; for Rome was at peace with all the world.

Questions—5. What of Rome at this time? What of the Capitol? 6. How was the Capitol saved? 8. Who conquered the Gauls? 9. What of the Romans? What of the war with the Samnites? 10. What of the kingdom of Italy? Where was Carthage? How far was it from Rome? 11. When did the first Punis war begin? How long did it last? 12. What of the Carthaginians? What of Regulus? 13. What of the temple of Janus? How long had the doors been open? Why were they now closed? When was the temple of Janus open? When shut?

HANNIBAL CROSSING THE ALPS

CHAPTER LXXI—EUROPE—Continued
Second and third Punic Wars

1. THE DOORS OF THE TEMPLE of Janus were soon flung wide open again; for a war broke out between the Romans and a tribe of Gauls. It ended in the conquest of the latter.

2. In the year 218 before the Christian era, another war with Carthage began. This was called the second Punic war. The Carthaginians were commanded by Hannibal, who proved himself one of the greatest generals that ever lived.

3. Hannibal transported his army across the Mediterranean Sea to Spain, and thence marched toward Italy. In his progress it was necessary that he should cross the Alps. The summits of these mountains are many thousand feet in height, and were covered with ice and snow; in some places Hannibal had to cut a passage through the solid rock.

Questions—CHAP. LXXI—1. What war now broke out? Which side was victorious? 2. When did the second Punic war begin? Who led the Carthaginians? 3. What did Hannibal do? How did his army cross the Alps?

4. After crossing these mountains, several battles were won by the Carthaginians. At length the two Roman consuls, with a large army, encountered Hannibal and his soldiers at Cannae. Here the Romans were defeated with dreadful slaughter. One of the consuls fled; the other was slain, and forty thousand men were left dead on the field.

5. Rome had now no army to protect it. If Hannibal had marched thither immediately, it is probable that he might have taken the city. But he delayed too long, and the Romans made preparation to defend themselves.

6. Hannibal never won such another victory as that of Cannae; for the Romans soon enlisted new armies, and fought more successfully than before. Scipio, their best general, sailed over to Africa, in order to attack Carthage. Hannibal immediately followed him.

7. A battle was fought between him and Scipio at Zama. The Carthaginians had a multitude of elephants. These animals were wounded by the Roman darts, and the pain made them rush through the field, trampling down whole ranks of Hannibal's army.

8. The Carthaginians were entirely defeated, and Hannibal himself barely escaped amid the rout and confusion. This battle put an end to the second Punic war.

9. But a third war between Rome and Carthage broke out in about fifty years. The Romans were commanded by another Scipio, who was as valiant as his namesake, but the Carthaginians had no longer a Hannibal.

10. This third Punic war ended in the destruction of Carthage. The city was set on fire, and continued to burn during seventeen days. Many of the citizens threw themselves into the flames, and perished. This happened in the year 146 before the Christian era.

11. Scipio returned to Rome, and was rewarded with a triumph. As this was the highest honor that a Roman general could attain, and as such triumphs were often given to successful commanders, I will tell my readers, in the next chapter, what Scipio's triumph was.

CHAPTER LXXII—EUROPE—Continued
Scipio's Triumph

1. Scipio, on his return from Carthage, stopped at the Campus Martius,

---

Questions—4. Describe the battle of Cannae. 5. What of Rome at this time? 6. What of Scipio? Who followed him? 7. Where was a battle fought? What of elephants? 8. Which side were defeated? What of Hannibal? 9. Who led the Romans in the third Punic war? What of the Carthaginians? 10. When was Carthage burnt? 11. How was Scipio rewarded?

which was a plain on the outside of Rome. From thence he was escorted into the city by a grand procession.

2. First came a band of musicians, playing their loudest strains on all sorts of instruments. Then followed a drove of oxen, which were to be sacrificed in the temples of the gods. Their horns were gilded, and garlands were wreathed around their heads.

3. Next came a train of cars, heavily laden with the rich spoils that had been taken at Carthage. There was gold and silver in abundance, and statues, pictures, and magnificent garments. The brilliant armor of the vanquished army was likewise piled upon the cars.

4. Then were seen some elephants, trudging along like moving hills. These huge animals were trained to war, and were able to carry a whole company of soldiers on their backs.

5. Next appeared a melancholy troop of the vanquished Carthaginians. Their chains clanked as they walked heavily onward. Among them were all the principal men of Carthage, and they drooped their heads in shame and sorrow, regretting that they had not perished in the flames of their city.

6. Behind the sad troop came another loud band of music, drowning the groans of the captives with the uproar of a hundred instruments. There were likewise dancers, whose garb made them appear like monsters, neither beasts nor men. These wore crowns of gold.

7. Then came a splendid chariot, adorned with ivory, and drawn by four white horses all abreast. In this chariot stood the triumphant Scipio, dressed in a purple robe, which was covered with gold embroidery. His face was painted with vermilion, and he had a crown of laurel on his head.

8. A golden ball hung at his breast; and in his right hand he held an ivory sceptre, with a golden eagle at the top. But in the same chariot stood a slave, who kept whispering to Scipio, "Remember that thou art but a man!" And these words seemed to sadden Scipio's triumph.

9. Around the chariot was a great throng of Scipio's relatives, and other citizens, all clothed in white. Next came the consuls and all the members of the Roman senate, in their robes of ceremony.

10. Last in the procession marched the victorious army. Their helmets

---

Questions—Chap. LXXII—1. Where was the Campus Martius? What of the procession? 2. What came first? What was done with the oxen? 3. With what were the cars laden? 4. What of elephants? 5. Describe the appearance of the captive Carthaginians. In what battle were they taken prisoners? 6. What of musicians and dancers? 7. How did Scipio appear? 8. What did the slave whisper in his ear? What was the effect of what he said? 9. What followed the chariot?

were wreathed with laurel. The standard-bearers carried eagles of gold and silver, instead of banners. As they moved onward, they sang hymns in praise of Scipio's valor, and all the Roman citizens joined their voices in the chorus. In this manner, the procession passed through the streets of Rome and entered the doors of the capitol.

CHAPTER LXXIII—EUROPE—Continued
Sylla and Marius

1. The Romans still continued to make conquests. Not long after the ruin of Carthage, the whole of Spain became a province of Rome. There was likewise a war with Numidia, a country of Africa, now called Algiers. Jugurtha, the Numidian king, was brought prisoner to Rome, and starved to death in a dungeon.

2. There was afterward a Social war, beginning in the year 91 B.C. This war was called Social, because it was between the Romans and the neighboring states of Italy, who had been their friends and allies. Three hundred thousand men were killed on both sides. Then there was a war with Mithridates, the powerful king of Pontus, in Asia Minor. He was not entirely vanquished till forty years afterward.

3. In the course of all this fighting, two Roman commanders acquired great renown. One was named Marius, and the other Sylla. Marius was a rude and daring soldier, knowing nothing but how to fight. Sylla was likewise a good soldier, but also a person of great elegance and of polished manners.

4. These two generals became so great and powerful that each was envious of the other. They therefore began a civil war, in which Romans fought against Romans. I will relate an incident in order to show the horrors of this war.

5. One of Sylla's soldiers had killed another that fought for Marius. He began to strip him of his armor; but on taking off the helmet which had concealed the dead man's face, he saw that it was his own brother. The wretched survivor placed the body on a funeral pile, and then killed himself.

Questions—10. Describe the victorious army. Where did the procession stop?

Chap. LXXIII—1. What of the Romans? What of Spain? Where was Numidia? *Direction from Rome? Carthage?* (See map p. 160). What of it? Its king? 2. When did the Social war begin? How many men were killed in this war? Who was Mithridates? Where was Pontus? 3. What of the Roman commanders? Marius? Sylla? 4. What war broke out in Rome? 5. Relate a horrible incident in this war.

152

6. In the outset of the struggle with Sylla, Marius was beaten; but he afterward gained possession of Rome. He now resolved to put to death every person that was not friendly to his cause. Senators and other distinguished men were publicly murdered. Dead bodies were seen everywhere about the streets.

7. But Marius could not escape the misery which his wickedness deserved. He was so tortured by remorse, that he contracted a habit of drinking immoderately. This brought on a fever, of which he died.

8. After the death of this wicked man, Sylla returned to Rome at the head of a large army. He declared himself dictator; and his word then became the sole law of Rome. Like Marius, he determined to massacre all his enemies. As fast as they were killed, their bloody heads were brought to him.

9. When Sylla had shed as much blood as he desired, he suddenly resigned his power. Everybody was surprised at this, but nobody lamented it; nor were there any mourners when this cruel and wicked man died, which happened soon after.

CHAPTER LXXIV—EUROPE—CONTINUED
Cneius Pompey and Julius Caesar

1. IF THE ROMAN people had loved liberty as well as they once did, they never would have borne the tyranny of Sylla and Marius. But they had become addicted to luxury, by the riches which they had acquired from their conquests in all parts of the world.

2. Owing to their continual wars, they had also accustomed themselves to consider successful warriors as the greatest men on earth. Soldiers must obey their leaders, without asking why or wherefore; and all the Roman people felt like soldiers. Thus, the very same causes which rendered the Romans so invincible to their enemies, made them liable to be enslaved by any great general who should be ambitious of enslaving them. And such a general soon appeared.

3. After the death of Sylla and Marius, the two most valiant and distinguished warriors were Pompey and Caesar. Pompey was the eldest. He had grown famous by vanquishing Mithridates, and by many other victories.

Questions—6. What did Marius do? 7. What was his fate? 8. What did Sylla do? Give an account of his proceedings. 9. What act of Sylla's surprised everybody?
CHAP. LXXIV—1. What of the Roman people? 2. What was the consequence of continual war?

153

He had conquered fifteen kingdoms, and taken eight hundred cities.

4. The name of this illustrious leader's rival was Julius Caesar. He was the most beautiful person in Rome. He had fought in Gaul, Germany, and Britain, and had overcome three millions of men, and killed one million. His soldiers idolized him.

5. At last, like Sylla and Marius, these two generals became so great and powerful, that the world was no longer wide enough for them both. They each collected great armies, in which all the Roman soldiers were enlisted, on one side or the other.

6. They encountered each other at Pharsalia, in Macedon. The best part of Pompey's army consisted of a multitude of the young Roman nobility. These youth had very handsome faces; and it was chiefly owing to this circumstance that Pompey lost the victory.

7. Caesar ordered his rough and weather-beaten soldiers to aim their blows right at the faces of their enemies. The latter were so afraid that their beauty would be spoiled, that they immediately turned and fled. A complete victory was gained by Caesar.

8. Pompey made his escape into Egypt, but was there murdered. His head was cut off and brought to Caesar, who turned aside his eyes from the bloody spectacle, and wept to think that so mighty a warrior had met with so sad a fate.

CHAPTER LXXV—EUROPE—CONTINUED
Caesar usurps the Supreme Power

1. WHEN THE ROMAN senate heard of Caesar's victory, they proclaimed a solemn thanksgiving to the gods. Supreme power was granted him for life, with the title of dictator. His person was declared sacred and inviolable.

2. His statue was placed among those of gods and heroes, in the Capitol. It stood next to that of Jupiter, and bore this impious inscription— "THE STATUE OF CAESAR THE DEMI-GOD." This proves that the Romans were already slaves, when they thus deified a mortal man.

3. Caesar had now but one other wish to gratify. He desired to bear the

---

Questions—3. What two generals appeared after Marius and Sylla? What had Pompey done? 4. What of Pompey's rival Julius Caesar? 5. What did these great generals do? 6. Where was a battle fought? What of Pompey's army? 7. By what means did Caesar vanquish the followers of Pompey? 8. What became of Pompey? Why did Caesar weep at his death?

CHAP. LXXV—1. What did the Romans do after Caesar's victory? 2. What of Caesar's statue?

name of king. He endeavored to gain the good-will of the soldiers and people, in order that they might gratify his ambition. For this purpose he spent immense sums in entertainments and magnificent spectacles.

4. On one occasion, he made a feast for the whole Roman people. Twenty-two thousand tables were set out in the streets of Rome. All sorts of delicious food and drink were heaped upon them. The meanest beggar was at liberty to sit down and eat his fill.

5. Most of the Romans had now lost the noble spirit which had animated their forefathers. They were willing to be governed by any man who would feed them with delicacies, and amuse them with splendid shows, as Caesar did. It must be owned, also, that Caesar had many noble and amiable qualities.

6. The people, therefore, had a fondness for their tyrant. They loved to behold him, at the public spectacles and entertainments, sitting in a gilded chair of state, with a golden crown upon his head. Had he asked it, they were even ready to fall down and worship him.

7. But there were a few Romans of the old stamp who loved liberty for its own sake. There were others, also, who hated Caesar because he had wronged them, or because he was more powerful than they. These two sorts of persons formed a conspiracy to kill him.

8. The two chief conspirators were Brutus and Cassius. Brutus was a sincere lover of liberty, and a true friend of Rome. He also loved Caesar, and was beloved by him. But he resolved to assist in slaying him in order that his country might be free.

9. Cassius formed the same resolution; but it was chiefly because he hated Caesar. Sixty other senators were engaged in the plot. Most conspirators endeavor to do their work in secrecy and at midnight. But the blood of Caesar was to be shed in broad daylight, and in the great hall of the senate-house.

CHAPTER LXXVI—EUROPE—Continued
Assassination of Julius Caesar

1. On the fatal morning, Caesar set forth from his mansion. There was a great throng of flatterers and false friends around him. As he came down

---

Questions—3. What did this great conqueror now desire? What did he do to obtain his wish? 4. Describe the feast. 5. State of the Romans at this time? 6. What did they like to see? 7. Who formed a conspiracy to kill Caesar? 8. Who were Brutus and Cassius? Why did they each determine to kill Caesar? 9. How was the conspiracy carried on?

155

ASSASSINATION OF CAESAR

the steps of the portal, a gray-bearded philosopher pressed through the crowd and put a paper into his hand. It contained an account of the whole plot. If Caesar had read it, it would have cost all the conspirators their lives, and have saved his own life. But he gave it to one of his secretaries, and walked onward.

2. As Caesar passed through the streets of Rome, he looked round at the crowd of obsequious senators, and listened to the shouts of the multitude. He felt that he was the most exalted man in all the world. But his heart was not at ease; for he also felt that he had enslaved his country.

3. The proud procession ascended the steps of the senate-house and passed into the hall. Along the sides of this hall were ranged statues of many famous Romans, and among them stood the marble image of Pompey, whose bloody head had been brought to Caesar. Just as Caesar was passing in front of Pompey's statue, Metellus Cimber, one of the conspirators, knelt down and took hold of his robe. This was the signal for the attack.

4. Casca, who was behind Caesar, drew a dagger and stabbed him in

---

Questions—CHAP. LXXVI—1. Describe Caesar's departure from his house. What happened as he came down the steps? 2. What did he see on looking around him? How did he feel? 3. Where did the procession march? What were ranged around the hall? What happened as Caesar was passing the statue of Pompey?

the shoulder. "Wretch! what doest thou?" cried Caesar, snatching the weapon. The other conspirators now rushed upon him. But he defended himself with the valor he had shown in a hundred battles.

5. At length Brutus pressed forward and struck him with his dagger. When Caesar saw that the hand of his dear friend was raised against his life, he made no more resistance. "And thou, too, Brutus!" he said, with one reproachful look.

6. Then covering his head with his mantle, that his enemies might not behold the death-pang in his face, he fell down at the pedestal of Pompey's statue. The marble countenance of the statue seemed to look down upon him, and Pompey was avenged.

7. The conspirators dipped their weapons in the blood that flowed upon the pavement. Brutus raised his dagger aloft, and called to Cicero, the illustrious orator and patriot. "Rejoice, father of our country!" he exclaimed, pointing to the prostrate form of Cæsar, "for Rome is free!"

8. But, alas! when the souls of a whole people are enslaved, it is not the death of any single man that can set them free. And thus, as my readers will perceive, the mighty victim died in vain.

CHAPTER LXXVII—EUROPE—Continued
Consequences of Caesar's Death

1. THE DEATH OF CAESAR took place forty-three years before the Christian era. The affairs of Rome were thrown into great confusion by it. Caesar's friends found no great difficulty in persuading the people that he had been unjustly murdered.

2. Brutus, Cassius, and the other conspirators were compelled to flee from the city. Three men then usurped the government, and were called triumvirs, or a triumvirate. Their names were Mark Antony, Lepidus, and Octavius. The latter was Caesar's nephew, and had been his adopted son.

3. The triumvirate resolved to secure themselves in power by murder-

Questions—4. Who first stabbed him? How did he defend himself? 5. Who gave Caesar the second blow? How did he receive it? 6. Describe his death. 7. What did Brutus and the conspirators do now? 8. Why did Caesar die in vain?

CHAP. LXXVII—1. When did Caesar's death take place? What of Rome? The friends of Caesar? 2. Who were obliged to fly from the city? Who now governed Rome? Who was Octavius?

157

ing all who were opposed to them. They made a list of three hundred senators and more than two thousand knights, and offered rewards for killing
them. They exulted when the heads of their victims were laid at their feet.

4. One of these wicked triumvirs presented the head of his own brother
to his colleagues. Another brought his uncle's head. No friend, nor relative, nor patriot was spared if he was suspected of being opposed to the
triumvirate.

5. In the mean time, Brutus and Cassius were in Greece. They had
collected an army of a hundred thousand men; Mark Antony and Octavius
marched against them: and a battle was fought at Philippi. Brutus and
Cassius being defeated, they both committed suicide.

6. The triumvirate had now got all the power into their own hands.
But they soon quarreled among themselves. Lepidus was turned out of office, and banished. Mark Antony and Octavius then made war upon each
other, like Marius and Sylla, and like Pompey and Caesar.

7. The good fortune of Octavius gave him the victory, and Antony killed
himself with his own sword, as I have related in the history of Egypt.
Octavius had no longer any rivals, and was now sole master of Rome and
its dominions. He was afraid to assume the title of king, but called himself
emperor, and Augustus Caesar.

8. In addition to several other titles, the senate gave him that of Paer
Patriae, or Father of his Country. This was merely a piece of flattery. Yet
there were now so few good men in Rome, that, perhaps, Octavius made a
better use of his power than any other would have done.

9. His reign from this time was peaceful and quiet, and offers few events
that need to be recorded in this brief history. Nearly the whole world was
under his sway, and, therefore, he had no occasion to increase his dominions by going to war. The greatest glory of his times consists in the works of
poets and other men of genius.

10. Octavius, or, as he is always called, Augustus Caesar, reigned forty-
one years, and died at the age of seventy-six, in the year 14 after the birth
of Christ. You will observe that it was during his reign that Christ appeared
in Palestine.

Questions—3. What did the triumvirate do?   4. What acts of cruelty did they
perform?   5. Where now were Brutus and Cassius?   Who opposed them?   Where was
the battle fought?   Fate of Brutus and Cassius?   6. What of the triumvirate?   7. Which
of the triumvirs triumphed?   What became of Antony?   What did Octavius call
himself?   8. What other name did the senate give him?   9. Describe the reign of Augustus.
10. How long did he reign?   When did he die?

CHAPTER LXXVIII—EUROPE—Continued
About the great Power and Extent of the Roman Empire in the Time of Augustus

1. As ROME WAS now at its greatest height of wealth and splendor, I shall try to give you some idea of the extent and power of this vast empire, and then, having told you a little more of its history, I shall say something about the manners and customs of the ancient Roman people.

2. In the time of Augustus, the Roman empire embraced all the nations of Europe, except a few northern tribes, who maintained their independence. It included England, France, Spain, Germany, all the states of Italy, Greece, the country now occupied by Turkey in Europe, beside many other nations.

3. In Asia, it embraced all the kingdoms from Asia Minor on the west, to India on the east. Of course, it included Asia Minor, Syria, Palestine, Arabia, Persia, Parthia, and many other countries.

4. It included the whole northern portion of Africa, from Mauritania, now Morocco, on the west, to Ethiopia on the east. This was the whole of Africa then known; the interior being only little inhabited by scattered bands.

5. It seems wonderful that one country could govern so many nations. This was done, however, by placing Roman governors over these various kingdoms; the governors being sustained by a multitude of Roman soldiers.

6. During this period, the people of Rome had great skill in architecture, sculpture, painting, and many other arts. These arts were extended to all parts of the empire.

7. Thus a multitude of cities in various parts of Europe, Africa, and Asia, were filled with costly temples and palaces of marble, with beautiful statues and valuable paintings. The splendor and magnificence of many of these cities, at this period, was, indeed, wonderful.

8. Nor was this all; the Romans built many public works of great utility; they constructed roads paved with stone; they built durable bridges, and made aqueducts for supplying the cities with water. So numerous and so permanent were these vast works, that the remains of them are still to

---

Questions—Chap. LXXVIII—2. What of Rome during the reign of Augustus? What did it include in Europe? 3. In Asia? 4. In Africa? What parts of Africa were then known? *Tell the direction of each of the countries named from Rome.* (See map, p. 160). 5. How did Rome govern all these nations? 6. What of the people of Rome? 7. With what were many cities filled?

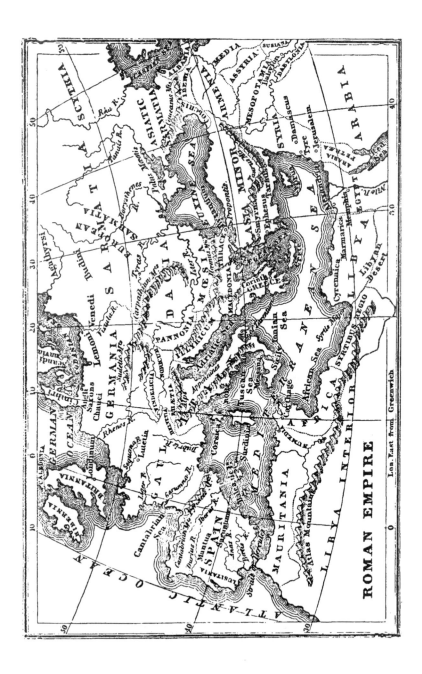

ROMAN EMPIRE

be found in most of those countries over which Roman dominion was then established, though they were executed nearly two thousand years ago.

9. But of all the cities in the world, Rome was itself the most wonderful. In the time of Augustus, it was fifty miles in circuit, and contained four millions of inhabitants.

10. Like all ancient cities, it was surrounded by high, strong walls of stone; for in those warlike times, as I have before said, walls were a necessary protection against the attacks of an enemy. The walls of Rome were entered by thirty-seven gates.

11. The interior of this wonderful city surpassed all description. The various generals who had conquered other countries, had robbed them of their choicest treasures, and these had been brought to Rome to decorate and enrich the capital.

12. There were beautiful statues from Greece, obelisks and columns from Egypt, and a great variety of curious and costly manufactures from Asia. Gold, silver, and precious stones had been gathered from every part of the earth.

13. The city was embellished with temples, many of them of marble, and beautifully sculptured; there were also theaters, amphitheaters, porticos, public baths, triumphal arches, and aqueducts.

14. In short, the city of Rome was enriched with the spoils of the whole world, and had that air of pomp and magnificence which suited the capital of the greatest empire the world ever saw.

CHAPTER LXXIX—EUROPE—Continued
The Means by which Rome acquired its Power

1. I TRUST YOU have now some faint idea of the extent, wealth, and power of the Roman empire. We cannot look back upon it but with feelings of admiration; yet when we consider the means which had been employed to establish this dominion, and reflect that the whole fabric was, ere long, laid in ruins, we feel that it rested on a false foundation, and that its destruction was like a just and inevitable retribution.

2. In the first place, the means used to aggrandize Rome were those of conquest. The Roman generals went abroad to subdue other countries, for

---

Questions—8. What of public works? What of aqueducts? 9. Describe the city of Rome. 11. How was the capital decorated? 13. What of temples? Other buildings? 14. What of the city?

CHAP. LXXIX—1. What must we feel upon reading the history of Rome?

no other purpose than to acquire fame and spoils for themselves, and power for Rome.

3. They slaughtered the inhabitants without mercy; they robbed them without scruple, and they subjected them to the Roman yoke without the slightest regard to the rights of mankind.

4. Such were the means by which the fabric of Roman power was erected. And what must have been the condition of mankind during the seven hundred years that Rome was carrying on its wars for no other purpose than to enslave the world?

5. It is true that a few men, generals, senators, consuls, and governors, might have lived in splendor, and enjoyed wealth and fame. Some of the Roman soldiers, too, might have led lives of adventure, gratifying to bold and restless spirits.

6. But how much suffering, sorrow, and despair must there have been among the millions of wounded men; among the millions who were bereaved of their friends; among the millions who were stripped of their fortunes; among the millions who were reduced to slavery.

7. The simple truth is, that the policy of Rome was wholly selfish. The Roman people, like the Greeks, Persians, Egyptians, and other ancient nations, had some notions of virtue, and occasionally displayed noble and generous qualities.

8. Yet, like all these nations, they were destitute of true morality; that morality which Christ has taught in a single sentence: Do to another as you would have another do to you. Like most other ancient nations, Rome was destitute of that true religion which teaches mankind, that all power founded in injustice must perish.

9. Splendid as the Roman empire was, it was destitute of real glory. Its splendor was acquired by robbery, and its fame, though it might dazzle a heathen, will be regarded as a false renown by the Christian.

10. In closing this chapter, it is proper to state a remarkable fact, that no heathen nation or country has ever existed, where the people were generally lovers of justice, truth, and charity. Public opinion in all heathen countries, ancient and modern, has been found to be an unsafe guide; it is only in Christian countries, where the laws of truth and morality are es-

---

Questions—2. By what means did Rome rise to such a high pitch of renown? What of the Roman generals? 3. What of Roman generals? 4. How many years was Rome at war with other nations? 5. What classes may have been benefited by these wars? 6. Who suffered from them? 7. What of Rome and her citizens? 8. Were the people either truly moral or religious? 9. What of the splendor of Rome?

tablished on the basis of the Bible, that the national faith can be trusted.

11. Such as it was, the power of Rome was destined to speedy decay. For a time after Augustus, the empire maintained its sway, and the magnificence of Rome continued. The luxury of the wealthy citizens even increased, and refinement in many respects was carried to a higher pitch than ever.

12. But the whole fabric was based on violence, selfishness, and wrong; and thus, as we shall see, in a few centuries imperial Rome was divided among a host of ruthless invaders.

CHAPTER LXXX—EUROPE—Continued
Rome under the Emperors

1. The Roman empire had now reached the height of its power, pomp, and splendor; but its decline had already commenced, because the people and their rulers were both corrupt. It was like a great tree with wide-spreading branches, but rotten at its trunk.

2. In the course of about three hundred and fifty years after the death of Augustus Caesar, there were thirty-six emperors of Rome; but I can mention only a few of them. They lived in great luxury and splendor, but they were generally such wicked persons that it would have been better for the world if they had never lived.

3. The next emperor to Augustus Caesar was Tiberius. He was a frightful-looking object, being bald and covered with sores, and his disposition was far more hideous than his aspect. This gloomy tyrant suspected everybody of plotting against his life.

4. He put so many people to death, that their dead bodies were piled in heaps in the public places. He once sentenced a poor woman to die merely for lamenting the death of her son. At last, he fell into a swoon, and his guards smothered him with his bed-clothes.

5. His successor was Caligula, who wished that the whole Roman people had but one head, that he might chop it off at a single blow. He also was murdered by his guards, and was succeeded by Claudius, an idiot. Claudius was poisoned by his own wife.

Questions—10. What may be said of heathen nations?   Christian nations?   11. State of Rome after the death of Augustus?   12. What was the final fate of Rome?

Chap. LXXX—1. To what can you compare the Roman empire?   2. How many emperors reigned after Augustus?   What of them?   3–4. Give an account of Tiberius.   5. Describe Caligula.

6. Nero was the next emperor. His whole reign was a scene of bloodshed. He murdered his mother and his wife. He set Rome on fire, merely for the pleasure of seeing it blaze. While the city was in flames, he sat on the top of a lofty tower, playing on a harp. Finally, he was dethroned, and condemned to be beaten to death with rods. To escape this torture, he killed himself.

7. The next two emperors were Galba and Otho. The first was killed by his soldiers, and the second committed suicide. The next was Vitellius. This monster delighted in visiting fields of battle, and snuffing up the odor of the dead bodies.

8. When the Romans grew weary of Vitellius, they put a rope round his neck and dragged him into the most public part of the city. There they bespattered him with mud, and then killed him in a most cruel manner. His head was put on a lance, and his body thrown into the Tiber.

9. But I am weary, my dear young readers! My old heart grows sick and sad while I speak to you of these evil and miserable men. Forget what I have told you. Forget that such monsters have ever existed in the world.

10. Or, if you must remember them, remember too that their frightful crimes resulted from the possession of more power than mortal man ought to possess. And, above all, remember, that if these tyrants were the scourges of their people, it was because the people had not virtue enough to be free.

CHAPTER LXXXI—EUROPE—Continued
Fall of the Western Empire of the Romans

1. YET THE PAGANS considered some of their emperors good men. Such were Vespasian, Titus, Antoninus, Marcus, Aurelius, Alexander Severus, Aurelian, and Diocletian. But these good men would doubtless have been better if their evil fortune had not made them emperors.

2. The first emperor who became a convert to Christianity was Constantine the Great. He began to reign in the year 306 after the Christian era. By him the seat of government was transferred from Rome to Constantinople.

3. The religion of Christ was planted in various parts of the Roman

---

Questions—6. What of Nero?   7. What of Galba and Otho?   Vitellius?   10. What may you remember of the reigns of these monsters?

Chap. LXXXI—1. What good emperors were there?   2. What of Constantine?   When did he begin to reign?   Where was the seat of government placed by Constantine?

empire by the apostles, but the first Christians were much persecuted. Some were whipped, many were imprisoned, and thousands were murdered.

4. Still their numbers increased. At length, the emperor Constantine ordered that the persecutions should cease, and he himself became a convert to Christianity. This took place in 311.

5. It is said that Constantine was one day riding at the head of his army, when he saw a splendid cross in the heavens, upon which was written, "Conquer by this sign." It is supposed that this vision persuaded the emperor of the truth of the Christian religion, and induced him to adopt it as the religion of the state.

6. From this period, Christianity flourished for a considerable time. The mythology of Greece and Rome, which had been extended throughout the Roman empire, gave way before it. Many of the temples were converted into churches, and the people who had been accustomed to bow down before the statues of Jupiter and other imaginary gods, knelt in humiliation at the foot of the cross.

7. In the year 364 after the birth of Christ, the Roman dominions were divided into the Eastern and Western empires. The capital of the Eastern empire, sometimes called the Greek empire, was Constantinople, formerly Byzantium. The fate of this will be briefly related in the history of the Turks.

8. The capital of the Western empire was Rome. But this imperial city was no longer powerful enough to defend itself against the nations which it had formerly conquered. It was ravaged by hordes of barbarians from the north of Europe, consisting of Huns, Goths, Vandals, etc.

9. Of these rude tribes I shall speak more particularly hereafter. It is sufficient for the present to say that they were bold warriors, and chose rather to obtain wealth by plundering the rich inhabitants of Italy, than by the cultivation of their own more sterile soil.

10. One of the first and fiercest of these northern invaders was Alaric, king of the Goths, who led a large army against Rome, and threatened the destruction of the city. The inhabitants were very different from the ancient Romans, and being overawed by the daring freebooter, promised him

Questions—3. What of the religion of Christ? First Christians? Persecutions? 4. What did Constantine do? 5. What is said to have happened to Constantine? 6. What of Christianity from this period? Mythology of Greece and Rome? Temples? People? 7. What took place 364 A.C.? What was the capital of the Eastern empire? The former name of Constantinople? What was the Eastern empire sometimes called? 8. Capital of the Western empire? How was it ravaged and laid waste? 9. What of the northern barbarians?

large sums of money. But this promise not being fulfilled, Alaric took the city and gave it up to plunder.

11. For six days imperial Rome was a scene of pillage and murder. Thousands of the citizens were slain, and a large portion of the place was reduced to ashes. This occurred in the year 410.

12. After a while, Alaric retired; but about the year 445, Attila, leader of the Huns, threatened to follow the example which Alaric had set. But in the midst of his projects he died, and Rome, for a time, was saved.

13. In the year 476, the whole Western empire, with Rome itself, was entirely subjugated by Odoacer, the leader of another northern tribe, called the Heruli; and it remained under this dominion for many years.

14. In the year 537, these barbarians were driven from Rome. This triumph was effected by Belisarius, an illustrious commander in the service of the emperor of the East. The Eastern and Western empires were then reunited, but only for a short period. Italy, as well as Rome, from this time frequently changed hands, being sometimes under the sway of northern kings, and sometimes under the Greek emperors.

CHAPTER LXXXII—EUROPE—CONTINUED
Progress of the Decline of Rome

1. IN THE TENTH CENTURY, the emperor of Germany claimed Italy as part of his dominions. Several cities resisted his authority. When the emperor, whose name was Otho, heard of it, he invaded Italy, and went to Rome.

2. He took possession of the palace, and prepared a magnificent feast. All the great men of Rome were invited. The emperor sat at the head of the table, on a splendid throne. The guests seated themselves, expecting to be feasted with luxuries.

3. But before they had eaten a mouthful Otho made a sign. Immediately the hall was filled with armed men. The emperor ordered the guests neither to move nor speak, on pain of death, whatever might take place. They trembled, and wished themselves away from the banquet.

4. One of the emperor's officers stood up and read aloud the names of all who had opposed his authority. These unfortunate men had been invited to the feast, and were now sitting at the table. The emperor com-

Questions—10. What of Alaric? 11. What occurred in 410? 12. What happened about the year 445? 13. What of Odoacer? 14. What happened in 537? Who was Belisarius? What did he do? What of the Eastern and Western empires? What of Italy? Rome? CHAP. LXXXII—1. What of the emperor of Germany?

manded them to be dragged into the middle of the hall and put to death. The executioner was in readiness, with a broad and heavy sword. One after another, the heads of the condemned persons rolled upon the floor of the hall. No mercy was shown to any of them.

5. When this dreadful scene was over, the emperor turned his attention to the banquet. His stern and wrathful aspect became mild and pleasing. He endeavored to make the other guests enjoy themselves; but probably their appetites were not increased by the sight of dead bodies on the bloody floor. This is a horrible story, and I only tell it to show you the barbarous and cruel character of the men of those times.

6. In the course of years, Italy was divided into several separate states, or sovereignties. The principal of these were Naples, Tuscany, Parma, Lombardy, Genoa, and Venice. Rome, with other territories, was given to the pope. Of these I shall hereafter give you a brief account; but before I proceed farther with the history of Rome, I will tell you something of the manners and customs of the ancient Romans.

7. Let me remark, however, that Rome was now totally changed from what it was in the days of Augustus. Not only was the empire broken in pieces, but the proud city of Rome itself had lost its former glory.

8. The number of its inhabitants had greatly diminished; many of its most splendid edifices were falling into ruins, and the people, having been long mixed with barbarians, had lost their former polish, and become partially barbarous themselves.

9. Even the language of Rome and of all Italy gradually became changed. The people had formerly spoken the Latin language; but this became mingled with the languages of the northern invaders, and thus the modern Italian was gradually formed. Such were the wonderful changes in Rome and Italy!

CHAPTER LXXXIII—EUROPE—Continued
Manners and Customs of the Ancient Romans

1. I AM NOW going to give you an account of the manners and customs of the great people whose history you have just read. I shall tell you about their domestic habits, and about their public observances; about their state

---

Questions—2–5. What did he do? Describe the banquet? 6. How did Italy become divided? 7. What of the changes in Rome? 8. What of the inhabitants, edifices, etc.? 9. The language of Rome?

of society, their agriculture, dresses, religion, marriage ceremonies, funeral rites, military institutions, and public edifices.

2. The people of Rome, as you know, were at first divided into two classes, the patricians and plebeians. It was to the struggles for power between these ranks that most of the difficulties in the state were owing. To these ranks a third was afterward added, called equites, or knights; the custom of making slaves of the subjects of conquered nations introduced a fourth division.

3. You have seen that the government of Rome was subject to very numerous changes. At one time it was under a king, at others under consuls, dictators, emperors, etc. The other officers of the state were numerous, and invested with different degrees of power.

4. The ministers of religion among the Romans did not form a distinct order of citizens, but were chosen from the most virtuous and honorable men of the state. These attended to the sacrifices of beasts to the gods, and other religious rites. The superstitions of the time also gave rise to the establishment of a college of augurs, whose business it was to explain dreams, oracles, and prodigies, and to foretell future events.

5. They drew their auguries, or presages concerning futurity, from the appearance of the heavens and inspection of the entrails of birds and beasts. Of course, they could no more divine the future than the old women you may sometimes meet with in our villages, who pretend to "tell you your fortune," by examining the grounds of coffee-cups.

6. The weakest and most ignorant are now too well informed to give credit to these pretenses. From this fact you can form some opinion as to the general intelligence of the ancient Romans compared with that of our own countrymen.

7. The augurs at Rome interpreted the will of the gods in the affairs of making war and peace, and none dared to dispute their authority. No business of importance could be proceeded in, without first consulting them; and their advice, whatever it might be, was, by a decree of the senate, to be strictly observed.

8. The office of an augur was important and honorable, and was sought after by many of the principal families in the Roman senate. Cato, the censor, was a member of their college, and Cicero also; though they both ap-

Questions—CHAP. LXXXIII—2. Into what four ranks or classes were the Roman citizens divided? 3. What of the government? Officers of state? 4. Ministers of religion? Superstitions? How did the augurs proceed? 6. What is said of these superstitions? 7. What more of the augurs?

168

pear to have been fully sensible of the extravagance and folly of the art they practiced. A remark is attributed to Cato, that he wondered how one augur could look in the face of another without laughing.

ROMAN SACRIFICE

CHAPTER LXXXIV—EUROPE—Continued
About Religion—Deities—Temples—Marriages

1. THE RELIGION of the Romans was borrowed from the Greeks, and included the worship of Jupiter, and a multitude of other deities. Every virtue and vice of the human heart, every faculty of the mind and body, every property of the real and imaginary world, was presided over by its peculiar god. Every grove, and mountain, and stream, had its nymph or naiad, and every hero and sage of the country was elevated to the rank of a divinity.

2. Every religious sect was tolerated at Rome except the Jews and the Christians. These were persecuted with unrelenting cruelty, until the mild precepts of the true religion triumped over superstition and ignorance. Christianity at length prevailed over conflicting opinions, and was adopted as the religion of the state, A.D. 311.

3. The number of deities whom the Romans worshiped occasioned the

Questions—8. The office of an augur? Cato and Cicero? Remark of Cato?
CHAP. LXXXIV—1. What of religion? 2. Toleration? Christianity?

erection of a great multitude of temples. Many of these were very splendid edifices, adorned with all the arts of sculpture, and filled with offerings and sacrifices. The priests attended at the temples, and sacrificed sheep, bulls, oxen, and other animals.

4. Those temples erected to the inferior deities were of less magnificence and grandeur, and were merely styled sacred houses. In the dwelling of every wealthy family there was a private chapel, in which they worshiped their household gods. Ancient Rome is said to have contained four hundred and twenty temples, dedicated to different deities.

5. Marriage was very much favored by the laws of Rome, and severe penalties were inflicted on those who remained single. At one period, the censors obliged all the young bachelors to make oath that they would marry within a certain time. Augustus increased the penalties on bachelors, and bestowed rewards on those who were parents of a numerous offspring.

6. The parties were betrothed some time before the actual celebration of the marriage. This was attended with many ceremonies, at which the priests and augurs assisted. The contract of marriage was drawn up in the presence of witnesses, and confirmed by the breaking of a straw between the engaged pair.

7. The bridegroom then presented his bride with the wedding-ring, and the father of the bride gave a great entertainment. The wedding-ring was worn on the third finger of the left hand, from a notion that a nerve of that finger communicated directly with the heart.

8. In dressing the bride, they never failed to divide her locks with the point of a spear, to signify that she was about to become a wife of a warrior. They then crowned her with a chaplet of flowers, and put on her a vail proper for the occasion.

9. Her toilet being completed, she was led in the evening toward the bridegroom's house, by three boys, whose parents were still alive. Five torches were carried before her, and also a distaff and spindle. Having come to the door, she herself bound the posts with wreaths of wool, washed over with melted tallow, to keep out witchcraft.

10. In going into the house, she was by no means to touch the threshold, but was to be lifted over by main strength. When she had entered, the bridegroom presented her with the keys, and with two vessels containing fire and water.

Questions—3–4. What is said of the Roman deities?   Their temples?   Household gods?
5. Marriage?   Penalties?   6–11. Describe the marriage ceremonies.

11. The bridegroom then gave a grand supper to all the company. The festival was accompanied with music and dancing, and the guests sang verses in praise of the new-married couple.

CHAPTER LXXXV—EUROPE—Continued
About Funeral Rites and Ceremonies

1. THE FUNERAL RITES of the Romans present a very interesting subject. Burning the dead, though practiced by the Greeks from very early times, was not adopted in Rome till the later ages of the republic. It afterward became universal and was continued without interruption till the introduction of Christianity. It then gradually fell into disuse.

2. Among the Romans, the bed of the sick was never abandoned to hired nurses and servants. It was attended by the relatives and intimates, who waited till the last hour, and bade a last farewell to their dying friend.

3. The body of the dead was bathed in perfumes, dressed in rich garments, and laid out on a couch strewed with flowers. The outer door of the house was shaded with branches of cypress. According to the heathen mythology, Charon would not convey the departed spirit across the Styx without payment of a fixed toll. A small coin was therefore placed in the mouth of the deceased to meet this demand.

4. The funeral took place by torchlight. The body was borne by near friends and relatives, on an open bier covered with the richest cloth. Lictors dressed in black regulated the procession. If the deceased had been a soldier, the badges of his rank were displayed, and the corps to which he belonged marched with their arms reversed.

5. Before the corpse were carried images of the deceased and his ancestors. Then followed musicians, and mourning women, who were hired to sing his praises, and dancers and buffoons, one of whom attempted to represent the character of the dead man, and imitate his manner when alive.

6. The family of the deceased followed the bier in deep mourning; the sons with their heads covered, and the daughters unvailed and with their hair disheveled. Magistrates and patricians attended without their badges or ornaments, and the procession was closed by the freedmen of the deceased, with the cap of liberty on their heads.

Questions—CHAP. LXXXV—1. What is said of burning the dead? 2. The bed of the dying? 3. The body of the dying? Notion in regard to Charon? 4–6. Describe the funeral.

7. The funeral ceremonies of a man of rank were distinguished by the oration in his honor, pronounced over the body by a friend. The scene of this display was the capitol, and in the later ages of the republic it became very common. While the practice of burial prevailed, the body was either interred without a coffin, or placed in a kind of deep chest called a sarcophagus.

8. On the termination of the rites, the tomb or sepulcher was strewed with flowers, and the mourners took a farewell of the remains of their friend. The attendants were then sprinkled with water by the priests, and all were dismissed.

9. When the custom of burning the body was introduced, a funeral pile was raised in the form of an altar, and the bier was placed upon it. The procession then moved slowly about, to the sound of solemn music, when the nearest relative advanced from the train with a lighted torch, and set fire to the pile.

10. Perfumes and spices were then thrown into the blaze, and the embers were quenched with wine. The ashes were collected and placed in a costly urn, which was deposited in the family sepulcher. In the funeral solemnities of a soldier, his arms, and the spoils he had won from the enemy, were sometimes added to the funeral pile.

11. It was a horrid belief of the heathen nations, that the spirits of the dead were pleased with blood. It was their custom to sacrifice on the tomb of the deceased those animals to which he was most attached during his life. In the more remote and barbarous ages, men were often the victims; so also were domestic slaves and captives taken in war; and sometimes friends gave themselves to be sacrificed from feelings of affection.

12. No burial was allowed within the walls of the city, except to the vestal virgins, and some families of high distinction. The tombs of military men were usually raised in the field of Mars, and those of private citizens in the gardens of their villas, or by the side of the public roads.

13. Some of these monuments are still standing, though in a ruinous state. The sepulchers of the great and wealthy were engraven with long and pompous lists of their titles, honors, and achievements. The tombs of the humble bore but a simple lesson to the reader, and some beautiful and touching expressions of sorrow or hope for the departed.

Questions—7. Oration 8. Conclusion of the ceremonies. 9–11. Ceremony of burning the body. 12. What is said of the burial-places? 13. Monuments?

CHAPTER LXXXVI—EUROPE—Continued
Roman Farms—Mode of Plowing—Farmhouses—Grain—Cattle—
Superstitions of the Farmers—Gardens—Vines

1. I AM NOW going to tell you about the farms and gardens of the Romans. In the early and more virtuous ages of the state, the cultivation of the fields, and a few rude trades connected with it, were the only occupations.

2. He who was the best husbandman was the most honored; and many of the most ancient families received their names from their success in the cultivation of plants or the rearing of cattle.

3. It is probable that at this period the ground was broken up only by the spade. Afterward, when the farms were enlarged, more expeditious means were discovered. Some of the Roman modes of plowing are still in use. They always plowed with oxen, a single pair, or sometimes three abreast, yoked by the neck and horns.

4. The farm-houses were at first little huts, but they were soon enlarged to suit the increasing possessions of the owners. We read, at a later period, of large store-houses and granaries, cellars for wine and oil; barns, together with separate buildings for the care and rearing of every species of domestic animal.

5. The kinds of grain in common cultivation were the same as those known in Europe, with the exception of maize, or Indian corn, which was first found in this country. The ancient mode of converting grain into meal was by pounding it with an instrument something like the pestle and mortar. Mills moved by cattle, and water, are later inventions.

6. Much care was paid by the Romans to the rearing of cattle. Sheep were secured under cover during the winter, notwithstanding the mildness of the Italian climate. Shearing time was a season of general festivity.

7. Goats were made as profitable to the farmer as sheep. Their hair was clipped every year and woven into a kind of coarse stuff, and their milk was the chief supply of the dairy.

8. The Roman farmers were very superstitious. They refrained from all labor on the fifth day of the new moon; on the seventh and tenth they planted vines, and harnessed young oxen to the yoke; on the ninth they commenced a journey.

Questions—CHAP. LXXXVI—1. What were the early occupations of the Romans? 3. What is said of their mode of plowing? 4. Their farm-houses? Other buildings? 5. What kinds of grain were cultivated? 6. What is said of cattle? 8. Superstitions of the farmers?

9. The skeleton of an ass's head was hung up at the boundary of the farm to enrich the soil and drive away the effects of blight. The same figure carved in brass, and crowned with vines, was affixed as an ornament to their couches.

10. In the remote ages, the gardens of the Romans contained only a few of the most common pot-herbs and orchard-trees. The more delicious fruits and more beautiful flowers were introduced at a much later period, from Persia and other parts of Asia.

11. The style of ornamental gardening was heavy and formal, producing a gloomy shade, rather than displaying beautiful scenery. It was the fashion to fill the gardens with dark walks shaded with evergreens, loaded with statues, and bounded by high clipped hedges.

12. It is supposed that the Romans obtained a knowledge of the cultivation of the grape, and the art of making wine, from Greece. They took great care of their vineyards, and labored in cultivating the plants with much art and industry.

13. The mode of gathering and pressing the grape was the same that is now practiced. The vintage was a time of festival, and the rustics made merry with the performance of a rude kind of comedy, and pouring out libations of new wine to Jupiter and Venus.

14. The wine appears to have differed from that of modern times; it was kept in jars formed like urns, some of which are said to have been so large as to have made, when filled, a load for a yoke of oxen. They were commonly ranged in cellars, but were sometimes buried in the earth, or even bedded in solid masonry. The wine was usually kept to a great age. It was held in less favor than the wine of Greece, and was much cheaper.

CHAPTER LXXXVII—EUROPE—CONTINUED
Country Houses—Description of Pliny's Villa—Aqueducts

1. I AM NOW going to describe the Roman villas, or country-seats. Originally they were nothing more than very humble farm-houses; but, with the progress of wealth and luxury, they were made by degrees more extensive and costly.

2. Some of them were surrounded by large parks, in which deer and

Questions—10. Produce of the gardens? From what countries did the Romans introduce the finer fruits and flowers? 11. Ornamental gardening? 12. What is said of the grape? Wine? 13. The vintage? 14. Wine jars?
CHAP. LXXXVII—1. What of the Roman villas?

174

various foreign wild animals were kept. Large fish-ponds were also not unfrequently attached to them, and were stocked at great expense. Generally, however, the villas were merely surrounded by gardens, and in size and appearance resembled those of modern Italy.

3. The philosopher Pliny the Younger was a nobleman and man of fortune, and the owner of four magnificent villas. Of two of these he has left minute descriptions. One of them I will now tell you about. It was seated on a rising-ground, facing the south, with the Apennine mountains raising their tall cliffs in the distant background.

4. A portico fronted the house, with a terrace before it, adorned with various figures, and bounded by a hedge of box. Hence you passed by an easy descent into a lawn surrounded by walks, and adorned with box cut into the shapes of various animals.

5. Beyond this lawn you entered a ground for exercise, laid out in the form of a circus, ornamented with well-trimmed box and other shrubs, and fenced with a wall covered by box. On the outside of the wall was a meadow, and beyond were other meadows, fields, and thickets.

6. Opposite the portico stood a square edifice which encompassed a small area of space, shaded by four plane-trees, with a fountain in the midst, refreshing the surrounding verdure. This apartment consisted of a bed-chamber and dining-room. A second portico looked out upon this little area.

7. Another room situated by the nearest plane-tree, enjoyed constant greenness and shade. In the same building were dressing-rooms, porticos, baths, and rooms for playing different games. The sides of one room were encrusted half way with carved marble; thence, to the ceiling, branches of trees were painted, with birds intermixed with the foliage.

8. In front of these buildings and porticos was a spacious circus, surrounded by plane-trees covered with ivy. Between these were planted box and bay trees, mingling their shade. The inward circular walks were perfumed with roses.

9. A thousand different fantastic shapes were given to the box that bordered the straight and winding alleys that crossed the grounds. At the end of one of these walks was an alcove of white marble, shaded with vines and supported by four pillars.

10. A fountain here emptied itself into a marble basin contrived with so much art as to be always full without overflowing. Sometimes Pliny

Questions—3. Pliny the Younger? 4. Describe his villa. 5. Ground for exercise. 6. Edifice opposite the portico. Rooms of this building. 8. Circus.

175

supped here with his friends, and then the basin served for a table, the larger vessels being placed about the margin, and the smaller ones swimming about in the form of little boats and water-fowl.

11. In front of the alcove stood a summer-house, of exquisite marble, with projecting doors which opened into a green inclosure. Next to this was a private recess, furnished with a couch, and shaded by a spreading vine which reached to the top. Here, also, a fountain alternately rose and disappeared. In different parts of the walks were several marble seats, and throughout the whole circus were small rills refreshing the grass and other plants.

12. Such is the description which Pliny has given us of one of his villas. You will see that it was very magnificent; and there were many others throughout Italy of equal splendor. You will perceive by this, that the wealthy Romans lived in a style of great luxury in the time of the emperors.

13. It was not till the year 441 after its foundation that Rome obtained its supplies of water by means of aqueducts. They afterward became so numerous that it has been calculated they furnished the city about five hundred thousand hogsheads every day. They were built of brick, and were sometimes thirty, forty, or even sixty miles in length.

14. The water was conveyed by reservoirs, and thence distributed through pipes over the town in great abundance. Only three aqueducts now remain for modern Rome; yet so pure are the sources from which they draw their supplies, that few cities can boast of such clear and healthful water.

15. Great attention was paid to ornament in the erection of the aqueducts. One built by Agrippa, when aedile under Augustus, contained one hundred and thirty reservoirs, and five hundred fountains, adorned with statues and columns. Remains of many of these great works, at this day, bear witness to their beauty and convenience.

CHAPTER LXXXVIII—EUROPE—Continued
Military Affairs of the Romans—Division of the Army—
The Imperial Eagle—Music—Arms—Dress—Military Rewards—
Crowns—The Triumph

1. You know that the Romans were almost continually engaged in wars.

Questions—10. Fountain? Basin? 11. Summer-house? Other ornaments? 13. Aqueducts? Quantity of water carried daily to the city? Describe the reservoirs. 15. Aqueduct built by Agrippa?

Their military affairs, therefore, occupied the attention of the most distinguished citizens. According to the Roman laws, every freeborn citizen was a soldier, and bound to serve in the army when called upon, from the age of seventeen to that of forty-six.

2. The Roman forces were divided into legions, each of which consisted of three thousand foot soldiers, and three hundred horsemen. The standard of the legion was the imperial eagle.

3. This was made of gilt metal, was borne on a spear by an officer of rank, and was regarded by the soldiers with a reverance which approached to devotion. The cavalry carried pennons, on which the initials of the emperor, or of the legion, were embroidered in letters of gold.

4. The only instrument of martial music among the Romans was the brazen trumpet. Some of the soldiers were armed with light javelins, and others with a heavy weapon of a similar description. All, however, carried shields and short swords, which they wore on the right side.

5. They were dressed in a metal cuirass, with an under covering of cloth, which was generally red, and hung loose to the knee. On the head they wore brazen helments ornamented with flowing tufts of horsehair. The uniform of the generals was an open scarlet mantle.

6. The cavalry wore a coat of mail, of brazen or steel scales, or of chain-work, sometimes plated with gold. Under this they wore a close garment which reached to their buskins. They rode without stirrups, and their saddles were merely cloths folded to suit the convenience of the rider. The disclipline of the army was maintained with great strictness and severity.

7. Rewards of various kinds were held out to those who distinguished themselves by an extraordinary exploit. A particular kind of crown was presented to him who in the assault first scaled the ramparts of a town.

8. A soldier who saved his comrade's life in battle was entitled to the civic crown, which was thought a distinction of the highest honor. The general who conquered in a battle was decorated with the laurel leaf.

9. But the highest ambition of every Roman commander was to obtain a triumph. This was the gift of the senate, and was only granted on occasions of splendid victory. When decreed, the general returned to Rome, and was appointed to the supreme command of the city on the day of his entry.

10. A sculptured arch was erected, under which the procession was to

---

Questions—CHAP. LXXXVIII—1. What is said of the military affairs of the Romans? 2. Divisions of the army? 3. Standard? Pennons? 4. Instruments of martial music? Weapons? 5. Dress of the soldiers? Generals? 6. Dress of the cavalry? 7. Rewards of the army? Crowns? 9–14. Describe the triumph of a victorious general.

pass, and scaffolding were raised for spectators in all the public squares and streets. The procession moved at daylight from beyond the walls of the city.

11. A band of calvary, with military music, took the lead. They were followed by a train of priests in their sacred robes, with attendants leading to sacrifice a hecatomb, that is, a hundred of the whitest oxen. Next came chariots laden with spoils, the arms and standard of the conquered, followed by long trains of the captives conducted by lictors.

12. Loud notes on the trumpet then announced the approach of the victor, dressed in a robe of purple, crowned with laurels, and bearing a scepter of ivory. He rode in a splendid car drawn by four horses, preceded by the Roman eagle, guarded by a troop of cavalry.

13. The most distinguished officers of the army, in their richest dress and trappings, surrounded him; a band of children clothed in white followed, flinging clouds of perfumes and flowers on the air, and singing hymns of praise to the conqueror.

14. Last of all came the victorious army, their weapons wreathed with laurel, and their burnished armor gleaming in the sunshine. Countless multitudes of the citizens lined the streets, and every window and every scaffolding shone with beauty. The procession was greeted on all sides by loud acclamations; joy and revelry reigned in the city, and a scene of magnificence was displayed hardly to be paralleled in modern times.

CHAPER LXXXIX—EUROPE—Continued
About Naval Affairs—The War Galley—Commerce—
Shows of Wild Beasts—Exhibitions of Gladiators

1. The first vessel of the Roman navy is said to have been built after the model of the Carthaginian galley taken in war. Their ships were roughly and slightly constructed, and, though very large, unfit to contend with boisterous and tempestuous weather.

2. They were clumsy and ill-fashioned, with a high stern and sides, and rowed with two or three tiers of oars on different decks. The prows of the ship were armed with iron, usually wrought into the shape of some animal's head; the upper deck was surmounted with a moveable turret, from which the soldiers could throw their weapons with advantage.

Questions—Chap. LXXXIX—1. First vessel of the Roman navy?   2. Describe the war-galley.

ROMAN SHIPS

3. The merchant-ships of the Romans were of a size corresponding with the purposes for which they were intended. Before the discovery of the magnet, by which the mariner can now direct his course in safety over the pathless waves, navigation was necessarily confined to the coast. These coasting-vessels were considered large if they reached the burden of fifty tons.

4. Rome was long supplied with the products of the East by the merchants of the maritime states of the Mediterranean. It was not till the conquest of Egypt by Augustus, that the trade became exclusively her own. Of this commerce Alexandria was the center.

5. The principal exports into Italy from India, consisted of drugs and spices; of cotton cloths and muslins, from the coasts of Coromandel and Malabar; of silk from China, and of large quantities of diamonds and pearls from Bengal and the pearl-fisheries near Cape Comorin. From Persia and Arabia they procured the richest carpets, silks, and embroidered stuffs, together with rice and sugar.

6. The first amphitheater erected in Rome, for the show of wild beasts and gladiators, was a mere temporary building of wood, probably erected by Julius Caesar. The Flavian amphitheater, bettern known by the name of Coliseum, was commenced in the reign of Vespasian, and is supposed to

---

Questions—3. What is said of the Roman merchant-ships? Navigation? Coasting-vessels? 4. How was Rome supplied with the products of the East? 5. What were the principal imports into Italy?

have been large enough to contain upward of eighty thousand persons. Its ruins are among the present wonders of Rome.

7. The wild beasts were secured in dens round the arena in the center, which was strongly fenced, and surrounded by a canal, to guard the spectators against their attacks. A vast number of wild beasts were made to destroy each other in these very cruel exhibitions.

8. Eleven thousand are said to have been slain during four months of triumph in honor of a conquest over the Dacians; and five hundred lions were killed in a few days on another similar occasion.

9. The first public combats of gladiators took place at Rome in the close of the fifth century from the foundation of the city. They were exhibited at a funeral. From that period they became frequent on such occasions, and afterward, on days of public festivals, were considered a material part of the ceremonies.

10. Five hundred pairs of these wretched beings have frequently been led to the public games to sacrifice each other for the amusement of barbarous spectators. They were at first taken from captives in war, or malefactors; afterward from slaves trained to the profession.

11. They fought with various weapons, some in complete armor, others with only a trident and a net, in which they endeavored to entangle their adversary and thus slay him.

12. It is needless to give a minute account of these inhuman customs. They were conducted with the most bloody and savage spirit, and are sufficient proofs of the degraded and brutalized condition of the period in which they were tolerated.

CHAPTER XC—EUROPE—Continued
Sports—Chariot Racing—The Circus—Carriages—
Private Entertainments—Supper Rooms—Convivial Parties—Luxuries

1. I will now change the picture, and give you an account of some of the less barbarous amusements of the Romans. Among these were several games of ball, played, as among us, both with the hand and foot. The young men chiefly engaged in sports in the open air that would make them more active and vigorous. Boxing, wrestling, and throwing the quoit, formed a

Questions—6. What is said of the first amphitheater? 7. Destruction of wild beasts? 9. Gladiatorial combats? 11. Weapons of the gladiators? What is said of these exhibitions?
Chap. XC—1. What is said of the games of the Roman youths?

180

prominent part of these amusements; but chariot driving took the lead of all others.

2. For the better enjoyment of horse and chariot races, there was an inclosed course immediately adjoining the city, called the circus. It was rather more than a mile in circumference, and was surrounded with seats and three tiers of galleries.

3. In the center was a barrier of twelve feet in breadth, and four feet high, around which the race was performed; and at one end was a triumphal arch, through which the successful charioteer drove, followed by the shouts and applause of the assembly.

4. Four chariots usually started together, the drivers of which were distinguished by dresses of different colors. Each color had its particular partisans, who betted largely on the success of their favorite. These sports were exceedingly popular, and were repeated in endless succession.

5. Of the carriages in use among the Romans, we have no very precise description. Some consisted of open and some of covered chairs and couches, borne on poles by slaves in livery. The couch was furnished with pillows and a mattress, and with feet of silver or gold to support it when set down. There were also close litters, drawn by mules, and carriages on two and four wheels, painted of various colors, and highly ornamented.

6. The horses were yoked to the carriage by means of a curved crossbar passing over their necks, and were directed by bridles and reins, which were sometimes of embroidered silk with gold bits.

7. Beside mules and horses, many other animals were occasionally used in carriages, such as dogs, goats, and deer, and even bears, leopards, lions, and tigers. But this of course was merely for a whimsical amusement, and not for real service.

8. When the Romans were poor and simple, they lived chiefly on milk and vegetables, with a coarse kind of pudding made of flour and water. But as they began to grow powerful, and to conquer the neighboring nations, they became acquainted with the luxuries of the people they subdued, and introduced them into their own state.

9. As they found in Greece models of the fine arts, so Asia furnished them with new and numerous sources of pleasure in the gratification of their senses. In the latter days of the republic, great attention was paid to

---

Questions—2–3. The circus?   4. The chariots?   Their drivers?   5. What is said of the form of the carriages?   6. How were the horses harnessed and managed?   7. What other animals were sometimes used?   8. Early living of the Romans?   Introduction of luxuries?

the arts of the cook, and various apartments were constructed in the houses of the rich for the entertainment of company.

10. The supper rooms of some of the emperors were hung with cloths of gold and silver, enriched with jewels. Tables were made for them of fine gold, and couches with frames of massive silver. The Romans always reclined on couches to take their meals.

11. At great entertainments the supper room was hung with flowers, and the guests were crowned with garlands. The floor was generally bare, though richly ornamented, and the ceiling was inlaid with fretwork of gold and ivory. Scented oil was used for lighting the apartments, and massive carved lamps of figured bronze reflected their brilliancy on the gay and beautiful scene.

12. Some of the more voluptuous and degraded of the Roman emperors, in the decay of the republic, were most extravagant and ridiculous in providing rare dishes for their tables. The livers and brains of small birds, the heads of parrots and pheasants, and the tongues of peacocks and nightingales, formed a part of their daily food.

13. But the most luxurious dish that graced the table of the Romans was an entire wild boar, roasted and stuffed with game and poultry. How miserable must have been the conditions of the people whose masters could lavish their wealth in such wanton and disgraceful indulgence of the appetite!

14. On one occasion, the senate was assembled to consult on the best mode of dressing an immense turbot which had been presented to the emperor. In our time, a council of cooks might have been called on an affair of so much importance, but it would hardly have been a subject to bring before the rulers of the people.

15. The Romans, however, would have been less rapidly enslaved and degraded, if their emperor and senate had always been employed as innocently as in discussing the most desirable manner of dressing a fish.

CHAPTER XCI—EUROPE—Continued
About Theaters—Clocks and Watches—The Fine Arts—
Books and Writing—Costume—Conclusion

1. Theatrical entertainments were first introduced into Rome in the

---

Questions—9. Arts of cookery? 10. Supper rooms? 11. Ornaments of the supper room? 12–13. Costly dishes of the Roman emperors? 14. Describe the consultation held by the senate upon cooking a fish. 15. What of the Romans?

182

year of the city 391. They were originally little more than dances to the sound of the flute. It was more than a hundred years before the drama attained to much dignity or excellence.

2. Actors were always held in contempt, but were enabled from the patronage they received to accumulate large fortunes. Theaters were at first built in the villages in the vicinity; the first permanent edifice of this kind in the city was built of stone, and calculated to contain forty thousand spectators.

3. The use of such clocks and watches as we have at present was unknown to the Romans. The sun-dial was introduced 440 years after the building of the city. About a century afterward, a kind of water-clock was introduced, which was contrived with much ingenuity, and answered all purposes for the measurement of time.

4. The fine arts were unknown in Rome till after the sixth century of her existence, when they were introduced by the successful captains of her armies, from the nations they had conquered. After a taste for the fine arts had been thus formed, large inclosed galleries were built around the mansions of the rich, and were adorned with the finest specimens of painting and sculpture.

5. In the dwelling of the most affluent patricians, these galleries also contained splendid libraries, which were open to the inspection of the learned and the curious. Collections of books were then of course very rare, on account of the great expense and difficulty of transcribing them.

6. They were sometimes written on parchment, but more frequently on a paper made from the leaves of a plant called papyrus. The leaves were pasted together at the ends, and then made up into a roll, which was inclosed in a covering of skin or silk, fastened with strings or clasps.

7. Writing was performed with a reed, split and pointed like our pen, and dipped in ink. Matters not intended for preservation were usually written with a pointed instrument on tables spread with wax. When letters were sent forward for delivery, they were perfumed, and tied with a silken thread, the ends of which were sealed with common wax.

8. The usual garments of the Romans were the toga and the tunic; the former was a loose woolen robe, of a semicircular form, and without sleeves; the latter, a close white garment, worn when abroad under the toga, but

---

Questions—CHAP. XCI—1. When were theatrical exhibitions introduced at Rome? What is said of them? 2. Actors? Theaters? 3. Clocks and watches? Sun-dials? Water-clock? 4. What is said of the fine arts? 5–6. Libraries? Books? Paper? 7. Writings? Letters?

alone in the house. The men usually went bareheaded.

9. For the feet, the usual coverings were the buskin and the sandal. The buskin reached about half way up the leg; the sandal was a mere sole, fastened to the foot by straps and buckles.

CHAPTER XCII—EUROPE—CONTINUED
Rome under the Popes

1. I WILL NOW PROCEED to finish the history of Rome. I have already had occasion to speak of the pope. This title was given to the bishops at a very early period of the Christian church. At first, the popes of Rome had no temporal power, but early in the eighth century they became possessed of a considerable portion of Italy, which they held until 1860, when most of it was taken away and added to the new kingdom of Italy, under Victor Emmanuel.

2. Thus we see that the popes, who claim to be the successors of the apostle St. Peter, ruled over Rome for over eleven hundred years. The pope may be a native of any country, and from any class of society, and is elected, when there is a vacancy, by the body of cardinals called the Sacred College, which consists, when full, of seventy members. But the popes for a long time have mostly been Italians, as the Romans were averse to the election of strangers.

3. Ancient Romans were first governed by seven kings for the space of two hundred and twenty years. During the next four hundred and forty-eight years, by consuls, tribunes, decemvirs, and dictators, in their turns. It was next governed by sixty emperors for five hundred and eighteen years, and lastly by one hundred and sixty-nine popes for over a thousand years.

4. But in the year 1517, a great excitement, called the Reformation, was commenced by a man called Martin Luther. He preached against the power of the popes, and all Europe was shaken with the convulsion which followed. The result was, that the authority of the popes was generally thrown off by the governments throughout Christendom, though it is known that many millions of people were killed in the wars that took place during this period of agitation.

Questions—8. Usual garments of the Romans?   9. Coverings for the feet?
CHAP. XCII—1. What of the popes of the early times?   2. What of the popes?   What may a pope be?   How is he elected?   3. How has Rome been governed since its foundation? 4.What took place in 1517?   What of Martin Luther?   What was the result of the Reformation?

5. In 1870, the Romans declared by a vote that they wished to join the new kingdom of Italy, and thus the pope lost the "temporal power," though remaining, as before, the head of the church.

6. Pius IX came to the papacy in 1847. He showed a desire to improve the political condition of the people, and hence acquired great credit, not only in Italy, but throughout the world. His efforts had a different effect from that intended, however. They awoke a spirit of liberty, and a rebellion followed. A republic was established in 1848, and the pope fled. He was soon brought back by the French, and the republic was overthrown. Pius IX died in 1878, and was succeeded by Leo XIII. Rome is the capital of the kingdom of Italy, Humbert I, son of Victor Emmanuel, being king.

7. Travelers who visit Rome at the present are wonder-struck by the existing tokens of the greatness of ancient Rome. But these ruins and relics are not the only remains of ancient Rome. There are many works still existing, written by the old Roman authors. These are in the Latin language, which, as I have before said, was spoken by the Romans. Many of them are very interesting, and from these, modern nations have derived a large part of their most valuable laws and institutions.

CHAPTER XCIII—EUROPE—CONTINUED
About several other Italian States

1. THE REVOLUTION IN ITALY in 1860 united Sardinia, Parma, Modena, Tuscany, Lucca, almost all of the States of the Church, and Naples, into one government, under Victor Emmanuel—embracing the two islands of Sardinia and Sicily, and all Italy, except Venetia and about one-eighth of the States of the Church.

2. The Kingdom of Naples, or the Kingdom of the Two Sicilies, formerly included the island of Sicily and the southern extremity of the peninsula of Italy. It embraced the foot of the figure of the boot which I have before mentioned. This kingdom had a population of eight millions five hundred thousand.

3. The history of Naples, after it was separated from the Roman em-

---

Questions—5. What happened in 1870?   6. What of Pius IX?   A Roman republic? Who succeeded Piux IX, and when?   The capital of Italy?   The king?   7. How are travelers affected in Rome?   What of ancient Roman works?   In what language are they written?   What have the moderns derived from these works?

CHAP. XCIII—1. What of Italy?   2. What did the kingdom of Naples include? Population?   *Direction of the city of Naples from Rome?*

pire, possesses very little interest. It passed first into the hands of one tribe of northern invaders, then into the hands of another, and then into the hands of another. After this it was subject to Spain and other countries, until at length it became an independent country.

4. In 1808, the emperor Napoleon gave the kingdom of Naples to one of his most distinguished generals, named Joachim Murat, who was the son of a pastry-cook. King Joachim was shot in 1816, and the two Sicilies were restored to the former king.

5. The history of Venice is very interesting. When the northern barbarians invaded Italy in 452, the inhabitants living in the vicinity of the present city of Venice settled in the marshes along the border of the sea, and supported themselves by fishing and making salt, and by commerce.

6. In the year 809, they commenced building the city of Venice on a little island called Rialto. To this place they transported their riches, and soon the new city became the capital of the Republic of Venice. The city and state increased, until at length Venice was one of the most powerful states in the world.

7. The inhabitants paid great attention to commerce, and such was the number of their ships, that in the eleventh century Venice sent a fleet of two hundred sail to assist in the First Crusade. It was on account of the interest which this state had in maritime matters that the Doge, who was the chief officer, used to "wed the city to the Adriatic Sea," in which it is situated.

8. The power of Venice continued to increase, and in process of time, the proud city of Constantinople was captured by its armies, aided by the crusaders. The spoils of the captured city, consisting of gems and jewelry, books, marbles, pictures, statues, obelisks, and other costly treasures, were chiefly carried to Venice.

9. The republic prospered for many years, and its wealth and power increased, though the people were often governed in the most cruel and oppressive manner. But I have only room to add, that toward the close of the last century, it fell a victim to the power of France, and in the year 1798 it was attached to the empire of Austria. Under this power it remained until 1866, when, in accordance with the terms of a treaty of peace between Prussia and Austria, Venetia was declared independent; and soon

---

Questions—3–4. What of the history of Naples? 5. What of the history of Venice? 6. When and where was Venice built? What did it become? 7. What of the commerce of Venice? Fleet? The Doge? 8. Power of Venice? What city was taken by Venice and the crusaders? What of the spoils of Constantinople?

after, by an almost unanimous vote of its people, it became a part of the kingdom of Italy.

10. Genoa, on the northwestern coast of Italy, formerly resembled Venice in its government, although it never was so powerful. In 1815, it was annexed to the territories of Sardinia. This kingdom originally consisted chiefly of the island of Sardinia in the Mediterranean, but it afterward comprised Genoa, Piedmont, and the island of Sardinia. The capital is the city of Turin. It is one of the most flourishing states of Italy.

11. Tuscany was a small state, and Florence was its capital. In former times it was celebrated for its wealth, its commerce, and its men of genius, who excelled in literature, sculpture, painting, and other arts.

CHAPTER XCIV—EUROPE—CONTINUED
About the Ottoman Empire—Turkey in Europe—Turkey in Asia—
About the Climate, People, and other Things

1. THE TURKISH OR OTTOMAN empire is divided into two parts, called Turkey in Europe and Turkey in Asia. It was formerly much more extensive than at present. It now embraces a large region of territory in Europe, lying between Greece on the south, and Russia and Germany on the north; this portion is called Turkey in Europe.

2. Turkey in Asia includes Asia Minor and Armenia, Syria, Palestine, Mesopotamia, etc. Egypt and the Barbary states in Africa were also subject to Turkey till within a few years.

3. The latter countries, together with Greece, have become wholly or partially independent of the Turkish dominion. The capital of this empire is Constantinople, which I have often mentioned before, and which at this day is one of the greatest cities in the world.

4. The chief ruler or king of the Turks is called the sultan. He lives at Constantinople, in a splendid palace. Like most Eastern princes, he has a great number of wives, whom he keeps shut up in a place called a harem.

5. The Turks have long beards, and most of them wear turbans on

---

Questions—9. What of the Republic of Venice for many years? What of France? What took place in 1866? 10. What of Genoa? Sardinia? 11. What of Tuscany?

CHAP. XCIV—1. What other name has the Turkish empire? How is the Ottoman empire divided? Where is Turkey in Europe? 2. What does Turkey in Asia now include? What other countries formerly belonged to the Turkish empire? How is Asia Minor separated from Turkey in Europe? 3. What of the countries that formerly belonged to the Ottoman empire? Capital of Turkey? What of Constantinople? 4. What of the sultan?

their heads, with loose, flowing robes over their under-dress. They sit on cushions instead of chairs, and take their food with their fingers instead of forks. They are fond of smoking very long pipes.

6. The sultan rules, not according to certain written or printed laws, but according to the customs of the country and his own will. The people generally do exactly what he requires; if they refuse to obey him, they may lose their property and their heads also.

7. If you were to go to Turkey, you would discover that the climate is mild, and the country naturally fertile; you would also see that the people are indolent and very grave. You would see that they have not many manufactures, and but little commerce. You would see that the lands are poorly cultivated, and that many tracts naturally fruitful are barren and desolate for want of tillage.

8. You would discover that the people dislike the Christians, and worship according to the faith of Mahomet. You would also remark that they have mosques instead of churches. At Constantinople there is a very splendid edifice, called St. Sophia. This was formerly a Greek church, but it is now converted into a Mahometan mosque.

CHAPTER XCV—EUROPE—CONTINUED

*About the Saracens—How the Turks overturned the Saracen Empire,
and how the Ottoman Turks founded the Ottoman Empire—
About the Bajazet, Timour, and other remarkable Characters*

1. IN THE HISTORY of Asia I have given you some account of the Saracens. These you will remember were Arabs, among whom Mahomet and his successors established an empire at the commencement of the seventh century.

2. The kings or rulers of the Saracen empire were called Caliphs, and resided at Bagdad, a splendid city which they built on the river Tigris in Mesopotamia. I have told you how these caliphs extended their empire over a considerable part of Asia and Africa, and some portions of Europe.

3. To the north of Mesopotamia, there were several tribes of Tartars,

---

Questions—5. Describe the Turks. 6. How does the sultan rule the Turks? What of the people? 7. Soil and climate of Turkey? The people? Manufactures? Commerce? Lands? 8. Religion of the Turks? What are their places of worship called? St. Sophia?

CHAP. XCV—1. What of the Saracens? When and by whom was the Saracen empire established? 2. What of the caliphs? Dominion of the caliphs?

among which were some called Turks. These were daring warriors, and such was their fame that the caliphs induced many of them to come to Bagdad and serve as soldiers.

4. In process of time, the Turks acquired great influence at Bagdad, and finally overturned the Saracen empire, made themselves masters of nearly all the Saracen possessions, and adopted the Mahometan religion. Thus the Turkish empire became the successor of the Saracen empire, and included in its dominions Asia Minor, Syria, Palestine, and other Asiatic countries, which the Saracens had conquered from the Greek empire.

5. After a while the Turkish empire, which had been thus established, was overturned by another tribe of Turks, who called themselves Ottomans. These came from the country east of the Caspian Sea, and laid the foundation for the present Ottoman empire. This took place in the year 1299; the founder of the empire being Othman the First.

6. The Greek empire had formerly included Asia Minor, but this had been taken by the Saracens, and afterward by the Turks. At the time of the Ottoman invasion, it included little more than what is at present called Turkey in Europe, with Greece.

7. Constantinople, the present capital of Turkey, was called Byzantium from Byzas, who founded it in 715 B.C. It was a flourishing city in the time of the early Greeks. The neighboring country was settled by colonies from Greece, and by other tribes. It was conquered by the Romans, and the name of Byzantium was changed to Constantinople, by the emperor Constantine, in 329.

8. It had before this period fallen into decay, but it was now revived, and Constantine removed thither with his whole court. It thus became the capital of the Roman empire. When that was divided into the Eastern and Western empires in 395, it was the capital of the former, which, as you know, was often called the Greek empire.

9. This continued, with various changes, to subsist as a distinct sover-

---

Questions—3. Where were the Turks? Where did they live? Why were they employed by the caliphs of Bagdad? 4. What did the Turks do? What of the Turkish empire? 5. By whom was the first Turkish dynasty overturned? When was the Ottoman empire founded? By whom? 6. What did the Greek empire formerly include? What did it include in 1299? 7. What of Constantinople? Who founded it, and when? What of it in the time of the early Greeks? When was its name changed? When and by whom was Byzantium called Constantinople? 8. What became of the capital of the Roman empire? What took place in 395? What was called the Greek empire? What countries did the Eastern empire of the Romans include? *Ans. Greece, Macedon, what is now called Turkey in Europe, Asia Minor, and other adjacent countries.*

eignty till the period of which I am now treating. It was, as I have said, on the brink of ruin, when the Ottomans, who had already established themselves in Asia Minor, and swallowed up the countries formerly belonging to the Saracen dominions, began to cast longing eyes upon the Greek empire in Europe.

10. The sultan, at this time, was Bajazet. He began to reign in 1389, and was so famous for his conquests that the Turks called him the Thunderbolt.

11. He was preparing to attack Constantinople, when a greater warrior than he came from Tartary and subdued him. This was Tamerlane, otherwise called Timour the Tartar, and sometimes Timour the Lame Man. He defeated Bajazet in a great battle, in which three hundred thousand men were slain.

12. It is said that when Timour the Lame Man had got Bajazet the Thunderbolt into his power, he put him into an iron cage, and carried him about for a show like a wild beast. Most conquerors have a resemblance to wild beasts, and it would be well if they could always be kept in cages.

13. The misfortunes of Bajazet prevented the Turks from conquering the Eastern empire of the Romans for a considerable time. But in 1453, when Mahomet the Great was sultan, they took Constantinople. The emperor, whose name was Constantine, was killed. From this time forward, the Turks were securely established in Europe, and the country which they inhabited was called Turkey.

CHAPTER XCVI—EUROPE—Continued
Sequel to the Turkish History

1. THE REIGNS OF MOST of the Turkish sultans have been full of crime and bloodshed. Sultan Selim, who began to reign in 1512, invaded Egypt and conquered it. The Egyptian soldiers were called Mamelukes, of whom I have told you in the history of Egypt. Thousands of them were taken prisoners.

2. After the victory the sultan ordered a splendid throne to be erected

---

Questions—9. What of the Ottomans?   10. Who was Bajazet?   When did he begin to reign?   What did the Turks call him?   11. What of Tamerlane?   12. How did Timour treat Bajazet?   What of conquerors?   13. What happened in 1453?

CHAP., XCVI—1. What of the reigns of some of the Turkish sultans?   What of Sultan Selim?   What of the Mamelukes?

on the banks of the river Nile, near the gates of Cairo [*ki´-ro*]. Sitting on this throne, he caused all the Mamelukes to be massacred in his sight, and their bodies to be thrown into the river.

3. Mohammed the Third, who ascended the throne in 1596, had nineteen brothers. All these he caused to be strangled, so that they might not attempt to rob him of his power.

4. Amurath the Fourth became sultan in 1621. This monster caused fourteen thousand men to be murdered. The sport that pleased him best, was to run about the streets at night with a drawn sword, cutting and slashing at everybody whom he met.

5. These facts will show the reader what kind of government the Turks have lived under. The father of the present sultan, whose name was Mahmoud the Second, ascended the throne in 1808. He was more enlightened than his predecessors.

6. But he was compelled to act with great severity. This was particularly the case in regard to the Janizaries. These were a large body of troops, established by Mahomet the Second in 1300, and who continued to be a very powerful body of soldiers for several centuries. Though called the sultan's guards, they became more dangerous than all the other subjects of the empire.

7. Sultan Mahmoud therefore determined to free himself from their power. Accordingly, in the year 1826, he ordered the rest of his troops to surround the Janizaries. This was done, and they were shot down and massacred without mercy. The sultan afterward endeavored to reform the manners of the Turks, and to make them adopt the customs of other European nations. In this he was followed by his successors, Abdul-Medjid and Abdul-Aziz; but the progress of the Turks in this direction has been very slow.

8. In 1854, Russia threatened an attack on Turkey, which resulted in what is called the Eastern War, one of the greatest struggles which the world has witnessed since the fall of Napoleon at Waterloo in 1815. By the aid of France and England, Turkey was preserved from being overwhelmed by Russia. In 1877, Russia again made war on Turkey, and took from her a large portion of her territory in Europe and Asia.

Questions—2. What did the sultan order? 3. When did Mohammed III ascend the throne? What crime did he commit? 4. Who became sultan in 1621? What of Amurath? 5. What of Mahmoud the Second? When did he ascend the throne? 6. What of him? Who were the Janizaries? When were they established? 7. What was done in 1826? 8. What of the Eastern War? War of 1877?

CHAPTER XCVII—EUROPE—Continued
Early History of Spain—The Moorish Conquest

1. The kingdom of Spain is separated from France by the range of mountains called the Pyrenees. It has Portugal on the west; its other boundaries are the Atlantic Ocean, the Bay of Biscay, and the Mediterranean Sea. The whole country forms a large peninsula.

2. Spain is a very remarkable country; it is full of wild, rocky mountains, with beautiful valleys between. The climate is warm and delightful. The country produces abundance of grapes, olives, lemons, almonds, figs, citrons, and pomegranates.

3. Spain is celebrated for a very fine breed of horses. It is also the country from which the merino sheep were first brought. There are many of these now in this country, and you know they produce the finest wool in the world.

4. Spain has about half as many inhabitants as the United States. The mass of the people are generally ignorant and superstitious, but they seem to be very honest, with an air of dignity and politeness in their manners. They are fond of gay dances in the open air. Madrid, the capital of Spain, is a very splendid city.

5. I must not omit the Gipsies, who are a race of strange, swarthy people, found in various countries of Europe, especially in Spain. Most of them wander about, carrying their property and children with them, and get a living by telling fortunes, and performing some services as mechanics. Some of them are addicted to thieving. For four or five hundred years these strange tribes have thus wandered about in Europe, and no one can tell whence they came. In Spain some of them have settled down and become good citizens.

6. Spain abounds in castles, churches, and palaces, built by the Moors, of whom I shall soon tell you the story. These edifices are some of the most wonderful buildings in the world. They are totally unlike those of ancient Greece and Rome. They bear some resemblance to what is called the Gothic architecture, specimens of which are to be found in some of our cities.

Questions—Chap. XCVII—1. How is Spain separated from France? Boundaries of Spain? 2. What sort of country is Spain? Climate? Productions? Should you not like to go to Spain and eat some of the fine fruits? 3. What of the horses of Spain? Merino sheep? 4. Population? What of the people? Capital? What of Madrid? *Which way is Madrid from you? From London? Paris? Rome? Algiers?* 5. What of the Gipsies? 6. What of the Moorish buildings in Spain?

A GIPSY FORTUNE-TELLER

7. If I had time and room, I should like very much to tell you a long story about Spain; but I shall be obliged to say very little of it, and leave you afterward to pursue the subject in some larger book.

8. Little is known about the history of Spain till the Phoenicians made voyages thither. They came from Phoenicia, which you know was close to the land of Canaan, a distance of two thousand miles, and built two columns at the Straits of Gibraltar. These columns were called the pillars of Hercules. The ancients did not dare to sail beyond them, into the broad Atlantic Ocean.

9. The Greeks founded several cities in Spain. Afterward, the Carthaginians acquired possession of the country; but it was taken by the Romans in 134 B.C., and they kept it till the year 406 after the Christian era. Spain was then invaded by barbarians from the north, called Suevi, the Alans, and the Vandals.

Questions—8. What of the early history of Spain? Where was Phoenicia? How far from Spain? What did the Phoenicians do in Spain? Where were the pillars of Hercules built? How far did the ancients venture to go in their vessels? 9. What of the Greeks? The Carthaginians? The Romans? What barbarians conquered Spain? About what time did they conquer Spain?

10. Some of these people continued in the country more than a hundred years. They were then driven out by another set of barbarians, called Goths, or Visigoths, who overran the whole of Spain. These became established in the country, and finally founded a kingdom there.

11. After the Goths had been in Spain about two hundred years, a king mounted the throne whose name was Roderick. This king grievously injured Count Julian, who was one of the most powerful of the Spanish or Gothic nobles. In order to avenge himself, Julian took steps which resulted in the ruin of his country.

12. In Mauritania, which I have already mentioned, on the northern coast of Africa, and not far from Spain, there was a nation of Saracens. They were called Mauri, or Moors, from the country which they inhabited. Count Julian invited them to cross the sea and invade Spain.

13. Accordingly, a great number of these infidels landed on the Spanish shores, under the command of a general named Tarik. King Roderick the Goth gathered an army, and encountered them at Xeres, in the south of Spain. Here a great battle was fought.

14. The Moors were completely victorious. The fate of Roderick was never known. His horse, and his sword, helmet, shield, and breastplate, were found by the side of a river, near the field of battle; but his body was nowhere to be seen. These events occurred about A.D. 712.

15. The Spaniards long believed that king Roderick was alive, and that, at some future day, he would again lead an army to battle against the Moors. But his war-shout was heard no more; and as the Gothic monarchy was ruined by his fall, he is called Roderick the Last of the Goths.

16. Pelagio, a prince of the blood-royal, took command of all the Gothic Spaniards who had not been slain by the Moors. He led them into the mountainous region of Asturias and Burgos [*boor´-goce*], and there founded a little kingdom. This was the only part of Spain which the Moors never conquered.

17. The successors of Pelagio enlarged the boundaries of his kingdom. But, for a long time, the Moors possessed three-fourths of Spain.

Questions—10. How long did the Suevi and other barbarians remain in Spain? Who drove out the Suevi and other barbarians? What of the Goths? 11. What of Roderick? Count Julian? What did he do? 12. What of Mauritania? *Its direction from Spain?* What of the Moors? Count Julian? 13. What did the Moors do? What followed? 14. Fate of king Roderick? How long ago did this happen? 15. What did the Spaniards believe? Why was Roderick called the Last of the Goths? 16. What of Pelagio? What was the only part of Spain not conquered by the Moors? 17. What of the successors of Pelagio? What portion of Spain did the Moors long possess?

CHAPTER XCVIII—EUROPE—CONTINUED
Wars between the Moors and the Spaniards

1. THE MOORS WERE a wild people when they first conquered Spain; but they soon became civilized and polished. There was more learning amongst them than in any other part of Europe.

2. In the city of Cordova, there was a library of six hundred thousand volumes. There were likewise seventy public libraries in other parts of the Moorish territories in Spain. The Moors were great lovers of poetry and music.

3. They built many noble edifices in Spain. The Alhambra, in the city of Granada, was the palace of the Moorish sovereigns. It was of marble, and ornamented with beautiful sculptures. The sultry atmosphere was cooled by fountains, which spouted continually in the chambers and halls. Beneath the Alhambra were vaults, which the Moorish kings had caused to be dug, that they might be buried there; for they loved the Alhambra so well, that they used it both as their palace and sepulcher.

4. But the Spaniards hated the Moors, and seldom were at peace with them. In their continual wars, the victory sometimes fell to one party, and sometimes to the other. Eighty thousand Moors were once slain in a single battle.

5. On the other hand, a Moorish hero, by the name of Almanzor, is said to have vanquished the Spaniards in more than fifty battles. He took the city of Compostella, and compelled his captives to carry the gates of a large edifice from thence to Cordova on their shoulders.

6. The most famous warrior that appeared on either side, was Don Rodrigo de Bivar, surnamed the Cid Campeador, or the Incomparable Lord. He gained so many battles against the Moors, that at last the Spaniards considered the victory certain whenever the Cid was at their head.

7. When the Incomparable Lord was dead, the courage of the Moors revived. They boldly attacked the Spaniards, and besieged the city where the Cid Campeador lay buried. The Spaniards went forth to meet them, and at their head rode an armed warrior, with a countenance like death.

8. The Moors recognized his features, and fled; for it was the Cid

---

Questions—CHAP. XCVIII—1. What can you say of the Moors?   2. What of libraries in Cordova?   In other cities?   What did the Moors love?   3. What did they build in Spain? Describe the Alhambra.   What were beneath the Alhambra?   4. How did the Spaniards feel toward the Moors?   What of their wars?   5. What of Almanzor?   What city did he take?   6. What famous warrior can you mention?   What of him?   7. What of the Moors after his death?   Who rode at the head of the Spaniards?

Campeador! The Spaniards had taken him from the tomb, and seated him on the war-horse which he had ridden in his lifetime. And thus the dead warrior won another victory.

9. Many other wonderful stories are told about the Moorish and Spanish wars. Sometimes, it is said, a saint came down from heaven, to lead the Spaniards to battle. Sometimes the sun stood still, that they might have time to kill their enemies. Sometimes they were encouraged by the appearance of a blazing cross in the sky.

10. But these are fables. It is certain, however, that the Moors gradually lost their Spanish territories, till nothing remained to them except Granada. And in the reign of Ferdinand and Isabella, they were wholly driven out of Spain. This event took place in 1492, nearly eight centuries after the overthrow of King Roderick the Goth.

11. It is the great glory of Ferdinand and Isabella that they gave encouragement to Christopher Columbus by means of which he discovered America. On the other hand, their memory is stained by having established the Inquisition in Spain, which became one of the most dreadful instruments of tyranny. This was a secret tribunal, which adjudged persons charged with heresy to various tortures and punishments, and to death itself.

12. It used torture to extort confession of guilt from the accused, but this horrid practice prevailed in other parts of Europe, and it has been shown that the Inquisition was little worse than some other tribunals of the age. It was established in Spain in 1478, and had power over all classes, nobles, clergy, monks, nuns, parents, and children, without any exception save the king and queen. It imprisoned Bartholomew Caranza, Archbishop of Toledo, where he died after seventeen years' confinement; and neither the efforts of Pope Pius IV, nor the protest of the council of Trent, of which he was a member, could procure his liberation.

13. The object that Ferdinand and Isabella had in establishing the Inquisition was to discover and punish the multitudes of Moors, who openly professed themselves Christians, to avoid being banished, but who were secretly zealous Mahometans, and doing privately all they could toward enabling their people in Morocco to reconquer Spain. Fifty years after its

---

Questions—8. How were the Moors affected by seeing the dead body of the Cid Campeador?   9. What stories are told of the Moorish and Spanish wars?   10. What at last remained to the Moors?   When were the Moors driven out of Spain?   11. What of Ferdinand and Isabella?   The Inquisition?   12. What further of the Inquisition?   When established?   What power?   Who did it imprison?

establishment it was unrelentingly and effectually used to prevent the introduction of Protestantism into Spain. It was abolished by Napoleon in 1808, re-established as a political institution in 1814 by Ferdinand VII, and finally abolished at his death in 1820.

CHAPTER XCIX—EUROPE—CONTINUED
The Invincible Armada—Curious Death of a Spanish King—Recent Affairs of Spain

1. ONE OF THE MOST powerful monarchs of Spain was Philip the Second. He was not only king of Spain, but he obtained the crown of Portugal also, in 1580; but Portugal afterward became a separate kingdom again. It had first been declared independent of Spain at the beginning of the twelfth century.

2. Philip intended to conquer England, and prepared a fleet of eighty ships for that purpose. This fleet was called the Invincible Armada. But it was conquered even without a battle, for a storm scattered it, and drove many of the ships on the British coast.

3. The son of Philip was a weak-minded man. The manner of his death was very singular. He was sitting one day in the council-chamber, which was warmed by a large stove. The heat and vapor of the stove affected his head.

4. He ordered the attendants to quench the fire. But the person whose duty it was to do this, happened not to be in the chamber, and the rules of the Spanish court were so strict, that it would have been unlawful for any other person to touch the fire.

5. Moreover, it would have been beneath the king's dignity to leave the chamber, or even to move his chair back from the stove. So the fire continued to grow hotter, and the poor king grew sicker and sicker, till at last it was impossible to cure him. And thus he died, by a kind of death that could have befallen nobody but a Spanish king.

6. In the year 1700, Charles the Second of Spain died without children. He was succeeded by a young French prince, named Philip, duke of Anjou [*an´-joo*], the grandson of Louis the Fourteenth. The kings of this family are called the Spanish Bourbons [*boor´-bons*].

Questions—13. What was the object in establishing the Inquisition?   What fifty years after?   Who abolished it?
CHAP. XCIX—1. What of Philip II?   What of Portugal?   2. What of the Invincible Armada?   3–5. Describe the death of Philip's son.   6. What happened in the year 1700?   Who succeeded Charles II?   Who were the Spanish Bourbons?

7. This event caused a long war in Europe. Charles, archduke of Austria, claimed the crown of Spain, and he and Philip of Anjou alternately drove each other out of Madrid. But Philip finally kept his seat on the throne.

8. Spain has often been at war with England. She united with France against that country during the American Revolution; but peace was concluded in 1783. Another war, however, began between England and France in about ten years afterward.

9. In 1808, when the emperor Napoleon was at the height of his power, he compelled the Spanish king to abdicate his throne. The name of this king was Ferdinand VII. Napoleon then placed the crown of Spain upon the head of his own brother, Joseph Bonaparte.

10. But most of the Spaniards refused to acknowledge king Joseph as their sovereign. A bloody war ensued. The English government sent armies into Spain and Portugal; and it was there that Lord Wellington gained his first victories over the French.

11. Ferdinand, the old Spanish king, was replaced upon the throne in 1814. He was, however, a tyrant and a bigot, and his reign was mischievous to the country. His death took place in 1833.

12. After this, Spain was ravaged by a civil war between Don Carlos and the young Queen Isabella II. The claims of Isabella were established, and she reigned till 1868, when she was dethroned and driven from the country. In 1870, Amedeo, son of the king of Italy, was invited to be king of Spain, and he consented. He only remained two years, however. Spain then declared itself a republic, afterward passed through a period of anarchy, and in 1879 became a monarchy again, with Alfonso, son of Isabella II, as king.

CHAPTER C—EUROPE—Continued
A Short Story about Portugal

1. Portugal lies to the west of Spain, and is bounded on the west by the Atlantic Ocean. The population of the country is about four millions.

Questions—7. Why did Charles and Philip go to war? Who triumphed? 8. What of Spain? When was peace concluded between France and England? 9. What did Napoleon compel the Spanish king to do in 1808? Who was Ferdinand VII? Whom did Napoleon make king of Spain? 10. What of the Spaniards? What of the English government? What of Lord Wellington? 11. When was Ferdinand replaced upon the throne? What of him? When did he die? 12. What of a civil war in Spain? Recent events?

The capital is Lisbon. This is a large city, and many of our vessels visit it for the purpose of getting wines, grapes, oranges, and lemons.

2. The climate of Portugal is like that of Spain. The people also resemble the Spaniards, but speak a language somewhat different.

3. Portugal was originally considered a part of Spain, and shared in the events of that country. In the twelfth century, it became independent. Since that time it has been considered a separate kingdom, though it has been subject to Spain for a portion of this period.

4. The history of Portugal is of little interest, till about the year 1400, when the Portuguese took the lead in navigating the Atlantic Ocean. At this time, this great sea was little known, and nobody had gone across it to America, nor had any one dared to sail around Africa.

5. But the little Portuguese vessels ventured out farther and farther, and finally one of them reached the Cape of Good Hope. After this, a Portuguese fleet passed entirely around Africa, crossed the Indian Ocean, and reached India.

6. These wonderful adventures and discoveries excited other nations, and in a few years Christopher Columbus discovered America. Thus the Portuguese may be considered as having led the way to the discovery of this vast continent on which we live, and which was unknown to the people of Europe, Asia, and Africa, till the year 1492.

7. I need not tell you of what happened in Portugal from this time till the year 1755. At that date, an earthquake took place, which shook down nearly the whole city of Lisbon. Houses, churches, and palaces were suddenly tumbled into heaps of ruins. Large chasms were opened in the earth, and hundreds of houses were plunged into them. The sea at first rolled back from the land, and then returned, sweeping every thing before it. In this awful calamity, ten thousand persons lost their lives.

8. The Portuguese founded a good many colonies in different parts of the world. One of these was in Brazil, in South America. To this place the king of Portugal retired with his family in 1807, and established his court at Rio Janeiro [*ri´-o ja-nee´-ro*], then capital of the country. This was done

---

Questions—CHAP. C.—1. Boundaries of Portugal? Population? Capital? What of Lisbon? 2. Climate of Portugal? The people? Language? 3. What of Portugal? When did it become independent? What of Portugal since the twelfth century? 4. What of the Portuguese after about 1400? What of the Atlantic at this time? 5. What of the Portuguese vessels? Their discoveries? 6. What consequences followed the Portuguese discoveries? What of America till 1492? 7. What happened in 1755? Describe the earthquake.

because Portugal had been invaded by the French.

9. The French being driven out in 1808, the king returned in a few years. After his death there was a struggle for the crown, but it was settled in 1834 upon Maria II, from whom it descended, in 1861, to Louis Philippe, the present sovereign.

CHAPTER CI—EUROPE—CONTINUED
Description of France—Its Climate—Cities—Manufactures—
Manners and Customs of the People

1. FRANCE LIES in the western part of Europe, and contains about thirty-seven millions of inhabitants. Paris, the capital, is a very large city, surrounded with walls of stone. It is full of fine houses, beautiful public gardens, pleasant walks, handsome streets, and interesting places of amusement.

THE ARCH OF TRIUMPH AT PARIS

2. Beside Paris, there are a great many other large and handsome cities in France. Among these are Rouen [*roo´-en*], where the people manufacture a great deal of handsome jewelry; Lyons, where they make beautiful silks; Marseilles [*mar-sailz´*], where the people deal in wines; and Bor-

Questions—8. Colonies of Portugal? What of the king of Portugal? When and why did he remove to Brazil? 9. What followed?
CHAP. CI—1. Population of France? Describe Paris.

deaux [*bor-do ´*], in the midst of a country which produces fine grapes, and other delicious fruits.

3. The climate of France is about the same as that of Pennsylvania, Maryland, and Virginia. The soil is fruitful, and yields abundance of food for the numerous inhabitants. The country produces many kinds of fruit in great perfection, such as cherries, pears, plums, peaches, and figs. It also yields immense quantities of grapes, from which many kinds of choice wines are produced.

4. The people of France are very gay and cheerful. They live a great deal in the open air, and it is common in all parts of the country to see both men and women at work in the fields. They do not labor very hard, and during the holidays, of which they have a great many, they walk about the streets, and dance in the public gardens or squares.

5. The French seem to enjoy themselves better than most other nations. They are fond of music, and delight to get together and talk about all sorts of things. They are very polite and always treat strangers with particular civility. The gentlemen are courteous to the ladies, and the ladies in return take every means in their power to make their society agreeable to the gentlemen.

6. The manufactures of France are numerous and valuable. The people have an excellent fancy in making jewelry, silks, laces, ribbons, clocks, watches, and many other ornamental things. These are sent to all parts of the world, and though they may not be considered very necessary, yet they give a great deal of pleasure, and thus have their use.

7. The French people are fond of dress, and the dressmakers of Paris set the fashions for the rest of the world. The milliners and mantua–makers of this city have more followers than any king that ever lived; for the gowns and bonnets of the ladies of Europe and America are made according to their direction.

8. The French nation, on the whole, are a very interesting and wonderful people. Though they might seem to be frivolous and thoughtless, yet France has produced many great men, and the history of the country displays many great and glorious actions.

Questions—2. What of Rouen? What of Lyons? What of Marseilles? What of Bordeaux? 3. Climate of France? Soil? Productions? 4. Characters and manners of the French people? 5. What of the gentlemen? The ladies? 6. Manufacture of France? What is the use of the fancy articles manufactured in France? 7. What of the French, as to dress? Milliners and mantua-makers? 8. What might seem to be the character of the French? What does their history display?

9. They have been represented as a nation of fiddlers, dress-makers, and dancing-masters; but if you look into their character, and read their story with attention, you will see that this is not just; they are in truth the most warlike nation in Europe; they take the lead in many arts and sciences; and if the people at large spend much of their time in amusement, it is not because they are deficient in genius for the highest pursuits of the mind.

CHAPTER CII—EUROPE—Continued

About the Gauls and other Tribes of Barbarians—
How the Southern Parts of Europe were first settled, and
how the Northern Parts were settled afterward

1. In the course of history, I have had frequent occasion to mention various northern tribes of Europe, called Barbarians, and perhaps I shall not find a better opportunity than the present to give you some account of them. You remember that Greece was settled before any other part of Europe. The first inhabitants were the descendants of Japheth. The descendants of these spread themselves over Greece, and probably other parts of Europe.

2. As the people increased along the shores of Asia and Africa, they sent colonies to different places along the shores of the Mediterranean. Some settled in Greece, some in Italy, some in Spain. These countries being warm, pleasant, and fruitful, were soon filled with inhabitants. Living upon the coast they had a great many ships, and carried on commerce with different countries.

3. In this way, after many years, they grew rich, and built large cities with fine houses, temples, and palaces. Such was the course of events in regard to all southern Europe, of which I have been telling you the story. But, while these things were going on, various tribes were emigrating into the more northern portions of Europe.

4. Here the climate was colder, and the soil less fruitful. Still the woods were full of elks, reindeer, fallow-deer, and the roebuck, wild bulls, wild boars, and many other animals. These supplied food for the inhabitants,

---

Questions—9. What of their talent for war?   Their genius for other things?
Chap. CII—1. What of Greece?   2. How were the shores of the Mediterranean settled? What of the people in these countries?   3. How were the northern portions of Europe settled?

and the chase furnished excellent sport to the adventerous people of those days.

5. Beside all this, in these regions unoccupied by man, the land was very cheap, and whoever would come and take it might have it. These circumstances invited the people to leave the soft, sunny regions of Greece, Italy, Spain, and also of Asia, for the colder and wilder realms of northern Europe.

6. Thus tribe followed tribe, and nation followed nation, until the whole country was occupied, from the Mediterranean on the south, to the Arctic Sea on the north. It was, in fact, very much such a course of events as you may have seen going on in our country.

7. Those portions of America first settled by the Europeans were along the Atlantic seaboard. Here they first built houses, and founded cities. After a while they went into the farther interior in search of wild game and new land. Thus they continued to push farther and farther into the country, and even now they are still advancing toward the far west.

8. In this same manner Europe was settled from Asia, some three or four thousand years ago.

CHAPTER CIII—EUROPE—Continued
Story of the Barbarians continued

1. I HAVE NOW shown you how the north of Europe was gradually settled by the tribes that emigrated from the south of Europe, and from Asia. These might be compared to a vast stream that continued to flow on, growing wider and advancing farther, until at length the whole country was peopled.

2. But you must remark one thing, that these emigrants were savages, and of a warlike character; they therefore did not mingle into one great nation, but each tribe remained distinct. As they increased in numbers they increased in power.

3. After a while, something would happen to bring two tribes living near each other into a state of war. Fierce battles would follow, and a great many would be killed. Sometimes one tribe would be vanquished, and they would all be slaughtered, reduced to a state of slavery, or driven out of their

---

Questions—4. Climate and soil of northern Europe?   What furnished subsistence to the inhabitants?   5. What of the land?   What induced the people to settle in northern Europe?   6. How does the settlement of America compare with that of Europe?   7. What of the Europeans in America?

Chap. CIII—1. How was the north of Europe settled?   To what may the emigration of the tribes be compared?   2. What of these emigrants?

country.

4. It was, in short, a state of things very much like that of our American Indians when this country was first settled by the white people. There was this difference, however, that the northern barbarians of Europe carried with them the knowledge of many arts. Their weapons of war, therefore were not merely the bow and arrow, but they had swords, spears, and shields.

5. They also built better houses than the wigwams of our Indians. Still they were a fierce people, and in many respects were as savage as the wild boars and wild bears which they pursued in the chase.

6. Among the most remarkable of these northern tribes were the Gauls, who were the first known inhabitants of France, and who came from Asia several hundred years before Christ; the Franks and Suevi, who inhabited Germany; the Goths and the Vandals, who inhabited Norway, Sweden, and Lapland, and afterward established themselves in Germany; and the Huns, who lived in Hungary. There were still many other tribes, but it is not necessary to mention them here.

7. Well, you must now imagine all the north of Europe inhabited by these wild tribes, spending their time chiefly in the chase, or in war, or other hardy pursuits, they became bold, daring, and adventurous. Their numbers also increased, and some of them became powerful nations.

8. They were, however, generally restless, and, like beasts of prey, were constantly looking out for some object upon which they might fall and devour it. So things went on, till at length these barbarians fixed their attention upon the rich cities, the fertile plains, and vine-clad hills of the south of Europe.

9. The Roman empire was now tottering to decay, and the Roman armies were no longer the dread of these tribes. About the year 400 they began to pour down their armies upon the plains of Italy. Alaric, king of the Goths, laid Rome under contribution, and less than fifty years after, Attila, king of the Huns, threatened the same city with destruction.

10. After this period, these restless invaders continued from time to time to attack the southern regions of Europe, till they made themselves masters of its finest portions.

Questions—3. What of their wars?   4. What did the state of these barbarians resemble? 5. What of them?   6. Which were the most remarkable of the northern tribes?   7. Describe their mode of life.   8. What at length attracted their attention?   9. What of the Roman empire?   When did the barbarians attack Italy?   What of Alaric and Attila?   10. What did the barbarians continue to do?

11. As the northern barbarians of whom I have been speaking had no books, and wrote no histories, their early story is little known. After getting possession of Rome, Spain, and other southern portions of Europe, they settled in these countries.

12. For a time, literature and learning, the arts of poetry, painting, sculpture, and music, which had been cultivated by the Romans, were unknown in the countries where they once flourished. But by degrees the new inhabitants became civilized and polished, and the modern nations which now occupy these regions may be considered as in part their descendants. It is now time to proceed with the history of France.

CHAPTER CIV—EUROPE—CONTINUED
The Gauls—Origin of the modern French Nation—Little King Pepin

1. THE ANCIENT NAME of France was Gaul, and the inhabitants were called Gauls. These were one of those warlike tribes of which I have just been speaking. At a very early date, they appear to have been numerous and powerful. In the year 390 B.C., they invaded Rome under Brennus, and took that city, but were expelled by Camillus.

2. Under another Brennus, they invaded Greece, as I have told you. In the time of Julius Caesar, the Gauls had made some little progress toward civilization; but they were still a barbarous people, and retained many practices that belong only to savages. The had, however, a good many cities, and these were defended with strong walls.

3. When Caesar entered the country, he found the Gauls sorely pressed by some of the German tribes. At first, he affected to be the deliverer of the Gauls from these troublesome enemies.

4. But the people soon discovered that Caesar's real design was to conquer them. They then began to resist, and for nine long years they fought Caesar and his armies with admirable skill and spirit. But the Romans were better versed in the art of war than the Gauls. Their soldiers were better trained, and their implements of war were superior to those of the Gauls.

Questions—11. Where did the northern barbarians settle? 12. What of them for a time? What happened at length? What of the modern nations of the south of Europe?
CHAP. CIV—1. What was the ancient name of France? Of the people? What did they do under Brennus? 2. When did they invade Greece? What of them in the time of Julius Caesar? What of their cities? 3. What did Caesar find on entering the country? 4. What did the people soon discover? What did they do? What of the Romans?

5. Notwithstanding all this, so brave and obstinate were the Gauls in the defense of their country, that it required all the genius of Julius Caesar, one of the greatest leaders that ever lived, aided by the immense power of Rome, to subdue them.

6. Caesar was occupied no less than nine years in conquering the Gauls, and it is supposed a million of men were slain in the bloody struggle. From the time of Caesar's conquest, about 50 years B.C., Gaul was a Roman province, and the people gradually adopted the manners and customs of the Romans. Even their language became changed, and assumed a resemblance to the Latin. But between the fourth and fifth century, the Franks, a German tribe whom I have mentioned, got possession of the greater part of Gaul.

7. It is said that the Franks who first established themselves in Gaul were led by Pharamond. He died in 428, and was succeeded by his son Clodion, who was celebrated for the beauty of his hair. Clodion died in 448, and was succeeded by Meroveus; Meroveus died in 458, and was succeeded by Childeric. Very little is known of these kings, except the last.

CHAPTER CV—EUROPE—Continued
About Clovis and Little King Pepin

1. Childeric is considered the founder of the French monarchy. He was succeeded by his son Clovis. When Clovis was only nineteen years old, he drove the Romans out of France. He afterward gained a great victory over the Germans.

2. As Clovis had married a Christian princess, he attributed his success to the God whom she worshipped. He therefore determined to become a Christian himself, and he was baptized, with three thousand of his subjects, on Christmas-day, in the year 496. After the death of Clovis, France was divided among several petty kings. They quarrelled among themselves, and caused great trouble to the nation. The wife of one of them was accused of murdering ten kings, or children of kings.

Questions—5. What of the Gauls? What was required to subdue them? 6. What was the consequence of this struggle between the Gauls and Romans? What of Gaul from this time? What of the Franks? 7. Pharamond? Clodion? Meroveus? What of these kings?

Chap. CV—1. Who was Childeric? What of Clovis? 2. Why did Clovis determine to be a Christian? When was he baptized? What of France after his death? What of the kings?

3. Little king Pepin, otherwise called Pepin the Short, thrust all the other kings from their thrones, and made himself sole ruler of France. He was a very small man, being only four feet and a half high; but he had a mighty spirit in that little body.

4. Moreover, he had an enormous deal of strength. Knowing that some of his courtiers made fun of his little size, he resolved to show them, that there was as much manhood in him as there could possibly be in a giant. He therefore invited them to see a fight between a lion and a bull.

5. The lion gave a tremendous roar, and leaped upon the bull's back, sticking his claws deep into the flesh. The bull also roared with pain and terror, as well he might. Then little king Pepin stood on tiptoe on his throne, to make himself as tall as he could; and he roared out to his courtiers, full as loud as either the bull or the lion:—

6. "Which of you all," cried he, "will make that lion let go his hold?" The courtiers all stood silent and abashed; for they had no notion of venturing within reach of the lion's claws. "Then I'll do it myself!" said king Pepin the Short. So the valiant little king leaped down from his throne, and drew a sword almost as long as himself. Brandishing it in the air, he ran up to the lion, who was still clinging to the mad bull's back.

7. When the lion beheld this terrible small champion, he opened his enormous jaws, as if he meant to snap him up at a single mouthful. But little king Pepin aimed a blow at him with his sword, and hit him fair upon the neck.

8. Down fell the lion's head on one side of the bull, and down fell his body on the other! And from that time forward, the courtiers would sooner have taken a roaring lion by the mane, than have laughed at little king Pepin.

CHAPTER CVI—EUROPE—Continued
The Reign of Charlemagne

1. KING PEPIN THE LITTLE had a son who was called Charlemagne, or Charles the Great. The epithet was given him because he was a mighty king and conqueror, but he also deserved it on account of his height, which was not an inch less than seven feet.

2. Charlemagne used to wear a sheep-skin cloak. Whenever he saw his

---

Questions—3–4. Describe little king Pepin.   What did he invite his people to see?   5–7. Relate king Pepin's encounter with the lion.   8. How did his bravery affect his courtiers? Chap. CVI—1. Who was Charlemagne?

courtiers richly dressed, he invited them to go a-hunting with him. Charlemagne took care to lead the way through all the thorns and bushes he could find, on purpose that his courtiers might tear their fine clothes in following him.

3. This king was continually at war. He subjugated the Saxons, and other tribes who lived in Germany. He likewise made conquests in Spain and Italy. At length, ruling over France, Germany, and other countries, he wished for the title of Emperor of the West.

4. Accordingly, he went to Rome, and knelt down at the high altar of the church as if to say his prayers. There was a large congregation in the church, and they were much edified by the devout behavior of Charlemagne. But while he was kneeling, the pope stole softly behind him, and placed the imperial crown upon his head.

5. This was the crown which all the old emperors of Rome had worn, and when the people beheld it on the head of Charlemagne, they shouted, "Long live the emperor!" Charlemagne pretended to be surprised and angry; but he took care to keep the imperial crown upon his head.

6. Charlemagne died in the year 814, when he was quite an old man. While he was alive, as I have mentioned, he wore a sheep-skin cloak. But after he was dead his attendants dressed him in robes of imperial purple.

7. They placed a throne of gold in his sepulcher, and set the dead body of the gray-bearded old emperor upon it. A sword was girded about his waist. He had a golden crown upon his head, a golden scepter and shield at his feet, a golden chalice in his hand, and a Bible upon his knee.

8. Over the sepulcher there was a magnificent triumphal arch, with an inscription to the memory of the mighty Charlemagne. And having wasted all this splendor upon the senseless corpse, the attendants shut up the tomb, and went to pay their court to Charlemagne's successor.

9. This was his son, entitled Louis the Mild. I know not wherefore he was called the mild, for one of the acts of his reign was to put out the eyes of another king whom he had taken prisoner. When Louis died, he left his dominions to his three sons. They immediately went to war with each other. It is said that a hundred thousand men were slain in one of their battles.

10. Some of the succeeding kings of France were Charles the Bald,

---

Questions—2. What of his dress? That of his courtiers? 3. What of Charlemagne? Over what countries did he reign? What did he wish? 4–5. What did he do? Describe his coronation. 6. When did Charlemagne die? How was his body dressed for his burial? 8. What was put over the sepulcher? 9. Who was Louis the Mild? What of him? What of his three sons?

Louis the Stammerer, Charles the Fat, Charles the Simple, Louis the Foreigner, and Hugh Capet. These sovereigns performed no actions that need to be recorded in my book.

CHAPTER CVII—EUROPE—CONTINUED
About the Crusades or Holy Wars

1. I MUST NOW GIVE you some account of the Crusades or Holy Wars, undertaken by the European nations for the recovery of Jerusalem, which was in the hands of the Turks. The Christians had a great reverence for this city, for here Christ preached, here he performed many miracles, here he was crucified, and here he rose from the dead.

2. On account of the pious reverence entertained for what they called the Holy City, many Christian pilgrims went on foot to visit it. It was very common for the Roman Catholic priests to impose this pilgrimage on persons who had committed some sin, as an atonement for the scandal they had caused, or the wrongs they had done, by their offences.

3. Now the pilgrims to Jerusalem were often treated with cruelty and scorn by the Turks, who held possession of Jerusalem and the country around it. The pilgrims returned to Europe and gave an account of the treatment they received. This excited the indignation of the Christians, and they were easily induced to unite in a great effort for taking the Holy Land from the infidel Turks.

4. The pope of Rome at this time greatly feared that the Mahometans would subjugate all Europe, and therefore gave the project all his influence. He also wished to place a Christian king over Palestine, should the country be taken.

5. Peter the Hermit was the principal agent in exciting the people to the first crusade. He was a half-starved monk, and went about bareheaded, with a rope round his waist, and wearing a garment of coarse cloth. This was so short that it barely covered his body, leaving his arms and legs naked.

6. It might seem that such a scarecrow as this would rather have excited ridicule than reverence. But Peter had been in Palestine, and had

---

Questions—10. Who were some of the succeeding kings of France?

CHAP. CVII—1. What were the crusades? Why were they undertaken? Why did the Christians reverence Jerusalem? 2. What of pilgrimages to Jerusalem? 3. How were the pilgrims treated? What did they do? What was the consequence of their representations? 4. What of the pope of Rome? 5. Describe Peter the Hermit.

experienced the insults of the Turks. He, therefore, spoke of things he had seen, and the people listened with a willing sympathy.

7. Thus Peter went from city to city, and everywhere crowds came to hear him. There was soon such a state of excitement, that the princes assembled, and armies were speedily gathered for the enterprise. Thus in the year 1096, Peter set out with two hundred thousand men at his heels. He carried a ponderous cross upon his shoulders, and his followers wore crosses of red cloth sewed upon their clothes.

8. But scarcely had his army landed in Asia, when sultan Solyman attacked them, and made a terrible slaughter. As a trophy of his victory over the poor wretches, he built a pyramid of their bones. Other armies of crusaders met with similar misfortunes.

9. It is computed that eight hundred and fifty thousand Christians lost their lives in the course of the first crusade. And all this slaughter took place before they had even come in sight of Jerusalem.

10. There was another army, however, belonging to the first crusade, that had better success. This consisted of eighty thousand men, and was led by a French prince called Godfrey of Bouillon [boo´-yong]. He proceeded through Asia Minor, took several cities, and captured Jerusalem in 1099. From this period till the year 1187, the Holy City remained in the hands of the Christians, when it was again captured by the Turks, in whose hands it has since remained.

11. No less than five other crusades took place; the last being commenced in 1248. This, with most of the others, proved unsuccessful. The whole number of men who lost their lives in these wild expeditions was not less than two million.

12. It appears that many of the crusaders were good men, and some, perhaps, were wise ones. Several of the leaders were brave knights, and they went forth clad in bright steel armor, and mounted upon fine horses. But a large portion of the armies were of a different character. Some were half-crazy people, filled with religious zeal, and a larger portion were thieves and robbers, who joined the expeditions that they might join in the plun-

---

Questions—6. What of him?   7. What effect had his preaching?   What took place in 1096?   8. Who attacked the army in Asia?   What did the sultan do?   What of other crusaders?   9. What of the first crusade?   10. What of the army under Godfrey Bouillon? What city did he take?   When did the Turks retake Jerusalem?   11. How many crusades were there?   When was the first crusade begun?   The last?   How many men lost their lives in the crusades?   12. What appears concerning many of the crusaders?   Their leaders?   What of a large portion of the armies?

der of cities that should be taken.

13. But although the motives of many of the crusaders were selfish, though the great object of these expeditions was not very important, and though much slaughter and bloodshed flowed from them; still the half-barbarous inhabitants of Europe brought from the East many arts that tended to refine and civilize the people. In this, and other ways, the crusades produced some good results.

CHAPTER CVIII—EUROPE—CONTINUED
About the Feudal System

1. I SUPPOSE YOU THINK it is now time to proceed with the history of France; but do not be impatient. It is not right for one who undertakes to tell the history of mankind, to speak only of kings and the great battles which they fight. We must not forget to consider how the people lived, and what they were about while their rulers were thus engaged.

2. If I were only to speak of little king Pepin and Charlemagne, and the popes and other rulers, and tell you what they did, you might still be ignorant of what their subjects were doing. You might not know whether they were happy or unhappy, whether they were in a state of poverty, whether they were in the enjoyment of freedom, or suffering the miseries of despotism.

3. I trust you will therefore excuse me for talking a little about the Feudal System, Chivalry, and a few other big words, which it is proper you should understand. I have told you that the northern tribes of Europe were fond of war, and were of a restless, roving character. War was indeed the chief business of the men. A few of them were engaged in agriculture; but a large portion of them led the lives of soldiers, either wholly, or at such times as their services were required.

4. A few were devoted to the building of houses, to the manufacture of armor, and such other articles as the simple manners of the people rendered necessary. But even these artisans occasionally bore arms and went with their countrymen to the field of battle if they were needed.

5. But, as I have said before, the great business of society in these time was war; either for defense against the attacks of other tribes, or for the purpose of conquering other tribes. The chiefs, or leaders, were generally

---

Questions—13. What good results did the crusades produce?

CHAP. CVIII—1. What must not be forgotten? 2. Why must the history of the people not be neglected? 3. What of the northern tribes of Europe? What of the men?

the bravest and strongest men, those who would be most likely in a battle of hard blows to insure some victory.

6. When a country was conquered, the lands, towns, cities, gold, silver, merchandise, horses, cattle, and all other property belonging to the conquered people, were considered the spoils of the victors. The people who were defeated, were either killed, driven away, or reduced to a state of servitude.

7. Strange as it may seem, this making of war and robbing people of their lands and possessions, was not only considered lawful, but it was reckoned grand sport. It is true, that the soldiers had often hard fare and hard knocks; occasionally they were wounded, and many of them were slain. But when the battle was over, those who survived celebrated their victory with feasting and drinking, and other amusements suited to the tastes of barbarous men.

8. Between the intervals of fighting, they had mimic battles among themselves, or two stout fellows would fight with swords in the presence of the whole people. At other times, during a wet day, or a dull night, they would prolong their festivities by telling stories of the great deeds they had done, or seen, or heard of, or by singing ballads of bloodshed and battle.

9. It frequently happened that some person in the camp had a great talent for singing and story-telling; he therefore would be often called upon to exercise his gift. So he would amuse the company with wild legends of the chase, in which a king or prince had a terrible battle with a fierce boar or a rough bear.

10. Or he would tell of some chief who had performed wonderful deeds, or perhaps he would weave some superstitious tale of ghosts that walked abroad by moonlight, or of some murdered prince whose spirit often came at night to haunt the castle where he once dwelt.

11. Such were some of the amusements which repaid these barbarians for the toils of war. But these were by no means all. The real object of most of the wars among these people was plunder. War took the place of trade and commerce among them, and the principal inducement to carry it on was to obtain the lands and the goods of other nations. It was, in short, a system of plunder, and the several tribes might be considered as so many

---

Questions—5. What was the great business of society in these times? What of the chiefs? 6. What of a conquered country? The people? 7. How were war and robbery considered? The soldiers? The survivors? 8. What was done in the intervals of fighting? 9–10. What of story-telling? 11. What was the real object of war among these ancient nations? What of war?

bands of robbers.

12. When a country was conquered, the spoils were distributed among the victors according to their rank. The king, or chief, had a large share, the inferior chiefs had a smaller share, and the common soldiers had still less. The lands were divided in this way; but it was always understood, that those who received the land were afterward bound to go and fight whenever called upon by their chiefs.

13. The lands were not held in those times as they are now among us; each individual did not own a piece of land and built upon it, or cultivate it as he liked. But a large tract might belong to the king, and a smaller tract might belong to the inferior chiefs or barons.

14. The king or baron built upon his land an immense strong castle of stone; around it, the people, who were called his vassals or slaves, built their little huts. These tilled the land, taking what was necessary for their own support, but giving the best of every thing to their liege lord.

15. Now what is meant by the Feudal System is this; that the vassals of a baron who lived upon his land were bound to do military service whenever the baron required it. So also the barons, under the Feudal System, were required to do military service, bringing into the field all the men they could muster, whenever their king required it.

16. In return for these services, the lord of the manor, or owner of the land, was expected to protect his people in time of war; and as the castle was usually large and strong, the people fled to it whenever an enemy appeared in sight.

17. Here in the castle they would make the best defense in their power. Sometimes they would be besieged for months; but so long as the wines lasted, and the stores of provisions held out, the besieged inmates of the castle would hold their revels, tell their stories, and sing their songs.

CHAPTER CIX—EUROPE—Continued
About Chivalry, or Knight-Errantry

1. I HOPE YOU now understand how matters and things went on among the rude tribes of France, Germany, and most other northern countries of Europe, in early times. I hope also you understand what is meant by the

---

Questions—12. What of the division of spoils? What of lands? 13. How were the lands held in those times? 14. What of a king or baron? The people or vassals? 15. What was the Feudal System? What were the vassals and barons required to do? 16. What was expected of the lord of the manor? 17. What of a besieged castle?

Feudal System.

2. If you will reflect a moment you will perceive that Europe at this time was divided among a great number of warlike tribes or nations; each tribe having a king, each king having under him several powerful barons, and each baron having a good many vassals.

3. You will remember, that the kings and barons dwelt in strong stone castles, and if you should ever go to Europe, you will see many of these still in existence, some of which were built more than a thousand years ago. Most of them are in ruins, but they are interesting on account of the tales and legends of the olden times which are connected with them.

4. It is not certain when the Feudal System commenced, but it appears to have been first in use among the German tribes, and was introduced into France by the Franks, who entered that country 420 A.D., and who laid the foundation of the French monarchy, about 486 years after Christ. It continued in full force in the time of Charlemagne, and, for some centuries after, it formed the basis of all the political systems of Europe.

5. Now I must tell you, that among the rough kings and barons of the feudal times, it often happened that private acts of violence and injustice took place. Sometimes a powerful baron would come suddenly upon a weaker one, seize his castle, and either murder him or shut him up in a dungeon. Sometimes one of these barons would carry off the beautiful daughter of another king or baron, and take her home to his castle.

6. Even in these rude times, such things were considered wrong, and sometimes a brave warrior, called a Knight, would take it upon himself to redress these grievances. He would perhaps go and challenge the baron, who had been guilty of injustice, to come out and fight with him, or in some other way would endeavor to repair the injury done.

7. The people applauded these knights, and cheered them on to acts of daring, in the cause of justice and benevolence. Thus, by degrees, their numbers increased, and about the time of the crusades, there appear to have been a great many of them.

8. The crusades themselves seemed to establish knight-errantry as a regular profession, and from the period 1100 after Christ, we may consider

Questions—CHAP. CIX—2. What can you say of Europe in feudal times? 3. What must you remember? 4. What of the Feudal System? Who introduced it into France? When? When was the foundation of the French monarchy laid? How long did the Feudal System continue? Of what did it form the basis? 5. What happened in feudal times? 6. How were such things considered? What would a knight sometimes do? 7. What of the people? Knights? 8. What of the crusades? When did knight-errantry become a regular profession?

214

it as one of the most remarkable institutions in Europe.

9. When knight-errantry, or chivalry, had become thus established, those who belonged to the profession were considered as under a religious vow to devote themselves to the cause of justice and humanity. If any person had suffered an act of injustice, they considered themselves bound to set the matter right. If any person was in distress, they were under obligation to peril their lives for his relief.

10. Besides this, the knights were required always to tell the truth, and always to perform their promises; they were expected to be full of generosity and courage, and never to be guilty of any act of meanness. They were, in short, expected to devote themselves to the cause of humanity, and remedy, as far as in their power, the injustice and violence which belonged to the age in which they lived.

11. Many of these knights spent their whole time in riding about the country in search of adventures. These were called knights-errant. If, in the course of their travels, they heard of any body in distress, they would offer their services for relief.

12. They were particularly devoted to the cause of ladies who had been stolen away, and shut up in castles. In behalf of these, they often performed wonderful feats of strength and valor. Sometimes, it is true, the knights acted wickedly, but in so doing they violated their vows.

CHAPTER CX—EUROPE—Continued
More About Chivalry

1. IF ONE KNIGHT-ERRANT chanced to meet another, they usually went to fighting, either for sport or renown. Some of them acquired great fame, and a multitude of songs and ballads were composed in celebration of their deeds.

2. The knights were very particular to ride fine, strong horses. Some of these are almost as famous in the legends of chivalry as their riders. The knight was powerfully armed, his chief weapon being a long-pointed lance. Beside this, he had a sword, dagger, battle-axe, and mace, which was a heavy sort of club.

Questions—9. What of those who belonged to the profession? 10. What was required and expected of the knights? 11. Who were knight-errants? 12. What did they perform for ladies?

CHAP. CX—1. What happened if two knight-errants met? What was done in celebration of their deeds? 2. What of their horses? How was the knight armed?

3. In addition to these weapons for attack, he had a defensive armor, consisting of a shield of metal, a helmet of steel, with a vizor to cover his face, a body-harness made of plates of steel, and sometimes a shirt of mail, consisting of a multitude of iron links, the whole fitting close to the body. Over all this, the knight wore a long flowing robe, which came down to his heels.

4. The horse also was carefully defended by mail or steel plates. His head, chest, and sides were usually covered, and sometimes the whole body was shielded by glittering steel. Nothing indeed could exceed the care and preparation usually bestowed by the knights in training their horses, in selecting their armor, in having it carefully fitted, and in keeping it bright.

5. They were also very attentive to their daily exercise, as well to preserve their health and acquire strength, as to keep themselves in perfect practice.

6. A knight was always attended by a squire, and sometimes by several squires. These attended upon their masters, and were considered as learning to become knights themselves. As the institution of chivalry advanced it became a matter of honor to be a knight; and therefore most kings, princes, and military leaders took upon themselves the vows of knighthood. The celebrated leaders of the crusades, Richard of England, Godfrey of France, and others, were knights.

7. In after times there were several orders of knights; those of each order taking upon themselves peculiar vows. Such were the Knights of St. John of Jerusalem, the Knights of the Cross, Knights Templars, etc.

8. When society had become somewhat more civilized, it was the custom in different parts of Europe to have tilts and tournaments. These were occasions of great ceremony, and multitudes of people collected together to witness them. They were often splendid beyond description. Kings, princes, and fair ladies delighted in these exhibitions.

9. They consisted of encounters between celebrated knights, clad in complete armor. They took place in some open plain, surrounded with tents and pavilions filled with spectators. The victorious knights were honored with applause from the people, and with marks of favor even from kings and queens.

10. Such was the institution of chivalry. If I had time I could fill a book

---

Questions—4. What of their horse's caparison?   Knight's armor?   5. What of exercise? 6. What of squires?   How was the profession of knighthood considered?   Who were some celebrated knights in the crusades?   7. What can you say of orders of knights?   8. What of tilts and tournaments?   9. Describe them.   What of the knights?

with stories of knights. A multitude of tales called romances were written in the age of chivalry. These recounted the deeds, or pretended deeds of celebrated champions. Some of them are very amusing, but they are nearly all filled with incredible fables.

11. Chivalry was at its height from the year 1200 to about 1400. From this latter period it rapidly declined, and in the time of Elizabeth of England, that is about 1600, it had ceased. If there were a few tilts and tournaments after this, they were only as relics of an age that had passed.

12. Thus have I told you about the Feudal System, the Crusades, and Chivalry; and I have told you of these things in connection with the history of France, because the people of that country were largely concerned in all these matters.

CHAPTER CXI—EUROPE—Continued
King Philip and Pope Boniface—Wars of the French and English

1. I WILL NOW GO on with my story about France. After Charles the Fat, Hugh Capet, and the other kings I have mentioned, there were many sovereigns, but I shall pass them over and come to Philip the Fair, who began to reign in 1285. He possessed great personal beauty, but had many bad qualities of mind and heart. The most remarkable event of his reign was a great quarrel with pope Boniface.

2. The pope thought the king was oppressing the clergy, and issued a bull excommunicating the king and commanding all the bishops of France to repair to Rome. Philip ordered the bull to be burned, and prohibited any of the bishops leaving the kingdom. He went himself, however, to Rome, and had the pope imprisoned, but as he had to leave Rome the pope got free.

3. He afterward imprisoned a number of knights templars, who had acquired great fortunes in the crusades, and whose vices and arrogance caused the order to be greatly detested. Philip, after a long imprisonment, caused these unfortunate men to be put to the most cruel tortures, and

---

Questions—10. What of romances? 11. When was chivalry at its height? What of it after 1600? When did it cease? 12. Why is the story of the Feudal System, Chivalry, etc., told in connection with the history of France?

CHAP. CXI—1. When did Philip the Fair begin to reign? What of him? 2. What of pope Boniface? What took place between him and Philip the Fair? 3. What of the king's treatment of knights templars who had returned from the crusades?

finally committed to the flames. But the same punishments were inflicted on them in other countries besides France.

4. The French have always been a warlike people. They have been so often at war with England, that Frenchmen and Englishmen used to think themselves born to be each other's enemies.

5. On the death of Charles the Fourth, in 1328, Philip of Valois became king of France. But Edward the Third, king of England, asserted that he himself was the rightful king of France, because his mother was the daughter of Philip the Fair. He undertook to enforce this claim by invading France with an English army.

6. King Edward challenged Philip of Valois to fight him in single combat; but Philip preferred to meet him with an army. At the bloody battle of Cressy, in France, in 1346, the French were defeated, with the loss of the bravest of their nobles, and thirty thousand men.

7. In 1350, John the Good, son of Philip of Valois, succeeded to the throne of France. The country was invaded by an English army under the eldest son of Edward the Third. He was called the Black Prince, on account of the color of his armor.

8. King John of France, with sixty thousand men, encountered the Black Prince of England, near Poictiers [poi-teerz]. The Black Prince had only eight thousand soldiers. But the English archers and cross-bow men let fly their arrows at the French, and made a dreadful havoc among them. King John was taken and kept prisoner four years in London.

9. John the Good was succeeded by his son Charles the Wise. King Edward of England had now grown old, and his son, the brave Black Prince, was dead. The French, therefore, got back all the territories which the English had won of them, except the town of Calais.

10. But when Charles the Well-beloved was king of France, the English renewed the war. Henry the Fifth, now king of England, invaded France. At the battle of Agincourt, he had but fifteen thousand men, while the French had nearly a hundred thousand.

11. Yet the English gained a glorious victory, with the loss of only forty

---

Questions—4. What of the French? How did the French and English consider themselves? 5. When did Charles IV die? When did Philip of Valois become king? What did Edward III claim? 6. What did king Edward do? What of the battle of Cressy? 7. Who became king in 1350? Who was the Black Prince? 8. Who encountered the Black Prince? Describe the battle of Poictiers? 9. Who succeeded John the Good? Why were the French able to win back their territories from the English? 10. Who was the next king of France? What battle was fought with Henry V?

men. On the side of the French there were seven princes, the high constable of France, and ten thousand gentlemen killed, besides many prisoners. In 1420, the English king entered Paris in triumph.

12. But Henry, king of England, died soon afterward; and then the French began to beat the English. The chief leader of the French at this time, was a girl of eighteen, named Joan of Arc, or the Maid of Orleans. She was very beautiful. The French believed that Heaven had sent her to rescue their country from the English invaders. The English believed her to be a witch, and that the Evil One assisted her in fighting against them.

13. For a considerable time it was found impossible to withstand holy Joan, the Maid of Orleans. She was clad in bright steel armor, and rode in front of the French army, on a snow-white horse. In her hand she carried a consecrated banner, on which was painted the image of our Saviour. But at last she was wounded and taken prisoner. The English condemned her to be burnt alive for witchcraft.

14. She was accordingly bound to a stake in the market-place of Rouen. The English army looked on, rejoicing, while the flames roared and whirled around her. When the fire had burned out, there remained nothing but ashes and whitened bones of the valiant Maid of Orleans.

CHAPTER CXII—EUROPE—Continued
The Reign of several French Kings

1. But though the Maid of Orleans was no longer their leader, the French were still successful. The English lost nearly all that Henry the Fifth had won. The French monarch was called Charles the Victorious, on account of his many triumphs.

2. Yet he was an unhappy king. His son hated him, and attempted to kill him by poison. After the discovery of this plot, the poor old king was afraid to take food enough to support life, lest he should take poison with it. So he wasted away, and died miserably.

3. His son Louis the Eleventh succeeded him in 1461. He was a crafty, treacherous, and cruel king. Once, when a nobleman was to be beheaded,

---

Questions—11. Which side won the victory? What was the loss of the French? What took place in 1420? 12. What happened after the death of Henry V? Describe the Maid of Orleans. What did the French and English think of her? 13. How did she appear at the head of the army? 14. What was her sad fate?

Chap. CXII—1. What of the French? The English? The French king? 2. What of Charles the Victorious? 3. What of Louis XI?

219

Louis ordered his infant children to be placed under the scaffold that they might be sprinkled with their father's blood!

4. One of the most famous of the French kings, was Francis the First, who ascended the throne in 1515. He fought against the Swiss, and against the emperor of Germany; but the emperor took him prisoner at the battle of Pavia, though he was soon released.

5. There was no war with England during the reign of Francis the First; but he once held an interview with the English king near Calais. So much magnificence was displayed on both sides, that the place of meeting was called the Field of the Cloth of Gold.

6. In 1560, Charles the Ninth became king of France. He was then a boy of ten years old. His reign was disgraced by one of the bloodiest scenes of history. It is called the Massacre of St. Bartholomew.

7. This bloody deed happened in consequence of a secret order of the king, to murder all the Protestants, and through which, from six to ten thousand are said to have been slain. This infamous decree was issued at the instigation of the king's mother, the notorious Catherine-de-Medicis.

8. The king himself sat at one of his palace windows, with a musket in his hand, and shot some of the poor wretches. But he was soon called to receive the recompense of his crimes. After the massacre he was afflicted with disease, and he died in 1574.

9. The next king but one was Henry the Fourth, who ascended the throne in 1589. He was a good king, a brave warrior, and a generous man. His subjects loved him, and the French have always been proud of Henry the Fourth.

10. Yet the affection of his people could not save his life. One day he was riding through the streets of Paris in his coach. Seven courtiers were with him. Other vehicles were in the way, so that the coachman was compelled to stop the horses. The king chose to alight.

11. There was a man near the coach, named Ravaillac. He was waiting for a chance to kill the king; and now, seeing him about to get out of the coach, he drew a poniard. All the power of France could not now be of any avail. The first blow of the poniard wounded the king, and the second killed him.

Questions—4. When did Francis I ascend the throne? What of him? 5. Describe the interview at Calais? 6. When did Charles IX come to the throne? 7. Describe the Massacre of St. Bartholomew. 8. When did Charles IX die? 9. When did Henry IV come to the throne? What of him? 11. How did he lose his life?

CHAPTER CXIII—EUROPE—Continued
The Reigns of Louis the Grand and his Successor

1. THE MURDERED HENRY was succeeded by his son, Louis the Thirteenth. The government was chiefly directed by Cardinal Richelieu, an ambitious priest. He grew more powerful than the king himself.

2. The next king was Louis the Fourteenth, whom the French call Louis the Grand. He was a very proud and haughty monarch. He endeavored to make France the greatest country on earth; not that he really cared for the welfare of his subjects, but because he wished to exalt himself above all other things.

3. He had a peculiar manner of walking, which would have been ridiculous in a common man, but it was thought extremely majestic in a king. He used to wear a large curled wig, and nobody ever saw him without it. He would never pull off his wig till he had got into bed and closed the curtains.

4. This king began to reign at five years old, and reigned no less than seventy-two years. He was continually at war. In the early part of his reign his armies achieved many splendid victories.

5. But, in the king's old age, the English duke of Marlborough wasted his troops, and reduced his kingdom to great distress. The French people now grew weary of their grand monarch.

6. And well they might be weary of him, for he had taken all their money, in order that he might have the means of going to war. He seemed to think it more necessary that he should have glory than that they should have bread.

7. At last, in 1715, the old king died. As he had been so grand in his lifetime, his courtiers deemed it proper that he should carry as much grandeur with him to the tomb as possible. They therefore prepared a magnificent funeral.

8. But wherever the procession passed, the people heaped curses on the royal corpse. They hissed so loudly, that, if the king had not been stone dead, he would have started up in his coffin. Thus ended the glorious reign of Louis the Grand.

9. All the sons and grandsons of old Louis the Grand had died before

---

Questions—CHAP. CXIII—1. Who succeeded Henry IV? What of Cardinal Richelieu? 2. Who was the next king? What can you say of Louis the Grand? 4. What of his wars? 5. What of the duke of Marlborough? 6. What of the French people? 7. When did Louis the Grand die? 8. Describe the funeral. 9. Who succeeded Louis XIV?

him. He was therefore succeeded by his great-grandson, a child of five years old, who now became Louis the Fifteenth.

10. Until the little king should become of age to take the scepter into his own hands, the duke of Orleans was declared regent of France. He was a profligate man. Instead of teaching the young king how to make his subjects prosperous and happy, he set him an example of all sorts of wickedness.

11. And Louis the Fifteenth turned out just such a king as might have been expected. In his whole reign of fifty-nine years he seems to have thought of nothing but his own selfish pleasures.

12. His kingdom was almost ruined and his subjects were starving. But if an earthquake had swallowed France and all its inhabitants, the king would hardly have cared. The reign of this odious monarch prepared the French to hate the very name of monarchy. He died in 1774, and was succeeded by his grandson, Louis the Sixteenth, who was then a young man of twenty.

13. Thus, by the extravagance of Louis the Fourteenth, and the profligacy of Louis the Fifteenth, a foundation was laid for what is called the French revolution, of which I shall tell you in the next chapter.

14. I should be very glad to pass by the story of that awful period, for I know it can give my reader no pleasure to read of violence and bloodshed. But it is necessary to know the dark as well as the bright pages of history.

15. We may learn from the French revolution how much evil may be brought upon a country by bad rulers, and as some of my young pupils will hereafter be men, and be called upon to assist in choosing rulers, they may be made to feel the duty of choosing good ones.

CHAPTER CXIV—EUROPE—CONTINUED
The French Revolution

1. LOUIS THE SIXTEENTH had no talents which could render him fit to govern a nation. But he was a man of good heart, kind disposition, and upright intentions. With all his defects, there has seldom been a better king; for, if he was unable to do good, he was unwilling to do harm.

2. The king was married to an Austrian archduchess, named Marie Antoinette. She had great beauty and accomplishments; but she was never a favorite of the French people.

Questions—10. What of the duke of Orleans?   11. What of Louis XV?   12. When did he die?   14–15. What of the French revolution?
CHAP. CXIV—1. What of Louis XVI?   2. What of Marie Antoinette?

3. Not long after this king and queen were crowned, A.D. 1775, the American revolution broke out. The United States declared themselves a free and independent republic. The people of France took a great interest in the affairs of America; and they began to think that a republic was a better kind of government than a monarchy.

4. They compared the tyranny under which they and their forefathers had groaned for ages, with the freedom which made the Americans so prosperous and happy. The more they reflected upon the subject, the more discontented they became with their own condition.

5. The French are a people whose minds are easily excited, and whenever any thing remarkable is going on among them, you would think that the whole nation was almost mad, or perhaps had been drinking too much wine. So it happened in this case. They now began to rave against the king, queen, and nobles, the priests, the gentlemen, and all others whom they formerly respected. They even blasphemed against Heaven itself.

6. In 1789, the mob of Paris tore down the Bastile. This was an old castle where the kings of France had been accustomed to confine such of their subjects as offended them. Many a poor wretch had been thrown into the dungeons of the Bastile, and never again beheld the sunshine.

7. The destruction of the Bastile was a good thing; and so likewise were many other of the first movements of the French revolution. But when the people had once begun to change their ancient government they knew not where to stop.

8. It was not long before blood began to flow. No man nor woman in the kingdom was now safe, unless they wore a red cap upon their heads, which was called the Cap of Liberty.

9. At this period it was no uncommon thing to see a mob of men and women in the streets of Paris, carrying a bloody head upon a pole. and those who looked at the features would perhaps recognize the countenance of some great nobleman or beautiful princess.

10. In a little while longer there were so many heads to be cut off that the work could not be done fast enough in the ordinary way. It was therefore necessary to do it by machinery; and a horrible instrument, called the guillotine, was invented for the purpose.

Questions—3. When did the American revolution begin? 4. What of the French people? 5. How do the French appear when any thing remarkable is going on? 6. What was done in 1789? What of the Bastile? 7. What of the destruction of this old castle? 8. What were people obliged to wear upon their heads? 9. What was common in Paris at this time? 10. Why was the guillotine invented?

11. This infernal contrivance was set to work upon the proud nobles, and the holy priesthood, and the beautiful ladies of France. Hundreds of their heads fell upon the pavement of Paris, and their blood ran like a river through the streets.

12. When many of the loftiest heads in the kingdom had been cut off, the people fixed their eyes on the head that wore a crown. "Off with the king's head too!" cried they. So they dragged the poor, harmless king before the National Convention, and he was forthwith sentenced to the guillotine.

13. As the poor king mounted the steps of the scaffold, he gazed around at the fierce and cruel multitude. It seemed all like a dream, that they, his born subjects, should be willing there to see him die. Then he looked at the guillotine, and beheld it stained with the blood of the thousand victims who had been dragged thither before him.

14. He could not yet believe but that his royal blood was precious to his people. He lingered—he was loth to lay down his head—he shivered with the agony of his spirit. There stood a holy priest beside him on the scaffold.

15. He whispered consolation to the unhappy king, and pointed heavenward. The victim mustered his fainting courage, and laid his head upon the block. "Son of Saint Louis," said the priest, "ascend to heaven!"

16. Down came the axe of the guillotine, and the head that had worn a crown was severed from the body! The blood of a kingly race gushed out upon the scaffold. Thus the crimes and misused power of many kings had brought vengeance on their innocent descendant.

CHAPTER CXV—EUROPE—Continued
The Rise of Napoleon Bonaparte

1. THE DAY OF THE KING'S execution was the 21st of January, 1793. Not many months afterward, the beautiful queen, Marie Antoinette, was likewise beheaded. France was now ruled by a succession of bloody monsters, who one day were sending crowds to the guillotine, and the next day were sent thither themselves. This anarchy was what the French called a Republic, but others called it the Reign of Terror.

2. In the mean time, war was breaking out on all sides. Austria, Prussia, England, Holland, Spain, and Russia sent armies against France. The French raised a million of men, and bade defiance to all Europe.

Questions—11. What use was made of it?   13–16. Describe the execution of Louis XVI.

CHAP. CXV—1. When was Louis XVI beheaded?   Describe the French republic.   2. What countries now went to war with France?

NAPOLEON

3. In the French army there was a young lieutenant of artillery, named Napoleon Bonaparte. When the war began he was an unknown and friendless youth. But he distinguished himself in every battle and every siege, till, in a very few years, the whole world had heard of Napoleon Bonaparte.

4. When he was only twenty-six years old he conquered Italy. The next year he compelled the emperor of Austria to make peace. In 1798 he invaded Egypt, and fought many battles in the sandy deserts and among the pyramids.

5. The French were now tired of being governed by men whose only engine of government was the guillotine. They wanted a ruler who would deserve their obedience by his sagacity and energy, and not merely compel them to obedience by the fear of having their heads cut off.

6. Napoleon Bonaparte was such a man. He was not a good man, nor a truly wise one. He was a selfish and ambitious despot. But perhaps he was a more suitable ruler for such a people as the French than if he had been a different man.

7. He saw that the French were now so excited that it would be difficult, perhaps impossible, to restrain them. He thought it better that they should make war on foreigners than slaughter each other, and with the sword rather than the guillotine. So, partly because he could not help it, but chiefly because he was ambitious, Napoleon Bonaparte became a mighty conqueror.

Questions—3. What of Napoleon Bonaparte? 4. What acts did Napoleon perform? 5. What of the French people at this time? 6. What of Napoleon? 7. What were his thoughts upon the French? What did he become?

CHAPTER CXVI—EUROPE—Continued
The Fall of Bonaparte

1. In 1802, Bonaparte was elected Consul of the French republic for life. Two years afterward he was proclaimed Emperor, by the name of Napoleon. He had now more power than any of the ancient kings.

2. I cannot follow this great general in his marches all over Europe, nor even number the victories which he won. Wherever he went, monarchs humbled themselves before him. He drove them from their thrones, and placed his own brothers and chief officers there instead. He gave away royal diadems like playthings. He was called the Man of Destiny, because fate seemed to have ordained that he should always be victorious.

3. But in 1812 the spell of his success began to be broken. He invaded Russia with a vast army, and penetrated to the city of Moscow. The Russians set the city on fire. Winter was coming on, and the French soldiers had nowhere to shelter themselves.

4. They retreated toward Poland. On their way thither, they fought many battles with the Russians, and the weather was so bitter cold that the bodies of the slain were frozen stiff. The snow was crimsoned with their blood.

5. Before they reached the frontiers of Poland, three-fourths of the army were destroyed. The emperor Napoleon fled homeward in a sledge, and returned to Paris. He soon raised new armies, and was ready to take the field again.

6. But all the nations of Europe were now allied against him, and, after a few more battles, he was driven from Germany into France. The enemy followed him. They compelled him to surrender the imperial crown of France in exchange for the sovereignty of the little island of Elba in the Mediterranean.

7. Napoleon went to Elba, and remained there almost a year. But in March, 1815, he suddenly landed again on the French coast. He was almost alone when he set foot on the shore. But there were a multitude of his grim old veterans throughout the country. These shouted for joy, and trampled on the white flag of the Bourbon kings who had succeeded him. In a few days, Napoleon's banner again waved triumphant all over France.

Questions—Chap. CXVI—1. What were the titles of Napoleon? 2. What happened wherever he went? What was he called? 3. What happened in 1812? 4. What of the French army? 5. What of Napoleon? 6. What happened to him? 7. How long did Napoleon remain at Elba? What of him in 1815? Describe his landing in France.

8. The nations of Europe now mustered their armies once more. They were led by the English Duke of Wellington. Napoleon marched into Flanders, or Belgium, to meet them. He was followed by almost every young Frenchman that could shoulder a musket.

9. The emperor Napoleon's last battle was fought at Waterloo, on the 18th of June, 1815. There he was utterly overthrown, and France was overthrown with him. The warlike emperor was sent to die on the Island of St. Helena, and the Bourbon king was again established on the throne of Louis the Sixteenth.

10. But a strange and interesting scene was witnessed nearly thirty years ago in France, relating to Napoleon. The French people did not like to think that the remains of Napoleon were far away upon the rock of St. Helena. So, in 1840, Louis Philippe, king of the French, sent his son in a national ship, and he brought the body of the late emperor back to France.

11. The people received the body with military honors, and many of Napoleon's old soldiers and officers rushed to the side of the coffin and wept over it as if he had been their father. With vast ceremony the body was taken to Paris, and there it is now interred, in the famous edifice called the Hotel of Invalids.

CHAPTER CXVII—EUROPE—Continued
Recent Affairs of France

1. Louis the Eighteenth, the new king of France, was a fat, quiet, respectable sort of old gentleman, and seems to have been chiefly distinguished for his love of oysters. He died in 1824, and was succeeded by his brother, Charles the Tenth.

2. It was said of all the Bourbon family that they had learnt nothing during their exile from France, nor forgotten any thing. And Charles soon proved that he had not forgotten that his ancestors had exercised absolute power, nor learnt that such power is very dangerous to possess or exercise.

3. In 1830, when Charles the Tenth had sat on the throne about six years, he forbade the printing of any newspapers, except such as praised his conduct and government.

Questions—8. Who led the nations of Europe against Napoleon? What did Napoleon do? Who followed him? 9. When was the battle of Waterloo fought? Fate of Napoleon? 10–11. What was witnessed in France in 1840?

Chap. CXVII—1. What of Louis XVIII? When did he die? 2. What was said of the Bourbon family? What did Charles X prove? 3. What took place in 1830?

4. The mob of Paris immediately rose and began a war against the royal troops. They beat out the brains of the king's soldiers with paving stones, and shot them from the windows of the houses. The old king, who had not forgotten the days of the revolution, began to tremble for his head.

5. In order to keep it on his shoulders, he took off his golden crown, and put it on the head of his grandson. But the French would not acknowledge the little fellow for their king. They raised large armies and drove Charles the Tenth and his family out of the kingdom.

6. They then asked the good and glorious La Fayette—the man who came and fought with our countrymen in the time of the Revolution—what sort of a government they should have. He would have chosen a republic like our own; but he knew that his countrymen were not like us.

7. He therefore told them that the government must be a limited monarchy, and that Louis Philippe, the Duke of Orleans, must be their king. Louis Philippe was accordingly raised to the throne.

8. He went on prosperously for a time, and was considered the most successful sovereign of the age. But in February, 1848, a revolution broke out in Paris, which extended over France.

9. In December, 1848, Louis Napoleon Bonaparte—a nephew of the emperor Napoleon—was elected President. He assumed the duties of the office immediately, thus becoming the first President of the New Republic of France.

10. In December, 1851, Louis Napoleon suppressed by violence the republic, and soon after was declared emperor, under the name of Napoleon III. The army, during his reign, was engaged in numerous wars—with the Romans, the Russians, the Austrians, the Mexicans, and finally with the Germans.

11. This last war came about in the following way. In 1870, Spain happened to be in want of a king, and proposed to take a Prussian prince. The French were exceedingly angry at this, for they were jealous of Prussia, and did not wish Spain to have a German king. So they said it should not be, and very soon they found themselves in a war with Prussia and her allies.

12. Little did they think what the end of this war would be. During the next six months Napoleon III was taken prisoner, and the Germans cap-

Questions—4. What of the mob of Paris? 5. What did the old king do? 6. What did the French ask La Fayette? 7. What did he tell them? Who was made king? 9. What happened in 1848? 10. In 1851? What of Napoleon III? His wars? 11. How did the Franco-Prussian war originate?

228

tured hundreds of thousands of men. They besieged Paris, took it, early in 1871, and marched through it. They then forced France to pay them one thousand millions of dollars damages, and to cede to Germany the territories of Alsace and Lorraine, containing one and a half millions of inhabitants.

13. France now became a republic, with Adolphe Thiers, a distinguished statesman, as President. He was soon succeeded, however, by Marshal MacMahon, a soldier, who was in his turn succeeded by Albert Grévy, a civilian. The country is now (1881) exceedingly prosperous. Napoleon III died in England in 1873.

CHAPTER CXVIII—EUROPE—Continued
About Germany

1. THE GERMAN EMPIRE is made of twenty-six different states, which united in 1871, as a consequence of the war with France. Prussia is the principal power in this confederation, and its king became the first emperor of Germany as William I.

2. The other principal states of Germany are Bavaria, Wurtemberg, Baden, and Saxony. The states of Germany are nearly all governed by kings, or grand dukes, or princes of some sort.

3. There are a great many large towns and cities in Germany. Among these are Hamburg, which forms one of the states of the empire, and carries on a good deal of commerce with this country; Munich, which is a very splendid city; Carlsruhe [karls 'roo], which has its streets arranged like the sticks of an open fan; Dresden, which is famous for the beautiful country around it, and Frankfort, which is encircled by a belt of fine gardens and public walks.

4. I could easily write a book about Germany, for it is full of curious and interesting things. In the cities there are a great many churches, in the Gothic style, which excite the wonder and admiration of a traveler, on account of their grandeur and the skill with which many parts of them are carved.

Questions—12. Its consequences? 13. What of recent changes in France?
CHAP. CXVIII—1. What of the German empire? Prussia? 2. Name some of the principal states. Their government? 3. Describe some of the principal cities of Germany. 4. What of churches?

CHAPTER CXIX—EUROPE—Continued
About the ancient Tribes of Germany, Charlemagne, etc.

1. In ancient days Germany, as I have told you, was inhabited by numerous tribes of barbarians. Among these were the Goths, Visigoths, Vandals, Suevi, Cimbri, Teutones, Heruli, Alemanni, and many others. As there was no Peter Parley among them to write their history in early times, we know little or nothing of them till two or three hundred years before Christ.

2. At this time they were numerous, but they were mere savages. They were clothed in the skins of wild beasts, and seemed to delight only in war and plunder. In the time of Caesar they were very powerful, but that famous conqueror marched against them, and, after many bloody battles, they were reduced to submission.

3. I have already told you that wherever the Romans extended their arms, they carried their arts. Thus the rude tribes of Germany became partially civilized; many of the people exchanged their skins of beasts for the Roman toga or gown. They also learnt how to make better weapons of war, how to build better houses, and how to live more comfortably.

4. But you remember that four or five hundred years after Caesar poor old Rome was tottering to decay. It was therefore unable to keep these restless tribes of the north in subjection; nay, Rome was now incapable even of defending herself.

5. The Germans soon discovered how matters stood. They saw that in Spain, Italy, and Greece, there were a great many rich cities, and pleasant towns, and fruitful valleys. They saw that in these countries the Romans had collected the wealth of the whole world, and these shrewd barbarians thought it would be a good speculation to go to these countries and live there.

6. They thought it would be much better to go and live in palaces and fine houses, and have a plenty of wine, and plenty of gold, silver, and jewels, than to live in their own less fruitful country, and earn their bread by toil, or by plundering each other.

7. Accordingly, some of them set out under their daring leaders, and marched into Italy. Others soon followed; and in the course of a few years

---

Questions—Chap. CXIX—1. How was Germany anciently inhabited? Mention some of the barbarian tribes. 2. What of them in ancient times? In the time of Caesar? 3. What of the arts of the Romans? How did the rude tribes become partly civilized? What did they do? 4. What of Rome several hundred years after Caesar? 5. What did the Germans soon discover? 6. What did they think?

these hordes had settled like swarms of bees in all the southern countries of Europe.

8. But still many remained behind in Germany, and these increased, so that in the time of Charlemagne they were numerous and powerful. But he conquered them, as I have said in the history of France. Thus, having made himself master of Germany, he became its emperor, and resided there. You will recollect that his empire included France, Germany, and many other countries.

9. The empire of Germany, thus established, was, however, composed of many separate sovereignties, each of which had its own ruler. In the year 912, it became the custom for these rulers to make choice of one of their number, and declare him emperor. He then presided over the whole of Germany. Thus Germany was what is called an Elective Monarchy, and so it continued, even so late as the year 1806.

10. Although the emperor was chief of the empire, supreme authority rested in the diet, which was composed of three colleges—the college of electors, the college of princes, and the college of imperial towns. The diet had the power of making peace or war, and regulating the important affairs of the empire; but their decisions had no effect without his consent.

11. The three principal religions are the Roman Catholic, the Lutheran, and the Calvinistic; but Christians of all denominations are tolerated on the same footing, and there are multitudes of Jews in all the cities and larger towns.

12. No people apply themselves more closely to their studies than the Germans. Every man of letters is an author, as no man can be a graduate of the university who has not published one disputation at least. This produces a multitude of books, and overstocks the book-shelves of Frankfort and Leipsic. The German language is a dialect of the Teutonic, which succeeded that called the Celtic.

13. In 1273, Rodolph of Hapsburg, a native of Switzerland, was elected emperor of Germany. He was the ancestor of the present sovereigns of Austria. Most of the German emperors, since his reign, have been his descendants.

Questions—7. What did some of them do?   What happened in a few years?   8. What of the barbarians that remained in Germany?   What of Charlemagne?   What did his empire include?   9. What of the sovereignties of Germany?   What was the custom in 912?   What of the emperor?   What was the government of Germany?   10. What of the diet?   Its power?   11. What of religion?   12. What of the German people in regard to letters?   The effect of this?   The German language?   13. Who was king of Germany in 1273?   What of him?

SCENE IN SWITZERLAND

CHAPTER CXX—EUROPE—Continued
Affairs of Switzerland

1. Until the year 1307, Switzerland was under the government of Germany. Switzerland, as you know, is a mountainous little country, which is hemmed in between Germany, France, and Italy.

2. As I have many kind wishes for my young readers, I hope it may be their pleasant fortune some day or other to visit Switzerland. When you go there you will find good roads, but I advise you to travel on foot. There are so many pleasant things to see; so many tall mountains looking like white clouds up in the sky; so many little blue lakes, seeming like mirrors, encircled with frames made of hills; so many bright green valleys; so many old ruinous castles; in short, so many interesting things to see, that you will be stopping every moment, and a carriage would therefore be a great trouble.

3. I have been over this country myself, and I went on foot. Switzerland seemed to me like a little world of itself. Every thing was strange, but still interesting. Among such wild mountains you would perhaps expect to meet with a wild and fierce people. Yet the Swiss are a gentle and honest race. I should like to visit the country again, but my old limbs will never more toil up and down those hills.

Questions—Chap. CXX—1. What of the government of Switzerland? Where is Switzerland? 2. Describe the appearance of the country there. 3. What of the people?

4. But I must now proceed with my brief account of the history of Switzerland. When Albert the First became emperor, in 1298, he acted like a tyrant toward Switzerland. He appointed governors, who were worse tyrants than himself. One of them, named Gesler, set his cap upon a pole, and ordered all the people to bow down to it.

5. The famous peasant, William Tell, would not bow down to Gesler's cap. My readers have heard the story, how Gesler commanded Tell to shoot at an apple on his own son's head, and how Tell hit the apple without hurting his son.

6. When the Swiss rebelled against the emperor of Germany, Tell was their principal leader. After sixty pitched battles with the emperor's troops, the liberty of Switzerland was established, and it became a free and independent republic.

7. It is said that some of the Swiss still believe that William Tell is not dead, though it is more than five hundred years since he was seen on earth. They suppose that he lies asleep in a cavern near the lake of Lucerne, with two other men who assisted in founding the empire.

8. These three slumberers are called the Men of Grutli. If ever Switzerland shall be enslaved, it is fancied that they will start from their sleep, and come forth with their ancient garb and weapons, and rouse up the people to fight for their freedom.

9. Since the time of William Tell, who died in the year 1354, Switzerland has generally been a free country. But during the French revolution it was conquered; it has since been restored to independence, yet the people are overawed by the kings that reign in the neighboring countries.

10. Many of the Swiss leave their beautiful but poor country to seek their fortunes in other lands. Some enter foreign armies as soldiers, and some go to Paris and London to sing songs, or carry about shows, and thus get a little money. You often find a Swiss boy in the streets of these great cities doing what he can to get a living.

CHAPTER CXXI—EUROPE—CONTINUED
Sequel of Germany History

1. I WILL NOW PROCEED with the history of Germany. Charles the Fifth was the most renowned of the emperors of Germany. He was likewise king

---

Questions—4. What of Albert I?   What of Gesler?   5. What of William Tell?   6. How did Switzerland obtain her liberty?   7. What legend have the Swiss concerning William Tell and his two companions?   9. When did Tell die?   What of Switzerland since the time of Tell?   10. What of the Swiss people?

of Spain, and ruler of the Netherlands and part of Italy.

2. When this great potentate was fifty-seven years old he grew weary of pomp and power. He therefore took off his crown, and gave it to his son Philip, and went to live in a monastery in Estremadura [es-tra-ma-doo´-ra], in Spain. He dressed very plainly, and busied himself in saying his prayers and working in a garden.

3. One day he wrapped himself in a shroud and lay down in a coffin, stretching himself out as if he were dead. He then ordered his attendants to carry him to the tomb. The reader must not suppose that the emperor meant to be buried alive. He merely wished to remind himself that his life must soon close. But the ceremony hastened his end; for it brought on a fever, of which he died, in 1558.

4. Ferdinand the Second, who began to reign in 1619, had nearly reduced all Germany under his power, when the Germans called to their aid Gustavus Adolphus, King of Sweden, who accordingly invaded Germany and defeated Ferdinand and his best generals.

5. The subsequent history of Germany does not abound with the sort of events which my young readers would be desirous of knowing. Few or none of the later emperors performed any remarkable actions. But they appear to have been better than most sovereigns, for they cannot be accused of great crimes.

6. The emperor of Germany, as I have mentioned above, was generally a prince of the Hapsburg family. The kingdom of Austria was enlarged by the successive emperors, and finally became great and powerful.

7. It was now able to carry on war by itself, and was at different times engaged in struggles with Turkey, with France and Spain, with Prussia, and sometimes with several of the sovereign states of Germany.

8. In 1792, Francis the Second became emperor of Germany. He undertook a war against Napoleon Bonaparte, but his armies were routed and in 1806 he was compelled to resign the title of emperor of Germany. From this time he was called Francis I, emperor of Austria. His empire, at the time of his death, which took place in 1846, was one of the most powerful sovereignties of Europe, and deserves a separate chapter.

Questions—Chap. CXXI—1. What of Charles V? 2. Relate an anecdote of him. 3. When did Charles V die? 4. When did Ferdinand II begin to reign? What of him? Who did the Germans call to their aid? 5. What of the late emperors of Germany? 6. What of the emperor of Germany? Kingdom of Austria? 7. With what countries has Austria waged war? 8. Who became emperor of Germany in 1792? What took place in 1806?· What of the Austrian empire?

9. After the revolution in France, in February, 1848, great agitation took place in several of the German states. A general diet, consisting of members chosen in general suffrage, was assembled at Frankfort; there was a free press throughout Germany, and most of the kings were compelled to give charters to the people. But a reaction took place, and the former despotisms were restored.

CHAPTER CXXII—EUROPE—Continued
About Austria, Hungary, etc.

1. Austria is an extensive and powerful empire, lying south of Russia and Poland, and north of Turkey. On the west it is bounded by the German States, Switzerland, and Italy.

2. Austria formerly belonged to Germany. It now includes Hungary, Bohemia, a part of Poland, and some other states which were formerly independent. Its present population is about thirty-four millions, including all these places.

3. Vienna is the capital of the empire of Austria, and is one of the most splendid cities in Europe. It is situated on the Danube, which is a large river. In winter, this is frozen over, and the people amuse themselves by sliding, skating, and driving upon it with various kinds of sledges or sleighs. The scene presented at such a time is very gay and pleasant.

4. In summer the inhabitants resort to the public gardens, which are extensive and beautiful. Here are fine walks, where you may see people of all kinds. There are ladies and gentlemen taking the air, boys and girls scampering about, men with monkeys taught to dance, and a multitude of curious sports. The gentlemen of Austria sometimes amuse themselves with hunting wild boars, which are common in some parts of that country.

5. In the German part of Austria, which is the western portion, the inhabitants speak the German language, and have the manners and customs of Germany. The history of this country has been partly told. In early times it was occupied by tribes of barbarians. At a later period it formed one of the states of the German empire.

Questions—9. What agitation took place? The consequences?
Chap. CXXII—1. Where does the empire of Austria lie? Its boundaries? 2. To what does Austria belong? What does it now include? 3. What of Vienna? What of the Danube? Amusements? 4. What of the public gardens? 5. What of the German part of Austria? What of it in ancient times? At a later period?

6. At that time it was called an Archduchy, and was governed by an Archduke, who was, however, subject to the emperor. Rodolph of Hapsburg succeeded to the government of the empire in 1273, as I have told you, and from him the sovereigns of Austria have since descended. After his time, Austria rapidly increased in power, and its archduke was at length considered as of course the emperor of all Germany.

7. It has since been engaged in many wars, particularly with Sweden, Turkey, and France. In 1688, the Turks pushed their arms into the heart of the empire, and laid siege to Vienna, but were finally driven back.

8. In 1809, Austria was involved in a war with Bonaparte. She had well trained soldiers and able generals, but the French emperor beat them in several pitched battles, and finally entered Vienna. Here he made peace with the emperor, but took from him a large portion of his dominions.

9. These, however, were afterward restored, and at the present day, Austria may be considered as one of the leading kingdoms of Europe. It is a curious fact that the emperors of Austria have had a great many beautiful daughters. Many of these have been married to the kings and princes of Europe, and it is owing to this, more than to success in war, that Austria has been able to acquire its vast possessions and extensive dominions.

CHAPTER CXXIII—EUROPE—Continued
About Hungary, Bohemia, the Tyrol, etc.

1. I MUST NOW GIVE you a very brief account of some of the dependencies of Austria. Hungary is an extensive country, and includes several provinces. Buda, the capital, is a fine city, situated upon the Danube.

2. The climate of Hungary is pleasant, and the soil yields very fine grapes, of which some choice wines are made. The mountains afford considerable quantities of gold and silver. The inhabitants are divided into two classes, the rich and the poor. The former live in splendid palaces, and the latter are but little better than their slaves.

3. The original inhabitants of Hungary consisted of several fierce tribes,

---

Questions—6. What was it called at this time? Who succeeded to the crown in 1273? What of Austria and its archduke? 7. What of the wars of Austria? What happened in 1688? 8. What happened in 1809? What did Bonaparte do? 9. How may Austria be considered at the present day? What is a curious fact?

Chap. CXXIII—1. What of Hungary? Its capital? 2. Climate and soil of Hungary? Mountains? Inhabitants?

who appear to have come from Asia into Europe at a very early date, by crossing the Altaï Mountains. They probably resembled those Tartar tribes called Turks, who fell upon the Saracen empire and established the empire of Turkey.

4. The principal of the Hungarian tribes were called Huns. An army of these, you will recollect, was led into Italy by the fierce and bloody Atilla, about 450. He had already fought many battles, and made the Greek empire a tributary. He now crossed the Alps, and pouring down upon the plains of Italy, spread terror and desolation among the inhabitants. He approached the city of Rome, but was compelled to retire. He died in 451.

5. For many years Hungary was the scene of perpetual wars. Its rulers did not acquire the title of king till the time of Stephen, who died in 1038, after a reign of forty-seven years. In 1563, Hungary became attached to the Austrian empire, and continues so to the present day.

6. Bohemia is a country surrounded by mountains, containing about five millions of inhabitants. It is rich in mines of silver, tin, and precious stones. Many of the present inhabitants are Jews. There are also a great many of those strange, wandering people, called Gipsies.

7. This country derives its name from a tribe of Celts from Asia, who settled there about 600 years B.C. About 450 after Christ, it appears that the Celts had been driven out, for the people at that time were Germans, under the government of a duke. Charlemagne rendered the country tributary, but it afterward became a kingdom. In 1526, it was attached to the house of Austria, and has continued so from that day.

8. I need not tell you more about the provinces of Austria. If I had room, I could give you an account of the brave Tyrolese, who live in the mountains between Italy and Germany, and of many other tribes under the government of Austria.

9. I can only add that great political agitation took place in Austria, and some of its dependencies, about thirty years ago. Hungary, and Venice, and Lombardy revolted, but after terrible bloodshed, they were compelled to submit. In 1859, however, Lombardy was ceded to Italy; and a war between Prussia and Austria in 1866 resulted in the liberation of Venice.

Questions—3. What of the original inhabitants? Their origin? Whom did they probably resemble? 4. What of the Huns? What of Atilla? Where did he die? 5. What of Hungary for many years? What of Stephen? What took place in 1563? 6. What of Bohemia? Population? Mines? Inhabitants? 7. What of a tribe of Celts? Who occupied the country in 450? What of Charlemagne? What took place in 1526? 8. Where do the Tyrolese live? 9. What of Austria about thirty years ago?

CHAPTER CXXIV—EUROPE—Continued
About Prussia

1. Though Prussia is part of the great German empire of which I have told you, its history is so important that I must speak of it separately. It was considered, even before the war with France, in 1870, one of the five great powers of Europe, and now that it is at the head of the empire, its importance is largely increased.

2. The kingdom of Prussia occupies a large tract in Central Europe, bounded north by the Baltic, east by Russia, south by Austria, the states of South Germany, and France, and west by the Netherlands and Belgium. Many of the smaller German states are entirely surrounded by its territory.

3. The capital of Prussia is Berlin, situated on the river Spree, a river, by the way, with a very merry name: it is, however, a very sober stream. The city is twelve miles in circumference, and is surrounded by a wall. It has a splendid palace, where the king resides, a fine university, where a great many young men are educated, and several places of public amusement. It is, on the whole, one of the most splendid cities in Europe.

4. Beside Berlin, there are many other fine cities in Prussia. Among these are Potsdam, where there is a royal palace, and Dantzic, a wealthy town and the chief sea-port of Prussia. At this place there is a powerful fortress with immense stone walls and a multitude of cannon. It is defended by a large garrison—that is, a number of soldiers, who always remain in it.

5. The inhabitants of Prussia are chiefly of Germanic origin, and speak the German language. These are industrious, and a multitude of schools having been established by the king among them, they are tolerably well educated. But they are not a free people; and without freedom even education cannot make a nation happy.

6. Beside the German population, Prussia has a good many Jews. There are also the remains of tribes that settled in the country long ago, who speak their original languages. These people are generally ignorant, and appear unwilling to be taught.

Questions—Chap. CXXIV—1. What of the history of Prussia? What was it considered? What of its increase? 2. How is the kingdom of Prussia divided? Bound the two portions. 3. Capital of Prussia? River Spree? What of the city? 4. What of Potsdam? Dantzic? What of the fortress? 5. What of the inhabitants of Prussia? Schools? Of what blessing are the people in want? 6. What of the Jews? Ancient tribes?

CHAPTER CXXV—EUROPE—Continued
History of Prussia

1. PRUSSIA DID NOT become a kingdom until the year 1701. Previous to that time it was governed by dukes. Its ancient inhabitants were called Borussi, from whom the country took the name of Prussia.

2. Frederic William the First, who ascended the throne in 1713, was a very odd sort of a king. He used to wear an old blue coat, which was ornamented with rows of copper buttons, reaching from his chin half-way down his legs. Whenever he got a new coat he made the tailor sew on these same old copper buttons.

3. He prided himself greatly on a regiment of his guards, which consisted of very tall men, many of whom were seven feet high. These gigantic fellows came from all parts of Europe; and if they would not come of their own accord, the king hired people to bring them by force.

4. Frederic William was in the habit of walking about the streets of Berlin, with a big cane in his hand, and if he happened to see any idle people, he would give them a sound thrashing. He beat his own son oftener than any body else. The princess, his daughter, got likewise a good many hard knocks.

5. When this ill-tempered old king was dead, his son Frederic came into possession of an enormous quantity of treasure, as well as an army of sixty thousand men. He soon found uses enough for his money and soldiers, in a war with Austria, Russia, and France.

6. The war between Prussia and these three kingdoms began in 1756, and was called the Seven Years' War. Saxony and Sweden joined the enemies of Frederic. At one time, he seemed on the point of losing all his dominions. But he finally brought the war to an honorable close. He was then the most celebrated sovereign of his time, and is known in history by the title of Frederic the Great.

7. He was almost as peculiar in his dress as his father had been. He always wore a uniform, consisting of a blue coat faced with red, a yellow waistcoat, and breeches of the same color. But his clothes were often torn, and generally soiled with snuff. On his head was a very large cocked hat,

---

Questions—CHAP. CXXV—1. When did Prussia become a kingdom? How was it previously governed? Its ancient inhabitants? 2–4. What of Frederic William I? When did he ascend the throne? Give an account of him. 5. Who succeeded him? In what wars did he engage? 6. What war began in 1756? What kingdoms joined the enemies of Frederic? What was he called?

and he wore a long cue behind.

8. When Frederic the Great was grown an old man, he used to sit in an easy chair, wrapped in a large cloak. He appeared to take no pleasure in his palace nor in all the pomp and power of his kingdom.

9. He looked very sad and wobegone, and might be heard muttering to himself: "A little while longer and I shall be gone!" He died in 1786, at the age of seventy-five.

10. He was succeeded by his nephew, Frederic William the Second, who reigned eleven years. The next king was Frederic William the Third. He had a large army, and thought himself powerful enough to withstand the emperor Napoleon.

11. But at the battle of Jena, in 1806, Napoleon wasted the Prussian army, and killed or wounded twenty thousand men. About forty thousand were taken prisoners. Frederic William was then deprived of a great part of his territories.

12. After the battle of Waterloo, and the final defeat of Napoleon, the losses of Prussia were repaired. Frederic William IV, who came to the throne in 1840, was a well-meaning man, educated under the guidance of Alexander von Humboldt. He declared that there should be a Bible in every cottage in his kingdom, and I believe he tried to keep his word.

13. Frederic William IV died in 1861, and was succeeded by his brother, William I, who is now emperor of Germany, as well as king of Prussia. I have told you how France made war on Prussia in 1870, and how all the German states joined together to assist the latter. Otto von Bismarck, a very able statesman, largely contributed to the formation of the German empire during the progress of this war.

CHAPTER CXXVI—EUROPE—Continued
Description of Russia

1. The Russian empire, like that of Turkey, lies partly in Europe and partly in Asia. The whole of the northern part of Asia belongs to Russia. This is thinly scattered over with a great number of different tribes, who chiefly wander about from place to place in search of food for their cattle.

Questions—7. What was the dress of Frederic the Great? 8. What of him when he had grown old? 9. When did he die? 10. What two kings succeeded him? What of Frederic William III? 11. What took place at the battle of Jena? What of the Prussian king? 12. What took place after the battle of Waterloo? What else can you say of this king? 13. Who became king in 1861? What happened in 1870? What of Bismarck?
Chap. CXXVI—1. What of the Russian empire? What of northern Asia? Tribes?

2. Siberia is a name given to nearly all the northern part of Asia. It is a bleak, cold region, and almost makes one shiver to think of it. The people are poor, and dress in the skins of wild animals, and for the most part live in poor huts. It is to this country of winter and poverty that the Russian emperor banishes those of his subjects whom he does not like.

3. I will now tell you of that part of Russia which lies in Europe. It is a vast territory, about two-thirds as extensive as all the United States, and embraces more land than all the other kingdoms of Europe. The population is not less than sixty millions.

4. You will see by this that the emperor of Russia is a very powerful king. He reigns over his subjects pretty much as he pleases, there being no law superior to his will. He is not only a despot in his own country, but he is a terror to all Europe.

5. He has a great many palaces in different parts of his kingdom, but he resides chiefly at St. Petersburg. He has an immense army, and is always surrounded with a great many soldiers.

6. By looking on a map, you will see that Russia in Europe extends from the Northern or Frozen Ocean on the north, to the Black Sea on the south, a distance of nearly two thousand miles. On the east, it is separated from Asia by the Ural mountains; on the west, it is bounded by the Gulf of Finland, the Baltic Sea, Prussia, Austria, and Turkey.

7. In such a vast territory as this, you may well suppose that the climate is various. Along the borders of the Frozen Ocean the lakes are covered with ice for nine months in the year. In the middle parts of Russia, the winter is about as severe as in Canada; in the southern parts the climate is very warm and pleasant. Here, grapes grow in abundance, with many other nice fruits.

8. The capital of Russia is St. Petersburg, situated on the river Neva, which flows into the Gulf of Finland. It is a splendid city, and contains almost as many inhabitants as New York. There is no place in the world where you would see more strange sights than in St. Petersburg. Here are a great many palaces, inhabited by people so rich, that some of them keep two or three hundred servants.

9. In the streets, you see a great many soldiers gayly dressed, gilt coaches

Questions—2. To what country is the name of Siberia given? What of the country? People? Russian emperor? 3. What of Russia in Europe? Its population? 4. What can you say of the emperor of Russia? 6. What is the extent of Russia in Europe? Boundaries? 7. Climate of Russia in Europe? Productions? 8. What of St. Petersburg? Palaces? People?

241

drawn by three horses, beggars covered with rags, and people dressed in all the strange fashions you can think of.

CHAPTER CXXVII—EUROPE—Continued
Description of Russia continued

1. Moscow is next to St. Petersburg in size, and contains about half as many inhabitants as New York. It is a famous old city, where the kings of Russia used to live. But in 1812 a great part of it was burnt, in order to drive out Napoleon and his soldiers, pretty much as people in our country sometimes set fire to a heap of brush in order to drive out a rabbit or a woodchuck. In this way Moscow was nearly destroyed, but it has since been rebuilt.

2. St. Petersburg carries on a great deal of commerce by sea, and many of our ships go there to get hemp, iron, hides, and other things. But Moscow is situated far inland, and therefore carries on no trade by sea.

3. There is no king in the world who reigns over so many kinds of people as the czar, or the emperor of Russia. In his European dominions he has at least sixty different tribes or nations under his sway, who speak different languages, and have different modes of life. In his Asiatic dominions he probably has nearly as many more.

4. In the northern part of European Russia there are a good many tribes of short, swarthy people, called Laplanders, Samoiedes, etc. These live almost in a savage state. Those that dwell near the sea live so much upon fish that they always carry about with them a fishy smell. These races resemble the Esquimaux [*es ´-ke-mo*] Indians who occupy the northern parts of our continent.

5. It would seem that these people would have a very dull time of it up in their cold country, where three-fourths of the time it is winter, and where the nights are sometimes six months long. But they appear to enjoy themselves pretty well. They have no books, but they tell long stories and crack their jokes as well as other people.

6. They have no history, for they seem to keep no more record of what passes among them than a hive of bees. One generation succeeds another,

---

Questions—9. What may you see in the streets?
Chap. CXXVII—1. What of Moscow? What was done in 1812? 2. What of the commerce of St. Petersburg? That of Moscow? 3. What of the czar of Russia? 4. What tribes live in European Russia? Whom do they resemble? 5. What of their employments? Their life?

and so things pass from age to age. They are not warlike, and have no great events to tell. Thus they go on, living as their great-grandfathers lived before them. They acknowledge the authority of the emperor; but the country is so cold he never comes among them, so they do pretty much as they please.

7. In the southern and western portions of European Russia there are a good many Tartars who are very fond of riding about on swift horses. Along the river Don there is a race of Cossacks. These, too, are fond of horses, and in battles fight terribly with long spears, which they hurl to the distance of two hundred feet.

8. Besides these tribes there are many Jews, several millions of Poles, a good many Germans, and some gipsies, in Russia. In the cities the people generally live pretty much as they like, each man pursuing what occupation he pleases.

9. But the country people who tilled the land were held in a state of bondage similar to that of the vassals in old feudal times. These were called *serfs.* The present emperor has emancipated them, and secured them land to live upon.

10. Russia has made astonishing progress in civilization within the last twenty years. Railroads have been extensively introduced and now connect the great cities. Arts and manufactures are encouraged, and a general state of improvement exists throughout the empire.

11. The late emperor Nicholas was ambitious of extending his empire, and his armies were greater than those of any other European power. I shall tell you more about him in another chapter.

CHAPTER CXXVIII—EUROPE—CONTINUED
The Reign of Peter the Great

1. ALTHOUGH RUSSIA is such an immense empire, its history will not detain us long. It was a country of barbarians till about one hundred and fifty years ago. It cannot be said to have taken a rank among civilized nations till Peter the Great ascended the throne.

2. Peter was a very strange man, and though he began the work of civilizing his empire he found it a more difficult task to civilize himself. In

Questions—6. Their history? 7. What of Tartars? Cossacks? 8. What of other inhabitants? 9. Who were the serfs? What of them? 10. What of the progress of Russia? 11. What of the emperor Nicholas?
CHAP. CXXVIII—1. What of Russia? Peter the Great?

fact, he was somewhat of a barbarian all his life.

3. The emperors of Russia are called czars. When the czar Peter was twenty-five years old he left his throne and traveled over Europe in search of knowledge. He did not go to any of the learned universities nor apply himself to the study of the dead languages.

4. That was not the sort of knowledge which Peter wanted. The first thing he did was to go to Holland, and put himself apprentice to a ship-carpenter. The house is still standing where he used to live while there. He afterward went to England, and followed the same trade as in Holland.

5. Beside learning the business of ship-carpentry he took lessons in other branches of mechanics, and also in surgery. In short, he neglected no kind of knowledge which he thought would be useful to himself or his subjects.

6. In a little more than a year he heard that his sister was endeavoring to make herself empress of Russia. This intelligence compelled him to break off his studies and labors, and hasten back to the city of Moscow. On arriving there he put some of the conspirators to death, and confined his sister in prison.

7. His time was afterward so much occupied in war, and in taking care of the empire, that he never had leisure to finish his education. But he had already learnt a great deal, and the effect of his knowledge was soon seen in the improvements of Russia.

8. Peter used to rise at five in the morning, and busy himself all day about the affairs of the empire. But in the evening, when his work was over, he would seat himself beside a big, round bottle of brandy and drink till his reason was quite gone.

9. This habit, together with the natural violence of his temper, rendered him almost as dangerous to his friends as to his enemies. He often said that he had corrected the faults of Russia, but that he could not correct his own.

10. Peter was in the habit of beating those who offended him with his cane. The highest nobleman in Russia often underwent this punishment. Even the empress Catherine, his wife, sometimes got soundly beaten.

11. It is supposed that the czar Peter ordered his own son to be put to death, and that he was himself privately executed in prison. He had many faults, and was guilty of some great crimes, but his name stands high on

Questions—2. What can you say of Peter? 3–7. Who are called czars? Describe the manner in which the czar Peter set about acquiring knowledge. 8–9. In what vice did Peter indulge? 10. What habit had he?

the list of sovereigns; for he was one of the very few who have labored hard for the welfare of his subjects. He did more for the good of Russia than all the czars who went before and have come after him.

CHAPTER CXXIX—EUROPE—Continued
The Successors of Peter the Great

1. PETER DIED IN 1725, at the age of fifty-three, and was succeeded by his wife, the empress Catherine. She had been a country girl, and the czar Peter had married her for the sake of her beauty. In some respects Catherine was a good sort of woman; but, among other faults, she was rather too fond of wine.

2. She reigned only about two years, and was succeeded by her husband's grandson, named Peter the Second. He died in 1730, and left the throne to Anne, duchess of Courland, his niece. This empress was a good sovereign, and performed many praiseworthy acts. None of her deeds, however, have been more famous than the building of a palace of ice.

3. This stately and beautiful structure was built on a frozen lake. Instead of wood or hewn stone it was composed entirely of blocks of ice. The furniture was likewise of ice; and even the beds were of the same material. When it was illuminated within, the whole edifice glittered and sparkled as if it were made of diamonds.

4. Bright as it was, however, I would far rather dwell in the meanest mud-cottage than in so cold a mansion. Yet, my dear readers, any other palace is almost as uncomfortable as the empress Anne's palace of ice. There is little in most palaces but cold and glittering grandeur.

5. The successor of Anne was the princess Elizabeth, a daughter of Peter the Great. She mounted the throne in 1740, and reigned twenty-two years. Her successor was Peter the Third, who began to reign in 1762.

6. He, like Peter the Great, had a wife named Catherine. They had not long sat together on the throne when she contrived to depose Peter, and make herself sole ruler of Russia. It is supposed that she afterward caused him to be murdered.

Questions—11. What is supposed to have been the fate of Peter's son? His own fate? The character of czar Peter?

CHAP. CXXIX—1. When did the czar Peter die? Who succeeded him? What of the empress Catherine? 2. How long did she reign? Who succeeded her? When did Peter II die? Who succeeded him? What of the empress Anne? 3–4. Describe the palace of ice. 5. Who succeeded the empress Anne? What of her? When did Peter III begin to reign? 6. What of his wife?

CROWNING OF ALEXANDER II

7. But although so wicked a woman, Catherine was endowed with admirable talents, and she became one of the most illustrious sovereigns in the world. Some people called her Catherine the Great Man; for many of her great qualities would have been more becoming in a man than a woman.

8. In 1796, when she died, Catherine was on the point of driving the Turks from their territories. If she had succeeded in doing so she would have governed the whole of the vast region between the Mediterranean Sea and the Arctic Ocean.

9. But death hurried the great empress away to answer for the murder of her husband, and many other crimes. She was succeeded by her son Paul, who was then forty-three years old.

10. The czar Paul possessed none of his mother's talents, and was of a

---

Questions—7. What can you say of her?   8. What plan had Catherine the Great before her death?   When did she die?   9. Who succeeded her?

very stern and unamiable disposition. People suspected him of being in-
sane. His conduct grew so intolerable that some of his principal nobles
conspired to kill him.

11. Paul was succeeded by Alexander I, his eldest son. This emperor
reigned from 1801 till 1825. He was engaged in war with the emperor Napoleon, who penetrated with his army to the city of Moscow, in 1812. But
the Russians burnt that ancient capital of their country; and its destruction ruined the French army.

12. Nicholas succeeded Alexander I in 1825; he was a man of great
abilities, and though of a despotic temper, greatly contributed to the ad-
vancement of Russia in civilization. In 1854, he became involved in a war
with Turkey, France, and England. The latter besieged the Russian town
and fortress of Sebastopol in the Crimea, and here about half a million of
men became engaged in the mighty contest. This was called the Eastern
War.

13. Sebastopol was taken in 1856. Nicholas died in the same year, and
was succeeded by his son, Alexander II. The latter freed the serfs and took
various measures to advance civilization in his empire. He was assassinated in 1881, by the agents of a set of people calling themselves Nihilists,
or Destructives. The murder of the czar brought down upon them the ex-
ecrations of the whole world. Alexander III, son of Alexander II, is now
emperor.

CHAPTER CXXX—EUROPE—Continued
About Sweden

1. The Swedish territories at present comprise Sweden, Norway, and
part of Lapland. These are bounded north by the Arctic Ocean; east by
Lapland, the Gulf of Bothnia, and the Baltic; south by the Baltic, the
Cattegat, and the Skagerrack; and west by the Atlantic.

2. Sweden is a cold and mountainous country, celebrated for its iron, of
which large quantities are brought to this country. The people are industrious, frank, and independent. A large part of the inhabitants live upon milk,
cheese, and fish. In winter they clothe themselves in furs and sheep-skin.

Questions—10. What of the czar Paul?   11. Who succeeded him?   What of Alexander
I?   How was the French army ruined?   12. What of Nicholas?   The Eastern War?   13.
What occurred in 1856?   What of Alexander II?   His death?   Who is the present czar?

Chap. CXXX—1. What do the Swedish territories comprise?   2. What of Sweden?   The
people?

3. The Swedes are a sensible people, and are disposed to make the best of everything. When their long winter goes away they celebrate the return of spring by dancing around a May-pole. They love their country, and insist that it is the pleasantest part of the world.

4. Though they dress in sheep-skins, and live in a homespun sort of a way, they are still very polite. They are, in short, much more amiable, respectable, and well-behaved than many of the kings and princes about whom I have been telling you.

5. I may not have a better opportunity to tell you that good manners are a great recommendation to every body; but they are especially necessary to people who are not rich. Rich people are sometimes haughty and proud. This is very wrong and very silly, and though every body despises such people, still their wealth will bring flatterers around them.

6. But people in more humble circumstances cannot afford to throw away the happiness, respectability, and comfort which arise from being amiable, gentle, and polite to every body.

7. Not much is known about the early history of Sweden. In ancient times it was under the government of Denmark. A Danish queen, called Margaret, ruled over Denmark, Sweden, and Norway, in 1387.

8. In 1518, the Danish king Christian caused ninety-four Swedish senators to be massacred in the city of Stockholm. Gustavus Vasa, the son of one of these senators, incited the Swedes to revolt against Denmark.

9. The king of Denmark sent an army to put down the rebels. But the ships in which the Danish soldiers had embarked, got imbedded in the ice, on the coast of Sweden. The inhabitants skated off from the shore, and set the ships on fire.

10. Gustavus Vasa succeeded in freeing his country, and was elected king. The next sovereign of Sweden who is worth mentioning was Gustavus Adolphus. He began to reign in 1611, at the age of eighteen.

11. This king was a great warrior, and vanquished the best generals in the service of the emperor of Germany. In 1633, he won the battle of Lutzen, but was killed at the moment of victory.

12. Gustavus Adolphus left a daughter named Christina, who was then only six years old. She was thought to possess remarkable talents, and great

---

Questions—3. What of the Swedes? 4. Their dress? Manners? 5. What of good manners? What of the rich? 6. People in more humble life? 7. History of Sweden? Who ruled in 1387? 8. What was done in 1518? What of Gustavus Vasa? 9. What of the king? The ships? 10. What of Gustavus Vasa? Who was king of Sweden in 1611? 11. What of Gustavus Adolphus? In what battle did he die?

pains were taken with her education. But she loved the study of languages and philosophy better than royalty.

13. After reigning a considerable time queen Christina became weary of the cares of government. She therefore abdicated the throne, and set out to seek a residence in some pleasanter country than Sweden.

14. On the death of her successor she asked to be received again as queen of Sweden, but without success. Afterward she spent the most of her time in the company of the learned in Paris, and died in Rome in 1689.

CHAPTER CXXXI—EUROPE—CONTINUED
Charles the Twelfth and his Successors

1. THE MOST FAMOUS sovereign that Sweden ever had, and one of the most famous in the world, was Charles the Twelfth. But my readers will long ago have become tired of hearing about conquerors; so that I shall speak very briefly of Charles.

2. He began to reign in 1697, at fifteen years of age. From his youth upward, he thought of nothing but being a soldier. When he was only about seventeen years old, the czar of Russia and the kings of Poland and Denmark made war upon him.

3. Charles beat them all in the first campaign. When he heard the bullets whistling about his ears, he showed great delight, and exclaimed, "That shall be my music!" And as long as he lived he never wished for any other music.

4. But it is a sad thing for a people when their king loves the whistling of bullets. Charles the Twelfth was a scourge to all Europe, and to his own kingdom more than any other. He delighted in war for its own sake, and not for any good which he expected to gain by it.

5. During the first few years of his reign Charles was constantly successful; but in 1709, the czar of Russia gained a great victory over him at Pultowa. Charles made his escape into Turkey.

6. He continued in that country five years, although, he might safely have returned home. He seemed to care nothing about his own dominions.

Questions—12. What can you tell of queen Christina?   14. What did she ask?   What of her subsequent life?

CHAP. CXXXI—1. Who was the most famous of the kings of Sweden?   2. When did he begin to reign?   What did he principally think of when a boy?   Who made war upon him?   3. What anecdote can you tell of him?   4. What can you say of him?   5. What of Charles XII for the first few years of his reign?   When was the battle of Pultowa?   Where did Charles fly?

When the Swedes sent to inquire what they should do in his absence, Charles answered that he would send one of his old boots to govern them.

7. At last, in 1714, he left Turkey and returned to Sweden. His first business was to make war again. But his warfare was now drawing to a close.

8. One night, while besieging a fortress in Norway, he advanced in front of his troops to see how the siege was going on. A cannon-shot struck him on the head and killed him. He was found grasping his sword, which was half drawn from the scabbard. Historians seem hardly decided whether to call Charles the Twelfth a hero or a madman.

9. One of his successors, named Gustavus the Third, was shot at a masquerade, in 1792. Gustavus the Fourth behaved in such a manner that his subjects were compelled to dethrone him. This took place in 1809.

10. The next king was Charles the Thirteenth. The emperor Napoleon caused a French general, named Bernadotte, to be declared Crown-prince of Sweden, and heir to the throne. In 1818, when Charles the Thirteenth died, Bernadotte succeeded him.

11. Though he had originally been only a common soldier, Bernadotte proved to be a better king than the most of the other European sovereigns, whose forefathers had worn crowns for a thousand years.

CHAPTER CXXXII—EUROPE—Continued
About Lapland, Norway, and Denmark

1. Lapland is the most northern country of Europe, and is divided between Russia and Sweden. The country is so cold that the hot liquor we call brandy sometimes freezes there. I am afraid, however, that the Lapps find means of thawing more of it than is good for them.

2. I have already told you something about the Laplanders. The men are about four feet high, and the women not much taller than a cider-barrel. The people have a great many reindeer, whose flesh supplies food, and whose skins furnish clothing. These also take the place of horses, and

---

Questions—6. How long did he stay in Turkey? What answer did he send to a message from the Swedes? 7. When did Charles return to Sweden? What of him when there? 8. How did he meet his death? What do historians think of Charles XII? 9. Who succeeded him? When did Gustavus III die? When was Gustavus IV dethroned? 10. Who was the next king? What of Napoleon? When did Bernadotte succeed to the throne of Sweden? 11. What of Bernadotte?

Chap. CXXXII—1. Where is Lapland? What of the climate?

SCENE IN LAPLAND

drag the people over the snow in sledges, at a rapid rate. These people have no history that is worthy of being related here.

3. Norway is an extensive country, bounded on the west by the Atlantic Ocean and on the east by Sweden. It is a cold, bleak, and barren region, but the inhabitants live pretty comfortably. They have very fine cows, from which they make the best butter in the world.

4. Bergen is the largest city, and has twenty thousand inhabitants. The houses are small, and generally built of wood. Fires sometimes do great damage, and therefore there are a good many watchmen who walk about the streets at night muffled up in thick great-coats. Every hour they cry out, "God preserve our good city of Bergen!"

5. Norway was early inhabited by rough tribes, who were adventurous seamen. There seems to have been now and then a pirate among them, for in 890, a pirate, named Naddodr, discovered Iceland, which was afterward settled by the Norwegians.

6. Norway was then conquered by Canute, king of Denmark, in 1030;

Questions—2. What of the Laplanders? Reindeer? History? 3. Where is Norway? What of the country? The people? Butter? 4. What of Bergen? Its population? What of the houses? What of fires? What of the watchmen? 5. How was Norway early inhabited? What was done in 890?

but six years after it became independent, and for many years it was governed by its own king. In 1397, it was incorporated with Denmark, and continued a part of that kingdom till 1814, when it was transferred to Sweden.

7. Denmark is a little kingdom lying between Sweden and Germany. It is a level country, nearly surrounded by the sea. The people have light complexions, and the skin of the ladies is said to be exceedingly white. The people have a great many cattle and horses, and they seem very fond of tilling the soil. Copenhagen, the capital, has one hundred and twenty thousand inhabitants. The whole population of the kingdom is two millions. The Danish language is spoken both in Denmark and Norway.

8. The three kingdoms of Denmark, Sweden, and Norway, were anciently called Scandinavia. In very early times these were occupied by tribes of Fins and Germans; afterward, the Goths conquered these countries. They were led by Odin, of whom many marvelous tales are told, and who seems to have been worshiped as a kind of Jupiter among these northern tribes. Skiold, the son of Odin, is said to have been the first king of Denmark.

9. All that we really know of Denmark at this early period is, that the people were composed of wild, adventurous warriors, who were generally considered by the more southern nations of Europe as pirates. About the time that the Roman empire fell, the Danes, Swedes, and Norwegians were known by the general name of Normans.

10. These bold freebooters sailed forth in their little vessels, and made conquests in different countries. Some of them settled in England, some in that part of France called Normandy, and some of them reached Spain and Italy.

11. In 920, the several Danish tribes appear to have been united under one government. Canute conquered Engand and a part of Scotland in 1016, and subdued Norway in 1030. Since his time, Denmark has had a great many sovereigns, and been engaged in several wars, but its history offers but little that is interesting.

Questions—6. When was Norway conquered, and by whom? When did it become independent? What of it in 1397? In 1841? 7. Where is Denmark? What of it? The people? What of Copenhagen? Its population? Population of the Danish kingdom? What language is spoken in Norway and Denmark? 8. What three countries were called Scandinavia? Who occupied it? Who led these tribes? Who was the first king of Denmark? 9. What of Denmark at this early period? What people were called Normans? 10. What of these freebooters? Where did they settle? 11. What took place in 920? What of Canute? History of Denmark?

CHAPTER CXXXIII—EUROPE—Continued
Brief Notice of several Kingdoms and States

1. THERE ARE SEVERAL countries in Europe of which my limits will not permit me to give a separate history. Some of them have been spoken of in connection with other kingdoms. The rest must be briefly noticed in one chapter. I shall first speak of Holland and Belgium, two little kingdoms which lie side by side, and which were formerly considered as one country, called the Netherlands.

2. If I had time I could make a long story about Holland, a country once covered by the sea, but which is now walled out by a vast dyke. The people are called Dutch, and are known all the world over as great smokers. They are, however, an industrious people, and I know of nothing more comfortable than the inside of a thrifty Dutchman's house in his own country. Amsterdam, the capital, contains two hundred thousand inhabitants.

3. In Belgium the people, strange as it may seem, appear to have a mixture of Dutch and French manners. They smoke a great deal of tobacco, yet speak the French language. The country is pleasant, and some parts are beautiful. Many of the cities are very interesting.

4. The Netherlands, or Holland, sometimes called the Low Countries, with Belgium, are bounded on the north by the North Sea, east by Prussia, south by France, and west by the English Channel and the North Sea. These territories belonged at one time to Rome, afterward to Germany, and finally to Spain.

5. In 1581, the Seven northern Provinces revolted against Philip of Spain, and formed themselves into a republic, which was then called Holland. During the seventeenth century it was a very powerful nation, especially by sea. At this time its ships often disputed, and sometimes successfully, with the British fleets.

6. The remaining provinces of the Netherlands were long under the government of Austria. In 1810, the whole of the Netherlands were united to France, but were afterward formed into a separate kingdom. In 1830, there was a revolution, and the country was divided into two kingdoms,

Questions—CHAP. CXXXIII—2. What of Holland? The people? What is the population of Amsterdam? 3. What of the people of Belgium? The country? The cities? 4. What of Holland and Belgium? How is the territory bounded? To whom has it belonged at different times? 5. What took place in 1581? When was Holland very powerful? 6. What of the remaining provinces of the Netherlands? What took place in 1810? In 1830?

253

the north being the kingdom of Holland and the south the kingdom of Belgium. In this condition they remain to the present day.

7. Poland was once a nation of Europe, but it is now no longer so. It was bounded north and east by the Russian dominions, south by the river Dniester [*nees´-ter*], and west by Prussia. In 1772, the sovereigns of Russia, Prussia, and Austria, seized upon Poland, and divided the greater part of its territories among themselves. In 1795, they seized the remainder. The inhabitants struggled bravely for their freedom, but in vain. They were cruelly treated by the emperor Nicholas, who sent thousands into exile, and banished thousands to other countries. Some of the Poles have fled from oppression to England, and some to this country.

CHAPTER CXXXIV—EUROPE—CONTINUED
Kingdom of Great Britain and Ireland

1. I HAVE NOW COME to the most interesting country in Europe; the country where there is more comfort, more good sense, more thorough civilization, more true religion, than in any other place in Europe, in Asia, or Africa.

2. The kingdom of Great Britain and Ireland embraces England, Wales, Scotland, and Ireland. The three first countries are upon the island of Great Britain. This island is on the western coast of Europe, and is separated by the English Channel from France. At the narrowest part this channel is twenty-five miles wide. Ireland lies west of Great Britain, at the distance of about sixty miles.

3. These two islands are small in extent, but they contain over thirty-one millions of inhabitants. Besides this the kingdom has colonies in various parts of America, Africa, and Asia, so that the sovereign rules over more than two hundred and fifty millions of people. Great Britain may be considered the richest and most powerful kingdom on the face of the globe.

4. I suppose you know that the first settlers of our country came from England. They brought with them the manners and customs of the country where they lived. Thus the United States became very much like En-

---

Questions—7. What of Poland? Its boundaries? What took place in 1772? In 1795? What of the Poles?

CHAP. CXXXIV—1. What is the most interesting country in Europe? 2. What is embraced in the kingdom of Great Britain and Ireland? What of the island of Great Britain? What of the English Channel? Ireland? 3. Population of Great Britain? Ireland? Colonies of Great Britain?

254

gland; the houses, the churches, the dress of the people in the two countries are nearly the same. Beside this, the people speak the same language.

5. But you must remember that England is an older and richer country than ours. It has larger cities, more splendid churches, more beautiful roads, finer gardens, and many other things superior to what can be found in this country.

6. Beside all this, England has a sovereign who has several magnificent palaces. England, too, has a great many noblemen, who live in costly and beautiful country-seats. These ride about in coaches, some of which, with their horses and harness, cost ten thousand dollars. Thus there is a great deal more splendor in England than we find here.

7. But, as an offset to this, there is more poverty there than in our country. Beggars throng the streets, even in London, and they are to be found in all parts of the kingdom. Thousands of people, too, who are not beggars, labor very hard, and yet are scarcely able to live. Sometimes people even die for want of food. Thus, England is a country which is wonderful for its magnificence and power, yet, with all its wealth, many suffer the pangs of poverty.

CHAPTER CXXXV—EUROPE—CONTINUED
About London and other Cities of England, Wales, Scotland, and Ireland

1. LONDON IS THE LARGEST and finest city in Europe, and contains about three millions of inhabitants. The Thames, a considerable river, runs through it. Across this, there are a number of handsome stone bridges. London has no wall around it like Paris, Berlin, and most large cities of the continent; but it is encircled by a beautiful country, dotted with villages, villas, and country-seats.

2. London seems like a world of itself; you might walk about for a year, and go into some new street every day. In some parts of the city there are such streams of people that it always seems there like our Fourth of July. The shops are filled with beautiful things, and the streets are crowded with coaches and carriages of all sorts.

Questions—4. How can you account for the United States resembling England? 5. How does the latter country excel the former? 6. What of the king or queen? Noblemen? 7. What of poverty in England? What can you say of England? *Where is London? Direction of the following places from London: Manchester? Birmingham? Sheffield? Edinburgh? Dublin? Wales?*
CHAP. CXXXV—1. Population of London? The Thames? Country around London? 2. Describe the appearance of London.

MAP OF THE BRITISH ISLES

3. The palace of St. James is a dark old building, but Buckingham Palace is new, and is very fine. Westminster Abbey is an old Gothic church, which strikes every beholder with admiration and wonder. St. Paul's is a more modern church, and is very handsome.

4. I have not time to tell you of the other wonderful things in London, nor can I tell you of the other beautiful towns and cities in England. You must read about them in some larger book, or come and see me some long winter night.

5. I will then tell you of Manchester, where they make beautiful ginghams, calicoes, and other goods; of Birmingham, where they make guns, pistols, swords, locks, and lamps; of Sheffield, where they make knives, forks, and scissors; and of other places, where they make a great variety of articles.

6. Wales is a country of mountains, lying on the west of England. Most of the people talk the Welsh language, which you could not understand. They are very industrious, and live in a comfortable manner. Their mountains are celebrated for producing coal, tin, iron, and copper.

7. Scotland is also a land of mountains. In the southern part the people speak the Scotch language, which perhaps you could partly understand. But in the highlands of the north, the inhabitants speak Gaelic, which would be as strange to you as the language of an Arab.

8. The capital of Scotland is Edinburgh, a fine smoky old city, with an immense, high castle in the midst of it. Beside this, there are many fine towns in Scotland. Glasgow is a large place, and celebrated for its manufactures.

9. Ireland is a bright, green island, containing six millions of people. It is the native land of those numerous Irishmen who come out to America. If their country were happily governed they would not be forced to come here; but the truth is, that Ireland has felt the miseries of bad government for many years, and a large part of the people are therefore kept in a state of distressing poverty.

10. The Irish are an interesting people. At home or abroad they seem to be full of wit and cheerfulness. It is by their lively disposition and cheerful turn of mind that they seem to soften the evils which too often pursue them.

Questions—3. Palace of St. James? Westminster Abbey? St. Paul's? 5. What of Manchester? Birmingham? Sheffield? 6. Where is Wales? What of the people? Mountains? 7. What of Scotland? Language? 8. What of Edinburgh? Glasgow? 9. What of Ireland? Government? 10. What of the Irish people?

11. Dublin is the capital of Ireland, and some of its streets are magnificent, but many portions of it are filled with inhabitants who present the most woeful aspect of raggedness and misery. Beggary is common in all parts of the kingdom.

CHAPTER CXXXVI—EUROPE—Continued
Origin of the British Nation—The Druids

1. It is supposed that Great Britain and Ireland were originally settled by a colony from Gaul. These were called Gaels or Celts. Their descendants are found at this day in Ireland and Wales, and the highlands of Scotland. Some of these still speak the ancient Gaelic or Celtic language.

2. Very little is known about these islands till the time of Julius Caesar. He invaded England in the year 55, before the Christian era. The country was then called Britannia or Britain. It was inhabited by barbarians,

DRUIDS

Questions—11. What of Dublin?
Chap. CXXXVI—1. What of the Gaels or Celts?

ANCIENT BRITONS

some of whom wore the skins of wild beasts, while others were entirely naked. They were painted, like the American Indians. Their weapons were clubs, spears, and swords, with which they fiercely attacked the Roman invaders.

3. The ancient Britons, like the other northern nations of Europe, were idolators. Their priests were called Druids. Their places of worship were in the open air, and consisted of huge stone pillars, standing in a circle. A large stone in the middle was used as an altar, and human victims were sacrificed upon it. The ruins of one of these temples still remain at Stonehenge, and are very wonderful.

4. The Druids considered the oak a sacred tree. They set great value on the mistletoe, a sort of plant which sometimes grows on the oak. Wherever they found mistletoe they held a banquet beneath the spreading branches of the oak on which it grew.

5. The Druids incited the Britons to oppose the Roman power. They fought fiercely, and the country was not entirely subdued till sixty years after the Christian era. Suetonius, a Roman general then cut down the

---

Questions—2. When did Caesar invade England?   What was Great Britain then called? What of the people?   3. Religion of the ancient Britons?   Who were the Druids?   What of their places of worship?   4. How was the oak considered by the Druids?   The mistletoe?   5. When was the country entirely subdued?   What of Suetonius?

sacred groves of oak, destroyed the temples, and threw the Druids into the fires which they had themselves kindled to roast the Romans.

6. The Scots, who inhabited the northern part of the island, were a fierce people, and were still unconquered. To prevent them from making incursions into Britain, the Romans built a wall from the river Tyne to the Firth of Solway.

7. The Britons remained quietly under the government of Rome for nearly five centuries after the Christian era, adopting during this period many of the Roman customs. They never attempted to free themselves. But at last the Roman empire became so weak, that the emperor Valentinian withdrew his troops from Britain.

8. The inhabitants had grown so unwarlike that when the Roman soldiers were gone, they found themselves unable to resist the Scots. They therefore asked the assitance of two tribes of people from Germany, called Saxons and Angles.

9. These people drove back the Scots into their own part of the island. Then, instead of returning to Germany, they took possession of Britain by the right of the strongest. It was divided by them into seven small kingdoms, called the Saxon Heptarchy.

CHAPTER CXXXVII—EUROPE—CONTINUED
Saxon and Danish Kings of England

1. IN THE YEAR 827 of the Christian era, all the seven kingdoms of the Saxon Heptarchy were united into one, under the government of Egbert. He was therefore the first king of England.

2. Egbert was a native of England, but had been educated in France, at the court of Charlemagne. He was therefore more polished and enlightened than most of the Saxon kings. During the reign of Egbert, and for many years afterward, the Danes made incursions into England. They sometimes overran the whole country.

3. Alfred, who ascended the throne in 871, fought fifty-six battles with them, by sea and land. On one occasion he went into the camp of the Danes in the disguise of a harper. He took notice of every thing, and planned an

---

Questions—6. What of the Scots? What did the Romans do? 7. How long did Rome govern Britain? What of the emperor Valentinian? 8. Whose aid did the Britons ask against the Scots? 9. What did these two tribes do? How was Britain then divided?

CHAP. CXXXVII—1. Who was the first king of England? What kingdoms did he govern? 2. What of Egbert? What of the Danes?

attack upon the camp. Returning to his own men, he led them against the Danes, whom he completely routed.

4. This king was called Alfred the Great; and he had a better right to the epithet of Great than most other kings who have borne it. He made wise laws, and instituted the custom of trial by jury. He likewise founded the university of Oxford. Nearly a hundred years after his death the Danes again broke into England. There was now no Alfred to oppose them. They were accordingly victorious, and three Danish kings governed the country in succession.

5. Canute the Great was one of them. He appears to have been an old pirate, or, as they were called in those days, a Sea-King. One day when he and his courtiers were walking on the shore, they called him king of the sea, and told him he had but to command, and the waves would obey him.

6. Canute desired a chair of state to be brought and placed on the hard, smooth sand. Then, seating himself in the chair, he stretched out his scepter over the waves with a very commanding aspect.

7. "Roll back thy waves, thou sea!" cried Canute. "I am thy king and master! How darest thou foam and thunder in my presence?" But the sea, nowise abashed, came roaring and whitening onward, and threw a sheet of spray over Canute and all the courtiers. The giant waves rolled upward on the beach, far beyond the monarch's chair. They would soon have swallowed him up, together with his courtiers, if they had not all scampered to the dry land.

8. In the year 1041, the Danes were driven out of England, and another Saxon king, called Edward the Confessor, was placed upon the throne. At his death in 1066, Harold, who was also a Saxon, became king.

9. But he was the last of the Saxon kings. No sooner had he mounted the throne, than William, duke of Normandy in France, invaded England, at the head of sixty thousand men.

10. Harold led an army of Saxons against the Norman invaders, and fought with them at Hastings [*haist´-ings*]. In the midst of the battle an arrow was shot through his steel helmet and penetrated his brain. The duke of Normandy gained the victory, and became king of England.

Questions—3. When did Alfred ascend the throne? What did he do? 4. Why was he called Alfred the Great? What of the Danes after his death? 5–7. Tell a story of Canute. 8. When were the Danes driven out of England? Who was then placed upon the throne? When did Harold become king? 9. Who now invaded England? 10. Where was the battle fought between Harold and William? Who became king of England?

CHAPTER CXXXVIII—EUROPE—CONTINUED
Norman Kings of England

1. WILLIAM THE CONQUEROR, as the duke of Normandy was now called, reigned about twenty years. He was succeeded by his second son, William Rufus, or the Red, who was so named from the color of his hair.

2. The Red king was very fond of hunting. One day, while he was chasing a deer in the forest, a gentleman by the name of Walter Tyrrel let fly an arrow. It glanced against a tree, and hit the king on the breast, so that he fell from his horse and soon died.

3. This took place in the year 1100, and William Rufus was succeeded by his brother Henry. This king was called Beauclerk [bo-clerc] or Excellent Scholar, because he was able to write his name. Kings were not expected to have much learning in those days. On the death of king Henry Beauclerk, in 1135, the throne was usurped by Stephen of Blois. But he died in 1154, and was succeeded by Henry the Second, grandson of the former Henry.

4. This monarch had a violent quarrel with Thomas Becket, archbishop of Canterbury. Hoping to please the king, four knights went to Canterbury and murdered Becket at the foot of the altar. But this bloody deed was a cause of great trouble to king Henry, from which he did not escape during the rest of his life.

5. He had four sons, and at one time he had a crown for each of them; but all four were guilty of rebellion against their royal father. Two of them came to an untimely end, and the unhappy king died of a fever caused by a broken heart, cursing his ungrateful children and the day he was born.

6. During the reign of this king, Ireland was conquered and annexed to the realm of England. It had previously been divided into several separate kingdoms.

7. Richard the Lion-Hearted was crowned king of England in 1189. He was a valiant man, and possessed prodigious strength; and he delighted in nothing so much as battle and slaughter. After gaining great renown in Palestine, as a crusader, he was, on his way back, taken and imprisoned for two years by the duke of Austria.

Questions—CHAP. CXXXVIII—1. Who succeeded William the Conqueror? 2. What was the fate of William Rufus? 3. When did Henry Beauclerk begin his reign? When did Stephen succeed to the throne? When did he die? 4. Who murdered Thomas Becket? 5. What happened to Henry II? 6. What of Ireland? 7. When was Richard made king of England? What of him?

8. The English obtained Richard's release by paying a heavy ransom; but soon afterward, while besieging a castle in Guienne, he was killed by an arrow from a cross-bow. The next king was Richard's brother, John, surnamed Lackland.

9. This epithet was bestowed on John because he lost the territories which the English kings had hitherto possessed in France. John was one of the worst kings that ever England had. Among other things, he murdered his nephew, Arthur of Bretagne [*breh-tan´*], who was rightful heir to the crown.

10. The barons of England were so disgusted with the conduct of John that they assembled at Runnymede and compelled him to sign a written deed, called Magna Charta [*kar´-ta*]. This famous charter was dated the 19th of June, 1215. It is considered the foundation of English liberty. It deprived John, and all his successors, of the despotic power which former kings had exercised.

11. King John died in 1216, and left the crown to his son, who was then only nine years old. He was called Henry the Third. His reign continued fifty-five years; but, though he was a well-meaning man, he had not sufficient wisdom and firmness for a ruler.

CHAPTER CXXXIX—EUROPE—Continued
English Wars and Rebellions

1. THE NEXT KING, Edward the First, was crowned in 1272. The people gave him the nickname of Longshanks, because his legs were of unusual length. He was a great warrior, and fought bravely in Palestine and in the civil wars of England.

2. Edward conquered Wales, which had hitherto been a separate kingdom. He attempted to conquer Scotland likewise, but did not entirely succeed. The illustrious William Wallace resisted him, and beat the English troops in many battles. But at last Wallace was taken prisoner and carried in chains to London and there executed.

3. Robert Bruce laid claim to the crown of Scotland and renewed the war against Edward. But old Longshanks was determined not to let go his

---

Questions—8. How was he killed?   9. Why was John called Lackland?   What of him? His crimes?   10. Who signed Magna Charta?   How is it considered?   11. When did king John die?   What of Henry III?

CHAP. CXXXIX—1. When was Edward I crowned?   What did the people call him? What of him?   2. What of Wales?   Who resisted Edward in Scotland?   Fate of William Wallace?

hold of poor Scotland. He mustered an immense army and was marching northward when a sudden sickness put an end to his life.

4. His son, Edward the Second, ascended the throne in 1307. He led an army of a hundred thousand men into Scotland. But he was not such a warrior as old king Longshanks. Robert Bruce encountered him at Bannockburn, with only thirty thousand men, and gained a glorious victory. By this Scotland was set free. Edward the Second reigned about twenty years. He was a foolish and miserable king. His own wife made war against him, and took him prisoner. By her instigation he was cruelly murdered in prison.

5. His son, Edward the Third, began to reign in 1327, at the age of eighteen. He had not long been on the throne before he showed himself very unlike his father. He beat the Scots at Halidon Hill, and afterward invaded France. I have spoken of his French wars in the history of France.

6. The king's son, surnamed the Black Prince, was even more valiant than his father. He was also as kind and generous as he was brave. He conquered king John of France and took him prisoner; but he did not exult over him. When they entered London together the Black Prince rode bareheaded by the side of the captive monarch, as if he were merely an attendant instead of a conqueror.

7. This brave prince died in 1376, and his father lived only one year longer. The next king was Richard the Second, a boy of eleven years old. When he grew up, Richard neglected the government and cared for nothing but his own pleasures.

8. During his reign a rebellion was headed by a blacksmith, named Wat Tyler. The rebels had also other leaders, nicknamed Jack Straw and Hob Carter. They marched to London with a hundred thousand followers, and did a great deal of mischief.

9. The king, attended by a few of his nobles, rode out to hold a conference with Wat Tyler. The blacksmith was very rude, and treated king Richard as if he were no better than a common man, or perhaps not quite so good. He even threatened the king with a drawn sword.

10. William Walworth, the lord-mayor of London, was standing near the king. He was so offended at Wat Tyler's insolence that he uplifted a

---

Questions—3. What of Robert Bruce? Death of Edward Longshanks? 4. What of Edward II? Battle of Bannockburn? How was Scotland set free? What happened to Edward II? 5. What of Edward III? When did he begin to reign? 6. What of the Black Prince? How did he treat John of France? 7. What of Richard II? 8–9. What of Wat Tyler's rebellion?

mace or club, and smote Wat to the ground. A knight then killed him with a sword.

11. When the rebels saw that the valiant blacksmith was beat down and slain, they gave an angry shout, and were rushing forward to attack the king's party. But king Richard rode boldly to meet them, and waved his hand with a majestic air.

12. "Be not troubled for the death of your leader!" he cried, "I, your king, will be a better leader than Wat Tyler!" The king's words and looks made such an impression that the rebels immediately submitted, and Wat Tyler's murder was unavenged.

CHAPTER CXL—EUROPE—Continued
The Lancastrian Kings of England

1. NOTWITHSTANDING HIS promise to the rebels, king Richard was not half so good a ruler as the blacksmith would probably have been. His subjects grew more and more discontented, and his cousin, the duke of Lancaster, formed the project of making himself king. Richard was dethroned, and imprisoned at Pontefract castle, where he was either killed or starved to death. The duke of Lancaster began to reign in the year 1400, and was called Henry the Fourth.

2. There were two rebellions against this king. One was headed by the earl of Northumberland, and the other by the archbishop of York; for, in those times, bishops often put on armor and became soldiers. Henry conquered the rebels and reigned several years in peace.

3. As long as his father lived the king's eldest son was a wild and dissipated young man. But no sooner was the old king dead than his character underwent a complete change. He now threw off his dissipation and devoted himself carefully to the business of governing his kingdom. He was crowned Henry the Fifth, in 1413. Two years afterward he invaded France.

4. I have already told, in the history of France, how Henry vanquished the French in the famous battle of Agincourt, and how he afterward nearly became master of the kingdom of France. His death took place in 1422, in the midst of his triumphs, at the age of thirty-four.

Questions—10. What did William Walworth do? 11. What of the rebels when Wat Tyler was killed? What did Richard do?

CHAP. CXL—1. What of England under Richard? Who dethroned him? His fate? Who was Henry IV? When did he begin to reign? 2. What rebellions were there against this king? 3. What of Henry V? When did he invade France? 4. Who fought the battle of Agincourt? When did Henry V die?

5. The new king of England, Henry the Sixth, was a baby only nine months old. At that tender age, while he was still in his nurse's arms, the heavy crowns of England and France were put upon his head. The ceremony of this poor child's coronation was performed in the city of Paris. He soon lost the crown of France. But the crown of England continued a torment to him as long as he lived, and it caused his death at last.

6. When he grew up he turned out to be a mild, quiet, simple sort of man, with barely sense enough to get along respectably as a private person. As a king he was an object of contempt. His wife had far more manhood than himself, and she governed him like a child.

7. During this king's reign began the War of the Roses. The reader will recollect that the duke of Lancaster had unlawfully taken the crown from Richard the Second. But he and his son reigned without much opposition, because they were warlike men, and could have defended the crown with their swords.

8. Henry the Sixth, on the contrary, was soft, meek, and peaceable, without spirit enough to fight for the crown which his father left him. The heirs of Richard the Second therefore thought this a proper time to get back their lawful inheritance. The duke of York was the nearest heir.

9. He began a war in 1445. If there had been nobody but Henry the Sixth to resist him, he might have got the crown at once. But Henry's wife, whose name was Margaret, and many of the nobility, took up arms for the king. Other noblemen lent assistance to the duke of York.

10. All the Yorkists, or partisans of the duke of York, wore white roses, either in their hats or at their breasts. The Lancastrians, or those of the king's party, wore a red rose in the same manner. Whenever two persons happened to meet, one wearing a red rose and the other a white, they drew their swords and fought.

11. Thus the people of England were divided into two great parties, who were ready to cut each other's throats, merely for the difference between a white and red rose.

CHAPTER CXLI—EUROPE—Continued
Wars of the Roses

1. THE WARS OF THE ROSES lasted thirty years. Sometimes the white

Questions—5. Describe the coronation of Henry VI. 6. What of him? His queen? 7. What of the duke of Lancaster? His son Henry V? 8. What did the heirs of Richard II do? 9. When did the duke of York begin the war? 10. What did the followers of the duke of York wear? Those of the king? What often happened?

266

rose was uppermost, and sometimes the red. The most celebrated general in these wars was the earl of Warwick [*wor ´ -rik*]. It was chiefly by his means that the soldiers of the white rose gained a decisive victory at Towton, in which thirty-six thousand of the red-rose men were killed. The young duke of York was then proclaimed king, under the name of Edward the Fourth.

2. This was in 1461. But not long afterward the earl of Warwick quarreled with king Edward and quitted the party of the Yorkists. He took king Henry the Sixth out of prison, and placed him on the throne again, and Edward was compelled to flee over to France.

3. As the earl of Warwick showed himself so powerful in pulling down kings and setting them up again, he gained the name of the King-maker. But he was finally killed in battle while fighting bravely for the Lancastrians; and then the white rose flourished again.

4. Henry the Sixth and his son were murdered in 1464, and Edward the Fourth became the undisputed king of England. He had fought bravely for the crown, but now that he had got firm possession of it he became idle and voluptuous.

5. He was a cruel tyrant, too. Having resolved to put one of his brothers to death, he gave him the choice of dying in whatever manner he pleased. His brother, who was a great lover of good liquor, chose to be drowned in a hogshead of wine.

6. Edward the Fourth died in 1483. He left two young children, the eldest of whom now became Edward the Fifth. But these poor children had a wicked uncle for a guardian. He was called Richard Crookback, duke of Gloucester. Most historians say that he was a horrible figure to look at, having a humpback, a withered arm, and a very ugly face. This frightful personage was determined to make himself king.

7. He took care that the little king Edward and his brother should lodge in the tower of London. One night while the two children were sound asleep in each other's arms, some villains came and smothered them with the bolsters of the bed. They were buried at the foot of a staircase. So Richard Crookback, the murderer, became king of England. He committed a thousand crimes for the sake of getting the crown, but he did not keep it long.

Questions—CHAP. CXLII—1. How long did the Wars of the Roses last? What of the earl of Warwick? 2. When was Edward IV made king? What did Warwick do? 3. What was he called? How was he killed? When did the party of the white roses flourish again? 4. What of Edward IV? 5. How did he treat his brother? 6. When did he die? What children did he leave? Describe Richard Crookback. 7. What cruelty did he commit? Did he become king?

8. Henry Tudor, the young earl of Richmond, was now the only remaining heir of king Henry the Sixth. The French supplied him with the means of making war against Richard Crookback. He landed in England and gained a victory at Bosworth.

9. When the soldiers of Richmond examined the dead bodies that lay in heaps on the battle-field, they found the humpbacked Richard among them, with the golden crown upon his head. They put it on the head of Richmond, and hailed him king Henry the Seventh.

10. The new king married a daughter of Edward the Fourth, and at their wedding they each wore a red rose intertwined with a white one, for the wars of the roses were now finished.

CHAPTER CXLII—EUROPE—Continued
Reigns of the Tudor Princes

1. HENRY THE SEVENTH, the former earl of Richmond, began his reign in 1485. He was a crafty king, and cared much more for his own power and wealth than for the happiness of his subjects. But for his own sake, he desired to reign peaceably, without foreign wars or civil commotions.

2. During his reign two imposters appeared in England, each of whom pretended that he had a better right to the crown than Henry the Seventh had. One was Lambert Simnel, the son of a baker; but he called himself a nephew of Edward the Fourth. The other was Perkin Warbeck, the son of a Flemish butcher. He pretended to be one of the little princes whom Richard Crookback had smothered in the tower.

3. Many knights and noblemen of England were led into rebellion by each of these imposters. But finally they were both taken prisoners. Perkin Warbeck was hanged, and Lambert Simnel was set to washing dishes in the king's kitchen.

4. Henry the Seventh died in 1509. He had been a great lover of money, and put all that he could lay his hands on into his own purse. A sum equal to fifty millions of dollars was found in his palace after his death.

5. His son, Henry the Eighth, began to reign at the age of eighteen. He was a haughty, stern, hard-hearted, and tyrannical king. Whenever he got

---

Questions—8. Who gained the battle of Bosworth? 9. Where was Richard found? 10. Who did Henry VII marry? Why were the Wars of the Roses now at an end?

CHAP. CXLII—1. When did Henry VII begin to reign? What of him? 2. What of two imposters? Their names? Whom did they pretend to be? 3. What became of them? 4. What of the riches of Henry VII?

angry, and that was not seldom, the heads of some of his subjects were sure to be cut off. This royal villain had six wives. One died a natural death; he was divorced from two, cut off the heads of two others, and one outlived him.

6. The reign of Henry the Eighth was chiefly remarkable on account of the Reformation in England. By this term is meant the substitution of the Protestant religion for the Roman Catholic. Until this period the pope of Rome had claimed authority over England, in matters of religion.

7. But Henry the Eighth took all the power to himself. If any of his subjects dared to have a religion unlike the king's they were either beheaded or burnt. The king was so proud of his religious character that he called himself Defender of the Faith!

8. The old tyrant died in 1547, at the age of fifty-six. One of his last acts was to cause the earl of Surrey to be beheaded although he was guilty of no crime; and with that innocent blood upon his soul, king Henry the Eighth was summoned to the judgment-seat.

9. His son, Edward the Sixth, was but nine or ten years old when he ascended the throne. He was a fine and promising boy, but lived only to the age of sixteen. His sister Mary succeeded him in 1553.

10. Henry VIII had left the crown to Mary, after Edward; but Edward was induced to alter the succession in favor of Lady Jane Grey, to the prejudice of Mary. The unfortunate legacy only brought Lady Jane a troubled reign of ten days, two rebellions in her favor, and death on the scaffold.

11. Mary determined to restore the old religion, of which she was a zealous member, to its former condition. But as the Reformers were equally zealous in their views, she caused numbers of them to be burned at the stake.

CHAPTER CXLIII—EUROPE—Continued
The Reign of Elizabeth

1. THE FAMOUS ELIZABETH succeeded Mary to the throne in 1558. She was a Protestant, and very quickly set aside all that had been done in favor of the Catholics during her sister's reign. She was, however, very severe on

Questions—5. When did Henry VIII begin to reign? What of him? What of his wives?
6. What great event occurred in his reign? What is meant by the Reformation? Who had claimed authority over England? 7. Why was the king called Defender of the Faith?
8. When did Henry VIII die? What was the last act of his reign? 10. To whom did he leave the crown? What did Edward do? 11. What of Mary?

269

all those who held a different faith from her own.

2. Elizabeth, however, in all that related to the power of England, was truly a great queen, and the nation was never more respected than while this mighty woman held the scepter in her hand. But she possessed hardly any of the kindly virtues that a woman ought to have. Yet she prided herself greatly on her beauty.

3. Many princes and great men desired to marry Elizabeth; but she chose to remain sole mistress of her person and her kingdom. And as she herself refused to take a husband, it made her very angry whenever any of the ladies of her court got married.

4. Philip the Second of Spain asked her hand in marriage. On her refusal he sent his Invincible Armada to invade England. But a storm destroyed part of the ships, and the English ships conquered the remainder.

5. Some of the actions of queen Elizabeth were almost as bad as those of old Harry, her father. When Mary, the beautiful queen of Scots, fled into England for protection, she caused her to be imprisoned eighteen years. And after those long and weary years the poor queen was tried and condemned to die.

6. Elizabeth was resolved upon her death, but she was loth to incur the odium of such a crime. She therefore endeavored to persuade the jailer to murder her. But, as he steadfastly refused, Elizabeth signed the death-warrant, and the unfortunate Mary was beheaded.

7. When queen Elizabeth grew old she could not bear to look at her gray hairs and withered and wrinkled visage in a glass. Her maids of honor, therefore, had all the trouble of dressing her. Part of their business was to paint her face. The queen of course expected them to make her cheeks look red and rosy.

8. But, instead of putting the red paint on her cheeks these mischievous maids of honor used sometimes to put it all upon her nose. So they set this great queen on her throne, in the presence of her court, with her nose as bright as if it had caught fire.

9. The courtiers often made a fool of Elizabeth by pretending to be in love with her, even when she was old enough to be their grandmother. Among others, the earl of Essex paid his addresses to her, and became her chief

---

Questions—Chap. CXLIII—1. When did Elizabeth ascend the throne? What was her religion? 2. What of her? 3. Why did she not marry? What made her angry? 4. What of Philip of Spain? What of the Invincible Armada? 5. What was one of the worst actions of queen Elizabeth? What was the fate of Mary queen of Scots? 7–8. What trick did the maids of honor put upon queen Elizabeth?

favorite. But at last he offended her, and was sentenced to lose his head.

10. When the earl of Essex was dead and gone, queen Elizabeth bitterly repented of her cruelty. She was now very old, and she knew that nobody loved her, and there were none that she could love. She pined away, and never held up her head again; and in her seventieth year she died.

11. The bishops, and the wise and learned men of her court, came to look at her dead body. They were sad, for they doubted whether England would ever be so prosperous again as while it was under the government of this mighty queen. And, in truth, of all the monarchs who have held the sceptre since that day, there has not been one who could sway it like the gray-haired woman whose spirit had now passed into eternity.

CHAPTER CXLIV—EUROPE—Continued
Accession of the House of Stuart

1. Elizabeth was succeeded by James Stuart, king of Scotland. He was the sixth James that had ruled over that kingdom, but was James the First of England. He began to reign in 1603. James inherited the English crown, because he was the grandson of a daughter of Henry the Seventh. His mother was Mary queen of Scots, whom Elizabeth had beheaded.

2. The whole island of Great Britain was now under the same government. This event put an end to the wars which had raged between England and Scotland during many centuries. But it was a long time before English and Scotch could live together like brethren.

3. As for king James, he was much fitter for a schoolmaster than for a king. He had a good deal of learning, and wrote several books. He delighted to talk Hebrew, and Greek, and Latin, and his courtiers were often puzzled to understand him.

4. James thought himself as wise as Solomon; and it must be owned that he possessed a sort of cunning which greatly resembled wisdom. This was seen in his discovery of the Gunpowder Plot. Some misguided Catholics had laid a plan to blow up the parliament-house at a time when the king, the lords, and all the members of parliament would be assembled there. If it had succeeded the whole government of England would have been destroyed.

Questions—9. What of the earl of Essex?   10. How did Elizabeth feel after his death? 11. How did the great men of the court feel when they saw Elizabeth's dead body?   What may be said of her government?

Chap. CXLIV—1. When did James I begin to reign?   Who was he?   2. What put an end to the wars between England and Scotland?   3. What of king James?   4. What plot had the Roman Catholics laid?

5. But king James smelled out the plot. He set people on the watch, and they caught a man by the name of Guy Fawkes, in a cellar, where thirty-six barrels of gunpower were concealed. Fawkes told the king the names of eighty of his accomplices. He and they were all put to death.

6. James had one good quality which kings have not very often possessed. He hated war. His reign was therefore peaceable. He died in 1625, and was succeeded by Charles the First, his son.

7. It was easy to foresee that this king would have a more troublesome reign than his father. There were now many Puritans in England. These people were opposed to the Church of England, to the bishops, and to all the ceremonies which had not been cast off when the Roman Catholic faith was abolished.

8. They likewise thought that the kings of England had too much power. They were determined that, thenceforward, the king should not reign merely for his own pleasure and glory, but for the good of the people. Charles, on the other hand, seemed to think that the common people were created only that kings might have subjects to rule over.

9. In the early part of his reign the king persecuted the Puritans. He would not allow the Puritan ministers to preach nor the people to attend their meetings. Their sufferings were great, although the king dared not burn them, as the bloody queen Mary would have done.

10. Many of them crossed the ocean and sought religious freedom in New England. John Hampden, John Pym, and Oliver Cromwell were once on the point of coming to this country. But the king prevented them, and these three persons afterward became his most powerful enemies.

CHAPTER CXLV—EUROPE—CONTINUED
Wars of the King and Parliament

1. TILL THE REIGN of Charles the First, the English parliament had hardly ever dared to oppose the wishes of the king. But now there were continual disputes between the king and parliament. And if Charles dissolved one parliament the next was sure to be still more obstinate.

2. Matters went on in this way till at length the quarrel grew too vio-

---

Questions—5. How did James discover the plot? What of Guy Fawkes? 6. What good qualities did James possess? When did he die? Who succeeded him? 7. What of the Puritans? 8. What did they think? What of Charles? 9. How did he treat the Puritans? 10. What did many of them do? What of three principal enemies of Charles? CHAP. CXLV—1. What of the parliament during the reign of Charles I?

lent to be settled by mere words. Both parties then betook themselves to their weapons. The king was supported by a great majority of the lords and gentlemen of England and Scotland, and by all the bishops and clergy of the English church. All the gay and wild young men in the kingdom likewise drew their swords for the crown. The whole of king Charles's party were called Cavaliers.

3. Some of the noblemen and gentry took the side of the parliament; but its adherents were chiefly mechanics, tradesmen, and common people. Because their hair was cropped close to their skulls their enemies gave them the nickname of Roundheads. The cavaliers dressed magnificently, and wore long hair, hanging in love-locks down their temples. They drank wine, and sang songs, and rode merrily to the battle-field.

4. The Roundheads wore steeple-crowned hats and sad-colored garments. They sang nothing but psalms, and spent much of their leisure time in praying and hearing sermons. They were a stern and resolute set of men, and when once they had made up their minds to tear down the throne, it must be done, though the realm of England should be rent asunder in the struggle.

5. The civil war between the cavaliers and roundheads began in 1642. Many battles were fought, and rivers of English blood were shed on both sides.

6. It was not long before Oliver Cromwell began to be a famous leader on the side of parliament. He pretended to fight only for religion and the good of the people. But he was an ambitious man, and meant to place himself in the king's empty seat.

7. Cromwell gained one battle after another, and rose from step to step till there was no man so powerful or renowned as he. Finally, in 1645, he defeated the king's army at the bloody battle of Naseby. King Charles afterward surrendered himself to the Scots, and they delivered him to the parliament.

8. The parliament brought the king to trial as a traitor. The court that tried him consisted of a hundred and thirty-three persons. They declared him guilty, and sentenced him to lose his head. When the people of England heard the sentence they trembled.

Questions—2. How was the king supported? What were the king's party called? 3. Who were on the side of the parliament? Describe the Cavaliers. 4. What of the Roundheads? 5. What war began in 1642? 6. What of Oliver Cromwell? 7. When was the battle of Naseby fought? 8. What was done to king Charles? How did the people feel when he was sentenced to death?

9. For it was a great and terrible thing that their anointed sovereign should die the death of a traitor. Many kings, it is true, had died by the hands of their enemies, but it had always been in darkness and secrecy. But king Charles was tried and condemned in the face of all the world.

10. On the 30th of January, 1649, they brought the king from his palace to the scaffold. It was covered with black cloth. In the center of the scaffold stood a block, and by the block stood an executioner, with an axe in his hand and a black mask over his face.

11. The steel-clad soldiers of Cromwell surrounded the scaffold. But the king walked to his death with as firm a step as when he went to his coronation. "They have taken away my corruptible crown," said he, "but I go to receive an incorruptible one."

12. When king Charles had knelt down and prayed, he cast a pitying glance upon the people round the scaffold; for he feared that direful judgments would come upon the land which was now to be stained with its monarch's blood.

13. But, as he saw that his enemies were resolved to slay him, he calmly laid his head upon the block. The executioner raised his axe and smote off the king's head at a single blow. Then, lifting it in his hand, he cried aloud, "This is the head of a traitor!" But the people shuddered; for they doubted whether it was the head of a traitor, and they knew that it was the head of a king.

CHAPTER CXLVI—EUROPE—Continued
The Protectorate and the Restoration

1. AND NOW THE THRONE of England was empty. The king, indeed, had left a son, but if he had shown himself in London, he would soon have died the same death as his father. The young prince was defeated in battle, and compelled to flee. At one time his enemies pressed him so hard that he climbed up among the thick branches of an oak and thus saved his life.

2. The government at this period was called a Commonwealth. There was no king, no lords, no bishops, nothing but the House of Commons, or the lower House of Parliament. All the real power of the kingdom was possessed by Oliver Cromwell, because he was at the head of the army.

Questions—10–13. Describe the execution of Charles I. In what year did it take place? CHAP. CXLVI—1. What of king Charles's son? 2. What was the government called at this time? Who had all the power?

3. No sooner did the parliament dare to oppose Cromwell's wishes than he led three hundred soldiers into the hall where they were sitting. He told the parliament men that they were a pack of traitors, and bade them get out of the house. When they were gone he summoned another parliament. The principal man in it was called Praise-God Barebone. This name sounded so well that it was bestowed on the whole parliament.

4. But Praise-God Barebone's parliament did not keep together a great while. At the end of five months they besought Cromwell to send them about their business and take the government into his own hands. This is just what Cromwell wanted.

5. In 1654, he was proclaimed Lord Protector of the Commonwealth of England. He held this high office four years. He was a sagacious and powerful ruler, and made himself feared and respected, both in England and foreign countries.

6. But he had no peace nor quiet as long as he lived. He constantly wore iron armor under his clothes, dreading that some of his enemies would attempt to stab him. He never enjoyed any quiet sleep, for the thought always haunted him that conspirators might be hidden in the closet or under the bed.

7. Cromwell was released from this miserable way of life by a slow fever, of which he died in 1658, at the age of fifty-nine. His son Richard succeeded him in the office of Lord Protector; but he had not ability enough to keep the kingdom in subjection.

8. Richard Cromwell soon resigned his office, and the government then became unsettled. The people began to think that England would never be prosperous again, unless the hereditary sovereigns were re-established on the throne.

9. The man who had most influence in the army after Oliver Cromwell's death was General George Monk. He invited the eldest son of Charles the First to return to England, promising that the soldiers would assist in making him king.

10. The banished prince had been living in different parts of Europe, and was reduced to great poverty. He lost no time in coming to England, and entered London in triumph. At sight of their new king it seemed as if

---

Questions—3. Describe the dispersing of the parliament by Cromwell. What parliament was then called? What of it? 5. When was Cromwell proclaimed Lord Protector? How long did he hold the office? What was his character? 6. What fears deprived him of peace? 7. When did he die? Who succeeded him? 8. What of Richard Cromwell? 9. What did General Monk do?

the people were mad with joy. He was crowned in 1660, by the title of Charles the Second.

11. Many of the persons who had assisted in dethroning and beheading the king's father were hanged. The body of Oliver Cromwell was taken out of the grave and hung upon the gallows, and afterward buried beneath it. Yet it would have been well for England if that stern but valiant ruler could have come to life again.

CHAPTER CXLVII—EUROPE—Continued
The Revolution of 1688 and other matters

1. Charles the Second had lived a careless and vicious life during his banishment, and his habits did not improve now that he was on the throne. He spent whole days and nights in drinking wine, and in all sorts of profligate pleasures.

2. In the year 1665, there was a great plague in London, of which nearly a hundred thousand persons died. The next year a terrible fire broke out, which consumed a great part of the city. But neither of these calamities made any impression on the king.

3. He suffered the nation to be ruled by unprincipled and wicked men. It was safer to be wicked in those days than to be virtuous and upright. Virtue and religion were looked upon as treason in the reign of Charles the Second. This good-for-nothing monarch died in the midst of his drunkenness and debauchery, in the year 1685. His brother succeeded him, and was called James the Second.

4. James was a Roman Catholic; and from the moment that he ascended the throne he thought of nothing but how to re-establish the Catholic religion in Great Britain. The attempt rendered him hateful to his subjects, and cost him his crown.

5. He had not been on the throne more than three years when some of the greatest men in England determined to get rid of him. They invited William Prince of Orange to come over from Holland and be their king.

6. The prince had no title to the crown except that he married the

---

Questions—10. What of the banished prince? When was Charles II crowned? 11. What of the body of Cromwell?

Chap. CXLVII—1. What of Charles II during his banishment? 2. What of the plague? What of a great fire? 3. What was the state of morals and religion during this reign? When did he die? Who succeeded him? 4. What did James wish to do? 5. What did some of the great men do? Whom did they invite from Holland?

daughter of James the Second. But no sooner had he landed in England than all the courtiers left king James and hurried to pay obeisance to the Prince of Orange. He and his wife were crowned in 1689, as king William and queen Mary. James had made his escape into France. Some of his adherents endeavored to set him on the throne again, but without success.

7. This change of government of which I have been speaking is generally called the Glorious Revolution of 1688. Some regulations were now adopted in order to restrain the royal power.

8. King William was very fond of hunting, and this amusement hastened his death. He was thrown from his horse in the year 1702, and died in about a month. His queen had died some years before him.

9. Anne, another daughter of the banished James, now ascended the throne. The reign of this queen was a glorious one for England. The renowned Duke of Marlborough gained many splendid victories over the French. But the chief glory of the age proceeded from the great writers who lived in her time.

10. Queen Anne reigned twelve years, and died in 1714, at the age of forty-nine. She was the last sovereign of England who belonged to the family of the Stuarts, which, as you remember, began to reign in England in 1603.

CHAPTER CXLVIII—EUROPE—Continued
The Hanoverian Kings of Great Britain

1. THE OLD BANISHED KING James had died in France in the year 1701. He left a son whom Louis the Fourteenth caused to be proclaimed king of England. But the English people called him the Pretender. They were determined not to have a Roman Catholic king. The nearest Protestant heir to the throne was the Elector of Hanover, a German prince, whose mother was a granddaughter of James the First. He was now about fifty-five years of age.

2. This old German Elector was proclaimed king of England by the title of George the first. With him began the dynasty of the House of Hanover.

Questions—6. What title had William to the throne? When was he crowned? What of the king James? 7. What of the revolution of 1688? 8. When did William die? 9. What of Anne? Her reign? What of the Duke of Marlborough? What was the chief glory of Anne's reign? 10. When did Anne die? When did the Stuarts begin to reign?

CHAP. CXLVIII—1. When and where did James II die? What did the English call James's son? Who was the nearest heir to the throne?

277

He could not speak a word of English, and knew nothing about the kingdom which he was to govern.

3. He spent much of his time in his native country, for he dearly loved Hanover, and could never feel at home in the palace of the English kings. He died in 1727, and was succeeded by his son, George the Second, who was likewise a native of Germany.

4. During part of George the Second's reign England was at war with Spain and France. The king commanded his army in person. The English were victorious in the battle of Dettingen, but they lost the battle of Fontenoy.

5. In 1745, the grandson of James the Second attempted to win back the crown of his ancestors. He landed in Scotland, and marched into England with a small army of Scotch mountaineers. But he was at last defeated, and forced to fly; and many of his adherents were beheaded or hanged.

6. In 1755, another war began between the French and English, and some of their principal battles were fought in America. The city of Quebec and the Canadas were conquered by the English during this war. Shortly after this event George the Second died, at the age of seventy-seven.

7. His grandson, George III, began to reign in 1760, when he was about twenty-one years old. No king ever ascended the throne with better prospects. Yet so many misfortunes befell him that it would have been far better for him to have died on his coronation day.

8. George the Third was a man of respectable common sense. In his private conduct he was much better than the generality of kings. But he was very obstinate, and often would not take the advice of men wiser than himself. Had he done so, it is probable that the American Revolution would not have happened in his reign.

9. I shall speak of this great event hereafter. The loss of America, together with many other troubles, contributed to drive George the Third to madness. His first fit of derangement happened in 1788, and lasted several months.

10. In 1805, he had another turn, and a third in 1810. From this latter period he continued a madman till his dying day. While the armies of En-

---

Questions—2. Who was George I? What of him? 3. When did George II come to the throne? 4. With what countries was England at war during his reign? What battle did the English gain? What did they lose? 5. What took place in 1745? 6. What of the war in 1755? What of Quebec and the Canadas? 7. When did George III begin to reign? 8. Character of George III? 9. What happened to him?

gland were gaining glorious victories, and grand events were continually taking place, the poor old crazy king knew nothing of the matter. Death released him from his miserable condition in the eighty-second year of his age.

11. The son of the old king was very wild in his youth, and he never became a really good man. He had been declared Prince Regent in consequence of his father's insanity. In 1820, he was crowned as king George the Fourth.

12. Even when he was quite an old man this king cared as much about dress as any young coxcomb. He had a great deal of taste in such matters, and it is a pity that he was a king, because he might otherwise have been an excellent tailor.

13. During his regency and reign, England combated the armies of Bonaparte. With her gigantic power, and aided by the other kingdoms of Europe, that famous conqueror was finally overthrown. The other events of king George's reign are so recent that they scarcely yet belong to history. He died in 1830, and was succeeded by his brother, William the Fourth; he died in 1837, and was succeeded by Victoria, the present queen.

14. Since her accession, the United Kingdom of Great Britain and Ireland, which is the title of her empire, has been very prosperous, and its power has been greatly extended. In the year 1840, queen Victoria married a German prince, by the name of Albert. She is very much loved in her own dominions, and is greatly respected throughout the civilized world.

CHAPTER CXLIX—EUROPE—Continued
The Story of Wales

1. IF YOU EVER GO to Wales and mingle with the people you will hardly believe that you are in any part of Great Britain. The names of the inhabitants are very different from English names. What would you think of Mr. Llewellyn ap Griffith ap Jones, and Mrs. Catesby ap Catesby? Yet such names are common in Wales.

2. Most of the people speak English, but some of them use the same language that was spoken by their ancestors. This is nearly the same as the original language of Ireland and the Highlands of Scotland. This seems to

---

Questions—10. What of his insanity? When did he die? 11. When was George IV crowned? 12. What of his taste in dress? 13. What events took place during his reign? When did he die? Who succeeded him? 14. What of queen Victoria?

Chap. CXLIX—1. What of the names in Wales?

show that the people are of the same stock as the Irish and the Scotch Highlanders.

3. The early history of Wales is involved in obscurity. When the Romans came to Britain, the Welsh mountains were inhabited by a rough set of people, who gave terrible blows with their clubs. They defended their mountains so fiercely that the Romans never got possession of the country.

4. When the Saxons came they subdued all England and a small portion of Wales; but the greater part held out against them to the last. Thus the Welsh princes maintained their independence, as well against the Romans as the Saxon invaders. These princes appear to have lived in strong stone castles, which, in time of war, were defended by the people around them. The ruins of some of these castles are still to be seen.

5. In these ancient times there was a strange set of men in Wales, called Bards. These sung songs and told stories about the brave deeds of the Welsh princes and heroes. The people loved to listen to these men, for their tales related to fierce war and bloody battles, of which rude nations are ever fond.

6. Some of these bards had a wonderful gift for singing and storytelling. They were often taken into the castles of the princes, and here they led a merry life, between singing and feasting. In order to keep up their influence they pretended to be prophets, and both the people and the princes believed they could foretell future events. Perhaps, too, the bards believed it themselves, for nothing is more easy than self-deception. At all events, the people paid them the greatest reverence.

7. There is nothing so troublesome to a king as a tribe of people maintaining their independence in his neighborhood. His pride is mortified, his indignation roused, by seeing people thus setting up for themselves. He thinks every body ought to bow to power, and feels toward them very much as an old hunter does toward a family of wolves or foxes, that persist in living among the rocks near him in spite of all his efforts to kill them.

8. So it was with the kings of England with regard to Wales. With a view therefore to subdue these Welsh wolves and foxes of the mountains, they sent a great many armies against them. But the mountaineers were too cunning to be caught, until about the year 1285. Edward the First was then king of England, and Llewellyn prince of Wales.

Questions—2. Their language? Of what stock are the Welsh people? 3. What of the early history of Wales? The ancient inhabitants? 4. What of the Saxons? What of the Welsh princes? 5–6. What of the bards? 7. What is very troublesome to a king? 8. What did the kings of England do? Who was the prince of Wales in 1285?

9. The bards were always great lovers of hard fighting, and therefore they incited the Welsh princes to the boldest deeds. Llewellyn had been told by one of these bards, that he should become master of the whole island of Britain.

10. Accordingly, when the army of Edward the First came against him, he rashly led his little army against the English and was defeated and slain. He was succeeded by his brother David, but he was taken and hung on a gibbet, for the crime of bravely defending his country.

11. King Edward was very angry at the bards for stirring up the people to resist his arms. He therefore caused them all to be assembled and put to death. These acts did not make the king a favorite, but the next king was born in Wales, and received the title of Prince of Wales. The Welsh people appear to have liked him a little better. From this time the eldest son of the king of England has been called Prince of Wales.

12. Thus, with the death of David, ended the line of Welsh princes, and thus ended the independence of Wales. Since that time the Welsh have been a part of the British nation, and they now weave stockings and dig coal and iron, instead of fighting, as their fathers did in the times of Llewellyn.

CHAPTER CL—EUROPE—Continued
The History of Scotland

1. THE FIRST INHABITANTS of Scotland appear to have been Celts, and probably were the same as the early Britons, Welsh and Irish. They defended themselves against the Romans, who could never subdue the people of the Highlands. They were so troublesome that the Roman generals caused a wall to be built from the Solway Firth to the river Tyne.

2. Thus the Scots were shut up in thir own country, like a herd of unruly cattle; but they contrived to get over the wall pretty often. In three or four hundred years after Christ a tribe of Goths, called Picts, came over from the continent and settled in the country. These inhabited the Lowlands, and lived by agriculture. The Scots dwelt in the mountains, carrying on war, and subsisting by the chase.

Questions—9. What did the bards do? What did one of them tell Llewellyn? 10. What did Llewellyn do? His fate? Who defeated him? What of his brother David? 11. What did king Edward do to the bards? Where was the next king of England born? 12. Since when have the Welsh become a part of the British nation? What of the Welsh people now?

CHAP. CL—1. What of the first inhabitants of Scotland? What did the Roman generals do? 2. What of the Picts? The Scots?

3. Thus the nation became divided into Highlanders and Lowlanders, and thus, to some extent, the people remain to this day. They live peaceably now, but in early days they quarreled very fiercely. I cannot undertake to tell you of their battles; indeed, we know but little about them.

4. In 839, it is said that Kenneth the Second, who was a Highland leader, subdued the Picts, and became the first king of all Scotland. From his time to Edward the First of England, there were a good many sovereigns, but their story is not worth repeating.

5. I have told you in the history of England, how Edward Longshanks, the same that subdued Wales, made war upon the Scotch, imprisoned Wallace, and had prepared a great army for the final subjugation of Scotland, when he died. I have told you how his son, Edward the Second, was beaten by Robert Bruce at the glorious battle of Bannockburn. This event occurred in 1313, and secured the freedom of Scotland, which had been threatened by the English kings.

6. From this time the history of Scotland tells of little but civil wars and bloody battles with England, till the time of James the Fifth. He assumed the reins of government in 1513, at the age of eighteen months. He afterward lost the confidence of his army, and they deserted him in the hour of need. This broke his heart, and he starved himself to death in 1542 at the age of thirty-one.

7. His daughter was the beautiful and unfortunate Mary Queen of Scots, as she is called, and whom I have mentioned in the history of England. She was educated in France, and was not only very handsome, but she was very accomplished. While she was yet a young lady she was taken to Scotland and became queen.

8. But beauty, accomplishments, and power, cannot insure happiness. Mary's kingdom was in a state of great trouble; the people were divided among themselves, and Mary found it impossible to govern them. At length she became afraid that they would kill her, and, to save her life, she went to England, and placed herself under the protection of Elizabeth.

9. This was about as wise as it would be in a fly to seek protection of a spider. Elizabeth treated Mary very much as a spider would a fly who falls into his power. She caused her to be put in prison, and finally took her life.

Questions—3. How was the nation divided? How did they live in the early time? 4. Who was king of Scotland in 839? 5. What can you tell of Edward Longshanks? Of Edward II? When was the battle of Bannockburn? Its effects? 6. How long were the Scots at war with the English? When did James V begin to reign? His fate? 7–9. Tell the story of Mary of Scotland.

10. The son of Mary, James the Sixth of Scotland, succeeded his mother, and after the death of Elizabeth he became king of England also, under the title of James the First. Though he lived in England he did not forget Scotland. He loved learning, and caused schools to be established in his native country, where all the boys and girls might learn to read and write. These schools continue to this day, and therefore it is very uncommon to meet with a Scotchman who is not a fair match for a Yankee.

11. From the time of king James, in 1603, Scotland has been attached to the British crown. She has sometimes rebelled, and in the cause of the Stuarts she fought a good many battles. But for many years Scotland has been a peaceful portion of the British kingdom.

CHAPTER CLI—EUROPE—Continued
About Ireland

1. THE HISTORY OF IRELAND—or "Green Erin," as it is called—is full of interesting matter, and I am sorry that I can only bestow upon it one brief chapter. The first inhabitants, like the Britons, were hard-fisted Celts, who fought with clubs, and seemed to love fighting better than even feasting.

2. They were divided into many tribes, and their leaders were called kings. These were constantly quarreling with each other, and thus the people had plenty of their favorite sport. The early Irish, like the other Celtic tribes, were devoted to the religion of the Druids, but about the year 430, a Christian missionary came into the country whose name was Patrick.

3. He seems to have been a wise and good man, and the people liked him very much. In thirty years he spread Christianity over all Ireland, and under its influence a part of the Irish gradually became somewhat civilized. Patrick lived to a great age, but at length he died and was buried at Doune [*doon*].

4. When he was gone, the people told pretty large stories about him and finally they considered him more holy than other men, and called him a saint. To this day many of the Irish regard St. Patrick as in heaven, watching over the interests of Ireland.

Questions—10. Who succeeded Mary? What did James do? 11. What of Scotland since 1603?

CHAP. CLI—1. What is Ireland called? Who were its first inhabitants? 2. What of the Celts? Religion of the early Irish? What took place in 430? 3. What of Patrick? What influence civilized the people? 4. What did the people think of Patrick? How do they regard him?

5. Among the curious notions still entertained by the Irish with regard to St. Patrick, is this: in Ireland there are no serpents or venomous reptiles, and the people firmly believe that St. Patrick put an end to them, and freed the island from them all forever!

6. In the time of Henry the Second of England, Ireland was conquered, and since that period has been under the English kings. It has, however, been very ill governed. King James the First did something toward improving the condition of the people, but neither he nor any subsequent king has been able to get what St. Patrick taught them out of their hearts.

7. The saint was a Roman Catholic, and the greater part of the people are Catholics to this day. They have been dissatisfied with the English government; and well they might be, for its conduct has been selfish and unwise. The people have often been in a state of rebellion, and though the leaders are constantly crushed by the power of the government, still others rise up to head the people.

8. Thus Ireland has been for years in an almost constant state of agitation. Thousands of lives have been lost in vain attempts to obtain the freedom of the country. In 1847, it was visited by famine and pestilence, which carried off a million of the inhabitants. Since that time vast emigrations have taken place, and the country seems now rising from its former state of depression.

CHAPTER CLII—EUROPE—Continued
Various Matters and Things

1. I HAVE NOW TOLD you something about England, Wales, Scotland, and Ireland; but it is impossible to do justice to so great a subject in this little book. I have told you something about the kings and the battles that have been fought.

2. But there are a great many interesting stories that I have been obliged to omit. If I had time I could give you a more particular account of the Celtic religion taught by the Druids, which was very curious, together with the manners of these Celts in other respects, which you would find very amusing.

Questions—5. What curious notion have the Irish with respect to St. Patrick? 6. When was Ireland conquered? How has it since been governed? What of king James I? 7. What is the religion of Ireland? Do the people like the government of England? What excites them to rebellion? 8. What is the present state of Ireland?
CHAP. CLII—2. What of the Druids?

3. I could tell you of Odin, or Woden, the Scandinavian hero, who established a strange mythology which pervaded the northern nations of Europe, and became, for a time, the religion of some of the inhabitants of Britain. I could tell you how Christianity was introduced into England sixty years after Christ; and how, at first, the people built rude churches of wood, and how they afterward constructed those fine Gothic buildings in which the people worship there.

4. If I had time I could tell of the Gipsies, a strange race of people to be found in most countries of Europe, but particularly in England, Spain, Hungary, and Bohemia; who wander from place to place, having no fixed homes; who come from some far land, but whether from Egypt or Asia none can tell; who continue from age to age the same, while the nations, among which they wander, rise and fall, flourish and decay.

5. If I had time I could tell you some curious stories about a famous robber by the name of Robin Hood, who lived in the woods, and performed strange things. I could also tell you of many celebrated people more worthy of being remembered than this freebooter.

6. I could tell you of Dr. Watts, who wrote that beautiful little book entitled Hymns for Infant Minds—a work which has given more pleasure and done more good than all the battles of the greatest conqueror that ever lived.

7. I could tell you of Hannah More, who wrote that beautiful story entitled the Shepherd of Salisbury Plain; of Miss Edgeworth, who wrote the story of Frank; and Daniel De Foe, who composed that beautiful fancy story called Robinson Crusoe.

8. It would be very pleasant to read about these people; they seem like friends to us, and we should like to know where they lived, how they looked, and what adventures they met with. But these and other matters relating to the history of that beautiful and interesting country from which our forefathers came, I must leave for the present.

9. I have then only to add, that while you can read the history of the British nation in books, you can best study the character and manners of the people at home in their own country. If you ever visit England you will certainly be delighted with the beauty of the country, and if you become acquainted with any of the people, you will be charmed by their hospitality.

Questions—3. Who was Woden? What did his mythology become? When was Christianity introduced into England? 4. What of the Gipsies? Where do they live? 5. Who was Robin Hood? 6. What of Dr. Watts? 7. What other celebrated writers could be mentioned? 9. What of Englishmen?

10. The Scotch are a shrewd, well educated, money-saving race, and may be called the Yankees of Great Britain, for they bear a considerable resemblance in their character, disposition, and religion, to the sober, sagacious, thrifty inhabitants of New England.

11. The Irish are much the same wherever they may be, cheerful and witty, if not wise. They are generally without education, but if ignorant they are perhaps better than most other ignorant people. They are of a race possessing fine natural qualities, but injured by ages of oppression. They are rapidly improving now, and their children—if educated in our schools—may be among our best citizens.

CHAPTER CLIII—EUROPE—Continued
Review—The Dark Ages—Important Inventions, etc.

1. Such is my brief story about Europe. I hope I have told you enough to excite your curiosity and lead you to read larger works than mine about the nations I have mentioned. You will find the subject very interesting and worthy of your careful study. I have room now only to mention a few things that have been omitted in the progress of my story.

2. You will remember that Greece was settled before any other portion of Europe, and that the Greeks became a polished and powerful people. You will remember that Rome became a mighty empire, and extended its sway over nearly all parts of the world that were then known.

3. You will remember that four or five hundred years after Christ the Roman empire was dismembered, and that the northern tribes of Europe spread themselves over Spain, Italy, and Greece. Thus the arts, learning and refinement, which had been cultivated in these countries, were for a time extinguished, and all Europe was reduced to a nearly barbarous state.

4. This period is called the Dark Ages, because the nations were generally ignorant, fierce, and barbarous. So things continued till about five hundred years ago, when the light of learning began to return. Since that time society has advanced in civilization till it has reached a higher state of improvement than was ever known before.

5. The history of the church of Christ is a subject at which I have been able only to take an occasional glance. After our Saviour's death, in the

---

Questions—10. What of the Scotch? 11. What of the Irish?

Chap. CLIII—2. Which of the nations of Europe was first settled? What of Rome? 3. What happened four or five hundred years after Christ? 4. What period was called the Dark Ages? How long is it since learning began to revive?

year 33, his apostles proceeded to spread the gospel throughout different countries. Paul was the most active and successful of these missionaries. He went several times through Asia Minor, traveled to Greece, and finally to Rome, everywhere preaching the truths of the Christian religion. He died at Rome, A.D. 61.

6. At first the Christians were persecuted by the Roman emperors, but the gospel continued to flourish until it pervaded most parts of the Roman empire. It was introduced into Britain in the year 60 A.D., and into most other parts of Europe at an early period. But it was not till the year 312, when Constantine adopted it, that it found favor with any king or prince in Europe.

7. From this period it advanced rapidly. The mythology of Greece and Rome gave way before it. The horrid sacrifices and gloomy superstitions of the Druids yielded to the gentle worship of one God, and the mysterious rites of Odin were forsaken for the religion of the cross.

8. The popes of Rome succeeded in placing themselves at the head of the Christian religion, thereby obtaining a controlling influence over mankind. They gradually acquired an immense political power, which, however, in process of time, was greatly lessened. A large part of the people of Christendom protested against their authority, and were thence called Protestants.

9. I have not had an opportunity to mention the Abbeys and Monasteries of Europe. These curious institutions, however, deserve notice. It appears that in most countries there have been some people who retire from the active business of life and shut themselves up for religious contemplation. Such has been the case in Asia; and among the worshipers of Brahma, Boodh, and Mohammed, they are still found. Such was also the case among the idolators of ancient Egypt, Greece, and Rome. Such was the case among the ancient Jews, and such has been the case among the believers of Christ from very early ages.

10. The first monastery was founded by St. Anthony, in Upper Egypt, A.D. 305. This consisted of a number of huts, in which several hermits dwelt, devoting themselves to penance and prayer. Another monastery was established in France, in the year 360, by St. Martin. From this time these insti-

---

Questions—5. When did Christ die? What of the apostles? Paul? 6. How did the Romans at first treat the Christians? When was Christianity introduced into Britain? What took place in 323? 7. What of the progress of Christianity? 8. What of the popes? Who were called Protestants? 9. What appears to be the case in most countries? Mention some instances.

288 ℒ Parley's History of the World

tutions were multiplied, and became established in all Catholic countries. From the eighth to the fifteenth century they received great encouragement, and many splendid edifices were erected for their use.

11. Some were called abbeys and some monasteries. Many of them were filled with monks and friars, and other with females, called nuns. The splendid remains of many of these edifices are still to be found in England, France, Germany, and other parts of Europe. At first the inhabitants of monasteries lived in a simple manner and devoted themselves to religious contemplations. Many of them were employed in transcribing books before the art of printing was discovered.

12. These institutions were, however, greatly encouraged, and it was not until the Reformation, in the sixteenth century, that they began to decline. They were abolished in England in 1539, and in France in 1790. In several other countries of Europe they have ceased, but still continue in Italy and Spain.

13. In the early ages war was carried on without guns and cannon. The Greeks and Romans were armed with swords, spears, and battleaxes, and they carried shields for defense. The troops of Egypt, Carthage, and Persia, were armed in a similar manner. In the year 1330, gunpowder was invented, and cannon began to be used some time after. They were first employed by the English at the battle of Cressy, in 1346. On that occasion king Edward had four pieces of cannon, which greatly aided in gaining the victory.

14. From this time fire-arms were rapidly introduced, and soon the whole art of war was changed. Bows and arrows, spears and shields were thrown aside, and contending armies, instead of coming up close to each other, and fighting face to face, learned to shoot each other down from a distance.

15. One of the greatest discoveries of modern times is that quality of the mariner's compass by which it always points to the north pole. This useful instrument, which enables the seaman to traverse the ocean, appears to have been in use as early as 1180.

Questions—10. Who founded the first monastery? When? Of what did it consist? When and by whom was a monastery established in France? What of monasteries from this time? 11. Who inhabited them? How did the monks and nuns formerly live? How in later times? 12. By whom were these institutions encouraged? When did monastic institutions begin to decline? When were they abolished in England? In France? Where do they still exist? 13. What of war in early times? Arms? When was gunpowder invented? When were cannon first used by the English? 14. What happened from this time? 15. What is a great discovery of modern times? When was the mariner's compass first used?

16. But a still more important invention was that of printing, in 1441. Previous to that time all books were written with the pen. A copy of the Bible was worth as much in ancient times as a good house or a good farm is now. Of course very few people could learn to read for the want of books. The other important inventions of steam navigation, railroads, and the electric telegraph, belong to the present century.

CHAPTER CLIV—EUROPE—Continued
Chronology of Europe

                                                                         B.C.
Greece founded by Inachus 1856
Athens founded by Cecrops 1556
Corinth founded 1520
Sparta founded by Lelex 1516
Thebes founded by Cadmus 1500
Argonautic expedition 1263
Twelve States of Greece unite 1257
Siege of Troy 1193
Phoenicians trade to Spain, about 900
Homer born about 900
Lycurgus gives laws to Sparta 884
Building of Rome by Romulus 752
Numa Pompilius made king of Rome 715
Tullus Hostilius made king of Rome 672
Solon, lawgiver of Athens 643
Bias the Greek philosopher flourishes 617
The Celts settle in Bohemia 600
Death of Tarquin, and his family expelled from Rome 509
The Carthaginians make conquests in Spain about 500
Tribunes chosen at Rome 490
Battle of Marathon 490
Decemviri chosen at Rome 451
Peloponnesian war begins 446
Censors established at Rome 437

Questions—16. When was printing invented?　How were books formerly made?　What of other important inventions?

Chap. CLIV—*The teacher may here examine the pupil carefully in the Chronological table.*

B.C.

Death of Pericles 429
General migration of Gauls to different parts of Europe 397
Italy ravaged by the Gauls and Rome taken 396
Battle of Leuctra 371
Death of Epaminondas 363
Theaters established in Rome 361
War between the Romans and Samnites 343
Battle of Cheronea 338
Death of Philip, king of Macedon 336
Death of Alexander, king of Macedon 323
Sundial introduced into Rome 312
Aqueducts built in Rome 311
The Gauls make incursions into Macedon and Greece .... 280 to 278
All Italy submits to Rome 270
First Punic war begins 264
Second Punic war begins 218
Spain subjected to the Roman power 206
A colony of Belgae settle in Gaul 200
Greece becomes a Roman province 146
Carthage destroyed 146
Spain becomes a province of Rome 134
The southern part of Gaul along the Mediterranean
       conquered by the Romans .... 128 to 122
Social war in Greece begins 91
War between Marius and Sylla 88
Pompey defeats Mithridates 63
Triumvirate formed in Rome 59
France invaded by Julius Caesar 58
Switzerland subdued by Caesar 57
Caesar invades Britain 55
Battle of Pharsalia and death of Pompey 48
Death of Caesar 44
All France finally conquered by the Romans 25
Hungary, anciently Pannonia, subject to the Romans 11

A.D.

Death of Augustus Caesar, emperor of Rome 14
Death of Tiberius, emperor of Rome 37
Death of Caligula, emperor of Rome 41

A.D.

England finally subdued by Claudius, a Roman General 44

Claudius, emperor of Rome 54

Death of Nero, emperor of Rome 54

Christianity introduced into England 60

Hygenus, first bishop of Rome who took the title of pope 154

Scotland receives the Christian faith 203

The Romans expelled from Germany 290

Constantine begins to reign 306

Christianity adopted by the emperor of Rome 312

Constantine moves seat of the Roman empire to Constantinople 329

Rome divided into the Eastern and Western empire by Theodosius 395

France invaded by the Goths and other Germanic tribes 400

Rome taken by Alaric 410

Pharamond, a Frank, becomes first king of France 418

Kingdom of the Visigoths founded in Spain 419

Venice founded 421

Germany conquered by the Huns 432

Hungary possessed by the Huns under Attila 433

Patrick visits Ireland 434

Italy invaded by Attila 445

The Saxons conquer England 445

Rome taken by Odoacer 476

Kingdom of Sweden begun 481

Monarchy of France established 486

Goths driven from Rome by Belisarius 537

The pope's supremacy over the Christian church established 607

Death of Mohammed 634

Roderick, king of Spain, defeated by the Moors 712

The first king reigns in Denmark 714

Gregory III, founder of the pope's temporal power, becomes pope 731

Pepin the Short, first of the Carlovingian race in France 751

The pope's temporal power established 755

Charlemagne begins to reign in France 772

Charlemagne crowned at Rome 800

Charlemagne master of Germany 802

Venice becomes an independent republic 803

Death of Charlemagne 814

Egbert I, King of England 827

A.D.

Kenneth II, first king of Scotland 839

Iceland discovered by the Norwegians 860

Alfred ascends the English throne 871

The Danes conquer England 877

Emperors first chosen in Germany 912

Canute, king of Denmark, conquers England 1016

Danes driven out of England.. 1041

Leo IX, the first pope that kept an army 1054

Henry IV, emperor of Germany.. 1056

Harold becomes king of England 1066

William the Conqueror ascends the throne of England 1066

Henry IV of Germany, obliged to stand three days at pope's gate 1077

Pope's authority introduced into England............................... 1079

Peter the Hermit heads the first Crusade............................... 1096

Godfrey of Bouillon [boo´-yong] takes Jerusalem 1099

Kingdom of Portugal founded 1139

Richard ascends the throne of England 1189

Chivalry at its height 1200

Magna Charta [kar´-ta] granted by king John 1215

Last Crusade begun 1248

Othman first emperor of Turkey 1268

Rodolph of Hapsburg is elected emperor of Germany 1273

Wales annexed to the crown of England 1283

Ottoman empire founded 1299

Residence of the pope removed to Avignon [a-veen´-yon] in
     France, where it remained seventy years 1308

Battle of Bannockburn 1313

Battle of Cressy [kres´-se] 1346

William Tell died 1354

Battle of Poictiers [poi-teerz] 1356

Norway incorporated with Denmark....................................... 1397

Battle of Agincourt [a-zhin-koor´] 1415

Joan of Arc raises the siege of Orleans 1428

The Turks conquer the Eastern empire 1453

Wars of York and Lancaster begun 1455

The Portuguese discover the Cape of Good Hope.................. 1481

The first court of the Inquisition of Spain 1481

Richard Crookback, king of England, dies 1485

A.D.

America discovered by Columbus 1492

The Moors of Granada driven out of Spain 1492

The Portuguese discover Brazil 1501

Reformation commenced by Martin Luther 1517

Gustavus Vasa expels the Danes from Sweden..................................... 1525

Rome sacked and pope Clement imprisoned 1527

Gustavus Vasa ascends the throne of Sweden 1528

Henry VIII of England dies 1547

Mary, queen of England 1553

The first czar reigns in Russia 1553

Elizabeth ascends the throne of England 1558

The republic of Holland founded 1581

Henry the IV ascends the throne of France.. 1589

James I ascends the throne of England 1603

Portugal becomes independent of Spain 1604

Henry IV of France, killed by Revaillac 1610

Gustavus Adolphus king of Sweden 1611

The Moors finally expelled from Spain 1620

Charles I ascends the throne of England 1625

Battle of Lutzen and death of Adolphus Gustavus 1633

Civil war begun in England between Cavaliers and Roundheads 1642

Charles I beheaded 1649

Cromwell made Lord Protector of England 1654

Charles II king of England 1660

Great Plague in London 1665

Great Fire in London 1666

The Turks lay siege in Vienna 1688

William and Mary crowned in England 1689

Peter the Great begins to reign... 1696

Prussia becomes a kingdom 1701

Anne ascends the throne of England... 1702

Peter the Great defeats Charles XII at Poltava [*pol-ta '-va*] 1709

Russia becomes an empire.. 1721

Peter the Great dies 1725

Hungary annexed to Germany... 1739

War between Austria, Russia, France, and Prussia 1756

George III king of England... 1760

Partition of Poland 1772

A.D.

American Declaration of Independence 1776

Political influence of the popes ceases in Europe 1787

The Bastile at Paris destroyed 1789

Execution of Louis XVI, king of France 1793

Catherine II of Russia dies 1796

Venice attached to Austria 1798

Switzerland conquered by the French 1798

Napoleon takes possession of Egypt 1798

Napoleon gains the battle of Marengo 1800

Napoleon created emperor of France 1804

King of Portugal removes to Brazil 1807

Joachim Murat made king of Naples 1808

Napoleon removes Ferdinand from the throne of Spain 1808

Austria at war with France 1809

The city of Moscow burnt 1812

Norway transferred to Sweden 1814

Inquisition abolished in Portugal 1815

Revolution in Portugal 1820

Inquisition abolished in Spain 1820

George IV made king of England 1820

Greece rises against the Turks 1821

Death of Lord Byron at Missolonghi 1824

Alexander, emperor of Russia, dies 1825

Nicholas ascends the throne of Russia 1825

Massacre of the Janizaries in Turkey 1826

Battle of Navarino [nav-a-ree´-no] 1827

Accession of Otho to the throne of Greece 1829

William IV ascends the throne of England 1830

Netherlands divided into Holland and Belgium 1830

Ferdinand VII, king of Spain, dies 1833

Victoria becomes queen of the British empire 1837

Revolution in France .... February 22, 1848

Republic declared at Rome 1849

The pope driven from Rome, but soon restored 1849

Louis Napoleon emperor of France 1852

Eastern war 1854

Nicholas, czar of Russia, dies; Alexander II succeeds 1855

Peace of Paris 1856

SCENE IN NORTH AMERICA

CHAPTER CLV—AMERICA
About America

1. WE HAVE LONG BEEN occupied with the three great divisions of the Eastern Continent, Asia, Africa, and Europe. Let us now leave these countries, cross the Atlantic, and come to the Continent of America.

2. This continent consists of two parts, North and South America. These are united by a narrow strip of land called the isthmus of Darien, about sixty miles in width; at the narrowest part it is but thirty-seven miles. Both parts of this vast continent are about nine thousand miles in length, and are nearly equal in extent to Asia. The whole population is estimated at fifty millions.

3. The northern part of America is excessively cold. Whether it is there bounded by the sea, or whether it extends to the north pole, we cannot tell. Greenland, the coldest inhabited country on the globe, was formerly considered a part of our continent, but it is now thought to be a great island.

Questions—CHAP. CLV—2. What does the continent of America consist of?   What of the isthmus of Darien?   Extent and population of America?   3. What is known of the northern part of America?   What of Greenland?

4. The countries of North America are the island of Iceland, Greenland, the Polar Regions, inhabited by the Esquimaux [es-ki-moz] and other tribes of Indians, British America, the United States, Mexico, and Central America.

5. Between North and South America are a number of beautiful islands, called the West Indies. South America is divided into Venezuela [ven-ez-wee´-la], New Granada, Ecuador [ek-wa-dor´], Peru, Bolivia, Chili [chil´-lee], the Argentine Confederation, Uruguay [oo-roo-gwi´], and Paraguay [pa-ra-gwi´]. These are republics. Brazil was formerly a province of Portugal, but is now an extensive empire. Patagonia, at the southern end of South America, is a land thinly settled by uncivilized tribes. Guiana belongs to Great Britain, France, and Holland.

6. I have said that it is extremely cold in the northern part of North America. In this dreary region no trees are to be found, no plants flourish. For nine months in the year the sea is frozen, and scarcely a living thing is able to dwell there. Even in summer, no animal is seen save here and there a lonely white bear, or a solitary reindeer feeding upon moss.

7. As you proceed south, you meet with a few stunted willow and birch trees, and some hardy plants. Still farther south, the vegetation improves, wild animals become abundant, and wild birds are seen swimming in the waters, or hovering in the air.

8. Here you meet with tribes of Esquimaux and Chippewa Indians. When you arrive at Canada, you find a fruitful country. When you get as far south as the United States, the climate becomes pleasant. In the West Indies, around the Gulf of Mexico, and througout all the northern parts of South America, the climate is that of perpetual spring or summer.

9. As you go further south, it grows cold, and when you reach Cape Horn, you will find it a desolate country, where winter reigns three-fourths of the year. The wild animals of America are very numerous. The bison, wild goat, wild sheep, antelope, many kinds of deer, several kinds of bears, wolves, foxes, and many smaller quadrupeds, together with birds of many kinds, are natives of North America.

10. But our domestic cattle, all our breeds of sheep, our horses, asses, mules, goats, hens, and cats, were originally brought from Europe. The domestic turkey, goose, and duck, are native birds.

Questions—4. Countries of North America? 5. What of the West Indies? Divisions of South America? Brazil? 6. What of the northern part of North America? 7. What of vegetation as you proceed south? 8. What of Indian tribes? What of the climate as you proceed south? Climate of the West Indies, etc.? 9. What of Cape Horn? Animals of North America? Birds? 10. What of cattle? Native birds?

11. The people of America may be divided into two great classes. First, the Indians, descendants of those who were found scattered throughout this continent when it was first discovered. They consisted of many tribes, living separately, and speaking different languages. And second, the descendants of the Europeans who have come to this country at various times, and settled here. To these we might add several millions of negroes, who have been brought from Africa as slaves, or their descendants.

12. America is remarkable for three things: it has the largest lakes, the longest rivers, and the longest chain of mountains to be found in the world. The largest fresh-water lake is Lake Superior; the longest river is the Mississippi; the longest chain of mountains is that which extends nearly the whole length of the continent, being called the Andes in South America, the Cordilleras in Central America, and the Rocky Mountains in the United States.

CHAPTER CLVI—AMERICA—CONTINUED
The first Inhabitants of America

1. WHEN WE LOOK AROUND US and see such cities as Boston, New York, Philadelphia, Baltimore, New Orleans, Chicago, St. Louis, and Cincinnati; when we see the whole country dotted over with cities, town, and villages, we can hardly believe that a little more than three hundred and fifty years ago our whole continent of America was unknown to the inhabitants of Europe, Asia, and Africa.

2. Such, however, was the fact. The country was indeed inhabited by many tribes of Indians, but these people had no books, and knew nothing of the rest of the world. Where they came from or when they first appeared in America no one can tell.

3. It appears that the northern portions of North America are inhabited by a race of people called Esquimaux. These differ from all the other Indians, and bear a close resemblance to the Laplanders. It seems likely, therefore, that these polar regions were settled by people who came from Europe in boats, many centuries since.

4. That such a thing is possible appears from the fact that the Norwegians are known to have discovered Iceland in the eighth century, and that

Questions—11. Describe the two classes of people in North America.   12. For what is America remarkable?

CHAP. CLVI—1. What of America three hundred and fifty years ago?   2. What of the Indians?   3. The Esquimaux?   What seems probable?

297

they actually made settlements in Greenland in the ninth century. It thus appears that portions of America were actually visited by these northern Europeans, who possessed no other than small vessels, and little knowledge in the arts of navigation.

5. But how did the other Indians get to this country? If you will look on a map of the Pacific Ocean you will see, at the northern part, that America and Asia come very close together. They are separated only by Behring's [*bee´-ringz*] Straits, which are but eighteen miles wide at the narrowest part.

6. Across the channel the people of the present day, living in the neighborhood, are accustomed to pass in their little boats. There is reason to believe, then, that many ages since some of the Asiatic tribes of Tartars wandered to Behring's Straits and crossed over to America. These may have been numerous, and consisting of different tribes. A foundation may thus have been laid for the peopling of the American continent.

7. That such was the fact there is little reason to doubt. There is considerable resemblance between the American Indians and some Asiatic tribes, and they appear to possess some singular customs known in Asia. Thus it would seem that Asia, which furnished the first inhabitants of Africa and Europe, also supplied this continent with the first human beings that trod its shores.

CHAPTER CLVII—AMERICA—Continued
Discovery of America by Columbus

1. IT HAS BEEN CONJECTURED that the ancient Carthaginians discovered South America, and made settlements there. But this is very unlikely; if it was the case, the event had been forgotten for two or three thousand years. The Norwegians, however, were great navigators of the northern part of the Atlantic, and about the year 1000 A.D., some adventurers from that country are believed to have discovered and settled in some part of New England.

2. But they soon left the country, and never made known their discovery. It is probable, therefore, that the first inhabitant of the Old World, who gave any information of what was called the New World, was Christo-

Questions—4. What of the Norwegians? 5. What straits separate Asia and America? Their width? 6. What is there reason to believe? 7. Whom do our Indians resemble? How was America probably first people?

CHAP. CLVII—1. What has been conjectured? What of the Norwegians?

298

pher Columbus. He may fairly be called the Discoverer of America.

3. This illustrious person was born at Genoa, in Italy, in 1435. As he grew up, he paid great attention to the study of geography. The idea entered his mind, that there must be vast tracts of undiscovered country, somewhere on the face of the broad ocean.

4. Columbus was poor, and had not the means of sailing in search of these unknown lands. He applied for assistance to the rulers of his native country; but they refused it. He next went to Portugal; but there he met with no better success.

5. At last he came to the court of Spain. Ferdinand and Isabella were king and queen of that country. The king, like almost every body else, treated Columbus with neglect and scorn.

6. But the queen thought so favorably of his project, that she sold her jewels to defray the expenses of the voyage. Three small vessels were equipped with ninety men, and with provisions for one year. Columbus took the command, and sailed from Spain on the 3rd of August, 1492.

7. He first held his course southward, and touched at the Canary Islands. Thence he steered straight toward the west. After a few weeks his men became alarmed. They feared they should never again behold their native country, nor any land whatever, but should perish in the trackless sea.

8. Columbus did his utmost to encourage them. He promised to turn back, if land were not discovered within three days. On the evening of the last day, at about ten o'clock, he looked from the deck of his vessel, and beheld a light gleaming over the sea. He knew that this light must be on land. In the morning an island was seen, to which Columbus gave the name of San Salvador.

9. This is one of the Bahama Islands. The natives thronged to the shore, and gazed with wonder at the three ships. Perhaps they mistook them for living monsters, and thought that their white sails were wings.

10. Columbus clothed himself magnificently, and landed with a drawn sword in his hand. His first act was to kneel down and kiss the shore. He then erected a cross, as a symbol that Christianity was now to take the place of paganism. He declared the island to be the property of queen Isabella. He then visited other islands, and returned to Spain, giving an

Questions—2. What of Christopher Columbus?   3–6. When and where was he born? Tell the story of Columbus till the time when he set sail.   7. Which way did he first steer his course?   What of his men?   8. How did Columbus encourage them?   What land was first discovered?   9. What of the natives?

account of the wonderful things he had seen. He made a second and a third voyage; during the last he discovered the continent of America.

11. No sooner had Columbus proved that there really was a New World beyond the sea, than several other navigators made voyages thitherward. Americus Vespucius, a native of Florence, came here and contrived to have the whole continent called by his name.

12. By degrees, discoveries were made along the whole coast of North and South America. People came from various nations of Europe, and formed settlements here. In relating the history of these settlements, I shall begin with the most northerly, although the earliest colonies were planted in the tropical regions.

CHAPTER CLVIII—AMERICA—Continued
A few words about Iceland and Greenland— Settlements of the French in America

1. I HAVE ALREADY TOLD you that the island of Iceland was discovered by a Norwegian pirate, in 860. After this, the Norwegians sent people to settle there. It is a cold, dreary country, and there is a terrible mountain in the island, called Hecla, which sometimes sends out fire, smoke, and ashes, and shakes the whole island with its frightful rumblings.

2. But still the inhabitants increased, and Christianity was introduced in 981. From that time to the present, they have continued a quiet, honest set of people. Their number is now sixty thousand, and they are under the government of Denmark. Greenland was discovered about the same time as Iceland, and settled soon after.

3. This colony continued to flourish till the year 1408. At this time, the winter was so severe as to block up the sea, and since that time nothing has been known of the colony of settlers. It is probable they all perished long since. This settlement was on the northeastern coast of Greenland. Another colony was settled in the southwestern part of Greenland; this continues to the present day, but the inhabitants are few in number. Many of them are native Esquimaux; the rest are the descendants of the Norwegian settlers.

4. The portion of America which is now under the government of Great

Questions—10. What did Columbus now do? 11. What of Americus Vespucius? 12. What of other discoveries?

Chap. CLVIII—1. When was Iceland discovered? What of it? Mount Hecla? 2. When was Christianity introduced into Iceland? The people? What of Greenland?

SCENE IN ICELAND

Britain, consists of Nova Scotia, New Brunswick, Newfoundland, Quebec, Ontario, and New Britain.

5. All these provinces together compose a tract of country equal in extent to the United States. They are bounded north by the Arctic Sea and Baffin's Bay, east by the Atlantic, south by the United States, and west by Alaska and the Pacific Ocean.

6. The first people who formed settlements in America to the north-ward of the present limits of the United States, were the French. Some-what more than three hundred years ago, they were in the habit of sending fishing-vessels to this coast.

7. In 1524, a Frenchman, named James Cartier, sailed up the St. Lawrence and built a fort, in which he passed the winter. Settlements were soon after formed in Canada and Nova Scotia. King Henry the Fourth of France appointed the Marquis de la Roche to be governor-general of Canada and the neighboring territories.

8. The city of Quebec was founded in the year 1608. It stands on the river St. Lawrence, about five hundred miles from the sea. Its foundation is on a rock of marble and slate.

9. The French settlers were on very friendly terms with the Indians.

Questions—4. What does British America consist of? 5. How large is it? Boundaries? 6. What of the French? 7. What was done in 1524? Who was appointed governor of Canada? 8. When and where was Quebec founded?

They purchased the furs which the Red Men obtained in their hunting expeditions. These were sent to Europe, and sold at a great profit. Some of the French were married to Indian wives.

10. When the English began to form settlements to the southward of Canada, the French incited the savages to make war upon them. Parties of French and Indians would sometimes come from Quebec, or Montreal, and burn the New England villages. The inhabitants were killed, or carried captive to Canada.

11. In 1629, Sir David Keith, a British officer, took Quebec; but it was afterward restored to the French. The people of New England made several attempts to get it back again.

12. In 1711, the British government sent a strong fleet up the St. Lawrence, under the command of Admiral Walker. There was an army of seven thousand men on board the ships.

13. If they had landed in safety, they would probably have succeeded in taking Quebec. But when they were entering the river, the vessels became involved in a fog. A strong wind began to blow, and drove eight or nine of the ships upon the rocky shore.

14. The next morning, the French found the dead bodies of a thousand men in scarlet coats, heaped among the rocks. These were the drowned English soldiers. This sad event caused the English to give up the design of conquering Canada.

CHAPTER CLIX—AMERICA—CONTINUED
The French Colonies conquered by the English

1. WHENEVER THERE WAS A WAR between France and Old England, there was likewise a war between New England and the French provinces in America. The French built strong fortresses, and the English, or Americans, made great efforts to take them.

2. The French had carefully fortified the city of Louisbourg, on the island of Cape Breton. In 1745, the New England people formed a project of taking it. They raised a strong army, and gave the command to a Boston merchant, named William Pepperell.

Questions—9. What of the French and Indians?   10. In what way were the English treated by them?   11. When and by whom was Quebec taken?   12–14. What was done in 1711?   Give an account of the expedition.   What was the object of it?

CHAP. CLIX—1. What was the consequence of a war between France and England?   2. Where was Louisbourg?   What was done in 1745?

3. The army sailed under the escort of an English fleet and landed on the island of Cape Breton. General Pepperell's men were merely farmers and mechanics, and he himself knew but little about taking fortresses.

4. But if the New Englanders had no skill, they had plenty of courage. They erected batteries, and cannonaded the city for about a fortnight, and then the French commander hauled down his flag. The conquest of Louisbourg was considered a very brilliant exploit.

5. Louisbourg was restored to the French at the close of the war. But it was again taken by General Wolfe, in 1758. The same general soon afterward led an army against Quebec.

6. This city was so strongly fortified that it appeared almost impossible to take it. It had a citadel, which was built upon a rock several hundred feet high, and there were strong walls all round the city. And beside the French garrison within the walls, there was a large French army on the outside.

7. But General Wolfe was determined to take Quebec or lose his life in the attempt. After trying various other methods, he led his army from the shore of the river up a steep precipice. When they reached the top they were on a level with the walls of Quebec.

8. This bold movement was performed in the night. As soon as the Marquis de Montcalm, who commanded the French army, heard of it, he marched to meet the British. A battle was begun immediately.

9. General Wolfe placed himself at the head of his troops, and led them bravely onward. Though he had received two wounds he refused to quit the field. At last a ball struck him on the body, and stretched him on the ground.

10. A few of his soldiers carried him to the rear. But, though the hand of death was on him, General Wolfe thought only of the battle that was raging around. He heard a voice shouting, "They flee! They flee!" and he asked who it was that fled.

11. "It is the French!" said one of his attendants. "They are beaten! The victory is ours!" A glad smile appeared on the general's face. "Then I die happy!" he cried, and expired.

12. The victory was complete. The Marquis de Montcalm was mortally wounded. In a few days after the battle, Quebec was surrendered. The whole province, and all the French possessions in the north, soon fell into the hands of the British.

Questions—4. Describe the capture of Louisbourg. 5. When was it restored to the French? When taken by General Wolfe? 6–7. Describe the capture of Quebec. 8. Who commanded the French army? 9–11. Describe General Wolfe's death.

13. They have ever since continued under the British government. When the other American territories of Great Britain became independent, these old French colonies still continued attached to the crown of Britain as they do now.

CHAPTER CLX—AMERICA—CONTINUED
Description of the United States

1. WE HAVE BEEN TRAVELING all about the world, but we have now got home again. We have been reading about countries where there are kings and emperors, but we have now come to a land where the people govern themselves in their own way, and get along very well without any king or emperor.

2. We have been listening to the story of nations who are governed by despots and tyrants; let us now hear what can be said about a land of freedom. Let us, in the first place, go to a map; for the first step in studying the history of a country should be to learn its situation, boundaries, shape, rivers, mountains, etc.

3. The United States, then, are bounded on the north by the British possessions, east by the Atlantic Ocean, south by the Gulf of Mexico and the state of Mexico, and west by the Pacific Ocean. The whole country is nearly as extensive as all Europe, and contains about fifty millions of inhabitants.

4. The United States are divided into thirty-eight states, each having a governor and a legislature to make laws. The whole are united under a national government, over which a president is placed as the chief ruler.

5. The United States are frequently spoken of under four sections. The Northern, Eastern, or New England states are Maine, New Hampshire, Vermont, Massachusetts, Rhode Island, and Connecticut. The Middle states are New York, New Jersey, Pennsylvania, Delaware, and Maryland. The Southern states are Virginia, West Virginia, North Carolina, South Carolina, Florida, Georgia, Alabama, Mississippi, Louisiana, and Texas. The Western states are Arkansas, Tennessee, Kentucky, Missouri, Illinois, Indiana, Ohio, Michigan, Iowa, Wisconsin, Minnesota, Kansas, Nebraska,

---

Questions—12. Consequence of the victory? French possessions? 13. To what are the old French colonies attached?

CHAP. CLX—1–2. What of the people of the United States? 3. Boundaries of the United States? Extent? Population? 4. What of the government? 5. Divisions of the United States? Name the New England states, Middle states, Southern states, Western states.

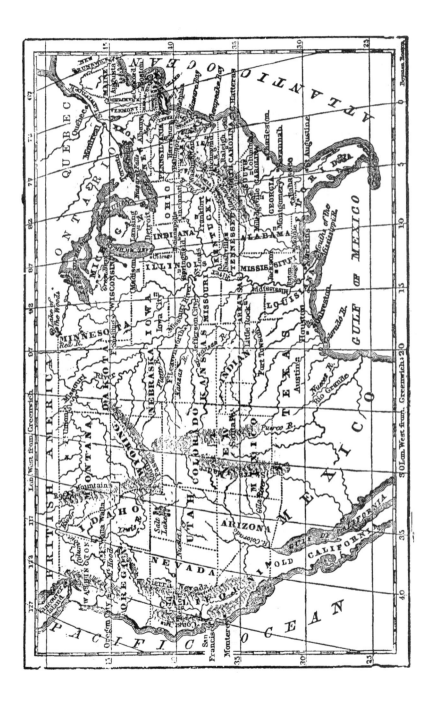

Oregon, Nevada, California, and Colorado. Besides these there are ten Territories, and the District of Columbia.

6. The United States are favored by a great many fine rivers, flowing through fertile valleys. There are many mountains, but none are so lofty as the Andes of South America, the Alps of Europe, or the Himalaya mountains of Asia. The climate of the north is temperate, and the soil yields apples, pears, peaches, and other fruits. In the south it is warm, and oranges, figs, and lemons flourish.

CHAPTER CLXI—AMERICA—Continued
Settlement and Colonial History of New England

1. Before speaking of the United States as one whole country, I must give a brief account of the settlements of the several colonies. I shall begin with New England, because that section of the Union is the most northerly, though not first settled.

2. New England, as I have said, contains the states of Maine, New Hampshire, Vermont, Massachusetts, Rhode Island, and Connecticut. It is bounded north by the province of Quebec, east by New Brunswick and the Atlantic Ocean, south by the Atlantic and Long Island Sound, and west by New York.

3. In the year 1620 a ship called the Mayflower arrived on the coast of New England. On board of this vessel were a number of pious men and women, with their ministers. They had also brought their children with them, for they never expected to return to their native land.

4. They had been driven from England by persecution, and they had come to this dreary wilderness, in order to worship God according to their own consciences. It was in the cold, wintry month of December when the Mayflower anchored in the harbor of what is now called Plymouth. The people went on shore, and the rock on which they landed has ever since been considered an interesting historical monument.

5. They went to work and built themselves some poor huts. At first they met with great difficulties and hardships. Many of them fell sick and died. The survivors were often in want of food, and were forced to dig for shell-fish on the sea-shore.

6. In addition to their other troubles, the wild Indians sometimes threat-

Questions—6. Face of the country? Climate? Soil? Productions?
Chap. CLXI—2. What of New England? Boundaries? 3. What took place in 1620?

THE PILGRIMS LANDED

ened to attack them. But the Pilgrims were as brave and patient as they were pious. They put their trust in God, and steadily pursued their design of making a permanent settlement in the country.

7. Soon after this settlement at Plymouth, other companies of religious persons came to different parts of New England. Some settled at Salem, and others at Boston. Thus a good many English people were established in the country. In the year 1635 sixty men, women, and children journeyed from Massachusetts to Connecticut, to make a settlement there.

8. They went through the woods on foot, and drove their cattle before them. At night they lay down to sleep, with no shelter but the boughs of the trees. When they reached the Connecticut river they began to build Windsor, Hartford, and other towns. These were the first settlements in Connecticut.

9. In 1636 a minister, named Roger Williams, was banished from Massachusetts. He went to Rhode Island, and settled at Providence. This good man was a great friend of the Indians, and they had a strong affection for him.

10. By degrees, villages were built all along the sea-coast of New En-

---

Questions—4–6. Describe the settlement of Plymouth.   7. What other settlements? What took place in 1635?   9. When and by whom was Providence settled?

gland, and settlements began to be formed inland along the rivers. But a thick and dreary forest still overshadowed the greater part of the country, and bears and wolves often prowled around the villages.

CHAPTER CLXII—AMERICA—Continued
Affairs of New England continued

1. The settlers of New England were good and pious people; but many of them seemed to have pretty much the same feelings toward the Indians that they had toward the bears and wolves. They considered them a sort of wild animal, or if men, very wicked ones.

2. The best friend that ever the Red Men had, was John Eliot. He considered them his fellow-beings, and went about preaching to them; and so he was called the Apostle of the Indians. He spent a great many years in translating the Bible into their language, and in teaching the Indians to read it.

3. There were, however, very few white men that loved the Indians; and the latter looked upon the settlers as their enemies. They were afraid that, in time, they would cut down all the trees of the forest, and change their hunting-grounds into cultivated fields.

4. The settlers had, therefore, many wars with the Indians; but the most terrible one broke out in the year 1675, and was called king Philip's war. King Philip, though an Indian, was a man of great sagacity, and it was his design to destroy all the settlers, and make New England a wilderness again.

5. King Philip first made an attack on the people of Swanzey, in Massachusetts, as they were coming out of the meeting-house, on Fast day. Eight or nine persons were shot. Many others were killed and scalped in different parts of the country, and many houses were set on fire.

6. Almost every man in New England now shouldered his musket, and went out to fight king Philip. Even the ministers, instead of teaching the Indians to read the Bible, as John Eliot did, now took their guns and sent bullets at them, whenever they had a chance.

7. In the course of the next winter, the settlers formed themselves into an army of nearly two thousand men, and drove king Philip and the other

Questions—10. What was done by degrees? What of the greater part of New England? Chap. CLXII—1. How were the Indians considered by the settlers? 2. What of John Eliot? 3. How did the Indians look upon the white men? 4. When did king Philip's war begin? What of king Philip? 5. When did he first attack the Americans? 6. What did the people do?

Indians into a strong fort, in Rhode Island. It stood in the midst of a swamp, and contained six hundred wigwams. All the Indian women and children had taken refuge there.

8. Four thousand Indian warriors were in the fort. But the settlers boldly attacked them, broke into the fort, and set the wigwams on fire. Many of the old and infirm Indians, as well as the women and poor helpless children, were burned alive.

9. A thousand Indian warriors were killed and wounded, and several hundred were taken prisoners. The remainder fled. The fort presented a horrible spectacle, with half-burned bodies of men, women and children, strewn among the ashes of the wigwams.

10. But still the war was not at an end, for king Philip was alive. The next summer, it was known that he had taken refuge at Mount Hope, in Rhode Island. Captain Church pursued him thither with a small party of men.

11. King Philip happened to come toward a clump of bushes, where an Englishman and a friendly Indian lay concealed. The Englishman fired at him, but missed. The Indian then took aim and fired, and the valiant king Philip fell dead.

12. After this war, the Indians were never again able to do so much mischief to the New England people. But, for many years afterward, they would sometimes steal out of the woods by night, set the villages on fire, and slaughter the inhabitants. The New England colonies, however, increased rapidly, and in time, the country had many pleasant towns and villages.

CHAPTER CLXIII—AMERICA—Continued
Early History of Virginia

1. THE COLONY OF VIRGINIA was settled some years before New England. Jamestown, on James river, was founded by captain Christopher Newport, in 1607. The first settlers of Virginia were not such grave, pious people as those of New England. They had not come to America for the sake of worshiping God, but were influenced by more worldly motives.

2. Many of them were wild young men, and it was difficult to keep them in order. Owing to this and other causes, the colony was sometimes

---

Questions—7. What did they do the next winter? What of the fort? 8–9. Describe the destruction of the fort. 10–11. Describe the death of king Philip. 12. What of the Indians after this war?

CHAP. CLXIII—1. When was Jamestown settled? What of the settlers of Virginia?

CAPTAIN SMITH AND POCAHONTAS

on the brink of ruin. The Indians gave the settlers great trouble, and would probably have destroyed them, if it had not been for Captain John Smith.

3. Captain Smith was a gallant man, and had been a warrior all his lifetime. Before he came to Virginia, he had fought against the Turks, and had cut off the heads of three Turkish lords, in single combat. He now showed himself equally valiant in his engagements with the Indians.

4. But one day, when Captain Smith was retreating from a large party of savages, he sank almost up to his neck in a swamp, so that he could neither fight nor flee. The Indians pulled him out of the swamp and carried him to their king Powhatan.

5. Powhatan was rejoiced to have Captain Smith in his power, for he had been more afraid of him than of all the other Englishmen together. In order to prevent any further trouble, he determined immediately to put him to death. Accordingly, Captain Smith was stretched on the ground, with his head laid on a large stone.

6. King Powhatan, who was a man of immense size and strength, then seized a great club, intending to kill Captain Smith. He lifted the club on high for this purpose; but just as the blow was falling, his daughter Pocahontas rushed forward.

7. This beautiful Indian maiden threw herself upon the body of Captain Smith. If Powhatan's club had fallen, it would have killed her, instead of the prisoner. Pocahontas besought her father to have mercy; and the

Questions—2. What of the Indians?   3. What of Captain John Smith?

fierce Indian could not resist her tears and entreaties.

8. Captain Smith was therefore released, and sent back to Jamestown. The name of Pocahontas will always be honored in America. She was afterward married to one of the English settlers, and her descendants are living in Virginia to this day.

CHAPTER CLXIV—AMERICA—Continued
Braddock's Defeat, and other Matters

1. I MUST PASS OVER the remainder of the history of Virginia, till the time of the old French war. This began in 1755. Not long after war was declared, the British general Braddock marched with an army to attack the French at Fort du Quesne [*du kane*]. This fort stood at the head of the Ohio river, where Pittsburgh is now situated.

2. Many Virginians and other colonists were in Braddock's army. Colonel George Washington, then a very young man, was one of his aids. Washington had already acquired much warlike skill; and if general Braddock had taken his advice, it would have saved his own life, and the lives of hundreds besides.

3. Braddock and his army marched onward, till they were within about seven miles of Fort du Quesne. Thick woods were all around them, and the settlements of Virginia were hundreds of miles behind. Suddenly, a terrible volley of musketry was fired at them from behind the trees.

4. General Braddock now knew that he had fallen into an ambuscade of French and Indians. He galloped about, endeavoring to encourage his men; but the bullets came so thick, that the bravest of them were appalled.

5. The general had five horses killed under him. At last, a fatal bullet struck him in the breast. Nearly all the other officers were either killed or wounded; but Washington remained unhurt. It seems as if he were preserved to be the savior of his country.

6. An Indian chief had taken aim and fired at him seventeen times, without once hitting him. It was Washington who rescued the army from total destruction. He and the Virginian troops kept off the Indians, and enabled the British to retreat.

7. I shall now proceed to speak of the other colonies. The first settlement in New York was made by some Dutch emigrants in 1613, on the

---

Questions—4–7. Relate the adventure of Captain Smith with the Indians.   8. What of Pocahontas? Her descendants?

CHAP. CLXIV—1. When did the old French war begin?   Where was Fort du Quesne?   2. What of Washington?   3–5. Describe the defeat and death of Braddock.

shores of the Hudson river, where Albany now stands. The city of New York, founded about the same time, was at first called New Amsterdam; it derived its name from the capital of Holland, for the early settlers, like those at Albany, were natives of that country.

8. In 1664, the province of New York was surrendered by the Dutch into the hands of the English. It grew and prospered very rapidly, and became one of the most powerful of the colonies.

9. Pennsylvania was settled in 1681. Its founder was William Penn, a Quaker, and all the earliest settlers likewise belonged to the sect of Quakers. When William Penn arrived in the country, he bought lands of the Indians, and made a treaty with them.

10. This treaty was always held sacred on both sides. The Indians saw that the Quakers were men of peace, and therefore they were careful never to do them any injury. There are no stories of Indian warfare with the Quakers of Pennsylvania.

11. The province of Maryland was given by Charles the First to Lord Baltimore. He was a Roman Catholic, and in 1634, brought over two hundred people of the same religion, and made the first settlement in Maryland.

12. Carolina first began to be permanently settled in 1680. In 1729, it was divided into North and South Carolina. The first settlement in Georgia was made in 1733. The principal founder was General James Oglethorpe. He came from England with one hundred and sixteen settlers, and founded the city of Savannah.

CHAPTER CLXV—AMERICA—CONTINUED
Causes which led to the Revolution

1. THE READER WILL HAVE learned, by preceding chapters, how the whole of the sea-coast, between New Brunswick, on the north, and Florida, on the south, became covered with colonies, which were all under the government of Great Britain. The inhabitants were constantly increasing in numbers.

Questions—6. What of Washington and his troops? 7. When and where was the first settlement in New York? What was the city of New York first called? 8. What of the province of New York? 9. When and by whom was Pennsylvania settled? How did William Penn treat the Indians? 10. What was the consequence of his treaty with them? 11. Who gave Maryland to Lord Baltimore? What of Lord Baltimore? When did he settle Maryland? 12. When was Carolina settled? When divided? First settlement in Georgia? Who founded it? What city did he build?

2. When the king of Great Britain and his ministers beheld the prosperous condition of the colonies they determined to derive some profit from them. For this purpose, in 1765, the British parliament passed what was called the Stamp Act.

3. Their object was to take money out of the pockets of the Americans for the use of the king and ministry. But the Americans were resolved that no king on earth should take their property without their own consent.

4. They made so strong an opposition to the Stamp Act that parliament was forced to repeal it. But a tax was soon afterward laid on tea, so that no American lady could give a tea-party without paying a tax to England. Soldiers were sent out to America to compel the people to obey these unjust laws.

5. In the year 1770 a quarrel took place between some of these soldiers and the inhabitants of Boston. A company of the British red-coats assembled in State-street, and fired upon a crowd of unarmed people. Three of them fell dead in the street, and five more were wounded. This affair was called the Boston Massacre.

6. But, instead of being affrighted by this bloodshed, the people grew more determined in their resistance to the tyranny of England. In the year 1773 some ships were sent from London to the colonies, laden with cargoes of tea.

7. Three of the ships arrived in the harbor of Boston. One night a number of persons went on board, in the disguise of Indians, and threw all the tea overboard. These Indian figures were never seen again, and, to this day, nobody can tell who they were.

8. When tidings of this event were carried to England, the king and ministry saw that they could never make slaves of the Americans unless by force of arms. They therefore sent over large bodies of troops to keep the people in subjection.

CHAPTER CLXVI—AMERICA—Continued
Account of the Battle of Lexington

1. In 1775 General Thomas Gage was the commander-in-chief of the

---

Questions—Chap. CLXV—2. What of the king and ministers of Great Britain? What did the parliament do? 3. Their object? What did the Americans resolve? 4. What did they do? What of a tax on tea? What of soldiers? 5. Describe the Boston Massacre. 6. What of the Americans? What happened in the year 1773? 7. Describe the destruction of the tea. 8. What did the king and ministers now do?

British forces in America. His head-quarters were at Boston.

2. On the night of the 18th of April General Gage sent a detachment of eight hundred grenadiers to seize some cannon and ammunition at Concord, about eighteen miles from Boston. The grenadiers marched all night, and reached the town of Lexington at sunrise.

3. Lexington is a village about twelve miles from Boston. A meeting-house stood by the road-side, and near it there was a level tract of grass. On this green space a company of American militia, who had heard that the British were coming, were drawn up.

4. Major Pitcairn was the British commander. As soon as he saw the militia he galloped forward, brandishing his sword, and drawing a pistol from his holster. "Disperse, you rebels!" he shouted. "Throw down your arms and disperse!"

5. As he spoke, without giving the militia-men time to run away, he discharged his pistol at them. The British soldiers followed the example of Major Pitcairn, and fired a whole volley at the Americans. Several of them were killed and wounded.

6. The British troops then continued their march to Concord. But the Americans were now collecting on all sides. When the British reached Concord they had a skirmish with a party of militia there. They now found it necessary to retreat as fast as possible.

7. As they marched along the road the people fired at them from behind the fences and stone walls, and out of the windows of the houses. At every step some of the British soldiers fell, but their comrades hurried on, without heeding them.

8. When General Gage heard what was going on, he sent Lord Percy out of Boston, with nine hundred men and two brass cannon. Lord Percy met Major Pitcairn and the grenadiers scampering back to Boston as fast as they could go, and, by firing his cannon, he kept the Americans off.

9. But the moment the troops resumed their march the Americans shot at them again from behind the fences. Before the British arrived in sight of Boston they had lost nearly three hundred men in killed, wounded, and prisoners. The loss of the Americans was much less. This was called the battle of Lexington.

10. The news of this battle spread all over the country, and wherever

---

Questions—CHAP. CLXVI—1. What of General Gage?   2. What did he do?   What of the grenadiers?   3–6. What took place at Lexington?   What followed?   7. How were the British annoyed in their retreat to Boston?   8. What did General Gage do?   9. What of the Americans and British?

the story was told the people quitted their business and turned soldiers; for now the Revolution had begun, and it was easy to foresee that there would be a bloody war.

THE BATTLE OF BUNKER HILL

CHAPTER CLXVII—AMERICA—CONTINUED
The Battle of Bunker Hill

1. IN A SHORT TIME after the battle of Lexington a large American army was assembled round Boston. The British troops could not venture out of the town. They found it difficult to get provisions enough to live upon.

2. On the night of the sixteenth of June Colonel Prescott marched with a thousand Americans to Bunker Hill, in Charlestown. On the summit of this hill, with their spades, they threw up a wall of earth and sod as high as their breasts.

3. They intended this as a fortification, from which they might fire upon the British fleet which lay in Boston harbor. No sooner did the British admiral see the wall of earth and sod than he began to batter it with cannon-shot and bombs. At the same time General Gage sent three thousand troops to take Bunker Hill by storm.

4. The troops landed in Charlestown, and marched boldly up the hill. They made a formidable appearance, moving in a long red line, with their glittering muskets. As they advanced the cannon-balls from the British fleet flew high over their heads, and struck among the Americans.

5. But when the British soldiers had come within twenty yards of the

---

Questions—10. What effect had the news of this battle?
CHAP. CLXVII—1. Where did an American army assemble? What of the British troops?
2. What did Colonel Prescott do? 3. What of the British admiral and General Gage?

fortification the Americans suddenly saluted them with a tremendous volley of musketry. The smoke cleared away, and there were the king's soldiers retreating in confusion to the water side.

6. But many of them lay dead or wounded upon the hill. In the mean time Charlestown had been set on fire by them, and was blazing like an immense furnace, and throwing clouds of smoke over the whole scene.

7. The officers encouraged the British troops and led them again into battle. But a second time they were driven back by the fire of the Americans with terrible slaughter. It was not till the third trial that the British were able to reach the breast-work.

8. The Americans had now fired away all their powder and ball, and were forced to retreat. General Warren was among the last to leave the breast-work. A British officer snatched a musket from a soldier and shot the gallant Warren dead.

9. But many a brave Englishman laid down his life that day, and blood enough had been shed to redden all the grass on Bunker Hill.

10. In about a fortnight after this battle General George Washington arrived at Cambridge. The continental congress at Philadelphia had appointed him commander-in-chief of the American armies. He managed matters so skillfully that the British were driven out of Boston in March, 1776.

CHAPTER CLXVIII—AMERICA—Continued
Progress of the War—Capture of Burgoyne

1. It was on the Fourth of July, 1776, that the continental congress declared the United States a Free and Independent Nation. This declaration caused great rejoicings all over America. Yet our affairs were not in a very promising situation.

2. After the enemy evacuated Boston General Washington marched from that town to New York. Some important battles were fought between our troops and the British; but Washington was finally compelled to retreat, by superior force. When winter came on the American soldiers were almost naked. Wherever they marched their bare feet left bloody tracks upon the frozen ground.

3. But, on a dark December night, Washington crossed the Delaware

Questions—4–9. Describe the battle of Bunker Hill.   10. What of General Washington? When were the British troops driven out of Boston?

Chap. CLXVIII—1. When were the United States declared free and independent?   2. What of Washington?   What of the American soldiers?

river with his troops, and marched to Trenton, in New Jersey. A large body of Hessian soldiers were encamped at this place. They were suddenly startled by the shouts of the Americans, who had broken into their camp, and they all laid down their arms.

4. Lord Cornwallis, the British general, was now in pursuit of the Americans; but Washington marched to Princeton, and attacked a party of the enemy who had taken post in the college edifice. Sixty of them were killed, and three hundred taken prisoners.

5. The next year, 1777, the gallant marquis de La Fayette came from France to assist the Americans. He was then only ninteen years old; but congress appointed him major-general, and he became one of the bravest and best in the army.

6. During this year the British General Burgoyne marched with a large army from Canada. He sailed down Lake Champlain, and went from thence to Saratoga. But General Gates was waiting for him there, with ten thousand American troops. Several battles were fought between them and the British under Burgoyne.

7. In one of these battles Colonel Cilley, an American officer, took a brass cannon from the enemy with his own hands. He immediately got astride of it, shouting and encouraging his men, and waving his sword, as if he were seated on a war-horse.

8. On the eighteenth of October General Burgoyne was forced to surrender. He and his aids rode out of the camp to meet General Gates, and Burgoyne took his sword by the point, and offered the hilt to the American general. At the same time all the British army grounded their arms.

9. This great success of the Americans induced the French to make a treaty of alliance with them, and to declare war against Great Britain. France sent a fleet, and afterward an army, to fight on our side.

CHAPTER CLXIX—AMERICA—Continued
The Story of Benedict Arnold and Major André

1. IT WOULD FILL a much larger book than mine, if I were to relate the particulars of all the battles, skirmishes, and other warlike events that occurred during the Revolution. I must therefore leave far the greater part of them unfold.

Questions—3. Describe the attack upon Trenton. 4. Attack upon Princeton. 5. What of La Fayette? 6. What of Burgoyne? General Gates? 7. What of Colonel Cilley? 8. Describe the surrender of General Burgoyne. 9. What did the French do?

2. One of the most interesting incidents in the whole war took place in 1780. General Arnold, who had shown himself a very brave officer, became discontented, and resolved to desert the cause of his country.

3. Pretending that his wounds rendered him unfit for active service, he requested that the command of West Point might be given him. This strong fortress was situated among the Highlands, on the shore of the Hudson river, above New York. Its loss would have been a severe misfortune to the Americans.

4. No sooner had Arnold got possession of West Point, than he sent to Sir Henry Clinton, the British general at New York, offering to surrender the fortress. Sir Henry sent a young officer, named André [an´-dray], to meet Arnold, and contrive the means of completing this treacherous business.

5. Major André had a meeting with Arnold, and they arranged the manner in which the fortress was to be given up to the British. André then wished to get on board the British ship Vulture, which had brought him up the river from New York.

6. But the Vulture had now sailed further down the stream, and it was necessary for Major André to return by land. He therefore took off his uniform and put on a common coat, in order that the Americans whom he should meet might not know that he was a British officer.

7. Then mounting a horse, he set out on the road to New York. He had to pass through a part of the country that was guarded by the American troops; but he traveled most of the way without any trouble or hindrance.

8. But when Major André reached a place called Tarrytown, he saw three young militia-men by the road-side. They came up to him and seized his horse by the bridle. Now André had a passport from General Arnold in his pocket, and if he had shown it to the militia-men, they would have let him go free. But instead of that, he asked them where they came from.

9. "From down the river," they replied. When André heard this, he mistook the three militia-men for Tories, or friends of the British. "I am a British officer," said he. "Let me pass on; for I am in haste."

10. But these words were fatal to poor André. The three men took him prisoner, and found some treasonable papers hidden in his boots. General Arnold made his escape to New York; but poor Major André remained in the hands of the Americans.

Questions—CHAP. CLXIX—2. What of General Arnold? 3. What did he request? 4. To whom did he send? What did Sir Henry Clinton do? 5. What of André?

11. He was tried as a spy, and condemned to death. Washington and all the army were sorry for him, but nothing could save him from the gallows. He was therefore executed.

CHAPTER CLXX—AMERICA—Continued
War in the South—Surrender of Cornwallis

1. IN THE LATTER PART of the war, many important events were transacted in the Southern states. In 1780, General Gates, the conqueror of Burgoyne, was defeated by Lord Cornwallis at Camden, in South Carolina. Congress then sent General Greene to command the army of the South.

2. General Greene had been a Quaker in his youth; but when the revolution broke out, he became the best officer in the American army, except General Washington. This was proved by his good conduct in the Southern states.

3. He fought several battles with the British, and though he was sometimes compelled to retreat by the enemy's superior force, yet they never gained any real advantage over him. By his skill and valor the British troops were finally driven into the city of Charleston. After this event, there was no more trouble with the enemy in the South.

4. Lord Cornwallis, with a large army, was now in Virginia. The American and French troops proceeded thither to attack him. General Washington had command of the whole; and, under Washington, the count de Rochambeau was commander of the French.

5. They besieged the British at Yorktown; for Lord Cornwallis did not feel strong enough to meet them in the open field. The Americans built breast-works round about the intrenchments of the British, and cannonaded them night and day.

6. Finally, on the nineteenth of October, 1781, Lord Cornwallis agreed to surrender his army. But he was ashamed to go through the ceremony of delivering his sword to the conqueror; and he therefore sent General O'Hara to do it in his stead.

7. General O'Hara accordingly marched forth at the head of the vanquished army. When he came into the presence of General Washington, he

---

Questions—6–11. Describe his journey and capture.

Chap. CLXX—1. What took place in 1780? 2–3. What of General Greene? 4. What of Lord Cornwallis? Who headed the Americans and French? 5. Describe the siege of Yorktown.

offered him the sword, in token of submission. But Washington pointed to General Lincoln; for it was not proper that he himself should receive the sword from any but Lord Cornwallis.

8. General Lincoln took General O'Hara's sword, and the whole British army grounded their arms, and yielded their banners to the victorious Americans.

9. After the surrender of Cornwallis, no important battles were fought, although peace was not declared until 1783. In the summer and autumn of that year, all the British troops sailed homeward, and left America free and independent.

10. Thus you see that the revolutionary war, which began by the battle of Lexington, in 1775, was terminated, after having continued eight years. The sufferings of our countrymen were very great, but the reward of their patience and patriotism was also great.

CHAPTER CLXXI—AMERICA—Continued
Affairs of the United States since the Revolution

1. WHEN THE REVOLUTIONARY WAR was over, the people of the United States found it necessary to adopt a constitution of government. The present Federal Constitution was prepared by some of the wisest men in the country. It went into operation in 1789.

2. The good and illustrious Washington was our first president. He came into office in 1789, and was re-elected at the end of four years. In 1797, John Adams was chosen to succeed him, and became the second president of the United States.

3. The most mournful event that had ever befallen America, was the death of Washington. It took place in 1799, when he was sixty-eight years old. The whole country was overwhelmed with sorrow. But Washington had done his work on earth, and it was fit that he should ascend to heaven.

4. The next president, after John Adams, was Thomas Jefferson. He served during two terms of office, and was succeeded by James Madison, in

---

Questions—6–8. Surrender of Lord Cornwallis? 9. When was peace declared? What of the British troops? 10. How long did the revolutionary war last? What of the sufferings of the Americans? Their reward?

Chap. CLXXI—1. When was the Federal Constitution formed? 2. Who was the first president? When did he come into office? When was John Adams chosen? 3. When did Washington's death take place? Effect of his death?

WASHINGTON

1809. The most remarkable event of Jefferson's administration, was the purchase of Louisiana from France, in the year 1803. This immense territory included the country between the Mississippi and the Rocky mountains. It was bought for fifteen million dollars. During the administration of Madison, the United States were on bad terms with Great Britain, and there was great reason to fear that hostilities would ensue.

5. Accordingly, on the eighteenth of June, 1812, Congress made a declaration of war. Troops were sent to invade Canada. There were several gallant conflicts on the Canadian frontier; but the Americans did not succeed in conquering the province.

6. Many glorious victories were won by the American navy, both on the ocean and the lakes. Hitherto, the British navy had always been triumphant; but now, our brave soldiers often compelled them to haul down their flag.

Questions—4. What did Jefferson purchase of the French? In what year? How large a country was it? What did it cost? When was Madison made president? What of the United States during his administration? 5. When was war declared? What of the war in Canada? 6. What of naval battles?

7. The last and most brilliant event of the war, was the battle of New Orleans. On the morning of the eighth of January, 1815, a strong British army advanced to take the city. But they were driven back with immense slaughter by the Americans, under General Jackson. Peace followed in a very short time after this battle. The United States have not since had any wars, except with the Indian tribes and with Mexico.

8. In 1817, president Madison retired from office, and was succeeded by James Monroe. During the eight years of his administration, the country was quiet and prosperous. John Quincy Adams became president in 1825. He was the son of old John Adams, who had been the next president after Washington. Neither the first nor the second president Adams continued in office longer than four years.

9. The next president was General Andrew Jackson. He was inaugurated in 1829, and began his second term of office in 1833. He was succeeded by Martin Van Buren, in 1837. William Henry Harrison became president in 1841, and died in thirty days after, being succeeded by John Tyler, then vice-president. James K. Polk became president in 1845, and Zachary Taylor in 1849. Millard Fillmore succeeded in 1850, and Franklin Pierce in 1853. James Buchanan became president in 1857. Abraham Lincoln in 1861, Andrew Johnson in 1865, and Ulysses S. Grant in 1869.

CHAPTER CLXXII—AMERICA—CONTINUED
The Great Rebellion

1. I MUST NOW TELL YOU something about Slavery in the United States, as it was this which led to the rebellion of 1861. Slaves, as you know, are persons—men, women, and children—owned as property by masters, for whom they are obliged to work. Slavery has existed in every civilized portion of the globe, except Australia.

2. African negroes were first introduced into the New World as slaves in the reign of Queen Elizabeth. The Queen herself took a share in the hazards of the enterprise. The slaves captured by the company were sold to the Spaniards in St. Domingo. Slaves were introduced into the English

---

Questions—7. Describe the battle of New Orleans. When did it take place? 8. What was done in 1817? In 1825? Whose son was John Quincy Adams? 9. When did Jackson become president? When was Martin Van Buren made president? What of Harrison? Tyler? Polk? Taylor? Fillmore? Pierce? Others?

CHAP. CLXXII—1. What of slaves? Where has slavery existed? 2. When were negro slaves first introduced into the New World? When into the English colonies?

colonies of America in 1620, a Dutch man-of-war having landed twenty in Virginia.

3. The traffic having thus begun, continued for some two hundred years. In the warm regions of the South, negro labor was found very useful in the cultivation of cotton, sugar, rice, etc.; and in 1860, there were four millions of slaves in the Southern states of the Union. In the Northern and Western states, there were few or none. The latter were called Free States; the former Slave States. The population of the free states was nearly double that of the others.

4. The people of the free states disliked slavery, and believed that it was wrong to hold any man in bondage. Still, they had no right to interfere in the matter, and could do nothing but *agitate,* that is, talk against it, print books and deliver speeches against it, seeking to show that slavery was injurious even to those who thought it a blessing.

5. The Southerners claimed the right to take their slaves into lands lately bought or acquired by the United States, to settle there with them, and thus to make more slave territory. This right a portion of the Northerners denied, and parties were formed holding these two opinions. In 1857, James Buchanan, a northern man, became president, elected by the Democratic party.

6. The agitation continued, and the number of those opposed to the extension of slavery increased. The Southerners believed the anti-slavery party would carry the next election, and that the new president would be able to prohibit slavery in the territories. They threatened in that case to secede from, or leave, the Union, and proposed to set up a government of their own.

7. This scheme had been long cherished by the South, and they now promised to carry it out. A vast majority of the people of the United States were not slaveholders. The Southerners asserted and generally believed that the Northerners were threatening their liberties and their honor, and that "secession" was not only a right granted by the Constitution, but a duty which they would be cowardly not to perform.

8. Abraham Lincoln was elected president in November, 1860, by the

---

Questions—3. What of slavery in the Southern states? How many slaves were there in 1860? What of the North and West? What were the two sections called? 4. What did the Northern people think of slavery? Had they a right to interfere? What could they do? 5. What did the Southerners claim? What parties were formed? What occurred in 1857? 6. What further agitation? What threats were made? 7. What of this scheme? What did the Southern people assert and believe?

party opposed to the extension of slavery into the territories. Though he was not to attain power for four months, and though, even then, the South would be in a majority in the Senate, they immediately seized the forts, arsenals, mints, custom-houses, and other United States property within their limits.

9. James Buchanan offered no resistance to these seizures. He took the ground that though the Constitution did not give the states the right to secede at their pleasure, still it did not give the government the right to "coerce" them, that is, to use force to prevent their seceding. So, when the Southerners had seized every fort except Fort Sumter in South Carolina and Fort Pickens in Florida, and erected batteries around these strong-holds, in order to drive out their small garrisons of United States troops, he allowed them to proceed unmolested.

10. So, when, upon the 4th of March, 1861, Abraham Lincoln was in-augurated as president, he found seven of these states had seceded, and four others preparing to follow them; a Southern government for these states being established in Alabama, with Jefferson Davis at the head of it. The president found that most of the ships of the United States navy had been sent to distant seas; and that the small garrisons distributed through the Southern states had either been captured or gone over to the enemy.

11. The two forts I have mentioned still held out, and these were the only points in the South where the United States flag was flying. Upon one of these flags the first shot was afterward fired.

CHAPTER CLXXIII—AMERICA—Continued
The Great Rebellion continued

1. FORT SUMTER, in Charleston Harbor, was garrisoned by seventy men under the command of Major Anderson. Their situation was painful in the extreme. Their provisions were nearly exhausted; they were cut off from all relief, were in the midst of enemies, and were surrounded by batteries and forts. General Beauregard, commanding the forces in Charleston, on being informed that an attempt would be made to throw supplies and re-enforcements into Fort Sumter, summoned Major Anderson to surrender on the 11th of April.

Questions—8. What of Abraham Lincoln? What followed his election? 9. What did Buchanan do? His opinions? What did he permit? 10–11. Describe the condition of the country when Lincoln was inaugurated.

CHAP. CLXXIII—1. What was the situation of Fort Sumter? What was Major Anderson summoned to do?

2. Major Anderson refused, and at half-past four on the morning of the 12th, the first shot was fired from Fort Moultrie, and the fight immediately began. There were seven thousand men on one side and seventy in the fort. In the afternoon of the second day, the garrison, exhausted, suffocated, and half blinded, capitulated and marched out with the honors of war. Not a man had been killed on either side.

3. The war thus commenced between the government and the South lasted just four years. I have not space in this book to write a full account of this terrible struggle, but will give merely an outline of the principal events. The president immediately called for troops, and soon, throughout the loyal states, nothing was thought or talked of but the raising and drilling of soldiers, the building of ships, and the forging of cannon.

4. One of the first measures resorted to was the blockade of the Southern ports. Men-of-war were stationed at the entrance of every harbor to prevent ships from going out or in. The English people, who are very fond of making money by trade, were very anxious to sell gunboats, cannon, soldiers' clothes, and muskets to the South, and to take cotton in exchange, and they built steamers expressly to carry on this traffic.

5. So eager were the English, that they continued the trade even after it was feared that it might lead to war between England and the United States. Many of their vessels were destroyed and many were captured by our navy; some succeeded in reaching port in safety, and their cargoes doubtless enabled the South to hold out longer than they could otherwise have done. No other nation but England behaved in this unfriendly manner.

6. In July, an army of some fifty thousnd men had been collected in the neighborhood of Washington, and, about the middle of the month, commenced to march upon Richmond, in Virginia, which had lately become the Southern capital. The battle of Bull Run ensued, in which the Union troops, having apparently won a decided victory, fell into disorder and panic upon an attack by fresh troops. The consequence was a retreat upon Washington and total defeat.

7. This seemed a terrible calamity, but it at once aroused the North to more energetic action, and to comprehend fully the magnitude of the struggle in which they were engaged. They saw that great sacrifices must be made, and they prepared to make them. Volunteers sprang to arms in great numbers, and the Army of the Potomac soon counted two hundred

Questions—2. Describe the battle and its result. 3. What of the war? 4–5. What of the blockade and the conduct of England? 6. Describe the battle of Bull Run. 7. What of the consequences of this defeat?

thousand men.

8. Battles were now fought, with varying results, all over the country; but it was not till January, 1862, that any definite purpose seemed to be kept in view by the military authorities. General Grant was, at this time, sent with forty thousand men from Cairo, in Illinois, to open the Tennessee and Cumberland rivers, which had been closed by the enemy's forts.

9. Fort Henry was captured upon the 6th of February, and Fort Doneldson on the 15th. The Union forces made a long stride into the hostile territory, the enemy falling back to the south. These two actions cleared the two rivers for hundreds of miles, and opened the Mississippi as far as Island No. 10.

10. In April, an attack was made upon the forts defending New Orleans by a fleet under flag-officer Farragut. After a six days' bombardment, the fleet ran by the forts, and after a terrific fight with the enemy's rams, fire-ships, and rafts, came to anchor within twenty miles of the city. A land force under General Butler immediately took possession.

11. In the same month, the Army of the Potomac, under General McClellan, moved from its winter quarters. Richmond was its proposed destination; and there were few persons in the North who did not believe that this magnificent body of men, equipped as no army was ever equipped before, would, no matter what resistance it might meet, overcome all obstacles, capture the enemy's capital, and summarily end the war. Never were high hopes destined to be brought so low.

12. The troops were carried by water to a point not far from Richmond. In less than three months, disease and battle had so reduced their numbers and their spirit, that the enemy no longer feared them, and having made Richmond safe, prepared to march upon Washington. Union troops under General Pope opposed them, but were compelled to retreat before the enemy. General McClellan was then ordered to evacuate his camp near Richmond, and bring his army to Pope's aid. Before this was done, Pope had been severely defeated at the second battle of Bull Run.

13. The enemy continued their march upon Washington, forded the upper Potomac, and met the Union forces under McClellan upon the banks of a stream in Maryland called the Antietam. The battle which followed was a bloody one, and victory perched upon the Union standard; but they

---

Questions—8. What occurred in January, 1862?   What was General Grant sent to do? 9. What captures were made?   The results?   10. Describe the capture of New Orleans? 11. What of the army of the Potomac?   What was expected of it?   12. Describe the campaign.   What did the enemy prepare to do?   What of General Pope?

made no pursuit, and the enemy crossed the river on the 18th of September unmolested.

CHAPTER CLXXIV—AMERICA—CONTINUED
The Great Rebellion continued

1. GENERAL BURNSIDE succeeded General McClellan in the command of the Army of the Potomac in November. In December, he fought the enemy at Fredericksburg, in Virginia, and was defeated with the loss of twelve thousand men. The same army, under General Hooker, again attacked the enemy in April, 1863, and again suffered defeat, losing eighteen thousand men.

2. General Lee, who commanded the enemy, believing the Union forces to be in no condition to make another fight, took his men across the fords of the Potomac in June. He met the Union army under General Meade at Gettysburg, in Pennsylvania, and on the 1st, 2nd, and 3rd of July, a terrible but decisive battle was fought. The enemy were totally defeated, their entire losses being fully thirty thousand men.

3. In the mean time, General Rosecrans had gained a splendid victory at Stone river, Tennessee; the Union army occupying Murfreesboro on the 4th of January, 1863. The Mississippi river had been opened in its entire length, except between Port Hudson on the south and Vicksburg on the north. To capture these two places and open the river completely was now the object of the government.

4. General Grant—one of the generals under him being General Sherman—got his army in the rear of Vicksburg, and, after a campaign of startling boldness, succeeded in investing the place, Commodore Porter's fleet occupying the water front. The stronghold surrendered on the 4th of July, the enemy losing in the series of battles thus closed forty thousand men and seven hundred guns. Five days later, Port Hudson surrendered to General Banks, and the great river was open from its source to its mouth.

5. Late in June of this year, General Rosecrans marched southward from Murfreesboro toward the enemy's flank, and entered Chattanooga on the 9th of September. The battle of Chickamauga stayed its progress for a time. General Grant succeeded General Rosecrans, and before the close of

---

Questions—13. What of the enemy? What battle followed? The result?

CHAP. CLXXIV—1. What of two battles fought by the Army of the Potomac? 2. What did General Lee do next? What battle ensued? The result? 3. What of General Rosecrans? The Mississippi river? 4. Describe the campaign against Vicksburg. Port Hudson?

the year the enemy in his front had been forced far down into the mountain fastnesses of Georgia.

6. In March, 1864, General Grant was made lieutenant-general, thus becoming commander-in-chief of the Union armies. From this time forward, the operations against the enemy all tended to one end, and are so simple that even a child can comprehend them. General Sherman was placed in command of the army at Chattanooga, his object being to march southward and destroy the great arsenal, storehouse, and railroad centre at Atlanta. General Grant cast his fortunes with the Army of the Potomac, on the Rappahannock, whose eyes were fixed, then as ever, on Richmond.

7. The two armies broke camp and started southward in the first week of May. From the 5th of this month to the 18th of June, Grant's forces were in constant collision with the enemy, certainly not less than one hundred thousand men losing their lives during these six weeks. The end of this period found the Union army besieging Petersburg, a little to the south of Richmond, and the key to that city. The hold was never once relaxed, though the enemy made terrible efforts to shake the assailant off.

8. Sherman's army, too, was in daily contact with the enemy, as it pushed on over hill and dale, through valleys and over mountains, across rivers and fords. A change of generals on the enemy's side assisted it greatly, for the new commander tried the experiment of throwing his army upon the Union lines, thus losing twenty thousand men in three days. Sherman entered Atlanta early in September.

9. The whole country was amazed by what followed, for it was far from expecting that anything so romantic, so apparently impossible, would be attempted. Sherman's men were observed to be cutting loose from their base of supply—a railroad which connected them with the north—and to be preparing for a march through the heart of the enemy's country. What they were preparing to do, they did. You will read of this wonderful march in larger books than this. The army reached and captured Savannah, on the Atlantic coast, before Christmas.

10. General Grant's object, in directing this movement, was now apparent to all. Sherman's army was clearly, after being rested and re-equipped, to turn to the north, and assist Grant in destroying the last army that defended Richmond. Abraham Lincoln had, in the mean time, been

---

Questions—5. What of Rosecrans' army? 6. What changes now occurred in the command of the armies? What is said of General Sherman? What was the object of each of the two armies? 7. Describe Grant's campaign. 8. Describe Sherman's campaign. 9. What followed? Describe the march to the sea.

re-elected president, Andrew Johnson, of Tennessee, being chosen vice–president.

11. Sherman's men now started for the north, and made their way through marshes and floods to the high lands of North Carolina. Cities fell before them, and many others which they did not even approach surrendered. When they were near the Virginia line, Grant fell upon his enemy at Richmond, pursued him remorselessly for a week, and received his surrender upon the 6th of April. This was the end of the rebellion.

12. The country was rejoicing over these auspicious events, when an event occurred which changed all its joy to mourning. Abraham Lincoln was shot by an assassin on the 14th of April, and died on the following morning. Andrew Johnson, elected as vice-president, succeeded him, becoming the seventeenth president of the United States. The government went tranquilly on, precisely as if nothing had happened, thus proving its strength in a moment of the greatest possible trial.

CHAPTER CLXXV—AMERICA—Continued
The Great Rebellion concluded

1. Very many important events happened during this war, which I have not been able to mention. You have all of you heard or will hear of the gallant fight between the little Monitor and the gigantic Merrimac; of the destruction of the ship Alabama, that was helping the South, by the American gunboat Kearsarge; of the passage of the forts in Mobile Bay by the fleet of Admiral Farragut—and of hundreds of incidents proving the coolness, daring, and endurance of the American citizen-soldier.

2. But there are one or two matters which I must mention here. Over a million men served in the Union armies during the four years of the war. The first two hundred thousand were volunteers, who received no wages but food, clothing, and thirteen dollars a month; the larger portion of the remainder were also volunteers, but they received what was called bounty money from their states and towns, to enable them to provide for their families during their absence. The remainder were either drafted men or their substitutes.

3. The expenses of the war were nearly three thousand millions of dol-

---

Questions—10. What was now evident?   What of the presidential election?   11. What of Sherman's march to the north?   How was the rebellion brought to an end?   12. What terrible event now happened?   Its effect upon the government?

Chap. CLXXV—1. What of other events of the war?   2. How many men served in the Union armies?   Describe the three ways of obtaining soldiers.

lars. About five hundred millions of this total were notes or bills issued by the government and declared to be money by law. These notes were, from their color, popularly called greenbacks. The remainder was obtained by borrowing from the people, who were willing to lend any amount to put the rebellion down. Of the debt thus incurred, a portion has already (1881) been paid, and the people have submitted willingly to be taxed, that the whole may be paid, perhaps in twenty, perhaps in thirty years.

4. The rebellion, which was begun for the purpose of perpetuating and extending slavery, ended, as many far-sighted persons said it would end, in the total destruction of slavery. On the 1st of January, 1863, Abraham Lincoln, in a paper called the Emancipation Proclamation, declared all slaves in the seceded states free. This he did as commander of the armies, not as president. It was a war measure, intended to weaken the rebellion by taking away a portion of its support.

5. Many of the slaves aided the Union armies throughout the war, guiding them, sheltering them, and finally enlisting in large numbers. At the close of the war, the people were desirous that slavery, which had been practically abolished, should be declared at an end in a legal and constitutional manner. All the required forms were duly complied with, and the spring of 1866 saw not a single slave within the borders of the Union.

6. The process of reconstructing the country has been begun, and will doubtless soon be completed. Difficult as it may be for those who have been fighting with each other for years to lay down their enmities with their swords, and to live together in amity, the difficulty will be overcome, as others have been; and we may confidently look forward to a period not far distant, when the whole country will be one in sentiment as it is one in interest.

7. The war has settled one thing for ever—namely, that this country is not a confederation, or league, but a nation. States may come in, but they cannot go out. The enemy looked upon the country as upon a stage-load of travellers—they had different destinations, and could separate when they pleased. The Unionists considered the tie that bound the states together as sacred as marriage, and what was once joined, they said, no man might sunder.

Questions—3. What did the war cost? What of the government notes or bills? What of borrowing? Taxation? The payment of the debt? 4. What did the rebellion destroy? What was the Emancipation Proclamation? Of what nature was this measure? 5. What of the slaves during the war? The final abolition of slavery? 6. What has been begun? What will doubtless be accomplished? 7. What has the war settled?

CHAPTER CLXXVI—AMERICA—Continued
General Remarks on the History of the United States

1. IN REVIEWING the history of our country, we shall notice that it has been involved in two foreign wars since it became independent. Previous to that event, the colonists had a great many battles with the Indian tribes, and they had a good deal of fighting to do in the old French war, which began about 1755.

2. The revolutionary war was a great affair. The people were fighting for independence, for liberty. America was poor and England was rich and powerful. In this struggle, our country may be compared to a stout boy in the grasp of a strong man, who is trying to bind him in chains. But the boy breaks the chains asunder, turns upon his oppressor, and drives him out of the country.

3. In looking back, then, we see that our forefathers toiled and suffered much to establish freedom in this country. We are now enjoying the fruits of their labors. Let us cherish their memory, for they were great and good men. Let us be thankful to Heaven, for it has smiled upon their labors.

4. Having taken a backward glance at the history of our country, let us consider for a moment its present condition. Look at the towns and cities that are scattered over the country. Look at the hills and valleys, covered with fruit-trees and gardens, and yielding their annual harvests.

5. Look at the rivers, plowed with steamboats; look at the canals, bearing along their burden of produce and merchandise; look at the steam-cars, hurrying along like birds upon the wing; look at our sea-ports, and see the forests of shipping that are crowding into their harbors.

6. Visit the city of New York, a busy, buzzing hive of men, containing nearly a million people. Observe its beautiful streets, its fine houses, the banks, the churches, and other public edifices.

7. Enter the shops and notice the beautiful articles of merchandise brought from China, from the great Asiatic islands, from India, from Arabia, from all the shores of the Mediterranean Sea, from England, France, Holland, and all the borders of the Baltic.

8. Go to the top of the Trinity Church, where you can have a view of the surrounding waters; notice the fringe of masts encircling the southern

Questions—CHAP. CLXXVI—2. To what may our country be compared in the revolutionary war? 3. What of our forefathers? 4–5. What shall we see in looking at our country? 6–7. What shall we observe in the city of New York?

portion of the city. See there the flag of every commercial country under heaven. See there, too, ships, sloops, schooners, and steamboats, coming and going like bees in a summer morning, all bringing their burden to the hive.

9. What a beautiful sight is this, and in a country, too, which has been settled but little more than two hundred and fifty years! And if you would know more of our country, get into a steamboat and sail up the Hudson, one of the finest streams on the face of the globe.

10. Visit Troy, Albany, Utica, Rochester, and Buffalo; all of them interesting and flourishing towns. Observe the numerous villages, the handsome houses, and the throngs of happy people that inhabit the state of New York.

11. If you are fond of traveling cross Lake Erie in a steamboat, and proceed through Ohio on the railroad. See there a country that has not been settled sixty years, now studded over with thriving towns and villages. Go to Cincinnati, Louisville, Nashville, St. Louis, and proceed on the bosom of the great Mississippi to New Orleans.

12. If you are not satisfied with all this, cross to the Pacific; visit the gold mines of California; proceed to Oregon, and from this point of view consider the extent and resources of these United States.

13. When you have seen these interesting things, go home and reflect upon them. Sit quietly down, review the past, consider the present, and look forward to the future. What a glorious prospect for our country, if our present government continues, if the people are true to their own interests, and maintain the liberty their fathers left them!

CHAPTER CLXXVII—AMERICA—Continued
About South America—El Dorado, and the Fountain of Youth

1. No sooner had Columbus discovered America than the pope of Rome claimed it as his own. None of the Catholic kings of Europe were supposed to have any right to plant colonies there unless his Holiness granted them permission

2. Alexander the Sixth was pope at that time. He very generously bestowed one-half of the new world on the king of Spain, and the other half

Questions—8. What shall we see on the waters around?   9. What of the Hudson?   10. Cities of New York?   11. What of the state of Ohio?   The Mississippi?   12. California? Oregon?
Chap. CLXXVII—1. What of the pope of Rome?

ENTRANCE TO THE KING'S PALACE IN EL DORADO

on the king of Portugal. These kings then sent out ships and men, who conquered immense territories, and reduced many of the inhabitants to slavery.

3. The Spaniards first took possession of the West Indies. They built the city of Havana, on the island of Cuba, and the Spanish governor had his residence there. Other nations afterward took possession of other islands. The great object of all who came to America at this period was to get gold and silver. The most wonderful stories were told about the abundance of these metals in some parts of the western continent.

4. There was supposed to be a kingdom called El Dorado, or the Gilded, which was thus described. The king was every day covered with powdered gold, so that he looked like a golden image. The palace of this glittering monarch was built of brilliant marble as white as snow. The pillars of the palace were porphyry and alabaster. Its entrance was guarded by two lions, who were fastened to a tall column by chains of massive gold.

5. After passing the lions a fountain was seen, from which gushed a continual shower of liquid silver, through four large pipes of gold. The interior of the palace was too splendid to be described.

6. It contained an altar of solid silver, on which was an immense golden sun. Lamps were continually burning, and their dazzling radiance was reflected from innumerable objects of silver and gold. Such was the splendid

Questions—2. What did pope Alexander do?   What of the kings of Spain and Portugal? 3. What of the Spaniards?   What was the great object of all who came to America?   What of gold and silver?   4–6. Describe the kingdom of El Dorado as it was supposed to exist.

fiction, invented by somebody, and believed in Europe.

7. Numbers of adventurers went in search of El Dorado, and some pretended that they had really visited this golden kingdom. But it has long since been ascertained that no such place ever existed.

8. Another thing which the Spaniards expected to find in America was the Fountain of Youth. Far away beneath the shadows of the forest, they had been told of a fountain, whose bright waters would wash away wrinkles, and turn gray hair dark again.

9. Oh, if there were any such fountain, old Peter Parley would journey thither, lame as he is, and plunge head foremost into its bosom! After a while the children of America would ask, "Where is that lame old gentleman who used to tell us stories?"

10. And there would be a youth among them, a stranger, whom they had never seen before. He would cry out, "I was old Peter Parley; but I have been bathing in the fountain of youth, and now I am a boy again! Come, let us see who will hop the farthest!" But I need not add that no such fountain of youth ever existed.

CHAPTER CLXXVIII—AMERICA—Continued
History of the Mexican Territories—Texas—Guatimala

1. Though there was no El Dorado in America, there was gold enough to satisfy even the Spaniards, if such rapacious people ever could be satisfied. The empire of Mexico contained immense riches.

2. This country is in the southern part of North America. It extends across from the Gulf of Mexico to the Pacific Ocean. Its capital city, which is likewise called Mexico, is one of the most magnificent in the world.

3. When America was first discovered, the city of Mexico was much more extensive than it is now. It had stately temples and houses, which were profusely ornamented with gold. Its inhabitants were more civilized than any other natives of America.

4. In the year 1519, Fernando Cortez, a Spaniard, invaded Mexico, with only about six hundred men. But, as his followers wore iron armor, and had muskets and cannon, they were able to fight whole armies of the Mexicans.

5. The emperor of Mexico was named Montezuma. He received Cortez

---

Questions—8–10. Describe the fountain of youth.

Chap. CLXXVIII—1. What of gold in Mexico?   2. What of Mexico?   The capital?   3. Describe the city of Mexico.   4. When did Cortez invade Mexico?

and his men with great civility, for he was afraid to quarrel with them. But, after a short time, Cortez threw Montezuma into prison, and loaded him with chains.

6. Finding himself in so unhappy a situation, Montezuma consented to become a vassal of the king of Spain. But the Mexicans raised an insurrection, and when Montezuma endeavored to quiet them, they uttered shouts of scorn and anger.

7. So offended were they, that they discharged arrows and stones at him. One arrow struck poor Montezuma in the breast, and stretched him on the ground. He would not suffer the wound to be dressed, and, in a few days, this ill-fated emperor died.

8. The Mexicans elected Guatimozin, son-in-law of Montezuma, to succeed him. He made a vigorous attack on the Spaniards, and drove them from the city of Mexico. But Cortez soon came back with an army, and conquered the whole country.

9. The emperor Guatimozin was taken prisoner. He refused to confess where his treasures were concealed. Some of the Spaniards then laid him at full length on a bed of burning coals. There Guatimozin writhed in agony, till he was delivered by Cortez, who had borne no part in this horrible cruelty. But, about three years afterward, Guatimozin was suspected of being engaged in a conspiracy, and Cortez sentenced him to be hanged.

10. It has been affirmed, that Cortez and his soldiers killed four millions of the Mexicans, in completing the conquest of the country. He pretended that his only object was to convert the people to the Christian religion. But he and his soldiers acted like fiends rather than Christians.

11. From the time of its conquest by Cortez, the Mexican empire continued under the government of Spain, till the year 1810. A revolution then took place.

12. In 1813, the Mexican provinces declared themselves free and independent. But their independence was not established till several years afterward. They are called the United States of Mexico. One of these provinces was Texas, which, after a severe conflict with the parent state, became independent a few years since.

Questions—5. What of Montezuma? Cortez? 6. What did Montezuma do? What of the Mexicans? 7. Fate of Montezuma? 8. What did Guatimozin do? Cortez? 9. What was done to Guatimozin? His fate? 10. What is said of Cortez? What excuse did he give for his cruelty? 11. How long was the Mexican empire under the government of Spain? What took place in 1810? 12. What in 1813? What is Mexico called?

13. In 1845, Texas was admitted as a state into our Union. In 1846, a war began between Mexico and the United States, which lasted for two years.

14. Our armies, under Generals Taylor and Scott, defeated the Mexicans in many battles, and finally their chief towns, including the capital, were in our hands. Peace was made in 1848, by which we gained California, the rich gold mines of which have produced a wonderful effect on the whole civilized world.

15. The country called Guatimala consisted of five provinces, Guatimala, San Salvador, Honduras, Nicaragua [*nik-ar-a´-gwa*], and Costa Rica [*kos-ta ree´-ka*]; these became independent states and were formed into a Republic, called the United States of Central America, the city of San Salvador being the capital. This general government, however, has been thrown off, and the several states are now independent of one another.

16. This country of Central America is very interesting on account of the ruins of several ancient cities, which are now found there. By these it appears that formerly—many ages ago—there lived in that region nations of Indians who had made considerable progress in civilization, but who have passed away, leaving no history behind them.

CHAPTER CLXXIX—AMERICA—CONTINUED
Spanish Peruvian Territories

1. A FEW YEARS AFTER the conquest of Mexico by Cortez, the Spaniards also conquered the vast empire of Peru, in South America. At the present day, Peru is bounded north by the republic of Ecuador [*ek-wa-dor´*], east by Brazil, south by Bolivia and the Pacific Ocean, and west by the Pacific. But when the Spaniards first invaded it, the Peruvian empire included a much larger space.

2. The sovereigns of this empire were called Incas, and the Peruvians believed that their first Inca was a Child of the Sun. The inhabitants were worshipers of the Sun.

3. Peru contained many magnificent cities, and gold was more abundant than even in Mexico. No sooner did the Spaniards hear of it, than they

---

Questions—13. What of Texas? 14. War? 15. What of Guatimala?

CHAP. CLXXIX—1. When was Peru conquered? What of Peru at the present time? What of it when the Spaniards first invaded it? 2. What of the native sovereigns of Peru? The people? 3. What did Peru contain? What did the Spaniards determine to do?

determined to make themselves masters of the country.

4. The first invader was Francis Pizarro. In 1531 he marched into Peru, and after a time took the Inca prisoner. The Inca's name was Atahualpa. To regain his freedom, he offered Pizarro as much gold as would fill a spacious hall of his palace, piled as high as he could reach.

5. But after the gold had been delivered, Pizarro refused to give the Inca his freedom. He was not satisfied with the Inca's treasure, but was determined to have his life. So he condemned him to death; and Atahualpa was accordingly strangled and burnt.

6. When he had conquered the Peruvians, Pizarro quarreled with one of his chief officers, named Almagro. They made war upon each other, and Pizarro caused Almagro to be beheaded. Soon afterward he was himself murdered.

7. In the course of time, the Peruvian empire was divided into several provinces. All of these were under the government of Spain. The Spanish territories comprised nearly all the western part of South America.

8. But after a time the kingdom of Spain became so weak that it lost its authority over these colonies. The first resistance to the government was made while Joseph Bonaparte was king of Spain; and the people would not return to their allegiance, when the former king was again seated on the throne.

9. The different states in America which were once Spanish provinces, comprise the States of Mexico, the Republic of Central America, New Granada, Venezuela, Ecuador, Peru, Bolivia, Chili, the Argentine Confederation, Uruguay, and Paraguay. All these have become independent states; but most of them are in a rather unsettled condition.

CHAPTER CLXXX—AMERICA—Continued
Account of Brazil

1. The vast country of Brazil is bounded north by New Granada, Venezuela, and Guiana; east by the Atlantic Ocean; south by the Atlantic, Uruguay, and Paraguay; and west by Bolivia, Peru, and the republic of Ecua-

---

Questions—4. When did Pizarro go to Peru? Who was the Inca? What did he do? 5. Fate of Atahualpa? 6. What of Pizarro and Almagro? What became of Pizarro? 7. What of the Peruvian empire? What of the Spanish territories? 8. What of the kingdom of Spain? The people? 9. What of the states in America which were once Spanish provinces?

Chap. CLXXX—1. Boundaries of Brazil? Extent?

dor. It is nearly as extensive as the whole United States together.

2. When the Spaniards were making conquests in other parts of America, the Portuguese came to Brazil. It is said that near the river Amazon they found a nation of women, whose lives were spent in war. This, however, is probably a mere fiction.

3. We do not read that the Portuguese committed such cruelties upon the natives as the Spaniards did. The reason was, that the inhabitants of Brazil possessed but little gold; and the Portuguese hardly thought it worth their while to colonize the country.

4. During many years the government of Portugal was accustomed to send nobody but criminals thither; so that to be sent to Brazil was considered almost as bad as being sent out of the world.

5. In 1548, a multitude of Jews were banished to Brazil. They planted the sugar-cane there and successfully cultivated it. When the king of Portugal found that the country was rich and fruitful, he sent over a governor, in order that he might not lose his share of the wealth.

6. France, Spain, and Holland, likewise attempted to get possession of Brazil. But the Portuguese resisted them, and finally became sole masters of the country. Perhaps, if the other nations had known of the hidden riches of Brazil, they would not have given up their claims so easily.

7. A long time after the settlement of the country, valuable mines of gold were discovered. Considerable quantities of this precious metal are also found in the beds of the rivers, mixed with sand and gravel. The topaz and the diamond are sometimes seen glittering among the gold.

8. The Rio Pardo, though it is a very small and shallow stream, produces a great number of diamonds. Other rivers are likewise enriched with them. Negro slaves are employed in washing the sand and gravel of these rivers, and when one of them finds a very large diamond, he receives his freedom.

9. In 1808, the king of Portugal removed to Brazil, and established his court in the city of Rio Janeiro. Fifteen years afterward he returned to Lisbon. His son Pedro was then proclaimed emperor of Brazil.

10. In 1831, the Brazilians became discontented with the government

---

Questions—2. What of the Portuguese? Amazons? 3. Why were the Portuguese not as cruel as the Spaniards? 4. Who were sent to Brazil? 5. What happened in 1548? What of the Jews? 6. What of other countries? 7. What were discovered in Brazil? 8. What of the Rio Pardo? What of the negro slaves? 9. When did the king of Portugal remove to Brazil? Where did he establish his court? When did he return to Lisbon? What of his son Pedro?

of Pedro. He therefore gave up the imperial crown to his son, who was then only five years old. This boy was styled the Emperor of Brazil; but the government was carried on by a council of regency, till the year 1841, when the emperor assumed the government. Since this time Brazil has gone on steadily in prosperity and improvement.

CHAPTER CLXXXI—AMERICA—Continued
The West Indies

1. I must not close my story about America, without giving you some little account of the West India islands, lying in the Atlantic Ocean between North and South America. These consist of three clusters, called the Bahamas, the Antilles, and the Caribbees. The Bahamas are the most northerly of the three groups, and lie near to Florida. They are about six hundred in number. Most of them are small, and consist chiefly of sand and rocks, and are uninhabited by man.

2. These, however, are the resort of a great variety of sea-fowl. Many of the birds which visit the lakes and shores of the United States in summer, retire to these lonely islands in winter, where they find a secure and pleasant abode. The Bahama islands belong to Great Britain, and contain about seventeen thousand inhabitants. The principal are Turks island, Providence, and San Salvador, or Cat Island. This last is that which Columbus first discovered.

3. The Antilles [an-teel´], occupying the middle portion of the West Indies, consist of Cuba, which is the largest, and belongs to Spain; Hayti, or St. Domingo, which is independent, and governed by blacks; Porto Rico, which belongs to Spain; Jamaica, which belongs to Great Britain, and a few smaller islands.

4. The Caribbee islands are very numerous, and lie to the southeast of the others. They stretch from Porto Rico in a semicircular group to the shores of South America. They belong to different European governments. The most celebrated of these islands are Martinique, Barbadoes, St. Thomas, Tobago, St. Lucia, St. Vincent, Guadaloupe [gua-da-loop], Antigua, St. Christopher, Dominica, Santa Cruz, and Trinidad.

Questions—10. What of the Brazilians in the year 1831? What did Pedro do? How is Brazil now governed?

Chap. CLXXXI—1. Where are the West India Islands situated? Of what three groups do they consist? What of the Bahama islands? 2. What of sea-fowl? To whom do the Bahamas belong? Which are the principal ones? 3. What can you say of the Antilles? 4. What of the Caribbee islands? The principal ones?

5. The climate of the West Indies is that of perpetual summer. Frost and snow never come to visit them. The trees are ever clothed with leaves, and many of the shrubs and plants continue at all times to be adorned with blossoms.

6. The fruits which are common to us, such as apples, pears, cherries, and peaches, are unknown in these regions; but oranges, figs, lemons, pineapples, and many other nice fruits, are abundant.

7. The people do not cultivate Indian corn, wheat, rye, oats, and barley; but they raise sugar-cane, from which they extract sugar and molasses, and they cultivate coffee, cotton, indigo, tobacco, cocoa, allspice, and other things.

8. The forests contain mahogany, lignum-vitae, iron-wood, and other woods useful in the arts. Among the birds are parrots of various kinds, some of which are not bigger than a bluebird. A friend of mine made me a present of one of these little fellows a few years since. Instead of sitting upon his perch, I have known him to hang by his claws to the top wires of his cage, with his head downward, and thus remain during the whole night.

9. Among the quadrupeds of the West Indies are some curious little monkeys, and several kinds of lizards. The chameleon is the most interesting of them. He was formerly supposed to live on air, and to have the power of changing his color at will. But it is now ascertained that he often makes a sly meal upon insects that come in his way, and that his color does not vary more than that of several other animals of a similar kind.

10. Although the West Indies are never disturbed by winter, they are often visited by terrible hurricanes. These sometimes come so suddenly as to tear the sails from the masts of vessels, and often overturn the houses and trees upon the land.

CHAPTER CLXXXII—AMERICA—Continued
West Indies continued

1. IF YOU WERE TO VISIT the West Indies at the present day, you would find them inhabited by Europeans and their descendants, together with a great many negroes. But you would meet with none of the native Indians. These have long since disappeared.

2. You already know that Columbus first discovered one of the Baha-

---

Questions—5. What of the climate of the West Indies? 6. Fruits? 7. Productions? 8. Forests? Birds? 9. What of monkeys? The chameleon? 10. What of hurricanes? CHAP. CLXXXII—1. How are the West Indies inhabited?

mas, to which he gave the name of St. Salvador, and which is now called Cat Island. Here he found a great many people who appear to have been nearly the same as the Indians who formerly inhabited our country.

3. After leaving St. Salvador, Columbus visited Cuba and St. Domingo. Both of these were thronged with Indians. It is supposed that Cuba alone contained several millions. They appeared to live happily, for the climate was mild, and the soil fruitful. They received Columbus with kindness, and rendered him every service in their power. They little thought of the cruel consequences which were soon to follow.

4. Not many years after the discovery of the West India islands, the largest and finest of them were taken possession of by the Spanish government. The Indians were a gentle race, and were easily subjugated. The Spaniards did not seem to regard them as human beings, but rather as wild animals, who were to be exterminated. They shot them down by thousands, and even trained blood-hounds to pursue them.

5. In this way, the numerous islanders who once swarmed like bees upon every hill-side and in every valley of these beautiful regions, were reduced to a very small number. Most of these were treated like slaves, and many of them were compelled to work in mines, where they soon perished from hard labor, to which they were unaccustomed, and for want of that free air which heaven had sent them before the Europeans came to deprive them of it.

6. Thus, by degrees, the native West Indians vanished, and their fair lands came into the possession of various European governments. Spain held Cuba and Porto Rico in her firm grasp. England got possession of Jamaica, the Bermudas, and some other islands. France had St. Domingo, Martinique [mar-tin-eek], Guadaloupe, and several others. Some of the smaller islands fell into the hands of the Dutch, Danes, Swedes, etc.

7. The first object of the Europeans after the discovery of America, was to obtain gold and silver. They seemed to imagine that all the hills and mountains in this continent were filled with these precious metals. But this illusion soon vanished, and in the West Indies the people began to cultivate the soil, instead of digging into the bosom of the earth for gold and silver.

Questions—2. What of Cat Island? What people did Columbus find there? 3. What islands did he next visit? What of the Indians? 4–5. What of the Spanish government? How did the Spaniards treat the Indians? 6. Which islands did Spain obtain possession of? England? France? What of smaller islands? 7. What did the Europeans expect to find abundant in America? Result of these expectations?

8. They discovered that the land was peculiarly suited to the raising of sugar-cane, oranges, pine-apples, and other productions of a tropical climate. To these, then, they devoted their attention, and the lands soon became very productive. In order to till them, the people sent to Africa for negroes, who were brought by thousands and tens of thousands, and compelled to work as slaves. In some of the islands slaves still perform the principal labor; in others they are emancipated.

CHAPTER CLXXXIII—AMERICA—Continued
West Indies continued

1. I shall not undertake to tell you of all the interesting events which have occurred in the West Indies. Several of these islands have often changed hands, sometimes belonging to one government, and sometimes to another. They have frequently been shaken by earthquakes, and often desolated by whirlwinds. But of these events I cannot tell you now.

2. I must not, however, overlook the story of Hayti. This fine island was discovered by Columbus on his first voyage, and here he left a part of his men, who made the first European settlement on this side of the Atlantic. The island was called Hayti by the natives, and Hispaniola by the Spaniards. The settlements increased rapidly, and soon the whole island became subject to Spain. In after times, the French obtained possession of a portion of the country, and until about forty years ago, it was shared between the French and Spanish governments.

3. But the negro slaves had become much more numerous than the white inhabitants, and, in 1791, they rose against their masters. France, at this time, was in a state of revolution, and could afford no aid to put down the insurrection. The negroes therefore slaughtered the white people by thousands, pillaging their houses, and then setting them on fire. A few escaped, but a large proportion were killed.

4. The negroes considered themselves independent, and began to form a government of their own. After various revolutions, the whole island was formed into a sort of Republic, the officers of which were negroes or mulattoes. After a time it became an Empire, and so it continues to this day.

Questions—8. What did they discover? What of negro slaves?

Chap. CLXXXIII—1. What of some of the West India islands? 2. Who discovered Hayti? What settlement was made? Names of the island? To what country did it become subject? What of France? 3. What was done in 1791? 4. What of the negroes? Their government? State of society?

5. Before I leave the West Indies, I must say a few words about the Buccaneers, a famous set of sea-robbers, who infested these islands during the seventeenth century. These at first consisted of men from England and France, who settled on the western coast of St. Domingo and the neighboring island of Tortuga, about the year 1630.

6. For a while, they lived by hunting wild animals, but when they became numerous, they procured vessels, and went forth upon the sea to rob and plunder whomsoever they might meet. This business succeeded so well, that a great many desperate adventurers from all parts of Europe united themselves to the buccaneers. They therefore procured larger vessels, which were equipped in the best manner for attack. These were filled with daring seamen, and commanded by bold leaders.

7. In this manner the buccaneers became very formidable. Their vessels hovered in the track of the merchant ships, ready, like hawks in the neighborhood of a barn-yard, to pounce down upon whatever might come in their way. They often captured ships laden with rich merchandise, and sometimes with gold and silver.

8. In this way, they amassed great wealth; and such was their power at one time, that they made successful attacks upon large cities, sometimes pillaging the inhabitants, and sometimes laying them under contribution. But, at length, the European governments were roused, by the violence and cruelty of these robbers, to measures of retaliation. They sent large vessels to cruise in the neighborhood of the West Indies, and after many struggles, the buccaneers were finally exterminated.

9. In later times, the West Indian seas have been infested with pirates, who have captured a good many trading vessels, but they are now seldom met with.

CHAPTER CLXXXIV—AMERICA—Continued
Chronology of America

A.D.

Iceland and Greenland settled 860

Christianity introduced into Iceland 981

Questions—5. What of the buccaneers? Where were they originally from? Where and in what year did they settle? 6. How did they live for a while? What did they afterward do? By whom were they joined? 7. What of the ships of the buccaneers? 8. What of the power of these pirates? How were they finally subdued? 9. What of other pirates?

Chap. CLXXXIV—*Let the pupil be examined in the Chronological table; and let him tell what was happening in Europe, as events were occurring in America.*

A.D.

Severe winter in Greenland, which destroys the colony 1408
Columbus born 1435
America discovered 1492
Cortez invaded Mexico 1519
French settlements made in Canada 1524
Pizarro goes to Peru 1531
First settlement in Virginia at Jamestown 1607
Quebec founded 1608
First settlement in New York 1613
Settlement at Plymouth 1620
Buccaneers first assemble at St. Domingo and Tortuga 1630
Maryland settled 1634
First settlement in Connecticut 1635
Providence settled 1636
English get possession of New York 1664
King Philip's war begins 1675
Carolina settled 1680
Pennsylvania settled 1681
The Carolinas divided 1729
Georgia founded 1733
Capture of Louisbourg 1745
Old French war begins 1755
Capture of Louisbourg by Wolfe 1758
Quebec taken by the English 1759
Stamp act passed 1765
Boston massacre 1770
Destruction of tea 1773
Commencement of the Revolutionary war 1775
British troops driven out of Boston 1776
Declaration of Independence, July 4 1776
La Fayette came to America 1777
André taken as a spy 1780
Gates beaten by Cornwallis 1780
Surrender of Cornwallis 1780
Peace between Great Britain and the United States 1783
Constitution of the United States went into operation 1789
Washington made president 1789
John Adams made president 1797

	A.D.
Death of Washington	1799
Jefferson made president	1801
Purchase of Louisiana	1803
King of Portugal goes to Brazil	1806
Madison made president	1809
Monroe president	1817
John Q. Adams president	1825
Andrew Jackson president	1829
Martin Van Buren president	1837
William H. Harrison president	1841
John Tyler president	1841
James K. Polk president	1845
Zachary Taylor president	1849
Millard Fillmore president	1850
Franklin Pierce president	1853
James Buchanan president	1857
Abraham Lincoln president	1861
War of the Rebellion	1861–1865
Andrew Johnson president	1865
U. S. Grant president	1869
Rutherford B. Hayes president	1877
James A. Garfield president	1881

CHAPTER CLXXXV—OCEANIA
About Oceania—The Malaysian Islands

1. HAVING NOW RELATED the history of Asia, Europe, Africa, and America, the reader will probably think that my History of the World ought to close here. But there is a Fifth Division of the globe, of which I must say a few words.

2. America ought no longer to be called the New World; for there is a newer one, composed of the islands which lie in the Pacific and Indian Oceans. The name of Oceania, or Oceanica, has been given to this region. If all the islands were put together, they would cover a space of at least four millions of square miles; that is a space larger than the whole of Europe.

3. There are three divisions of Oceania. Those islands which lie in the Indian Ocean, near the continent of Asia, are called Malaysia. The largest of them are Borneo, Sumatra, and Java. Scarcely any thing has been written about the history of Malaysia, for the islands are chiefly inhabited by the natives, who keep no record of passing events, and have no desire to know the deeds of their forefathers.

4. The history of Java is best known, but it is not very important or interesting. It was discovered by the Portuguese, in the year 1510. They found it an exceedingly fertile island, producing abundance of sugar, coffee, rice, pepper, spices, and delicious fruits. There were also mines of gold, silver, diamonds, rubies, and emeralds.

5. The island is six hundred and fifty miles in length. Soon after its discovery, the Dutch got possession of a large portion of it. They built the city of Batavia, on the northwestern coast of the island.

6. The city is situated on a low, marshy plain, and canals of stagnant water are seen in many of the streets. But the edifices were so splendid, that Batavia was called the Queen of the East. Its beauty was much increased by the trees that overshadowed the streets and canals.

7. In the year 1780, the population amounted to a hundred and sixty thousand. People from all the different parts of the world were among them. But the Europeans were the fewest in number, although the government was in their hands.

8. For a time Batavia rapidly declined; the climate was so unhealthy,

---

Questions—CHAP. CLXXXV—2. What of Oceania? Extent of Oceania? 3. What of Malaysia? The natives? 4. What of Java? When was it discovered? What are its productions? Mines? 5. Length of Java? Who built Batavia? 6. Describe the city. 7. Population of Batavia in 1780?

that strangers were attacked by dreadful fevers. Of late years the city has been rendered more healthy by drainage.

9. In the year 1811, the English took possession of the island of Java. They kept it till 1816, and then restored it to its former owners. The Dutch are said to exercise great tyranny over the natives.

CHAPTER CLXXXVI—OCEANIA—Continued
The Australasian Division of Oceania

1. THE SECOND DIVISION of Oceania is called Australasia. This comprises the great island formerly called New Holland, but now called Australia, with New Guinea, Tasmania (or Van Diemen's Land), New Zealand, and other islands in the vicinity. Australia is an immense island, containing three millions of square miles, and is about as extensive as all the United States.

2. The natives of Australia are described as the most degraded people in the world. They are black, and have frizzled hair like negroes; and they have very lean arms and legs.

3. This great island was discovered by the Dutch, in 1610, but the whole of it is now claimed as a territory of Great Britain. Captain James Cook, the celebrated navigator, took possession of it in 1770.

4. It is divided into North Australia, Western Australia, South Australia, Victoria, Queensland, and New South Wales. The latter began to be settled in 1778. It was then called Botany Bay.

5. The first colonists were not a very respectable sort of people. The English government conceived the plan of sending criminals to Australia, instead of keeping them in jail, or sending them to the gallows. Accordingly, ship-loads were transported every year.

6. This cannot be considered a severe punishment, for the soil of Australia is fertile, and the climate is delightful. Perhaps the English would have acted more equitably, if they had transported the honest poor people who were starving at home.

7. But during many years there were hardly any honest men in the

Questions—8. What of this city of late years? Its climate? 9. What happened in 1811? In 1816? What of the Dutch?

CHAP. CLXXXVI—1. What is called Australia? What is the size of Australia? 2. What of the natives? 3. When and by whom was New Holland discovered? Who now hold it in possession? When was it taken by Captain Cook? 4. What of the divisions of Australia? When was New South Wales settled? What was the settlement called? 5. Who were the first colonists? Who were sent every year to Botany Bay?

SCENE IN AUSTRALIA

new colony. Few of the inhabitants felt any reluctance to commit crimes, or were ashamed to be found out; for they knew that their neighbors were as bad as themselves.

8. In later years, however, the people began to improve. The children of the convicts were now growing up, and their parents had taught them to be more virtuous than they themselves had been.

9. A young girl, who was born in Australia, was once asked whether she would like to go to England. "Oh, no!" said she; "I should be afraid to go there, for the people are all thieves!" The child knew that a gang of thieves arrived in every ship which came from England, and she naturally supposed that the English were all thieves alike.

10. Criminals became so numerous in Australia, that it was found necessary to plant new colonies of them; and in 1804 Tasmania was appropriated to that purpose. In the year 1853 the home government abandoned the practice of transportation for crime.

11. In 1850, rich gold mines were found in Australia, which caused a

---

Questions—7. What can be said of the colonies for some years? 8. What of them in later years? 9. Relate the anecdote of the young New Holland girl. 10. What became necessary on account of the number of criminals sent to Australia? What was done in 1804? What took place in 1853?

sudden and extraordinary prosperity in these colonies. Many millions of dollars, in gold, are now sent from this island to Great Britain every year.

CHAPTER CLXXXVII—OCEANIA—CONTINUED
Polynesia—The Sandwich Islands

1. THE THIRD DIVISION of Oceania is called Polynesia. It consists of many groups of small islands, which are scattered over a large extent of the Pacific Ocean. None of them are wholly occupied by civilized people.

2. The Sandwich islands are among the most important in Polynesia. They consist of ten islands, of which Owhyhee, or Hawaii [*ha-wi´-ee*], is the largest. These islands were discovered by Captain James Cook, in 1778.

3. He found them inhabited by a race of people whose forms were very beautiful, although their complexions were darker than our own. They appeared to be of a gay, friendly, and sociable disposition.

4. But there were some shocking customs among them. They were in the habit of feasting on human flesh, and offering human sacrifices to their idols. They were also great thieves, and had many other vices.

5. The natives at first behaved in a very friendly manner to Captain Cook. But, after some time, a part of them stole one of the boats belonging to his vessel. The captain went on shore, intending to take the king of Hawaii prisoner, and keep him till the boat should be returned.

6. But when he had landed, the natives mustered in great numbers. Captain Cook found it necessary to retreat toward his own men, who were waiting for him in a boat near the shore. The natives followed him, shouting, throwing stones, and brandishing their weapons.

7. Captain Cook pointed his musket at them, but it only made them more tumultuous and violent. He then took aim and shot the foremost native dead. In a moment, before the smoke of his musket had blown away, the natives rushed upon him. One of them beat him down with a club, and then stabbed him with a dagger. His men fired their muskets at the natives, but could not rescue him.

8. The Sandwich islands soon after became the resort of whale-ships,

Questions—11. What of gold mines?

CHAP. CLXXXVII—1. What of Polynesia? Its inhabitants? 2. Which are the most important islands of the group? Which is the largest of the Sandwich islands? Who discovered these islands in 1778? 3. What people did Captain Cook find inhabiting the Sandwich islands? 4. What were some of their customs? 5. What took place between the natives and Captain Cook? 6–7. What did Cook find it necessary to do? Relate what then happened.

and of all other vessels that voyaged in that part of the Pacific Ocean. But the inhabitants did not derive any advantage from their intercourse with civilized people.

9. On the contrary, they became a great deal more vicious than ever they were before. They contracted so many diseases, that their numbers were reduced from four hundred thousand to less than a hundred and fifty thousand. There was reason to fear that the islands would be depopulated.

10. Some American missionaries crossed the ocean, in hopes to save these poor islanders from destruction. They preached the gospel to them, and established schools, in which the natives were taught to read the Bible.

11. Kaahumana, the queen-regent of the Sandwich islands, adopted the Christian religion. By her assistance, the missionaries met with great success. A number of schools were established. It appeared probable that the whole people would be civilized and Christianized.

12. But Kaahumana died, and her death was a great misfortune to the Sandwich islands. Many of the natives relapsed into their former vices. But the missionaries labored earnestly for their good; and such has been their success, that the natives are, in a degree, Christianized and civilized.

13. Many white people settled in these islands, and after a time, churches and newspapers were established, and a considerable trade with the civilized parts of the earth is now carried on there.

CHAPTER CLXXXVIII—OCEANIA—Continued
Polynesia continued—The Society Islands

1. THE SOCIETY ISLANDS likewise belong to Polynesia. They are situated about a thousand miles south of the equator, which is nearly the same distance that the Sandwich islands are north of it.

2. The largest of the Society islands is called Tahiti [ta-hee´-tee], or Otaheite. It is a hundred miles in circumference, and is inhabited by about ten thousand people. Like the natives of the Sandwich islands, they are generally handsome, and of agreeable manners.

3. A very interesting event took place among these islands many years ago. The brig Bounty, belonging to the British navy, was went to the Soci-

---

Questions—8. What ships soon resorted to the Sandwich islands?   9. What was the consequence of the intercourse of the natives with the whites?   10. What of American missionaries?   11. What of Kaahumana?   12. Consequences of her death?   What of the missionaries?   13. What of white people, etc.?

CHAP. CLXXXVIII—1. Where are the Society islands?   To what group do they belong? 2. What is the size and population of Tahiti or Otaheite?   What of the natives?

ety islands in order to carry bread-fruit trees from thence to the West Indies. Her commander was Lieutenant William Bligh.

4. He arrived at Otaheite in 1788. His crew were delighted with the island. The air was balmy and full of sunshine. Fruits grew abundantly on every tree. There was no need of toiling for bread, since there were trees enough which produced it ready made, and almost as good as if it had been baked.

5. The natives of Otaheite received the Englishmen with kindness. The women behaved with great affection toward the poor storm-beaten sailors. In short, the crew spent their time so pleasantly, that they were very reluctant to depart.

6. They desired to spend their whole lives in these sunny islands, instead of wandering any more over the wide and dreary sea. When the Bounty sailed, they cast many a sad glance at the pleasant shores which they were leaving. They had not sailed many days, before they formed a resolution to return.

7. A young man by the name of Christian was an officer on board the Bounty. He was not on good terms with Lieutenant Bligh, and he incited the crew to mutiny against their commander, and take possession of the vessel.

8. One morning, before sunrise, Christian and his associates entered Lieutenant Bligh's cabin while he was asleep. They bound his hands behind his back, threatening him with death, if he made the least resistance. He was then put into a leaky boat, with eighteen other persons who refused to join in the mutiny.

9. I can only say of Lieutenant Bligh and his companions, that they arrived safe in England, after severe hardships. After a time the British frigate Pandora was sent to Otaheite in search of the mutineers, that they might be brought to justice.

10. The frigate arrived at Otaheite and found fourteen of the mutineers. She took them on board and sailed for England, but was wrecked on her passage. Four of the mutineers were drowned. The other ten were carried to England, where three of them were hanged.

Questions—3. What of the brig Bounty?   Who was her commander?   4. When did he arrive at Otaheite?   How did his men like the island?   5. How did the natives treat the Englishmen?   6. What of the crew of the Bounty?   What resolution did they form?   7. What did Christian do?   8. How did he treat Lieutenant Bligh and eighteen others?   9. Did they arrive in England?   What ship was sent to Otaheite?   10. What happened to the Pandora?   What became of the mutineers?

11. Christian, the ringleader of the mutiny, had not been taken prisoner by the Pandora; for he and several companions had sailed from Otaheite in the Bounty. They had taken with them a plentiful supply of hogs, dogs, cats, and fowls, and also a number of Otaheitan men and women.

12. For a great many years, nobody could tell what had become of Christian and his friends, and of the brig Bounty, in which they had sailed away. As no news was heard of them, people universally believed that the vessel had gone to the bottom, with all her crew.

CHAPTER CLXXXIX—OCEANIA—Continued
Story of the Bounty concluded

1. But, after twenty years, when people had long ago done talking about the Bounty, it was found out what had become of her. In the year 1813, a British ship of war was sailing from the Marquesas [*mar-ka´-sas*] islands to the port of Valparaiso [*val-pa-ri´-so*], in South America. The captain of the vessel was Sir Thomas Staines. In the course of his voyage, he happened to cast anchor off Pitcairn's islands.

2. This small island lies many leagues to the southwest of Otaheite. It was first discovered by Captain Carteret, in 1767; but very few people had since visited it, for it produced no valuable commodities, and it was supposed to be uninhabited.

3. But, as Sir Thomas Staines looked from the deck of his vessel to the shore, he was amazed to perceive that the island was cultivated, and that there were small houses on it. These houses were better built than are those of the savages generally, and they looked something like the dwellings of poor people in England.

4. While Sir Thomas Staines and his sailors were wondering at these circumstances, a small boat put off from the shore. The waves rolled very high, but the boat skimmed like a sea-bird over the tops of them, and soon came alongside of the vessel.

5. The boat was rowed by two young men. They were handsome, though of a rather dark complexion. When they came near the vessel, one of them called out, in good English—"Won't you throw us a rope, friends?"

Questions—11. What had Christian and his companions done? 12. What was supposed to have become of them?

Chap. CLXXXIX—1. What happened in the year 1813? 2. Where is Pitcairn's island? When was it discovered? 3. What was seen from the deck of the ship? How did the houses appear? 4. What of a boat from shore? 5. Describe the young men who rowed it. What did they call out?

6. A rope was thrown to them, and they took hold of it and clambered on board of the vessel. Sir Thomas Staines asked them who they were, and how they came to be living on that lonely island. The mystery was soon explained.

7. When Christian and his companions left Otaheite, they had steered for Pitcairn's island, and had run the Bounty on the rocks and set her on fire. They had then built houses on the island, and had married the Otaheitan women whom they brought with them.

8. Christian and all his associates were now dead, except one old man, whose name was John Adams. But they had left children and grandchildren, so that there was now quite a flourishing colony on the island.

9. These people increased in numbers, and in 1856 there were nearly two hundred of them. At their request, they were then removed by the British goverment to Norfolk island, which lies to the east of Australia, and is about five miles long, and contains nine thousand acres of land. It is fruitful, and has a charming climate, and here, no doubt, these people will be very happy.

CHAPTER CLXL—OCEANIA—Continued
Chronology of Oceania

A.D.

Java discovered by the Portuguese	1510
New Holland discovered by the Dutch	1610
Batavia, the capital of Java, built by the Dutch	1619
Captain Cook took possession of New Holland	1770
Botany Bay, in New South Wales, settled	1778
Sandwich Islands discovered by Captain Cook	1778
Death of Captain Cook	1779
Ship Bounty arrives at Otaheite	1788
Convicts sent to Van Diemen's Land	1804
The English take Java from the Dutch	1811
Sir Thomas Staines reaches Pitcairn's island	1813
The Dutch take Java again from the English	1816
Missionaries established at the Sandwich islands	1820
The inhabitants of Pitcairn's island removed to Norfolk island	1856

Questions—7. Where had Christian and his companions steered on leaving Otaheite? What did they then do?   8. Who alone remained of the mutineers?   How was they colony peopled?   9. What of Norfolk island?

CHAPTER CLXLI
General Views

1. I WILL NOW GIVE you some account of the origin of Government, Architecture, and other things. At the present day, some nations are governed in one way and some in another. In our country, the people are governed by rulers of their own choice, and according to a constitution of their own formation. This government is called a Republic.

2. Some nations are governed by kings or emperors, who rule according to their own good will. These are called Despotic Monarchies. Other nations are ruled by kings or emperors, whose power is restrained by legislative assemblies, who make laws for the country. These are called Limited Monarchies.

3. In very early ages, there were no kings or emperors. A father would rule over his family, or a grandfather would rule over all his descendants. This kind of government was called Patriarchal. It existed before the flood, and continued in some parts of Asia long after that event.

4. But when the people became divided into nations, they went to war with each other. The boldest and strongest man would become the leader. Having the soldiers at his command, he would acquire great power, and become a King or Chief. As the people became rich, he would build palaces and live in great pomp.

5. When a king conquered several nations he would be styled Emperor. Thus you perceive that the rulers went on acquiring power, until they made slaves of the people. In Europe and Asia, nearly all the nations are governed by Kings or Emperors.

6. At various times, the people have become tired of being governed by selfish monarchs, and have established governments for themselves. In ancient Greece and Rome, the people threw off the yoke of their tyrant kings, and for a time enjoyed freedom. But it always happened that ambitious men led the people astray and enslaved them. It is to be hoped that the Americans will not thus part with their liberty.

7. In looking round upon the world, and observing the multitude of cities filled with beautiful buildings, you would hardly imagine that man-

---

Questions—CHAP. CLXLI—1. What of the government of different nations? Government of the United States? 2. What of Despotic Monarchies? Limited Monarchies? 3. What of Patriarchial Government? 4. What of Kings and Chiefs? 5. What of Emperor? Governments of Europe? 6. What of the people as to selfish rulers? What of ancient Greece and Rome?

PRIESTESS OF DELPHI

kind once dwelt in huts, grottos, caverns, and tents; yet such was the case in early ages.

8. But as people grew more civilized, they made themselves more comfortable houses. At first these were of stone or wood, rudely put together; but after a time they learned to make them more neatly.

9. Having built good houses for themselves, they began to erect temples for their gods. Thus architecture was improved and became a great art. The ancient Egyptians, Babylonians, Assyrians, Persians, and Phoenicians filled their cities with splendid edifices. But of all the ancients, the Greeks built the most pleasing and elegant structures.

10. The most famous of all the temples of ancient Greece was at Delphi or Delphos, on the south side of Mount Parnassus. Here a priestess pretended to announce the will of heaven. But these gods of the Greeks have passed away forever, and the temples reared in their honor are in ruins.

11. The Romans, carrying their conquests over the civilized world, copied and combined the architecture of different countries. Many of their edifices were exceedingly splendid, but not so chaste and beautiful as those of the Greeks.

12. Agriculture was one of the first arts of man. The Bible tells us, that Cain was a tiller of the ground, and that Noah was a husbandman, and

Questions—8. What of the people as they became more civilized?   9. What of temples? The structures of the Greeks?   10. What of the Greek temple of Delphi?   11. What of the Roman architecture?

PERSIAN WAR VESSELS

planted a vineyard. For many ages, agriculture was almost the only art practiced by mankind.

13. The Chinese, Japanese, Chaldeans, Egyptians, and Phoenicians, held husbandry in high estimation, in the earliest ages. The Greeks had but few farming tools; but the Romans used a great variety. They particularly venerated the plow.

14. The first mention made of nations trading together appears in the book of Genesis, chapter xxxvii. 25, when Joseph's brethren sold him to a band of Ishmaelites, who were conveying spices, balm and myrrh into Egypt. The balm was from Gilead, and the myrrh was the produce of Arabia. They were going through the land of Canaan into Egypt, which was then a highly cultivated kingdom.

15. The central situation of Egypt made it the ancient emporium of commerce. By caravans, the treasures of Asia and Africa were brought thither. Trade was held in great esteem there, because of the wealth it brought. Tyre and Sidon, cities of Phoenicia, were early devoted to commerce; and Solomon carried on an extensive trade with them.

16. The Persians, as far back as the time of Xerxes, had also consider-

---

Questions—12. What of agriculture? 13. What of the Chinese, Japanese, etc.? The farming tools of the Greeks? Of the Romans? 14. What of the first mention of commerce? 15. What of trade of Egypts Caravans? Trade of Tyre and Sidon?

356

able trade by sea, and in the wars with the Greeks their ships amounted to many hundreds. They were, however, small and insignificant in comparison with the ships of the present day.

17. The Greeks had a very extensive commerce along the borders of the Mediterranean Sea. The Carthaginians were also a highly commercial people. The Romans preferred acquiring wealth by conquest and plunder, rather than by trade. Of all modern nations Great Britain and the United States are the most commercial.

18. I have not space to tell you the history of Music, Painting and Sculpture. Egypt was the birth-place of the arts and sciences, but most of the great nations of antiquity made some progress in them. The most beautiful specimens of sculpture in existence are those produced by Greek artists at least two thousand years ago. In painting, the modern Italians have excelled all other nations.

19. In looking back at the ancient nations we see many things to admire, but still they were greatly behind the moderns. They had no printed books; no chimneys in their houses; no glass to their windows—no railways, no steamboats, no electric telegraphs. All these, and a thousand other inventions, which greatly contribute to the comfort of mankind, are of modern origin.

Questions—16. Ships of the Persians?   17. What of the commerce of the Greek?   Of Great Britain and the United States?   18. What of Egypt as to the arts?   Sculpture of the Greeks?   Painting of the Italians?   19. What of the ancients as compared with the moderns in respect to many inventions?

INDEX

A

Aaron 44
Abbas 38
Abbeys 287
Abd-el-Kader 98
Abel 21
Abercrombie 95
Aboukir [*a-boo-keer´*] 95
Abraham 40
Absalom 54
Abyssinians 86
Achaia 127
Adam 20, 22, 78
Adams, John 320
Adams, John Quincy 322
Adrian 62
Adriatic Sea 186
Aegean Sea 74
Aesop 75
Africa 85
Agincourt [*a-zhang-koor´*] 218
Agis 134
Agrippa 176
Alabama 304
Alans 193
Alaric 166
Albans 167
Alcibiades 114
Alemanni 230
Alexander 37, 58, 77, 123, 129
Alexander II 247
Alexander Severus 164
Alfred the Great 261
Algeria 98
Algiers 96
Alhambra 195
Ali 71
Almagro 337
Almanzor 195
Amenophis 92
America 295
Amphictyonic Council 127
Amsterdam 253
Amurath IV 191
Anacreon 124
Anaxagoras 121
Ancus Martius 143
André [*an´-dray*], Major 317
Angles 260
Anne, Empress of Russia 245
Anne, Queen of England 277
Anthony, Saint 291
Antioch 73

Antiparos 106
Antipater 58
Antoinette, Marie 222
Antoninus 164
Antony, Mark 93, 157
Apis 34
Apollo 118
Arabia 69, 159
Arabs 69
Ararat 22
Arbaces 30
Archias 115
Architecture 354
Ardysus 74
Argonautic Expedition 110
Aristides 113
Arkansas 304
Armada, the Invincible 197
Armenia 22, 32
Arnold, General 318
Artaxerxes 36
Asher 42
Ashur 25
Asia 19
Asia Minor 72
Assyria 25, 29
Asturias 194
Athens 109
Athos 36
Attila 166
Augurs 168
Augustus Caesar 158
Aurelian 164
Aurelius 164
Australasia 347
Australia 347
Austria 186, 234
Ayesha 71

B

Babel 23, 25, 109
Bacchus 118
Bagdad 38
Bajazet 190
Balbec 74
Baltimore, Lord 297
Bannockburn 282
Barbarians 133
Barbarossa 97
Barbary States 97
Barebone, Praise-God 275
Barnabus 76
Bastile [*bas-teel´*] 223
Bavaria 229

Beaumont, Marshal 98
Belgium 105
Belisarius 166
Belshazzar 33
Belus 26
Bengal 179
Benjamin 42
Bergen 251
Berlin 238
Bethlehem 58
Bias 120
Birman Empire 78
Biscay, Bay of 192
Black Prince 218, 264
Black Sea 74
Bligh, Lieutenant 351
Boeotia 115
Bohemia 235
Bolivia 296, 337
Bonaparte, Joseph 198, 337
Bonaparte, Napoleon 94, 224
Boniface, Pope 217
Bordeaux [bor-do´] 200
Boston 297, 307
Botany Bay 347
Bounty, Ship 350
Braddock, General 311
Brazil 337
Brennus 133, 147
British America 296
Brutus 155
Brutus the Elder 145
Buccaneers 343
Bucephalus 129
Buddha 81
Bunker Hill, Battle of 315
Burgos [boor´-goce] 194
Burgoyne, General 317
Byzantium 165

C

Cadmea 115
Cadmus 109
Caesar 153
Caillié [kah-yay´] 99
Cain 21, 355
Cairo [ki´-ro], Grand 95
Calais 218
California 306
Caligula 163
Caliphs 188
Callisthenes 131
Cambyses 33, 90
Camillus 148
Campus Martius 150
Canaan [ka´-nan] 41, 45
Canada 296, 301

Cannae 150
Canton 66, 68
Canute 251
Cape of Good Hope 99
Cape Town 99
Carlsruhe [karls´-roo] 229
Carteret, Captain 352
Carthage 97, 148
Carthaginians 357
Cartier, James 301
Casca 156
Caspian Sea 33
Cassander 133
Cassius 93, 155
Cat Island 339
Catherine 244
Cato 168
Cavaliers 273
Cecrops 109
Celts 258
Central America 336
Ceres 118
Chaeronea [ker-o-ne´-a] 128
Chaldea [kal-de´-a] 40
Charlemagne [shar-le-mane´] 207
Charles, Archduke of Austria 198
Charles I 272
Charles II 276
Charles II of Spain 197
Charles IV 218
Charles IX 220
Charles the Bald 208
Charles the Fat 208
Charles the Simple 208
Charles the Victorious 219
Charles the Well-beloved 218
Charles the Wise 218
Charles V of Germany 233
Charles X 227
Charles XII of Sweden 249
Charlestown 315
Charon [ka´-ron] 171
Chaus 64
Childeric 206
China 64, 67
Ching 64
Ching-tsa 66
Chivalry 211
Chosroes 37
Christ 61
Christian 351
Christian Era 83
Christianity 164, 300
Christina of Sweden 248
Chronology 81
Church, Captain 309

Cicero 157
Cid Campeador 195
Cilicia [si-lish´-e-a] 93
Cilley, Colonel 317
Cimber 156
Cimbri 230
Cimon 113
Claudius 163
Cleombrotus 115
Cleopatra 92
Clinton, Sir Henry 318
Clitus 131
Clodion 206
Clovis 206
Cochin China 77
Codrington, Sir Edward 136
Coliseum 179
Collatinus 145
Columbus 196, 298
Comorin, Cape 179
Compostella 195
Concord 314
Confucius 65
Confusion of Tongues 81
Connecticut 304
Constantine the Great 164
Constantinople 164, 186, 187
Cook, Captain 347
Cordova 195
Coriolanus 146
Cornwallis 317, 319
Coromandel 179
Cortez 334
Cossacks 243
Costa Rica [kos-ta ree´-ka] 336
Creation 19, 81
Cressy, Battle of 288
Croesus 75
Cromwell, Oliver 272
Crucifixion 60
Cupid 119
Curiatius 142
Cushing 67
Cydnus 93
Cyrus 32, 75

D

Dacians 180
Dagon 48
Damascus 73
Dan 42
Danes 252
Daniel 59
Dantzic 238
Danube 235
Darien, Isthmus of 295
Darius 59, 112

Dark Ages 286
David 60
David of Wales 281
De Foe, Daniel 285
Decatur 97
Delilah 48
Delphos 118
Deluge 22, 81
Democritus 121
Demosthenes 128
Denmark 252
Diana 118
Diocletian 164
Diogenes [di-oj´-e-nes] 123
Discovery of America 298
Don Carlos 198
Don, River 243
Doune [doon] 283
Draco 111
Dresden 229
Druids 259
DuQuesne, Fort 311

E

Eastern Empire 135
Eastern War 191
Ecuador [ek-wa-dor´] 296
Edgeworth, Miss 285
Edinburgh 257
Edward I 263
Edward II 264
Edward III 264
Edward IV 267
Edward the Confessor 261
Edward V 267
Edward VI 269
Egbert 260
Egypt 25, 31, 42, 86, 356
El Dorado 334
Elam 32
Elba 226
Elijah 59
Eliot, John 308
Elisha 59
Elizabeth, Queen of England 269
Empedocles 122
England [ing´-land] 254
Epaminondas 115
Ephesus 75
Epimenides 120
Erostratus 76
Esau 42
Esquimaux [es´-ki-mo] 296
Essex, Earl of 270
Ethiopia 95
Etna 139

Etruria 145
Euphrates 20, 23, **25**, **33**, 78
Europe 103
Euxine Sea 74
Eve 20, 78
Exmouth, Lord 98

F

Fayette 317
Ferdinand II 234
Ferdinand, King of **Spain** 196
Ferdinand VII 197
Feudal System 211
Field of the Cloth of **Gold** 220
Fillmore, President **322**
Florence 137
Florida 304
Fohi 63
Fountain of Youth **334**
France 200
Francis I 219
Frankfort 229
Franks 204
Frederic the Great **239**
Frederic William I **239**
Frederic William II 240
Frederic William III 240
Frederic William IV 240
French Revolution **222**

G

Gabriel 70
Gaels 258
Gage, General 313
Galba 164
Gates, General 317, 319
Gauls 133, 204, 205
Gaza 48
Genghis Khan 66
Genoa 167, 187
George I 277
George II 278
George III 278
George IV 279
Georgia 304, 312
Germany 229
Geshen 96
Gesler 233
Gibraltar, Straits of **103**
Gideon 47
Gilboa 53
Gilead 356
Gipsies 192
Glasgow 257
Godfrey of Bouillon [*boo´-yong*] 210
Goliath 51
Goths 165, 204, **230**, 252, **281**
Government 354

Granada 196
Grand Cairo [*ki´-ro*] 95
Great Britain 357
Great Britain and Ireland 254
Greece 25, 35
Greek Empire 135
Greene, General 319
Greenland 295
Gregory III 291
Grutli, Men of 233
Guatimala 336
Guatimozin 335
Guillotine 223
Gunpowder, Invention of 288
Gunpowder Plot 271
Gustavus Adolphus 234
Gustavus III 250
Gustavus Vasa 248

H

Hagradin 97
Ham 23, 86
Hampden, John 272
Hannibal 149
Hanover 277
Hapsburg, Family of 234
Harrison, President 322
Havana 333
Hawaii [*ha-wi´-ee*] 349
Hayti 342
Hebrews 40
Hebron 42
Hecla 300
Hegira 83
Heliopolis 74
Hellespont 36, 130
Henry Beauclerk 262
Henry II 262
Henry III of England 263
Henry IV of England 265
Henry IV of France 220
Henry IV of Germany 292
Henry Tudor 268
Henry V 218
Henry VI 266
Henry VII 268
Henry VIII 268
Hephestion 132
Heraclitus 121
Hercules 119
Herod 58
Heruli 230
Hindostan 77
Hiram 55
Hispaniola 342
Hob Carter 264
Holland 105

Homer 110
Honduras 336
Horatius 142
Hugh Capet 209
Hulaki 72
Hungary 235
Huns 237
Husseyn 39
Hyksos 87

I

Iceland 296
Illinois 304
Independence, Declaration of 344
India 77
Indiana 304
Indians of America 297
Inquisition 196
Iowa 304
Ireland 254
Isaac 41
Isabella II 198
Isabella, Queen of Spain 196
Isdegerdes 38
Ishmael 38
Isis 91
Ispahan 39
Israel 46
Israelites 47
Issachar 42
Italy 104

J

Jack Straw 264
Jackson, General 322
Jacob 42
James I 271
James II 276
James VI of England 283
Jamestown 309
Janus 148
Japan 77
Japheth 23, 25
Jefferson, Thomas 320
Jerusalem 20, 57, 209
Jesus Christ 61, 83
Jews 338
Jezebel 59
Joab 54
Joan of Arc 219
John, King of France 264
John Lackland 263
John the Good 218
Jonah 59
Jonathan 53
Jordan 59
Joseph 42
Joshua 46

Judah 57
Judas Maccabeus 58
Judea 61
Jugurtha 152
Julian, Count 194
Julius Caesar 205
Juno 118
Jupiter 118
Jupiter Ammon 131

K

Kaahumana 350
Kenneth II 282
Kentucky 304
Khosrou 37
Kleber 95
Knight-Errantry 213
Knights of St. John 216
Knights of the Cross 216
Knights Templars 216
Koran 71
Kouli Khan 39

L

La Fayette 228, 317
Lacedaemon 110
Lama, Grand 81
Lambert Simnel 268
Lancaster, Duke of 265
Lapland 204
Laplanders 242
Lassa 81
Layard 32
Lelex 110
Leonidas 36
Lepidus 157
Leuctra 116
Levi 42
Lexington 314
Lexington, Battle of 313
Lictors 171
Lincoln, General 320
Lisbon 199
Llewellyn 279
Locrians 127
Lombardy 237
London 255
Louis Napoleon 228
Louis Philippe 200
Louis the Foreigner 208
Louis the Grand 221
Louis the Mild 208
Louis the Stammerer 208
Louis XI 219
Louis XIV 221
Louis XV 221
Louisbourg 302
Louisiana 304

Lucretia 145
Luke, Saint 73, 76
Luther, Martin 184
Lutzen 248
Luxor 91
Lycurgus 110
Lydia 74

M

Macao 68
Maccabeus, Judas 58
Macedon 37
Machpelah 42
Madison, President 320
Magna Charta [kar´-ta] 263
Mahmoud [mah-mood´] 39
Mahmoud II 191
Mahmud [mah-mood´] Gazni 71
Mahomet the Great 190
Maid of Orleans 219
Maine 304
Malabar 179
Malaysia 346
Malta 61
Mamelukes 94, 191
Mantinea 117
Marathon 112
Marcus 164
Margaret 248
Maria II 200
Marie Antoinette 222
Marius 152
Mark Antony 93
Marlborough, Duke of 221
Marquesas [mar-ka´-sas] 352
Mars 118
Marseilles [mar-sailz´] 200
Mary, Queen of England 269
Mary, Queen of Scots 282
Mary, Queen of William 277
Maryland 304, 312
Massachusetts 304
Massacre of St. Bartholomew 220
Mauri 194
Mauritania 97, 194
Mayflower 306
Mecca 69
Media 31
Medina [med-ee´-na] 70
Mehemet Ali [ah´-lee] 95
Memnon 92
Menelaus 110
Menes 86
Menou 95
Mercury 118
Meroveus 206
Mesopotamia 32

Messiah 61
Metellus 156
Mexico 334
Michigan 304
Midianites 47
Miltiades 112
Minerva 118
Misraim 86
Mississippi 304
Missouri 304
Mithridates 75, 152
Mohammed 38, 40, 69, 79
Mohammed III 191
Monasteries 287
Monk, George 275
Montcalm, General 303
Montezuma 334
Moors 192
More, Hannah 285
Morocco 96, 97
Moscow 226, 242
Moses 43, 45
Mostasem 72
Mosul 32
Mount Ætna 122
Munich [mu´-nik] 229
Murat, Joachim 186
Music 357
Mutius Scævola 145

N

Nabis 134
Nankin 67
Naphthali 42
Naples 137, 167, 185
Napoleon 94, 224
Natolia 74
Navarino 136
Nebuchadnezzar 57
Nebuzaradan 57
Neptune 119
Netherlands 253
Neva 241
New Britain 301
New Brunswick 301
New England 306
New Hampshire 304
New Holland 347
New Jersey 304
New Orleans 321
New York 297, 304, 331
Nicaragua [nik-ar-ah´-gwa] 336
Nicholas 243, 247
Niger 99
Nigritia 99
Nile 42
Nimrod 26

Nineveh 20, 25, 30, 32
Ninias 29
Ninus 28
Niphon 77
Nitocris 87
Noah 22
Norfolk Island 353
North Carolina 304
Northumberland, Earl of 265
Norway 251
Nova Scotia 301
Nubia 86, 95
Numa Pompilius 142
Numidia 97, 152

O

Oceania 346
Octavius 94
Octavius Caesar 158
Odin 285
Odoacer 291
Oglethorpe, James 312
O'Hara, General 319
Ohio 304
Orleans, Duke of 221
Ormuz, Gulf of 69
Osiris 91
Otho 136
Otho, Emperor 166
Ottoman Empire 187
Ottomans 77, 189
Owhyhee 349

P

Painting 357
Palatine 140
Palestine 41, 45
Palmyra 74
Pandora 351
Papyrius 147
Paraguay 296
Paris 200
Paris, Trojan Prince 110
Parma 167
Parthia 32, 76
Patricians 168
Patrick, Saint 283
Paul, Emperor of Russia 246
Paul, Saint 61, 73, 76
Pausanias 128
Pavia 220
Pedro, Don 338
Pekin 66
Pelagio 194
Pelopidas 115
Peloponnesus 114
Penn, William 312
Pennsylvania 304, 312

Pepin, King of France 206
Pepperell, William 302
Percy, Lord 314
Pergamos 76
Pericles 113
Perkin Warbeck 268
Persepolis 36, 40, 130
Persia 31, 32
Peru 336
Peter II 245
Peter III 245
Peter, Saint 73
Peter the Great 243
Peter the Hermit 209
Petersburg, St. 241
Pharamond 206
Pharaoh [fa´-ro] 43
Pharsalia 290
Philadelphia (Asia Minor) 76
Philip II of Spain 197
Philip, Indian King 308
Philip of Macedon 127
Philip of Valois [val-wah´] 218
Philip the Fair 217
Philippi 158
Philistines 47
Phocis 127
Phoebidas 115
Phoenicia 55
Phrygia 114
Picts 281
Pierce, President 322
Pilate, Pontius 61
Pillars of Hercules 193
Pindar 124
Pisgah 46
Pisistratus 112
Pitcairn, Major 314
Pittacus 120
Pizarro 337
Plague in London 276
Plataea 36
Plato 123
Plebeians 145
Pliny the Younger 175
Pluto 119
Plymouth 306
Pocahontas 310
Poictiers [poi-teers´] 218
Poland 254
Polynesia 349
Pompey 153
Pontius Pilate 61
Pontus 75
Popes of Rome 184
Portugal 198

Portuguese 38, 338
Porus 130
Potsdam 238
Powhatan 310
Preble, Commodore 97
Prescott, Colonel 315
Pretender 277
Prexaspes 33
Printing Invented 288
Protectorate in England 274
Providence 339
Prussia 229, 238
Psammenitus 92
Ptolemais 74
Ptolemy 92
Pul 31
Pultowa 249
Punic Wars 146, 149
Pygmies 98
Pym, John 272
Pyramids of Egypt 91
Pythagoras 121

Q

Quebec 301
Quebec, Capture of 302

R

Ramses 88
Ravaillac [rav-i-yac´] 220
Red Sea 44
Red-Beard 97
Reformation 184
Regulus 148
Rehoboam 57
Reign of Terror 224
Remus 140
Restoration in England 274
Reuben 42
Revolution in France 222
Rhode Island 304
Rialto 186
Richard Crook-Back 267
Richard II 264
Richard the Lion-Hearted 262
Richmond, Earl of 268
Rio Janeiro [ri´-o ja-na´-ro] 199
Robert Bruce 263
Robin Hood 285
Robinson Crusoe 285
Rochambeau 319
Roderick 194
Rodolph of Hapsburg 231
Roman Empire 159
Rome 104, 137
Romulus 140
Rouen 200
Roundheads 273

Russia 240

S

Sabines 140
Sahara 86
Salamis 36
Salem 307
Salvador 341
Samaria 57
Samnites 148
Samoiedes 242
Samson 47
Samuel 51
San Salvador 336
Sandwich Islands 349
Saracens 71, 79, 188
Sarah 41
Sardanapalus 30
Sardinia 185
Sardis 76
Saul 51
Saxon Heptarchy 260
Saxons 260
Saxony 229
Scævola, Mutius 145
Scipio 150
Scotland 254, 257
Scots 260
Scott, General 336
Sculpture 357
Scythians 33, 76
Sea Kings 261
Semiramis 28
Sennacherib 31
Servius 144
Sesostris 88
Seth 21
Seven Wise Men of Greece 120
Shahs 38
Shalmaneser 31
Sheba, Queen of 56
Shem 23, 25, 32
Shepherd Kings 87
Shinar 23
Shishak 57, 92
Siam 77
Siberia 78
Sicily 139, 185
Sidon 74
Sigiven 65
Silas 76
Simeon 42
Sinai 46
Siroes 37
Siva 80
Slave Trade 100
Smith, Captain John 310

Social War 152
Society Islands 350
Solomon 54
Solomon's Temple 55
Solon 111
Solyman, Sultan 210
Sophia, St. 188
Sophis 38
South Carolina 304
Spain 192
Sparta 36, 110
Sphinx 91
St. Helena 227
Staines, Sir Thomas 352
Stamp Act 313
Stephen 237
Stephen of Blois 262
Styx 171
Suetonius 259
Suevi 193, 204, 230
Suez 85
Sweden 247
Switzerland 232
Sylla 152
Syria 72

T
Tadmor 73
Tahiti [ta-hee´-te] 350
Tamerlane 190
Tarquin the Proud 144
Tarsus 76
Tartars 38, 77
Tartary 63
Taylor, General 336
Taylor, President 322
Tea 69
Teheran 39
Tell, William 233
Temple of Apollo 127
Tennessee 304
Terah 40
Teutones 230
Texas 304, 336
Thales 120
The Crusades 209
Thebes 90
Thebes in Greece 115
Thermopylae 36
Thomas Becket 262
Thrasybulus 114
Thyatira 76
Tiber 164
Tiberius 163
Tibet 63, 81
Tiglath Pileser 31
Tigris 25

Timandra 114
Timbuktu 99
Timothy 76
Timour 190
Titus 62, 164
Tomyris 33
Tournaments 216
Trinity Church 331
Tripoli 96
Trojan war 110
Tullia 144
Tullus Hostilius 142
Tunis 97
Turin 187
Turkey 71
Turkish Empire 189
Turks 38, 74, 77, 79, 135, 189
Tuscany 185, 187
Tyler, President 322
Tyre 55
Tyrol 236

U
United States 304
Uruguay 296

V
Valentinian 260
Van Buren, Martin 322
Van Diemen's Land 347
Vandals 165, 193, 204, 230
Vati 65
Vatican 139
Venezuela 296
Venice 139, 186, 187, 237
Venus 118
Vergilia 146
Vermont 304
Vespasian 164
Vesta 118
Vesuvius 139
Veturia 146
Victoria 279
Vienna 235
Virginia 304, 309
Vishnu 80
Visigoths 194
Vitellius 164
Volsci 146
Vulcan 118

W
Wales 254, 257, 263, 279
War of the Roses 266
Warren, General 316
Warwick [war´-rik], Earl of 267
Washington, George 311, 316, 319, 320
Wat Tyler 264
Waterloo 191

Watts, Dr. 285
Wellington, Lord 198
Welsh Bards 280
West Indies 296
West Point 318
Western Empire 164
William IV of England 294
William of Normandy 261
William Prince of Orange 276
William Rufus 262
William Wallace 263
William Walworth 264
Williams, Roger 307
Wisconsin 304
Woden 285
Wolfe, General 303
Wurtemberg 229

X

Xerxes 35, 113

Y

Yong-tching 66
Yorktown 319

Z

Zama 150
Zebulon 42
Zedekiah 57